CITY LIMITS

City Limits

Perspectives on the Historical European City

Edited by

GLENN CLARK, JUDITH OWENS, AND
GREG T. SMITH

McGill-Queen's University Press
Montreal & Kingston • London • Ithaca

ISBN 978-0-7735-3651-7 (cloth)
ISBN 978-0-7735-3652-4 (paper)

Legal deposit first quarter 2010
Bibliothèque nationale du Québec

Printed in Canada on acid-free paper that is 100% ancient forest free (100% post-consumer recycled), processed chlorine free

McGill-Queen's University Press acknowledges the support of the Canada Council for the Arts for our publishing program. We also acknowledge the financial support of the Government of Canada through the Book Publishing Industry Development Program (BPIDP) for our publishing activities.

Library and Archives Canada Cataloguing in Publication

City limits : perspectives on the historical European city / edited by Glenn Clark, Judith Owens, and Greg T. Smith.

Includes bibliographical references and index.
ISBN 978-0-7735-3651-7 (bnd)
ISBN 978-0-7735-3625-4 (pbk)

1. Cities and towns – Europe – History. 2. City and townlife – Europe – History. 3. Europe – Social life and customs. 4. Europe – Social conditions. 5. Europe – History, Local. I. Owens, Judith II. Smith, Greg T. (Greg Thomas), 1967– III. Clark,Glenn (Glenn Jeffrey)

HT131.C568 2010 940.09173'2 C2009-905280-6

Typeset by Jay Tee Graphics Ltd. in 10.5/13 Sabon

Contents

Figures and Tables

FIGURES

TABLES

Acknowledgments

Any volume that originates in an academic conference incurs a wealth of debts before it appears in public. The editors of *City Limits* take pleasure in expressing their gratitude to the institutions and people who have given time and money to this project. The original conference was generously supported by a grant from the Social Sciences and Humanities Research Council of Canada as well as financial assistance from the following units within the University of Manitoba: the Office of the Vice-President (Academic), the Faculty of Architecture, the Faculty of Arts, the Faculty of Graduate Studies, the Institute for the Humanities, St John's College, the School of Art, the Department of English, and the Department of History. We would also like to thank the members of the conference organizing committee: Jim Bugslag, Roisin Cossar, Pam Perkins, Vanessa Warne, Johannes Wolfart, and Arlene Young. The conference ran more smoothly than it might have thanks to the help of graduate students Judith Anderson and Jacqui Nadiger and, especially, with the dedication and organizational expertise of Natalie Johnson of the University of Manitoba Institute for the Humanities.

City Limits has grown in many ways since the conclusion of its initiating conference in 2004. We would like to thank John Zucchi, acquisitions editor at McGill-Queen's University Press; Joan McGilvray, our co-ordinating editor; and Joanne Richardson, our copy-editor, for their valuable support and guidance.

The two anonymous readers for the press helped focus and tighten a lengthy draft manuscript. Generous financial assistance towards the publication of the volume has been provided by several units within the University of Manitoba, including the Office of the

Vice-President (Research); the Dean of Arts; the Department of English, Film, and Theatre; and the Department of History. Our final and most profound thanks go to our contributors, writers of both chapters and prefaces, for their support and patience.

Finally, Glenn and Judith would like to thank Greg for taking on the herculean task of preparing the manuscript for submission.

Glenn Clark
Judith Owens
Greg Smith

CITY LIMITS

Introduction

The city ... consist[s] ... of relationships between the measurements of its space and the events of its past.

Italo Calvino[1]

Relationships – of space and time, place and actor, proximity and distance, material and immaterial – are by no means as uncomplicated as the (seemingly) straightforward syntax of our epigraph might suggest. How *does* one measure a city's spaces? Architects can supply one means of measurement, sociologists, poets, surveyors, labourers, tourists, and so on, quite other. And, if the verb "consists" posits the city as a stable, finally realized object of inquiry, such entelechy is always just receding into the future because the past is always forming just behind us. The human agency, which is implied but not expressed by the balanced abstractions of Calvino's sentence and which is instrumental (*someone* measures, *someone* acts the events) but unnamed, haunts these abstractions with the particularities of motive, cause and effect, design, intention, and accident. And just what is it that constitutes an "event"? The phrase "events of the past" is sufficiently general to include not only the public acts of an individual or group but also the private acts of an individual or group. Relationships between space and time (those "measurements" and "events") are complicated further by the traditional tenets of urban morphology, according to which a city's physical spaces can continue to conform, in perpetuity almost, to the purposes for which those spaces were initially laid out, while institutions and cultural practices change, often rapidly, over time. From this perspective, spaces and events might always be just out of synchronization (although in ways quite different from the lack of fit that some theorists ascribe to postmodern architectural space). Such an understanding of the city's spaces and time is indeed just permitted by Calvino's sentence if the slightly ambiguous syntax is taken to mean *both* that the city consists of relationships between spatial measurements and events *and* that it consists of its spatial relationships, on the one hand, and its events, on the other. Even without putting any strain on the syntax, it still becomes evident that relationships between space and time are complicated by the recognition that those relationships represent multiple, sometimes conflicting, uses of the same city spaces. Above all, as the play of singular and plural nouns (and the mono- and multisyllabic words) in Calvino's sentence intimate, the city accommodates pluralities.

To tease these implications from Calvino's sentence is not only to gesture towards humankind's continuing fascination with the city. More pertinently for our purposes, it is to stress that the city supports often contradictory meanings, thus providing a topos within which individual scholars can test the limits of a discipline and towards which a collection of chapters such as those that appear here can develop an interdisciplinary perspective. Almost as soon as we started to plan a conference on the historical European city, we included "limits" in the title and punctuated it with a question mark, precisely in order to destabilize the limits of inquiry, whether disciplinary, epistemological, or ontological. A central aim of our project has been to posit the city as fruitful ground for interdisciplinary exploration. Our aim was realized. We received submissions from scholars in six disciplines, some of whom individually developed interdisciplinary perspectives in their chapters. In organizing *City Limits*, which includes some of the conference papers (substantially revised) as well as chapters solicited specifically for the volume, we maintained the emphasis on interdisciplinarity. The result is a collection of chapters whose individual interests range from historiography to architecture, from social practices (of inclusion *and* exclusion) to tourism, from governance to protest, from high culture to subculture, from popular culture to journalism, from ways of thinking about the city to ways of being in the city.

In *City Limits*, the limits in question are not only spatial and administrative but also conceptual, psychological, and socio-economic. This volume demonstrates that the city both consolidates and destabilizes a variety of perceptible but provisional spaces, categories, and identities, whether political, administrative, religious, cultural, aesthetic, vocational, or corporeal and gendered. The titles of parts 1, 2, and 3 represent one attempt to reflect on urban limits without reifying them or the spaces they provisionally mark. "Placing the City" suggests that European cities did indeed produce and sustain various aspects of urban identity and place, including "places" in the rhetorical sense of conceptual topics. Such topoi are sustained as a result of the enduringly complex phenomena of urban life. Part 1 reminds us that cities, with their multitudinous components, were hardly ephemeral and that civic identity and the dynamic inclusiveness of urban spaces were objects of desire. Moreover, it suggests that security and confidence adhered to civic identity and that such confidence created the conditions for the growth and naturalization of urban values. In turn, we might also recognize that urban success has provided the conditions for urban critique.

Part 2 picks up at this point. "Gender, Mobility and the City" gestures to the mutual constitution of personal identity and the identity of cities, but it also attends carefully to the ambivalences and fragmentations of civic and personal identity in terms of gender and embodied life. Urban subjects are formed in the city, but those subjects have the agency to reform, to mobilize, the broad cultural vision of the city. Similarly, the chapters in part 3, "Redressing Boundaries," envision the city as a space of competition and contrariety, challenge and resistance. Urban boundaries, categories, and identities are often productively destabilized, and, however paradoxically, it is at least partly because of this destabilization of limits that the values imagined in the chapters in part 1 come to be established. Our three parts do not imply any teleology, and, in fact, we intend them to resist simple narratives of progress or corruption. The parts themselves are by no means absolutely distinct. Multiple points of intersection exist between parts as well as between the individual chapters composing them. As in cities themselves, patterns can be discerned and "places" (in the rhetorical sense) can be located. We would emphasize only that these patterns are no more hegemonic, definitive, or unchallengeable than are the urban spaces, categories, and limits the chapters and parts of this volume seek to sketch.

The European city has, of course, attracted significant scholarly attention. Urban historians have been able to reconstruct the structural and organizational features of medieval and early modern cities. The historical demography of key European cities, their economic and political developments, their administrative and governmental structures, and their patrician or plebeian citizens, have captured the attention of many academics.[2] Rather than adding small contributions to that vast literature, we hope to complement it with chapters that explore the cultural experience of the city, a dimension of urban history that has been relatively underexplored. A number of our contributors offer close readings of select urban centres as sites of cultural production or as the settings for spiritual or emotional engagement among people on a scale not found in physically smaller and less populous places. Our goal in this collection is to build on the impressive literature on European cities that emerged in recent years. As the recent multivolume *Cambridge Urban History of Britain* demonstrates, constructing a comprehensive survey of even one nation's urban history is a monumental undertaking.[3] Inevitably, then, an approach that includes various parts of western Europe must be selective. In the chapters presented here, we offer a fresh set of perspectives on the lived experience of urban actors in the early modern European city and on their material and mental environments. The originality of these insights comes from an interdisciplinary approach to urban phenomena understood more in terms of discourse and representation than in terms of data analysis. Our humanities-based interdisciplinarity helps reveal the lived experience of the city.

Interdisciplinarity is not an end in itself, however. Its high, and rising, stock across academic disciplines comes from its demonstrable usefulness in advancing knowledge. Because the city not only accommodates but also, in a very real (if ungrammatical) sense, *is* pluralities, interdisciplinarity proves an exceptionally effective heuristic tool. In their cumulative and interactive effect, the chapters gathered here enable us to comprehend the historical European city in new ways. Interdisciplinarity makes visible what is both "early" and "modern" in the early modern European city by highlighting the inaugural moments in continuities; it represents the complexity of the city by engaging multiple sites, jurisdictions, communities; it recovers the particularities of motive, effect, accident, and design – that is, the multiple human agencies – that do not always emerge in the study of the abstract idea known as the city.

As Peter Laslet observed many years ago in *The World We Have Lost,* continuity (however attenuated) in traditions and easy familiarity with long-established patterns of behaviour can create a curious kind of blindness about the past, a condition in which "the force of the contrast between our world and the world which the historian undertakes to describe" becomes "indistinct."[4] This blurring of distinctions applies with particularly insidious consequence to questions of origins. To see little difference between then and now can be to neglect to look for how things started and to regard as "natural," and so inevitable, the conditions and structures of contemporary urban, or civic, life. With its intersecting angles of vision, interdisciplinarity brings into sharp relief the contrasts between then and now, highlighting as it does so the moments and conditions from which emerged now-familiar structures of experience. Several of the chapters in our collection, for example, consider the formation of civic identity and the relationship, in turn, between civic and national exigencies as well as the relationship of these exigencies to modernity. The chapters collected here approach these questions from a variety of disciplines, from the perspectives afforded by the study of the confessional imperative in urban chronicle-writing (Wolfart); by the translation of civic into national values via journalism (Bailey); by the provocative mingling of rational design and thrilling sensation in urban tourism (Perkins); by the engaging of past and future in Romantic poetry (Saklofske); by the creative exchange of music and musicians linking a northern European city to a southern one (Hammond); and by the struggle of fin-de-siècle women artists to negotiate the ambiguous or contradictory pressures of city life (Johnson). These chapters thus intersect to illuminate various ways in which cities become communities, help to shape national character, and herald modernity. Perhaps even more important, these chapters register the urgency, excitement, and sense of discovery that attended inaugural moments.

Interdisciplinarity advances knowledge most substantially not when it blurs beyond recognition the lines that distinguish disciplinary aims and practices but, rather, when it generates productive critical conversations by respecting the strengths of discrete disciplines. To address the historical European city from methodologically and epistemologically distinct perspectives enriches our understanding by foregrounding *for us* the complexity of that urban experience and by according value to the myriad ways in which the *citizens* experienced, shaped, and represented their world. Thus, for example, a theatre historian can take us inside the performative, material, textual creation, and experience of civic authority (Blackstone), while a historian of political economy can clarify the surprisingly fixed structural features of civic government

(Friedrichs). While historians of the Victorian city have imagined the movement of women through London streets, a scholar of Victorian literature (Warne) can lead us to understand how disabled people moved, or were hindered in moving, through those same streets.[5] A scholar of the new Atlantic history (Land) can follow the shifting boundaries, and fortunes, of "sailortown" to emphasize its synecdochal relationship to the city; a musicologist (Fisher) can attune us to the soundscapes of biconfessional cities to remind us that religious and civic identities formed in myriad ways; a scholar of Henry James's aesthetic vision and practice (Hoople) can trace in stones the spiritual aspirations of a city's buildings; a historian of Jewish neighbourhoods in Amsterdam (Coenen Snyder) can trace the fascinating and potentially liberating dialogue between travellers and civic edifices.

As the chapters cited above suggest, one of the largest returns on interdisciplinarity is the extent to which it recovers, even discovers, human agency, motivation, and affect within so (potentially) monolithic a structure as the city. This is especially true when, as is frequently the case in these chapters, the marginalized actors who are not always accorded agency within the grand narratives of urban development emerge into view, crossing boundaries and extending limits. People move a lot and insistently in these chapters: out of economic necessity, out of social or cultural imperatives, out of religious, moral, or political conviction. They move out of, into, and through the spaces of the city. All this movement emphasizes the dynamism of city life, certainly; however, more to the point adduced at the start of this Introduction, this movement reminds us that relationships between spaces and events, people and places, are never inert.

If the title of our volume licensed the testing, crossing, and extending of limits, it also set chronological and geographical limits. One of our goals in drawing these scholars together, as we have indicated, was to mount a direct challenge to the fixed notions of what the city was and to test our understanding of the boundaries or limits of city life, city culture, city space, and/or city jurisdiction. Nevertheless, these chapters are still very much engaged with the city as a given, with the city as a site for understanding those things in the past. Thus, in all but two of the chapters (and even these develop comparative analyses of European and other cities), we are concerned with the historical European city. We chose these limits, the historical European city circa 1400–1900, not only because our own teaching and research interests centre here but also because these parameters allowed us, implicitly, to pose certain theoretical, methodological, and ideological questions, not the least of which are the kinds of questions that arise when subjects are distanced from investigators by time and place. Our time frame, while it does not seek to mute or deny any continuities with the periods that precede 1400 or follow 1900, was selected to encompass the long transformative era in which most European cities emerged from their particular medieval or ancient origins into something closer to the densely populated, industrialized, and heterogeneous social and economic units that would continue to grow and command power and attention into the modern era. Our breadth encourages recognition of both the "early" and the "modern" in the early modern city. The peculiar and particular dynamics that made urban spaces in the past variously exciting, stimulating, inspiring, or dangerous (among many other things) are reflected in various ways in the following chapters.

Our decision to restrict inquiry to European cities also rested, in part, on our wish to bracket out questions of what might be called teleological trans-Atlantic influence in order to avoid the temptation to understand cities primarily in terms of the forms and functions they came to assume in North America. As productive and vital as is that inquiry, it can produce severe distortions by flattening historical depth and by looking back only in order to find the seeds for what was to come, thereby making those eventualities seems inevitable. For much the same reason, we restricted the period of inquiry to, roughly, 1400–1900, that is, from the start of the early modern period to the start of the modern period. To broach urban history of the twentieth and twenty-first centuries is necessarily to enter into debates about modernity and postmodernity, debates that are immensely important but that, again, produce certain kinds of distortions and occlusions.

The history of the European city is, of course, inextricable from the history of Europe. Their developments may be traced from the same broad processes. There are also many variations on this theme, and so, naturally, historical approaches to the city and to urban life in

Europe have produced a deep and wide-ranging scholarship. The city as a subject of historical inquiry has generated a legion of administrative studies, political histories, religious histories, biographies of civic leaders, and military analyses of successful or unsuccessful responses to attack, not to mention social and economic histories of the citizens, their work, and their personal lives. One of the themes that has sustained much critical work on the city is the role it plays in the creation of a political population. Cities, from their pre-European origins, have functioned as spaces for the political organization of and politicization of society. From early on, cities developed inherently utilitarian roles. People came to associate certain functions and particular powers with city administration. From the beginning of the period covered by these chapters, it is possible to examine the lives of the inhabitants of the European city in some detail thanks to the survival of written sources generated to support those administrative functions. That very fact of record survival alone speaks to the growing administrative and organizational demands and functions of the emerging European city.

The development of cities as administrative centres, then, was a common feature of European history and is reflected even in the physical geography and architecture of cities. Urban centres usually have one or more squares or "places" where commercial and social concourse was expected and encouraged and where a central, civic building – variously styled the town hall, Rathaus, hôtel de ville, guildhall, or stadhuis – housed the political leaders. These physical manifestations of city space may be found across Europe and were designed and built to fix in place the locale for important civic functions and rituals, from the political (council meetings), to the legal (courts of law), to the cultural/social (weddings), to the inevitable (tax payments). Thus, cities came to be associated with deliberate sites for the transaction of business and the interaction of people generally. Explaining the city as a nexus of exchange was and remains a strong theme underlying how cities are written about.

Other overarching themes, such as crisis and conflict, which sparked much investigation in urban history and the social and economic circumstances of city life, have latterly given way to culturally informed analyses of the psychic, intellectual, and/or ontological city. And the growth of interdisciplinary approaches has resulted in works of urban history that now explore the politics of local religion, the gendered discourses of urban space, and/or the economics of civic rituals. By continuing in this interdisciplinary vein, the chapters collected here help to deepen our understanding of the dynamic and creative power of the city, especially in a period that many historians would identify as critical in shaping the features of modern urban life. Over the period stretching from the early fifteenth century to the cusp of the twentieth, the European city came fully into being as a forum for social, commercial, intellectual, and political concentration. To be certain, such concentrations of people for the purposes of social organization were certainly not unique to Europe. Edo (Tokyo) had a population of roughly 400,000 by the 1640s and perhaps 900,000 by 1700. Indeed, before the early nineteenth century, other European capitals, such as Vienna, Moscow, and Berlin, were smaller than both Osaka and Kyoto.[6] Indian cities such as Varanasi (Benares) and Madras were thought to have had populations of between 400 and 500,000, according to early nineteenth-century estimates.[7] It is likely, too, that late Ming China also had large cities other than Peking/Beijing, which is estimated to have had between 600,000 and 1 million inhabitants circa 1640.[8] But population alone is only part of the story. Worth exploring further are the multiple ways in which the experience of dense urban living began to shape connections among and between people. In the European case we find that city dwellers were beginning to exhibit some common traits, evident in the spread of religious and secular ideas as well as in the adaptation of architectural styles. The physical geography of Europe should also be borne in mind as it facilitated the uniquely European character of urban development. Along with its concentrated size, the accessible topography and navigable rivers of Europe made travel between cities both easy and likely.

What have been identified as "key" civic centres in western Europe have received the most scholarly attention, from the Venetian city states to trade hubs like Cologne, Danzig, Milan, Magdeburg, Antwerp, Paris, and London. This is to be expected; these cities were exceptional entities because, in both quantitative and qualitative terms, Europe before 1900 remained overwhelmingly rural. Dense urbanization was geographically spotty, with few cities topping the 100,000 mark before the eighteenth century. The exceptions were usually the capitals of London, Madrid, Paris, and Rome, which were long established as centres of political administration and religious organization as well as loci for trade, finance, and the making of law. The greater cities were a constant source of wonder, delight, and fear for newcomers and rural visitors, and even for those whose urban experiences were of the more modest-sized towns and villages. Conurbations of more than ten thousand inhabitants would have been considered substantial towns by contemporaries, and even those of up to half that number would have seemed congested, noisy, and bustling to those used to leading altogether more bucolic lives. Some regions and countries were more urbanized than others, at least by the sixteenth and seventeenth centuries, and by the start of the eighteenth century the number of European cities with populations of five thousand or more was around 555. By the year 1800, that number had nearly doubled to 908, and by 1890 there were four European cities with populations of over 1 million.[9]

The concentration of energy, resources, and ideas in larger European centres made for a new kind of public sociability, a body politic, that was more carefully attuned to the internal needs of urban organization and order and that became increasingly separated from the seasonal cycles of the rural world, which were still driven by the rhythms of the harvest. City life created and required kinds of association, patterns of operational logic, and grids of coherence that were different from those possible in rural life. Certainly the growth of cities created a new kind of dependence on the countryside as demands for food and raw materials expanded along with urban economies. But the dominance of the city as the core rather than the periphery of this relationship became fixed over the period considered here.

Indeed, over the long time period covered by this volume there were important developments in economic, social, and political structures of European societies that had profound consequences for the life patterns of many women and men. The movement of people into and out of urban centres was a defining feature of the early modern European experience, but the increasing tendency of those moving people to stay put and to make a home in those urban centres triggered a series of changes to the urban environment to accommodate and cater to the multiple and growing needs of city dwellers. The migration of skilled workers in and around Europe had been a feature of the medieval urban economies, especially in the wake of disease or war. Such patterns not only intensified in the fifteenth and sixteenth centuries but also became supplemented by the movement of cultural products, including books, art, and music. European cities were both the sites and sources of a great deal of this production of cultural capital.

The changes wrought by the movements of people to urban centres reverberated through every level of society, a point recognized in the wide range of topics pursued by scholars of the city. For example, the physical geography of cities has attracted interest from those seeking to understand both the processes for creating the built landscape and the psychic and social impact of spaces as they develop in ways planned and unplanned. In some cases, the boundary between city and environs was unequivocal. Many cities were enclosed by walls punctuated by a limited number of gates, creating a permeable but identifiable physical space against which multiple claims could be asserted, justified, or denied. The fixed boundaries of the physical city thus provided certain kinds of identity. The physical confines of the city that created spaces according to which one might identify his or her status, rights, or duties were thus a direct consequence of that physical reality.

But other groupings were also possible, within the larger civic entity, with their own kinds of ethereal borders constructed by language, religion, or by micro-networks of quotidian sociability, commerce, and dispute. Neighbourhoods were less explicitly demarcated by physical borders of streets or party walls, as what made for neighbours or neighbourliness was dependent to a large part on the social and familial relationships established by and between residents. What constituted a neighbourhood or neighbour, then, was contingent upon much more than physical proximity of living quarters. As some of our contributors demonstrate, the boundaries, or "limits," of the physical city could provide the necessary dividing line for creating betwixt-and-between spaces in which the identities defined by the city were more diffuse and constantly contested. In some cases, there was a deliberate attempt by some residents of certain urban locales to unmake the traditional neighbourhood or to find ways constantly to blend and reconfigure the nature of urban, public relationships through a series of coded and intentionally opaque displays of behaviours.

The mutability of these urban identities reminds us of another organizing concept that emerged as a common theme in a number of chapters, the theme of space and movement. Many of the authors are concerned with the flow of people and ideas through urban spaces and how the city acted as both a generator and a consumer of such ideas. To this end, these chapters contribute to a growing literature concerned with the cultural dimensions of urban life in the past. As scholars in many disciplines have pushed beyond the structural-functionalist analyses of societies characteristic of the pioneering works in urban history and historical geography, and as interdisciplinarity as a heuristic device is no longer being merely encouraged but actively implemented in the methodological approaches and research questions being asked, this new scholarship is now bearing fruit.

The city has proved itself to be an enduringly productive topos for exploring the material, social, and ideological contexts through which we now understand texts to be structured and to which they, in turn, contribute. The ever-increasing breadth of conversation among scholars of the literature and culture of the city arises from the complexities we have already discussed: as a historical phenomenon, the city is marked by ambiguity. Much like texts themselves, it is a place of boundaries, differences, and identities, of mobility and fixity, of contestation and stability. As a topic, the city reveals simplifying and ultimately misleading binaries, such as those that privilege court culture or any single urban institution. A foundational axiom for current approaches to the city and its culture was articulated in the 1970s by Raymond Williams, who argued that the English town or city – in contrast to the culturally mystified countryside – "made evident ... the decisive relations in which men actually lived." Thinking of Wordsworth's evolving representations of the city, Williams significantly recognized that "in the transforming experience of the city, appeared [the] shock of recognition of a new dimension ... The objectively uniting and liberating forces were seen in the same activity as the forces of threat, confusion and loss of identity."[10] While not all scholars share a Marxist view of the "decisiveness" of the economic, we should acknowledge Williams's influential critical vision, in which the city makes important relations "evident." Few would now disagree that the materiality of urban social relationships and identities is an important factor in the structural relationship between city and culture. Just as significant is Williams's attention to the representation of the phenomenological experience of the city, the "shock" that accompanies cultural recognition of the profound ambivalence of urban life.

An analysis of the ambivalence experienced by humans beings in the Western city, and of the nearly essential ambiguity found in representations of the city in literary and cultural texts, might well begin with Gail Paster's description of the city of classical literature as "not just a symbol for order but an expression of human mastery over time and nature as well."[11] A lengthy tradition of urban panegyric extols the human urban accomplishment. The city is, and is represented as, a place of accumulation of material and cultural resources, and of a corresponding intensity of human experience. The urban environment is rich in many senses. But it is precisely this attempt at mastery, this challenge to nature, that also generates discontent about the city. The triumphal and monumental symbols of human power, accomplishment, and accumulation that compose the city – the modern as well as the ancient – generate a corresponding distaste, a sense of insecurity in the face of hubris. From this insecurity springs the ancient tradition of urban dystopia and satire, given generative force by the biblical Book of Revelation and St Augustine's *City of God*. Both works memorably contrast the heavenly city to the corrupt worldly city.[12] We need only remember the profound contempt released in John Milton's phrase "luxurious Cities" to feel the literary impact of this force.[13]

A more sociological account of urban ambivalence might begin with Richard D. Lehan's formulation of the purpose and significance of the city in Western history. According to Lehan, the city represents "the attempt to impose order on nature [which has] worked within limits."[14] For Lehan, the city is always a place of regulation and discipline, of order imposed by authority, though not without broad social consent precisely because such order offers various kinds of security. But, inevitably, there are limits to the degree that the city can exclude the uncontrollable forces of nature, and those forces may be embodied by the resistance of citizens to the imposed order of the city. The city is a place of paradox, a place in which competing and contradictory forces of regulation and liberation, celebration and demonization, mobilize enormous cultural energy. Urban culture and its texts embody the surprise, the pleasure, and the anxiety of the city itself.

Perhaps because so much European literature of the past five hundred years has been structured by the material and social relations of the city, and perhaps even because writing originated in the city, writing and urban life are frequently brought together as mutually explanatory phenomena in urban studies and literary criticism. The development of sociology as a twentieth-century academic discipline is deeply intertwined with the study of urban experience. Lewis Mumford, writing in the 1930s of an ideal city first given sociological force by Max Weber, argues that "mind takes form in the city; and in turn, urban forms condition mind ... The city is both a physical utility for collective living and a symbol of those collective purposes and unanimities that arise under such favoring circumstance. With language itself, it remains man's greatest work of art."[15] For Mumford, the city as symbol of collectivity, as work of art, conditions minds to produce more symbols, which, in turn, enhance the status of the city as work of art and reinforce the collective functions of the ideal city. While today we might take pleasure in noting that Mumford finds himself influenced not only by Max Weber but also by Renaissance humanist urbanism, we would surely find ourselves deeply sceptical of his organicist and functionalist idealism. Nonetheless we might also recognize in Mumford's sophisticated texturing of the city an anticipation of poststructuralist cultural theory.[16] Mumford imagines urban culture as exchange: as mind shapes city, so city shapes mind, and from this exchange come symbol, trope, text, and art. The city and the text are mutually reproducing. Much more recently, Lawrence Manley begins his compelling study of literature and culture in early modern London with a very similar idea: "Like the language, London was undergoing rapid growth and change, offering new possibilities for exchange and combination, producing signs, symbols, civic habits, and systems of order."[17] From here, Manley proceeds to explain the vast breadth of literary form in London as structurally related to civility and settlement within a discontinuous historical process of private capital accumulation and state centralization. Manley's urban symbols are generated in a city far less unified in collective intent than Mumford's ideal city, but both recognize the relationship between urban symbolic exchange and artistic, textual production.

The mutual constitution of urban exchange and textual trope is sufficiently compelling that it offers the possibility of transforming a complex causal relationship into metaphor: the city, or its social networks and symbolic exchanges, *as* textual production, and textual production *as* a city. In an important attempt to theorize the influential literary-critical method called New Historicism, Stephen Greenblatt uses urban metaphors to describe the ideologically sustained but necessarily incomplete (or false) separation of artistic practices from general cultural practices:

> Now the demarcation is rarely, if ever, absolute or complete, nor can we account for it by a single theoretical formulation. We can think up various metaphors to describe the process: the building of a set of walls or fences to separate one territory from adjacent territories; the erection of a gate through which some people and objects will be allowed to pass and others prohibited; the posting of a sign detailing the acceptable code of behavior within the walled territory; the development of a class of functionaries who specialize in the customs of the demarcated zone; the establishment, as in a children's game, of ritualized formulas that can be endlessly repeated.[18]

Greenblatt is not particularly interested in the urbanity of literature as such. In fact, he does not even note that his descriptive metaphors are drawn from urban structure and experience (though he surely realizes it). What is important for our purpose is that Greenblatt finds that the city provides an ensemble of practices that is adequate to metaphorizing the relations between a society and its art and literature. What makes the metaphors work is not simply the theme of the wall and gate but, rather, the implied actions of disciplining and identifying, of separating, allowing, prohibiting, demarcating, and ritualizing. For Greenblatt, profoundly influenced by Michel Foucault's theorization of the disciplined subject as well as by the formal and deterministic anthropology of Clifford Geertz, the city is metaphorically adequate to the task of describing textual production because both spheres of human culture are primarily disciplinary and controlling in nature. This is again a very different approach to the culture of the city from that taken by Lewis Mumford, in whose ideal city "the ways of the village cease to be coercive."[19]

However, poststucturalist theories of resistance also find important expression in the metaphorical substitutability of city and text. Michel de Certeau, for example, conceptualizes the urban tactics of the weak and disempowered in terms of rhetoric, poetry, and intertextuality. Such tactics constitute resistance to the strategic and architectural organization of urban space by the powerful:

> The walking of passers-by offers a series of turns (*tours*) and detours that can be compared to "turns of phrase" or "stylistic figures" ... I would add that the geometrical space of urbanists and architects seems to have the status of the "proper meaning" constructed by grammarians and linguists in order to have a normal and normative level to which they can compare the drifting of "figurative" language ... The long poem of walking manipulates spatial organizations, no matter how panoptic they may be ... It creates shadows and ambiguities ... It inserts its multitudinous references into them ... These diverse aspects provide the basis of a rhetoric.[20]

For de Certeau, the city is no more a site of unified purpose or identical interests than the poststructuralist literary work is the site of organic form or single-authored intention. As many critics have noted, the understanding of texts and the understanding of cities have evolved together, and, for many literary specialists, the mutually illuminating approaches to city and text centre on issues of coercion, resistance, pluralization, and liberation.

Theorization of the mutually sustaining relationship between urban life and textuality, and the metaphorical intensification of the significance of this relationship, discloses an all-important fact: the texts of the city, its symbols, its figures, tropes, genres, and modes, are consistently engaged in the ideological work of perpetuating or challenging the social constitution of the city. While urban literature is engaged in what historian Jan de Vries calls "behavioral urbanization" – the assuming of civic expectations – it is also and equally engaged in promoting critique.[21] One way of assessing the significance of the relationship between city and text, therefore, is to consider the social and political stability of the city. Indeed, this is precisely why critics attentive to the place of the city in literary and cultural history find that they are either explicitly or implicitly engaged in the historiographical debate over the relative stability of the European city. For example, Manley's argument for the ideological power of early modern London's literature and culture to (on the whole) promote the urbanization of a population "lacking indigenous traditions of *urbanism*" is premised on the relative stability of early modern London.[22] The work of urban historian Ian W. Archer offers the most reliable current assessment of this debate for Elizabethan London. Archer argues that, while London was essentially stable during this period, there was nonetheless a perceived socio-political and economic crisis.[23] Other historians have doubted the overall stability of early modern London.[24] The question is equally open and suggestive for other cities and other time periods.[25]

Archer has cautioned that strong advocates of urban stability tend to overlook a variety of problems and tensions, and certainly literary and cultural critics often find that what Archer calls the perception of crisis or instability is an especially important condition of possibility for cultural and literary innovation. On the other hand, it is important to remember that major European cities – indeed, major cities throughout the world – have preserved themselves over time, and literary and cultural critics ought to take account of the role of various kinds of texts in sustaining long-term stability. As de Vries rightly states, urbanization is a "general historical process, but one whose specific characteristics vary over time."[26] Current analyses of urban literature are especially interested in the historical particularity of ideological or behavioural urbanization. The question of stability in the urban environment offers an intriguing point of engagement for all specialists in urban literature, culture, and urbanization.

Analysis of the cultural work of literature in the historically specific urban environment by no means excludes analysis of form and formal innovation. Monumental, architectural, spatial, ritual, and literary forms in the city change under pressure from concurrent transformations. As the chapters collected here show, human density and migration patterns; ethnic, national, or religious mixture and conflict; responses to disease; political organization; military power; capital accumulation; status mobility; and the development of class and economic rationalization – and this list is not exhaustive – shape cultural form. A survey of approaches to the culture and texts of urbanization prior to the twentieth century shows that literary specialists have found that material change in the city is perhaps most clearly reflected, sustained, and challenged during a few eras of intensified cultural production and innovation. These include, most notably, the development of a professional theatre and innovation in dramatic and ritual form in quickly growing late sixteenth- and early seventeenth-century London, and developments in the novel stemming from the industrialization and rationalization of nineteenth-century London and Paris. However, as the variety of chapters in this collection show, London and Paris, or theatre and novel, present only the tip of the iceberg in terms of possible approaches to cultural developments in the historical European city. Even within these areas of unflagging interest, intellectual exchange offers many possibilities for critical innovation.

Current approaches to the city, literature, and culture tend to reflect developments and interests in the field of literary criticism and cultural studies more generally, while maintaining a strong commitment to historical accuracy and particularity. A partial list of areas of broad critical interest currently informing work on urban literature and culture might include the related studies of everyday life and the lives of subalterns, attention to particular material objects and their associated social networks, phenomenology, the study of representations of emotion, and studies of religious or confessional change. These areas of current interest often inflect or accompany more familiar critical themes.

As a whole, the chapters in the present volume can be read like the city: as individual components in modifying relation to each other and as an accumulated whole. The breadth and complexity of this collection is appropriate to its subject: the city is a human artefact whose qualities depend on its historical particularities. This is why the city generates powerful responses that cannot be simplified or reduced.

NOTES

1 Calvino, *Invisible Cities*, 13.

2 Recent studies include de Vries, *European Urbanization, 1500–1800*; Hohenberg and Lees, *The Making of Urban Europe, 1000–1950*; Friedrichs, *The Early Modern City, 1450–1750*; Cowan, *Urban Europe, 1500–1700*; Le Galès, *European Cities*; Lees and Lees, *Cities and the Making of Modern Europe, 1750–1914*.

3 Clark, *Cambridge Urban History of Britain*.

4 Laslett, *The World We Have Lost*, 7.

5 On Victorian streets and movement, see Walkowitz, *City of Dreadful Delight*; Walkowitz, "Going Public"; Nord, *Walking the Victorian Streets*.

6 Rozman, "Edo's Importance in the Changing Tokugawa Society," 93n7; Yonemoto, *Mapping Early Modern Japan*, 17; Hanley, "Urban Sanitation in Preindustrial Japan," 3–4.
7 Bhattacharya, *Report of the Population Estimates of India*, 405–6, 452–3.
8 Naquin, *Peking*, 126; Robinson, "Banditry and the Subversion of State Authority in China," 527.
9 de Vries, *European Urbanization*, 70, table 4.12.
10 Williams, *The Country and the City*, 54, 151.
11 Paster, *Idea of the City*, 15.
12 Ibid., 1–32.
13 Milton, *Paradise Lost*, bk. 1, line 498.
14 Lehan, *The City in Literature*, 20.
15 Mumford, *Culture of Cities*, 5. For a history of urban sociology, see "An Introduction" to Sennett, *Classic Essays on the Culture of Cities*.
16 On humanist urbanism, see Paster, *Idea of the City*, 21–32.
17 Manley, *Literature and Culture in Early Modern London*, 1.
18 Greenblatt, *Shakespearean Negotiations*, 13.
19 Mumford, *Culture of Cities*, 4.
20 de Certeau, *Practice of Everyday Life*, 100–1.
21 de Vries, *European Urbanization*, 12.
22 Manley, *Literature and Culture*, 15.
23 Archer, *Pursuit of Stability*, 1–17.
24 Griffiths, *Lost Londons*.
25 Steve Rappaport, for example, contrasts his vision of sixteenth-century London's stability with the considerable evidence for instability in various Continental cities of the same century. See *Worlds within Worlds*, 6–7.
26 de Vries, *European Urbanization*, 13.

PART ONE

Placing the City

PREFACE

Placing the City

PETER LAKE

Life in a number of so-called world cities has come to epitomize the modern, and indeed the postmodern, encapsulating all that is best and worst and, thus, most distinctive in life on the cusp between the present and the future. The city has therefore moved to the centre of scholarly concern in a number of disciplines and, indeed, in a number of sites of interdisciplinary activity. The result, typically, has been a resurgence of interest in the past of cities. The sense of the city as a place where all the different aspects of modern life are condensed and experienced in their most intense, complex, and alternately exhilarating and disorientating forms has come to inform the investigation of the urban past. This development also reflects developments within the discipline of history over the past few decades. The study of cities as places of manufacture and exchange, of trade and consumption, was central to the emergence of economic and social history and theory. There is now a massive and sophisticated literature on a variety of different cities written in that mode. Central to the emergence of urban history as a subdiscipline were a series of definitional and typological questions about the nature of the city (and indeed of the town) – questions that continue to be of relevance to modern scholars, as Johannes Wolfart's discussion of the urban-ness of southern Germany attests.

Answering such definitional and typological questions has always implicitly, and very often explicitly, involved an exercise in comparative history. Christopher Friedrich's chapter continues that tradition, moving out of national or regional fields of vision to encompass both Europe and Eurasia in the early modern period. But while Friedrich's piece represents the continuation of long-standing traditions of social, economic, and institutional analysis, his key concept is "political culture." This approach refers to a major shift in the historiography of the last few decades: the rise of cultural history and the broadening definition of what constitutes the cultural domain. The historian's basic materials have broadened from the sorts of cultural commodities, artefacts, and performances that cities have always produced and sold, circulated and exchanged, to include the whole range of performative and signifying actions with which and through which the inhabitants of cities organized, interpreted, and gave meaning to their lives – actions in and through which the city represented itself to itself and to the wider world, or, to put it another way, in and through which different groups competed for inclusion, status, and power within the city thus constituted.

Here attention might be paid to the formal performances of cityness and urban identity put on by various groups within the city – the royal entries, the mayoral shows, the religious festivals and processions. And a range of historians have tried to read off a variety of meanings and messages from the often fragmentary and always problematic sources that such necessarily evanescent occasions left behind them. The problems did not go away but, rather, merely mutated when the surviving scripts for such performances were at their most complete. For here was evidence of how certain people either pro- or retrospectively wanted the event to appear. The gap between script and performance always gaped before the historian, anxious, as ever, to get at "what really happened" but with that prospect receding at a rate of knots the more carefully he or she pursued it through ever more rigorous and critical readings of the evidence. The consequent interpretative difficulties were exacerbated by the necessity to build into the account the always partial and widely divergent experiences of different groups or individuals within the audience. It might well be argued that different individuals' exposure to, experience of, participation in, and interpretations of the event varied to such an extent that the event itself would scarcely have existed as a unitary whole for many or most participants or viewers. Such questions of audience and reception link the study of this aspect of cities very closely to studies of the drama, on the one hand, and, on the other, to various sorts of social theory concerned to recuperate the fractured and fragmentary ways in which the "social reality" of the city is experienced and, indeed, created by its inhabitants as they negotiate their way through its streets and neigbourhoods transacting the business of the everyday. Mary Blackstone's analysis of the performance of authority and identity in Mary Tudor's Norwich addresses all these questions.

However, cities exist or come to exist not only in and through the quotidian lives of their inhabitants but also through the reflections on the nature of this or that city – on the nature of urbanity and on the different styles of urban existence and culture lived in or represented by different cities and by the subsequent study of such studies and comparisons. As centres of innovation and generators of wealth and display, of conspicuous consumption and of "taste," on what were very often unimagined scales of magnitude, cities have always attracted the attention of those either exhilarated or worried by change.

Early modern London attracted a literature of denunciation and complaint, often expressed in a prophetic key, a literature that almost doubled as a paean of praise to the sheer size, exorbitance, and corruption of the city. Intellectuals, concerned to characterize, comment upon, and even shape the times in which they lived, have thus been fatally attracted to cities not only as places in which to live and interact with other like-minded persons but also as objects of study and comment, as ideal types in and through which they can capture the essence of what is happening now and what is about to happen next. Both Robin Hoople and Melanie Bailey capture this process occurring in the reflections of Henry James on Florence and New York and in Gaultier's, Berlioz's, and Foucault's use of Paris as both the home and also the producer of a new model Frenchman. On their view, Paris – or, rather, certain sections of Paris society concerned with the production and consumption of certain types of culture and knowledge – was the great engine of change and of enlightenment in and through which first France and then Europe and finally the world would be transformed. James, of course, framed his (very different) notion of the modern and the future around a different city – New York – and used travel to and reflection upon Florence to come to a series of rather less upbeat conclusions.

Great cities, of course, always exist in relation to and, very often, in considerable tension with a variety of hinterlands. A crucial aspect of the experience and impact of the urban has always turned on people and goods moving into and out of the city. As centres of production and exchange, as nodes of communication, points of departure and arrival, cities have always been dynamic and interactive places; their effects on neighbouring places are often seen to be transformative, in either beneficent or malign ways, according to the perspective of the viewer. The relation between Paris and its hinterland France was conceived by Bailey's intellectuals as one between an innovating and improving centre and a periphery needing to be innovated upon and improved.

In Bailey's chapter, the central issue is the connection between certain notions of Paris and the Parisian, on the one hand, and France, on the other; however one of the central features of the city is that it is a node of communication and exchange whose impact on and contact with the wider world cannot be restricted to one national context. Cities, precisely because they are based on trade and exchange, consumption, and display, tend to be international, and the historians of great cities thus tend to transcend the national historiographies in which the rest of us spend so much of our time.

In a period as obsessed as ours is with the transnational, the hybrid, and the metropolitan, it is entirely natural that this aspect of the study of cities should be booming. The result, as Susan Hammond may be taken to suggest, is that musical exchange between early modern Copenhagen and Venice can emerge as constitutive of musical practices and texts inexplicable outside the nexus of exchange that linked the two cities in the late sixteenth and early seventeenth centuries. If exchange between disciplines and national historiographies, if the study of the transnational and the hybrid, are indeed to become central features of the historical scholarship of the coming decades, then, as these chapters all show (in their different ways), the study of the city is, in turn, likely to be central to those enterprises.

I

What Made the Eurasian City Work? Urban Political Cultures in Early Modern Europe and Asia

CHRISTOPHER R. FRIEDRICHS[1]

What makes cities work? This deceptively simple question lies at the heart of almost every study of urban history. A city in any urbanized culture is a densely built physical space whose inhabitants belong to a variety of identifiable and overlapping social groups, each with its own objectives and interests. These groups may be diverse in terms of function, origin, or belief systems, but they are alike in attempting to pursue their interests by exploiting whatever social resources seem most strategic or promising. The process by which these often powerfully competing interests are articulated, pursued, and adjudicated is, in fact, urban politics. And the practice of urban politics is what makes cities functional for their inhabitants – simply put, it is what makes cities work. But did cities work in quite the same way in early modern Europe and Asia? That is the question that this chapter sets out to consider.

To answer this question requires us to confront and overcome some significant obstacles – "city limits," in fact. Of course cities in the past were often characterized by physical and socio-political limits. The physical limits were the walls, rivers, or canals that might demarcate the boundary between the urban core and surrounding districts or separate one neighbourhood within the city from another. The socio-political limits were the rules, customs, and practices that distinguished the various groups and subcommunities that made up every urban society and structured the interactions between them. We cannot begin to understand the way cities worked until we know something about these limits and how they operated.

But to compare the political cultures of European and Asian cities requires us to recognize and overcome a very different kind of "city limit" – a limit to the historical imagination. For all too often historians and theorists of the city have been hampered by deep-seated assumptions about some fundamental difference in character between the "occidental" and the "oriental" city. Of course there were real differences between European and Asian cities of the past. When historians focus on formal structures of political participation as the key to understanding the character of urban politics they are rightly struck by differences between cities in Europe and Asia. Such observations are important, but they can also limit our understanding of what really mattered in urban politics. If we can overcome this obstacle and focus on other analytical categories for thinking about how cities actually worked in the past, we may begin to see things very differently. This is precisely why it is important for historians of the European city to look beyond Europe. For, ultimately, our understanding of how cities functioned in Europe can only be enriched if we see the European city as part of a much broader historical category: the Eurasian city.

The history of politics in European cities of the early modern era is richly documented. European cities were clearly defined entities governed by collective bodies, which, by the late Middle Ages, had become accustomed to maintaining detailed written records of their transactions. Account books, council minutes, judicial records, lists of office-holders, chronicles, and countless other written sources have survived to form the basis for detailed analyses of the distribution of power, the issues that animated town dwellers, and the conflicts that emerged among them in the cities of early modern Europe.[2]

The same cannot be said for cities everywhere else in early modern Eurasia. For certain parts of Asia – Japan, for example – detailed records sometimes make possible the description of urban politics on a level of precision that often corresponds to what is known about European cities. Yet, for many Asian polities, urban records range from spotty to almost non-existent. Sometimes cities were not differentiated administratively from their hinterlands, making it difficult to extract specifically urban data from the surviving records. Some cities were governed in ways that discouraged the maintenance of written administrative records. Many records have been lost or destroyed. For much of premodern Asia, it is difficult or impossible to reconstruct the day-to-day details of urban politics. Anecdotal accounts may suggest broader patterns, but the specifics will remain lost until new sources are found or new ways of understanding the existing records emerge.

Yet, even when it is difficult to reconstruct the details of urban politics, it may be possible to say something about urban political cultures. Politics involves specific issues, conflicts, and personalities. Political cultures, by contrast, have to do with the broader spectrum of norms, practices, and beliefs that shape the interplay of everyday politics. Even if records of urban politics as such are unevenly distributed, we know enough to be able to compare the fundamental features of urban political cultures in the major polities of early modern Eurasia. In short, even if we cannot always find out what happened in cities at particular times, we can study and compare how cities worked. And if we do so, we will find that some long-standing assumptions about the differences between cities in Europe and Asia may require substantial revision.

To explore this topic is certainly a form of world history. But it is important to make clear what kind of world history it is. There is one great tradition of world history – embodied, for example, in the classic works of William McNeill or in more recent studies of the "Eurasian exchange" – that emphasizes contact between different cultures and the way in which cultures are reshaped by that contact.[3] Certainly the early modern era, with its ever-expanding volume of intercontinental exchanges, raises a vast number of interesting questions about how contact between cultures changed political and social and religious norms.[4] But there is also another approach to world history, one that is essentially comparative: to examine how different cultures or civilizations dealt with the same kinds of issues or resolved the same kinds of problems. These cultures may have experienced some contact, but in this approach the issues arising from that contact are not the central ones. The main problem here is to see how two or more cultures with different institutional and ideological foundations addressed the same situations. So this is the question to be considered here: to what extent were the political cultures of cities in widely separated parts of Eurasia during the early modern era significantly different and to what extent were they essentially the same?

Obviously, differences matter. Even looking just at European cities one cannot help but be impressed by the variety of structures and practices that typified their political procedures and processes. Yet, as I have argued elsewhere, all of these differences masked some fundamental uniformities in the way in which European cities were governed in the early modern era.[5] Now I want to ask whether we can identify any fundamental uniformities in the way cities were governed in the early modern era that go beyond Europe itself. Are there any meaningful commonalities in the urban political cultures of all the major Eurasian civilizations?

To pose this question is not simply to imply that by knowing something about Europe we can learn more about Asia. Indeed, the reverse is just as likely to be true: by learning more about Asian urban history we may be able to understand more about the European city. In reading about cities in early modern Asia, I have been struck by how often historians seem to make reference to European cities: some observation about urban life in Tokugawa Japan or Ming China or Mughal India will be reinforced by a reference to the literature about London or Paris, Florence or Venice, Rome or St Petersburg. But the reverse is rarely the case. How often is a discussion of European cities enhanced by drawing a comparison to Edo or Kanazawa, Nanjing or Ahmedabad? It may be time for historians of European cities to start doing so.[6]

Obviously, there are some pretty fundamental differences between European and Asian civilizations of the early modern era. But historians are increasingly inclined to draw attention to the underlying uniformities among the major Eurasian civilizations before 1750. Much recent discussion has focused on the similarity of core economic attributes in European and Asian societies prior to the "great divergence" of the nineteenth century.[7] To be sure, the extent of these similarities remains a subject of vigorous debate – but when it comes to cities there are undisputed commonalities that make it particularly meaningful to enter into comparisons. Western and Central Europe, the Ottoman Empire, South Asia, China, and Japan were all highly urbanized societies in the early modern era – Japan, in fact, may have been the most urbanized of all.[8] All of these societies were highly monetarized, with complex regional economies in which cities played a crucial role as centres of production and nodal points for transit of goods. All of these societies had highly developed state systems that made heavy fiscal demands on urban communities. They also had religious systems that were often linked to but never totally integrated with the state. And, in all of these societies, urban populations were highly mobile, with a constant influx of new inhabitants. All Eurasian cities needed some kind of mechanisms for absorbing and integrating newcomers, for facilitating and controlling social mobility, for alleviating the poverty and distress caused in many cases by excessive immigration, and for regulating conflicts between different groups identified by occupation, religion, place of origin, or some other defining characteristic. So all of these cities confronted some comparable problems.

But if urban problems were often the same, what about the solutions? Of course not all urban issues are "political" in the narrow sense. Obviously, many problems were tackled and resolved by families, religious institutions, or other non-governmental structures. But, in fact, the concept of political culture should be understood broadly to encompass the whole set of rules, customs, and practices by which societies and communities respond to the various pressures and issues that beset them.[9] And if those pressures and issues were broadly comparable in early modern times, then clearly we should ask to what extent cities in Europe and in various parts of Asia had similar political means for dealing with them.

This is not an entirely new question. In a sense it was posed and even answered a century ago by Max Weber. It was Weber, after all, who articulated the classic difference between what he called the occidental and the Asiatic city, and the key difference between them, according to Weber, was political. All cities, Weber said, share some defensive and economic functions – but only some cities, in his view, were true urban communities. What made them urban communities was a substantial level of political and juridical autonomy along with "administration by authorities in the election of whom the burghers participated." According to Weber, "an urban 'community,' in the full meaning of the word, appears as a general phenomenon only in the Occident." By contrast, "with possible isolated exceptions, the cities of Asia were not urban communities at all even though they had markets and were fortresses."[10]

This definition has remained highly influential, and it continues to inform much writing about Asian cities. But it has also stirred deep resentment. Indeed, historians writing about Middle Eastern or Asian cities often attack Weber in painfully bitter tones for allegedly regarding Asian cities as inferior to European ones because they lacked fully urban characteristics.[11] Such writings may involve a well-founded rebuttal of certain statements that Weber made about non-European cities. But the heartfelt defenders of the urban characteristics of Asian cities often overlook what Weber actually said about the *European* city. They simply assume that Weber's well known description of the occidental city applied to every city in premodern Europe. But this was by no means the case. For Weber's definition of "urban community" was actually so narrow that it did not encompass all European cities: in fact, Weber argued that, in terms of his own definition, "the 'cities' of the Occidental Middle Ages only qualify in part as true cities; even the cities of the eighteenth century were genuine urban communities only in minor degree."[12] Weber was certainly correct in implying that many great cities in eighteenth-century Europe had lost so many of their erstwhile powers of self-government that they could not fit his own definition of "urban community." But if eighteenth-century London and Paris were not true cities, then the notion that there was some fundamental character of "European" cities that made them different from "Asian" cities surely loses all meaning.

Now it is true that European cities were characterized, at times, by certain features not normally found in premodern Asian cities. These features can be defined as administrative autonomy, citizenship, elections, and collective structures of decision making. Some of these features were emphasized by Weber; some were not. Some were common to all European cities; some were not. But all of these features were rarely found elsewhere in Eurasia.

Cities in Asia were typically governed by office-holders who held their appointments directly from the ruler or as part of an administrative hierarchy ultimately responsible to the ruler. By contrast, the classic European urban commune – the true Weberian city – was a corporate entity that strove to minimize direct intervention by officials of the state. The less interference of that sort that a city had to endure, the more "autonomous" it was. The struggle to achieve more autonomy forms part of the grand narrative of European urban history in the Middle Ages. But such autonomy was not permanent. In fact, the attempt by rulers to diminish this autonomy forms part of the grand narrative of European urban history of early modern times. Perhaps there were some moments when, in the words of Bernard Chevalier, some cities had achieved an "accord parfait" in their relations with the state.[13] But, if so, this never lasted for long. The normal state of affairs was an ongoing struggle over autonomy, which, in the long run, most cities ended up losing. Even Venice, the very epitome of the autonomous city, finally lost its independence in 1797.

And even in its heyday Venice was a rare exception among European cities. Its government did not have to answer to any higher authority. Normally, autonomy was a relative rather than an absolute quality. Even the "free" cities of the Holy Roman Empire were generally subject to interference from above.[14] It is true enough that these cities are often described as city-states; however, historians are increasingly aware that "autonomy" in the modern sense of political sovereignty is an occasional attribute rather than a defining characteristic of city-states.[15]

The second distinct feature of European urbanism was citizenship – the special status of those adult male householders who were acknowledged members of the urban commune. Even when, as was often the case, most citizens had little actual part in governing the city, they were still understood to have a distinct status and a unique stake in the affairs of the community. The proportion of householders who enjoyed this status varied enormously, and there were always some householders who were not citizens. Occasionally, this was even by their own choice, as a way of avoiding civic responsibilities.[16] Yet everywhere in Europe municipal citizenship – a status unknown elsewhere – was one of the fundamental building blocks of urban identity.

The third feature was elections. In many – though by no means all – European cities, citizens participated in direct elections of certain municipal office-holders or the indirect selection of electors who would, in turn, choose the civic authorities. Electoral procedures varied widely, from elaborate systems of secret balloting to an open show of hands. The merits of each system of voting were subjects of lively debate in early modern times.[17] The actual consequences of such elections were limited – specific procedures as well as entrenched habits of deference ensured that magistrates in cities with elections almost always came from the same social groups as magistrates in cities without them. But the existence of electoral procedures for choosing city-wide officials was quite unknown in Asia – except of course in colonial cities whose white inhabitants were granted European-style forms of government.[18]

Finally, cities in early modern Europe were governed not by individuals but by collective bodies.[19] Every European city had a council, senate, or similar body whose members, whether chosen by election or by co-optation, were members of the citizenry and were considered to act on behalf of their fellow citizens in making decisions about municipal affairs. Though they often shared power with some other sources of authority – with agents of the king, lord, or bishop, for example – these collective bodies were central to the administration of the European city. By contrast, collective structures of municipal governance whose members derived their authority by belonging to the citizenry were unknown outside Europe.

In short, there were indeed some fundamental differences in the constitutional and organizational structures of European and Asian cities. But this does not legitimate the argument wrongly attributed to Weber – that there was a fundamental difference between the political cultures of all European and all non-European cities. For constitutional structures, important as they are, represent only a small part of what makes up any political culture. If a political culture is the system of norms and patterns by which groups identify their interests and use available resources to pursue them, then participation in the selection of municipal authorities may be one such resource – but it is only one. In fact, the inhabitants of every city belonged to a variety of identifiable groups and associations, defined by occupation, location, origin, religion, and other criteria, and many of these groups were able to articulate common needs and pursue common goals. In doing so they always had to deal with the urban authorities. These authorities might be imposed from above, chosen from below, or sustained in power by a process of self-selection. But no matter how they derived their power, they had to deal with comparable groups and confront comparable problems in administering their communities. Once we step back from the question of what legitimized urban authority to look at urban politics as a process of interest-group formation and problem solving, we will start to find some striking similarities in the character of urban political cultures and in the way that political action was actually carried out in Asian and European cities of the early modern era.

Politics always involves an alternation between "normal" times, when the system functions according to rules that are accepted by most participants, and "crisis" periods, when the rules are challenged by a sufficient number of people or groups to generate a breakdown or disruption of the system. It may seem obvious that any attempt to describe a political culture should begin by focusing on periods of "normal" functioning. But, in fact, moments of crisis or breakdown may form the best point of entry into understanding a political system because sometimes this is exactly when norms and assumptions that otherwise remain unspoken are articulated and described. So it may be instructive to begin our consideration of early modern urban political cultures by describing a particular episode of crisis. The case to be discussed relates to one of the most typical manifestations of urban political crisis: a series of riots that broke out when the customary means of conflict resolution had failed to operate successfully. Indeed, the structure of such riots is one of the most intensively studied aspects of early modern European urban history. This particular case may be useful in setting up some categories of analysis for us to consider.

The episode concerned took place in the year 1582. I will leave the location unmentioned for the moment, but the sequence of events may have a familiar ring.

For many years preceding these events, two issues in particular had animated the political life of this city. One was the property tax on all households. Over the years this tax had risen steadily, in ways that put a greater burden on poorer householders. There had been frequent discussions about this problem and some changes had been made, but most of the city's ordinary householders continued to resent the structure of the tax system.

Yet, an even more contentious issue had to do with the obligation of householders to contribute to the safety and security of the city by performing mandatory communal service as night watchmen. Every night, gates between different parts of the city were closed and the conscripted watchmen had to man the gate towers in their neighbourhoods. This might have been more acceptable if every householder had shared this obligation equally, but in fact the rich could hire substitutes or bribe city clerks to drop their names from the duty list. So the burden fell chiefly on the poorer householders.

An outspoken schoolteacher – an immigrant from the countryside who had acquired some prestige in his neighbourhood as a spokesperson for ordinary residents – took it upon himself to deal with this issue. He submitted numerous petitions to the officials asking for reform of the mandatory night patrol duty system. At one point, he was punished for doing so and was sent back to his home district, but he soon returned to the city and resumed his efforts. Eventually, some different officials took a more sympathetic view of his complaints and changes were made. In the late 1570s, the conscription of residents as watchmen was cancelled and replaced by a system by which people were paid for this work. But then, in 1580, the system of required community service was reinstated. As a result, the poorer householders had to do patrol duty again, while the paid watchmen were suddenly out of work. This generated widespread resentment.

The actual uprising broke out in May of 1582. It began with a mutiny by soldiers garrisoned in the city, whose pay and food rations had been reduced. An official of the central government was sent to quell the uprising, and he immediately offered the soldiers redress of their complaints. The soldiers' uprising died down. But their agitation seems to have triggered a resolve among *civilian* inhabitants – ordinary householders, retailers, craftspeople, and the like – to launch a protest against the hated watch patrol system. The schoolteacher suddenly began to make inflammatory public speeches. He was arrested, whipped, and placed in a pillory in front of the court of justice. Though this public exposure was obviously intended to intimidate others, it also meant that he could continue to harangue the crowd. His very words are recorded: "My appeal over the night patrol duty was made for you! Now I alone must suffer! Why don't you do something to help me? ... It was for you that I appealed over night patrol duty, but I alone am bound in shackles and have been whipped. Can you bear this?" The crowd responded by attacking the pillory, tearing it down, and releasing him. Within hours hundreds of rioters were rampaging through the city. They began by burning down the watchtowers. They then attacked and burned the homes of about forty of the city's leading families. Other elite homes were spared, but their owners were ordered to have their cooks lay out great feasts for the schoolteacher, who was paraded from one mansion to another to partake of the delicacies – in short, it was a humiliation ritual for members of the municipal elite.

The government official who had been sent to put down the soldiers' mutiny had by now been promoted to governor of the province. He returned to the city to deal with the civilian uprising. Lacking any military backup, his first ploy was to try to appease the rioters. Addressing the crowd in person, he offered to deal with their complaints and promised that if they dispersed peacefully only a few ringleaders would be punished. But the rioting continued. So he tried a different approach: he met with the leaders of the military uprising that he had recently suppressed, offered the soldiers even more favourable terms, and got them to help him crush the civilian uprising. Once he had secured the military force he needed, the rioting was swiftly quelled: 150 people were arrested and fifty of them – including the schoolteacher – were beheaded and their heads placed on public display. Yet this did not result in a total defeat for the rioters. For, at the same time, the governor kept his promise and redressed the major complaints. Not only did he cancel the conscripted watch patrol duty and reinstate the paid watchmen, but the hated householders' tax was also abolished. So, in some ways, the inhabitants had achieved their goals – at the cost of the lives of fifty of their leaders.

Many elements in this episode will sound familiar to anyone who has studied the history of popular uprisings in early modern Europe. The ritual procession in which the rebel schoolteacher was taken from one mansion to another and feasted by the wealthy homeowners who hated him sounds like it could have been lifted right from the pages of Natalie Zemon Davis's work on ritual violence during the French Wars of Religion.[20] The ambivalent response of the authorities, wavering between appeasement of the rioters' legitimate demands and ruthless suppression of the insurrection, sounds like a passage from William Beik's great book on urban protest in seventeenth-century France.[21] The educated immigrant who became the charismatic spokesperson for the poorer householders of the community would have been right at home in one of my own studies of German urban conflicts in the early seventeenth century.[22]

But, in fact, this episode did not take place in Europe at all. It took place in the city of Hangzhou in China, about one hundred miles south of Shanghai. My summary of what happened there is based on the work of two historians, Susuma Fuma and Richard von Glahn, who have both studied this event in detail.[23] Obviously, some elements in the story are distinctive to the Chinese situation. Above all, political authority in the city was essentially exercised from above through the series of officials – national, provincial, municipal – who were part of the famous Chinese system of bureaucratic administration. But these officials, just like European magistrates, knew that their authority was to a large extent dependent on the consent or complicity of the community. They acknowledged the right of the inhabitants to petition not just for redress of specific grievances but also for fundamental changes in the tax system or in the allocation of civic responsibilities. The authorities had to respond to such concerns not because of any theoretical notions about governing with the consent of the governed but, rather, because they could not impose their will otherwise. Even when soldiers were garrisoned in the city, as was the case in Hangzhou, they could not automatically be relied upon. In the long run – as in any European city that experienced a similar uprising – the authorities could always find the military force needed to impose their will and to restore order. But, in the short run, the authorities were hostage to the inadequate command of police power that characterized municipal governments in early modern Asia as well as Europe. Inevitably, then, at the height of the riot the new governor had to promise reforms, and even after the riot was suppressed – even as he ordered a brutal round of reprisals for the ringleaders – he found it prudent to keep the promises he had made.

The structure of the riot itself also echoed themes that are familiar to us from the intensively studied conflict situations in European cities. As in many European cases, when the rioters resorted to violence their targets were carefully chosen: the forty houses that were burned in Hangzhou belonged to members of the city's social and economic elite – the "gentry" – rather than the officials in whom the rioters initially reposed some unrealistic hopes of support. Obviously, the rioters made some serious miscalculations (or fifty of them would not have been executed), but the main point is that the riot did involve elements of political choice rather than directionless rage. It was, in its own way, a classic case of "rational" urban violence.

Riots like these have often, and understandably, evoked the close attention of historians. This particular sequence of rioting, like so many other cases, is instructive both because it exposes the mentality of the participants and because it shows how limited the authorities' resources were in dealing with a crisis that had been allowed to escalate to this point. Yet riots of this sort were relatively rare – in Asian as well as in European cities – for they signalled the breakdown of urban political systems whose very purpose was, in part, to prevent such outbursts. After all, the maintenance of order was the primary object of urban governance. Events such as these showed what could happen when the authorities intervened too late, offered too little, acted too hesitantly, or otherwise responded ineffectively to the articulated interests of urban groups. Yet, normally the system did not break down. This is precisely what makes it important to focus on the institutions that generally preserved political stability.

In doing so, one must always look at two aspects of urban politics. On the one hand, we must consider the structures of authority; on the other hand, we must look at the means by which the rest of any city's inhabitants attempted to articulate their interests and get the authorities to respond to them. Obviously, such a binary division of cities into governors and governed grossly oversimplifies the complexities of urban politics. But it does give us a point of entry for understanding and comparing urban political cultures.

It is in the structure of municipal administration that we generally see the sharpest distinctions between European and Asian cities – although those distinctions should not be exaggerated. As already noted, the central institution of governance in every European city was a council – or in some cases an overlapping set of councils – generally made up of members of the wealthier sectors of the citizenry who were chosen by some process of election or co-optation. In Asian cities, by contrast, authority in cities was invested by the ruler or the state. In China, in all but the smallest towns municipal administrators were members of the state bureaucracy. They were even supposed to be posted from another province so as to ensure that their decisions would not be affected by personal bias. In Tokugawa Japan, municipal administrators were samurai, members of the warrior class, who would not necessarily have had any local roots. In India, the top municipal administrators, such as the *kotwal* and *kazi*,[24] were appointed on an individual basis by rulers or provincial governors. In Ottoman cities, the governor and the *qadi*, the chief judge, were also imperial appointees. In contrast to the meritocratic Chinese model, in the Ottoman Empire such positions might be filled quite simply by sale to the highest bidder.[25] Typically, the governors of Ottoman cities were outsiders, though this was not always the case: in Mosul, for example, a wealthy local family monopolized the position of governor for most of the eighteenth century.[26] In short, the basis for appointment as municipal authorities varied substantially among various Asian societies; however, in all of these cases officials might be expected to make decisions less on the basis of local custom or need than in accordance with their own interests or those of the ruler who had named them.

Yet, even so, it would be unrealistic to posit a simplistic difference between municipal power invested from "below" in Europe and from "above" in Asia. After all, in many European cities the municipal council was by no means the only source of authority as the state was often represented on the local level by officials who shared authority with the municipal council or, in many cases, wrangled with the council over issues of jurisdiction and competency. And no matter how firmly a city's political autonomy might be upheld by privileges and charters, rulers often interfered in the procedures by which mayors and members of municipal councils were chosen. There were hardly any true "free cities" in which the state exercised no influence over the workings of the municipal administration.

And, of course, in Asia the state was not an abstract mechanism that simply imposed itself from above without responding to local interests. Take, for example, the system of municipal governance in Mughal India. In principle, the basis of municipal authority was radically different from that of European cities with their elected or co-opted councils. It was also radically different from that of China, where every official occupied, at least in theory, a clearly defined position in a hierarchically ranked system that stretched from the imperial court down to the individual neighbourhood.[27] The leading officials of a Mughal town held their appointments directly from the emperor or, in some cases, the provincial governor. Yet, even at the height of their powers, the Mughal emperors did not enjoy an entirely free hand in the selection of municipal officials. As M.P. Singh has shown, in a number of cases – especially but not only in towns on the periphery of the empire – pressure from the community or from members of the urban elite could lead to the dismissal of an unpopular *kotwal* or the reinstatement of a popular one.[28] Nor did any one official ever enjoy a free hand in carrying out his duties. The *kotwal*, *kazi*, *muhtasib*, and other leading officials had to defer to each other with regard to each one's sphere of responsibility, while all of them were subject to the ceaseless surveillance of paid informers who submitted weekly reports to the imperial government. Municipal government in Mughal India was by no means immune from corruption, but local complaints about abuses of power were taken seriously by the imperial government and could result in officials being dismissed or demoted.[29]

In China and Japan, municipal administrators, even if they had no personal roots in the community, could not govern cities effectively without close cooperation from the local elites. The leading merchants and, in China, members of the local gentry always had to be consulted and conciliated. And, as in most premodern societies, members of the lower orders were always entitled to submit petitions, which officials were expected to review with care.

In fact, no matter what was the source of their authority or how they came to be chosen, all municipal administrators had to be responsive to pressure from the various interest groups, constituencies, and subcommunities that made up the early modern city. These groups differed enormously in their degree of cohesiveness, visibility, and exclusivity – and in the nature of their political role. In some cases, they simply served to give expression to the interests of their members; elsewhere they played a formal role in helping to govern the community or they were assigned specific administrative responsibilities. But in all cities groups like these played an intrinsic role in the functioning of urban politics. So it may be instructive to identify and briefly consider some of the most fundamental forms of group solidarity in the early modern city.

ELITES

To anyone whose conceptions of urban politics are primarily shaped by a knowledge of European cities, it may seem perplexing to identify urban elites as associational groupings distinct from structures of urban authority since, in the case of Europe, the categories of "urban elite" and "urban authorities" so often overlapped.[30] Indeed, in a few cases, such as Venice, these two categories virtually merged into each other. But even so, an analytical distinction must always be drawn between urban elites and municipal authorities. Indeed, the structure of urban politics only makes sense if we are able to perceive urban elites as distinct interest groups with their own political, economic, or social objectives. So it may be useful to identify specific types of urban elites.

The first and perhaps most familiar category consists of the mercantile elite. Every Eurasian city, from Aberdeen to Edo, had merchants. Some of these merchants were very wealthy. Of course, then as now, wealth was only one social resource – honour, education, and ancestry were useful as well – but it was a particularly effective one. All of the early modern Eurasian polities shared a profound respect for private property. Private wealth could be diminished by taxation, confiscation, or other forms of coercion, but, on the whole, merchants everywhere retained a large amount of what they earned, and they deployed their wealth effectively to achieve their economic and social objectives.

A second category within the elite consisted of those whose wealth was derived not from commerce but from income on property. Often this took the form of landed property, and the individuals concerned might spend part of their lives in the countryside where their principal holdings were located. But the assumption that people whose wealth was largely derived from land always preferred to spend their time on rural estates is misleading. In Europe, those who commanded rural wealth often maintained urban homes and formed part of the urban elite. In many parts of Asia, the preference for living in cities was even more pronounced. One reason for this is that, in many cases, a sharp line could not be drawn between those whose wealth was based on land and those whose wealth was based on commerce. Indeed, in some cities merchants and rentiers formed a single social group. In other cities, however, their identities remained separate, and occasionally their interests were even distinct or incompatible.

A third category consisted of those whose elite status was derived from intellectual or religious authority. In Muslim cities, of course, religious and intellectual authority remained virtually identical throughout the early modern period: the *ulama* formed a single group. Elsewhere, a distinction could be made between the religious authority of priests or clerics and the secular authority of jurists, literati, scholars, and the like. In some societies, notably Europe and China, the attainment of clearly defined educational qualifications was a resource that created specific occupational opportunities for jurists or administrators.

Finally, in some cities, personal ancestry could confer elite status. In Europe, noble status – available chiefly by birth but increasingly also by achievement, by service, or even by purchase – was a powerful personal resource. In Ottoman cities, membership in families descended from the Prophet played a comparable role. In China after 1644 and in Japan throughout the early modern era, inherited membership in a military elite conferred substantial personal advantages that might compensate, in part, for a lack of personal wealth.

These elite groups were familiar across the Eurasian cityscape. Sometimes these groups overlapped, sometimes their interests were specifically antagonistic. Where lines of identity were strictly drawn, membership in one group might preclude membership in another. Sometimes particular forms of activity – commerce, say, or military service – were limited by law to members of particular elite groups. In some European cities, merchants had to surrender their involvement in trade in order to be accepted as having noble status, and nobles were threatened with loss of aristocratic rank if they engaged in trade. Such rules were known elsewhere as well. In Japan, for example, a samurai might have to surrender his membership in the knightly class in order to engage in trade.[31] Indeed, issues and conflicts around group identity were subjects of obsessive concern to members of these urban elites.

But in almost all cities the lines that demarcated specific urban groups were more fluid than the prevailing social theories of the day ever allowed. Recent studies of the prosperous Chinese city of Yangzhou in the early modern era document the extent to which two elite groups – merchants and literati – interpenetrated each other. The late seventeenth century was, in the words of one historian, an age of "permeable categories and fluid boundaries" in the composition of the Yangzhou elite.[32] To another author, the influential role of salt merchants at the pinnacle of Yangzhou's society in the eighteenth century – something that "contradicted the formal hierarchy of Chinese society" – led inevitably to the "blurring of social boundaries between literati and merchants."[33] Nor did this apply only to China. In fact, though local details always differed, comparable formulations could be applied to cities all across Eurasia in the early modern epoch.

Elite groups had two forms of relationship to urban authority. Sometimes, as in Europe, their members attempted to become the authorities themselves, and often they were successful in doing so. Elsewhere, it was more common for urban elites to deploy their resources to persuade or to coerce the authorities to confer benefits on them. In the pursuit of such advantages, different elite groups frequently worked together, but sometimes they found themselves in bitter conflict with each other. Yet, when conflicts occurred, they did not necessarily pit definable social categories against each other – rentiers versus merchants, for example, or merchants versus literati. The conflicts might also be along factional lines, pitting two or more powerful families – each with its own network of retainers, clients, dependents, and servants – against one another. Indeed, factional conflicts could become an important form of urban politics. Sometimes these conflicts lasted for decades as successive generations of powerful families and their clients would sustain the struggle to secure strategic appointments or lucrative privileges.[34]

But even so, factional conflicts were only part of what urban politics was all about. For urban politics did not only involve the efforts of the powerful to secure or retain their economic and social advantages; it also involved the efforts of less obviously powerful but still significant urban groups to achieve their often more modest goals. Everywhere, the authorities had to pay close attention to the needs and interests of these groups because, without their cooperation, it would have been impossible to maintain order, regulate commerce, collect taxes, or generally sustain the complex machinery of urban life. So it is crucial to identify at least some of the other important forms of associational grouping in the early modern Eurasian city.

GUILDS

Historians of the Ottoman Empire as well as of East and South Asia have long used the term "guild" to refer to certain urban associations that had much in common with the European organizations for which the same term is used. Consider, for example, this description of early modern Indian guilds from Kenneth Gillion's classic study of the town of Ahmedabad in Gujarat:

> Admission to a guild was hereditary or by purchase. Expulsion was an occupational and often a social disaster. The guilds con-

> trolled admissions, restricted competition, maintained joint charities through levies on their members, kept up standards, determined wages, controlled prices (sometimes), set holidays, and safeguarded the interests of their members against the government, other guilds and outsiders.[35]

This summary of a guild's functions and powers is, in fact, so uncannily similar to descriptions of European guilds that one might suspect that the author was to some extent influenced by European models. But, in fact, there is no question that, in Ahmedabad as in other towns of Gujarat, the guilds – or *mahajans*, to use the local term – played this role.[36] Of course, findings from one city or region cannot simply be generalized to India as a whole, but, as a rule, north Indian cities had recognized occupational groups whose headmen, or *chaudhuris*, had to be consulted by the municipal authorities when relevant issues emerged.[37] And, in south India, artisanal associations not only structured their members' religious devotions and festive activities but also functioned as interest groups that fought effectively against excessive taxation or other perceived injustices.[38]

Guilds played a major role in cities of the Ottoman Empire. In fact, the formation of occupational organizations was strongly encouraged from above as they were an administrative convenience for the authorities. But guilds were not just conduits for the implementation of policies or, in some parts of the Ottoman Empire, the allocation of taxes. They also played a role in regulating the purchase of raw materials or the sale of finished goods, arbitrating disputes, structuring mutual assistance, and framing formal displays of group identity.[39] They selected their own leaders and made their own rules, though these choices often had to be confirmed by government officials. As Abraham Marcus notes for eighteenth-century Aleppo, "The guild system operated outside government, but not independently of it."[40]

Guilds were, if anything, even more important in Chinese cities of the late Ming and early Qing eras. In China, however, the guilds were not necessarily organized around shared economic functions. The guilds were associations of individuals who shared either a common economic activity or a common place of origin – or, in many cases, both, because immigrants from one region or district often enjoyed a virtual monopoly on some particular economic activity in the city to which they had come. The guilds were chiefly fraternal associations that offered their members mutual aid in times of distress and the opportunity for shared religious observances. However, they also functioned to protect their members' economic interests by preventing competition from outsiders or unfair practices by their own members. They could act as pressure groups, and, in small towns where local leaders rather than imperial officials ran the municipal government, they may even have played some role in local administration.[41]

Yet, ultimately, guilds never played as significant a role in the political life of Middle Eastern, South Asian, or East Asian cities as they did in European cities of the early modern era. For it was only in Europe that it was possible for guilds to secure a recognized place within the constitutional order, as happened in many central European towns in the late Middle Ages when guilds were accorded a specified number of council seats. Even in those cities, of course, the political power granted to guilds as a whole tended to drift steadily towards their richest members. In the mid-sixteenth century, many guilds were ejected from their role in German municipal governments, and even where this did not happen the guilds sometimes ceased to be authentic associations of members of the same craft or trade.[42] Yet, despite all that, guilds retained a potential for direct or indirect political power in Europe that was never rivalled in Asia.

NEIGHBOURHOODS

A second form of association played a much bigger political role in many parts of Asia: the urban neighbourhood. Of course, wards, quarters, or parishes afforded many European town dwellers an opportunity for some degree of self-government on the neighbourhood level. It would have been impossible, for example, to administer a growing metropolis like London without the participation of householders who routinely held minor offices in their wards or parishes.[43] Yet nowhere in Europe did neighbourhood self-government play as important a role as it did, say, in early modern Japan. The administration of Japanese cities in the seventeenth century might be thought of as involving two intersecting structures, one organized from the top down and the other from the bottom up. The well studied case of Kanazawa in western Japan may be taken as typical.[44] The top-down structure was the municipal administration, which functioned under the authority of the regional lord, the *daimyo*, and was staffed almost entirely by samurai: the lord's council of advisors gave direction to the city magistrates who, in turn, supervised constables, inspectors, and hundreds of clerks and other officials in the City Office. But the town dwellers themselves were entrusted with major responsibilities. A single street would constitute a household group with responsibility for fighting fires, preventing crimes, and settling minor disputes under the direction of a headman chosen by the householders themselves. The next level of self-government consisted of wards, headed by ward representatives who investigated complaints, mediated disputes, and supervised ward patrols. At the top of this structure stood the city elders, who were appointed to represent the inhabitants and present their petitions and concerns to the municipal administration. Not surprisingly, the much larger capital city of Edo had a more complex system, but the basic principles were much the same: substantial powers of self-administration were entrusted to residential quarters and the five-family groups into which they were divided.[45] In fact, with inevitable local modifications, similar structures were the norm in most Japanese cities of the Tokugawa era.[46] Some Japanese historians have argued that, during the early modern era, the smallest units of government in Japanese cities were, in fact, "entirely autonomous neighbourhoods ... which had their own police forces, financial organizations, and meeting halls."[47]

There was probably no other early modern society in which neighbourhood government played quite as significant a role as it did in Japan since, normally, there were too many other competing forms of association for the neighbourhood to command such a strong sense of identification. However, in South Asian cities as well, though the element of self-administration was not nearly so visible, the urban neighbourhood could play an important role in structuring the lives of town dwellers. One contributing factor was that the neighbourhood was often physically demarcated by its own walls and gates and its own marketplace. The gated *pol*, or house group, in Ahmedabad may have represented an extreme case as here even house property was, to some extent, held in common by the inhabitants.[48] But certainly the typical *mahallah* in a north Indian city would have not only a distinct sense of identity but also its own council, or *panchayat*, and its own headman, or spokesman – the *mohulladar* – who would represent the neighbourhood's interests to the higher levels of government. And even in capital cities like Shahjahanabad, where patron-client relationships formed the basis for much of urban politics, the neighbourhoods that developed around the great houses of members of the imperial entourage still provided the framework for urban administration and group identity.[49]

CASTE

There is no universal agreement among social scientists about the meaning of caste, but those who lean to a broad definition of the term would agree that a caste is a social group whose members inherit an immutable personal status and are barred by powerful taboos from marrying, eating with, or engaging in any other close personal contact with members of other groups. Membership in a caste is often linked to specific occupational roles. Most societies in the premodern world had some castes, though generally these were only marginal groups. In the case of Europe, two such caste groups were strongly represented in certain cities. The first such group consisted of the Jews. Like members of castes in other societies, they were barred from engaging in certain occupations but were allowed or even encouraged to practise others. Wherever Jews were permitted to live, they not only practised a highly developed form of communal self-government but also formed a powerful and articulate interest group in their relations with the host communities.[50] The second caste group was found only in the Germanic lands of central Europe. It consisted of the members of the "dishonoured trades," such as executioners and carrion-removers. Their services were acknowledged as indispensable to their home communities, but they were strictly barred from intermarriage or interdining with other members of the community.[51] They were less persecuted but also less well organized and less politically effective than were the Jews.[52]

Castes existed elsewhere as well. In Japan, members of shunned hereditary castes of professional beggars as well as *tōnai* – people employed as gardeners, jailers, and police informers – lived in cities. They were subject to close regulation, but through their headmen they could articulate their concerns and put some pressure on the municipal government.[53]

But, of course, castes played a much greater role in South Asia as the caste system encompassed the entire Hindu population. Castes were major interest groups in Indian cities, and their status was usually recognized without hesitation by the Muslim administrators of north Indian cities. But it is difficult at times to demarcate castes clearly from other interest groups in the Indian city as caste was strongly associated with occupational roles and often linked to residential patterns as well. So a particular *mahallah* might consist largely – though never, it seems, entirely – of members of a single caste who were engaged in a common trade. Caste councils, or *panchayats*, were recognized institutions in Indian cities. Often these councils had to regulate internal caste disputes regarding marriages and ritual practices, but they might also represent the caste group in its dealings with the larger community. And this often meant defending economic rights, such as the monopoly enjoyed by members of the caste on some particular trade or service.

Significant as castes were, it would be a mistake to assume that political interests could not be articulated across caste lines. Christopher Bayly has demonstrated that many north Indian cities of the eighteenth century had associations or assemblies of merchants or other notables who belonged to different castes but worked together to protect common economic interests. In Benares, in fact, beginning in the mid-eighteenth century a cross-caste association of leading merchant families not only served as a powerful interest group for its own members but also functioned as an unofficial commercial court for the city as a whole.[54] Even more striking was the situation in some south Indian cities, where the whole population was often divided into two bitterly hostile multi-caste associations, each of which encompassed a whole range of castes from high to low. Historians have struggled, apparently without success, to find an economic or social rationale to explain why particular castes would belong to one or the other association. But it is clear that being part of these associations – in whose internal deliberations leaders of every caste could participate as equals – gave members of low-status castes the advantage and gratification of belonging to a larger, more powerful political entity.[55] Thus, caste could even form the basis for powerful associational groupings that were not limited to members of a particular caste.

RELIGION

Religious institutions played a major role in urban life in all of these societies. Priests, monks, nuns, or other clerics associated with houses of worship, shrines, temples, or monasteries were powerful urban interest groups with, in most cases, devoted and influential supporters within the lay population. But in many towns an even more assertive interest group consisted of members of non-established or minority religious communities. We must keep in mind that all of these societies – with the possible exception of Japan after the expulsion of the Christians – were characterized by religious pluralism. Short-lived campaigns to extirpate all religious diversity could erupt at any time, but they generally gave way to begrudging acceptance of religious pluralism. Often the multiplicity of cults was simply part of the routine fabric of urban life. In China, for example, Confucian, Daoist, and Buddhist shrines (not to mention the occasional mosque) could typically be found in any large city.[56] In cities of the Ottoman Empire, long-established Muslim, Christian, and Jewish communities existed side by side.[57] But the religious spectrum was normally hierarchical, with some cults or sects favoured over others. Often there was an established religion, practised and privileged by the ruler. Normally in such situations the municipal administration was controlled by members of the established religion, while adherents of the tolerated sects had to settle just for the right to live, work, and, if possible, worship in the city. This even applied when, as was often the case, the established religion was practised only by a minority of the inhabitants. In cities all over northern India, for example, the machinery of government was controlled by members of one religion while the majority of inhabitants belonged to another. Such situations were known elsewhere as well.

Members of tolerated sects or religions often compensated for their lack of political authority by engaging in particularly vigorous economic activity and by functioning as articulate and assertive interest groups. In this they were aided, in many cases, by the financial, political, or moral support they received from like-minded coreligionists in other communities. Whether we are looking at the Sephardic Jews of Amsterdam, the Mennonites of Hamburg, the Jains of Ahmedabad, or the Hindu merchants of Benares, we tend to find much the same pattern.

But these arrangements were never entirely stable. Indeed, the very roots of religious pluralism often lay in the disruptive episodes that transformed religious allegiances since, from time to time, in almost every Eurasian society, there might occur sudden outbursts of intense religiosity. Under the inspiration of charismatic religious leaders, groups of townspeople might commit themselves with unprecedented fervour to an existing system of belief or even join an entirely new sect or religion. These episodes of heightened religiosity might override or eclipse previous associational allegiances, making the objectives of the religious community all-important in ways that could challenge the comfortable arrangements that normally linked religious and political authority structures. The success or failure of such movements often depended on whether powerful social groups saw the religious upheaval as an opportunity to promote their interests or as a threat to their well-being. But movements of heightened religious intensity are by definition transitory. Sooner or later either the traditional religious arrangements were restored, sometimes by force, or a new set of arrangements was institutionalized, with a differently configured set of religious subcommunities and a new ranking of hierarchical relationships among them.

OTHER GROUPS

The list of such groups could go on. But we need mention just two others: military associations and ethnic subcommunities. Many Eurasian cities had military associations that functioned as urban interest groups. The most notable example is represented by the Janissaries in cities of the Ottoman Empire. Originally, of course, the Janissaries were an elite corps of conscripted soldiers under the direct control of the sultan. By the seventeenth century, however, in many cities the Janissaries had become a group of privileged inhabitants whose members participated avidly in local economic life and took advantage of their armed status to vigorously pursue their interests in local politics.[58] In Tokugawa Japan, the samurai often lived in cities as an entrenched urban interest group whose members tried to exploit their military status as an economic or political resource. In Europe, the long-standing obligation of citizens to bear arms in defence of their community sometimes led to the emergence of militia companies, which could become major players in urban politics. Indeed, in some cities, especially in northern Europe, the militia companies became the main instrument through which citizens attempted to articulate their interests or participate in municipal decision making.[59]

In the increasingly globalized milieu of early modern Eurasia, ethnic subcommunities became an increasingly common presence in major port cities or trading centres. Such communities, whose core members were usually merchants or traders, were often granted commercial and even juridical privileges. The special role of Hanseatic traders in cities like London or foreign mercantile communities in Venice are familiar themes of European urban history. But this was an Asian phenomenon as well. Consider Masulipatnam, the thriving commercial entrepôt on the southeastern coast of India. In the seventeenth century, Masulipatnam belonged to the kingdom of Golconda. The governors were Indian Muslims, the majority of the inhabitants were Hindus. But the most dynamic economic group consisted of Persian merchants who enjoyed the status of a quasi-autonomous subcommunity with their own force of guards and cavalrymen. At various times during the seventeenth century the city also included English, Dutch, French, Danish, Armenian, and other subcommunities, each with its own stoutly defended economic and social privileges.[60] In fact, the political history of seventeenth-century Masulipatnam is largely the story of the dizzyingly unstable relationship between successive governors and the most assertive or aggressive of the foreign communities, which gave the city its distinctive – but far from unique – "multi-ethnic, plural character."[61]

Associational groupings of various kinds formed the institutional framework through which much of urban politics was carried out in the early modern world. This is not to say that every aspect of personal identity could provide the basis for the formation of such groups. Women, children, servants, slaves, or transient visitors to the city did not form groups. Women – especially those who had inherited substantial property or high social status – might exert great personal power as members of a family or household, but aside from occasional participation in devotional associations they never belonged to associations that pursued common interests based on their gender. Children, servants, or slaves were even more thoroughly excluded from any opportunity to articulate common interests. But adult males who lived in a city for any length of time were almost always able to pursue their interests through some form of association. And, normally, they belonged to more than one such grouping.

Numerous instruments of political practice were available to these groups. Only one form of collective action – the drafting and submission of petitions – was universally accepted by the holders of authority in early modern cities as a legitimate form of political action.[62] Other forms of collective action were more problematic, but they could be highly successful. Litigation or appeals over the heads of local authorities might be undertaken. There could be strikes or boycotts. In India entire subcommunities – all the members of a particular craft, say, or all of a city's merchants – might close their shops or even leave en masse and settle elsewhere until their demands were met.[63] And then there was the politics of the street: mass demonstrations with the implied threat of violence or, of course, actual violence itself. Urban groups were often led by shrewd tacticians who knew how to calibrate collective action to maximize the likelihood of concessions, how to forge alliances with other groups, and how to articulate demands in ideological terms most likely to resonate effectively with the authorities. But sometimes mistakes were made. When alliances broke down, actions got too violent, or demands moved beyond specific grievances to the reordering of social relations, brutal reprisals might ensue. Usually in such cases the urban authorities called on assistance from elites outside the community who were likely to fear the destabilizing impact of any challenges to constituted power.

The tortuous history of popular politics in Kyoto during the epoch of political instability in Japan that lasted from the mid-fifteenth to the mid-sixteenth century is an apt case in point. As Mary Elizabeth Berry has shown, the commoners of Kyoto were adept at using not only petitions and litigation – "word wars" – but also mass demonstrations and even acts of violence to extract concessions from the authorities or to achieve redress of grievances. But this worked only up to a point. When, in the mid-1530s, an uprising inspired by the religious enthusiasm of the Hokke sect seemed to challenge fundamental power relations in the community, members of previously hostile elites joined forces to ruthlessly crush the revolutionary movement.[64] By chance, much the same thing happened at exactly the same time in the north German town of Münster: in 1535, Roman Catholic and Protestant princes overcame their mutual antagonisms to obliterate an urban religious movement that had spiralled out of control and seemed intent on restructuring basic political and property relationships.[65]

Yet, such cases are significant chiefly because of their infrequency. Just as urban authorities knew when it was prudent to concede a reduction of taxes or redress of grievances, urban groups normally knew how far they could push their demands without seeming to challenge basic power relationships. Associational groups normally accepted the legitimacy of the existing regime. They promoted the interests of their members by appealing to the urban authorities for protection and privileges. In doing so, however, they often found themselves in conflict with other associational groupings. Indeed, one of the main jobs of urban authorities was precisely to adjudicate such conflicts between groups within the community. Complex legal cases were bound to ensue, for example, when two guilds claimed the right to produce the same goods or provide the same services, or when some privileged association felt that its exclusive rights were being undermined by interlopers. Mostly such disputes were resolved peacefully. But they could become violent, especially when identity issues rather than economic advantages were at stake. The transgression of protected space or misappropriation of emotionally charged symbols by members of a rival group was particularly likely to trigger a cycle of violence. The way in which religious processions or ritual mockery could lead to riots in sixteenth-century France will be familiar to every student of early modern European history.[66] But French and British colonial administrators were confronted with exactly the same phenomenon in eighteenth-century Pondicherry and Madras, when holding a wedding procession or carrying an umbrella in the wrong part of town could lead to rioting between left-hand and right-hand caste agglomerations.[67] And while communal violence between Hindus and Muslims was less common in early modern Indian cities than it became later on, it was certainly not unknown.[68]

If the municipal administration was perceived as a neutral arbiter in such disputes, it could often be successful in adjudicating conflicts and restoring peace between the aggrieved interest groups. On the other hand, if the municipal administration was seen as being too partisan or itself became the object of grievances, there might be an appeal to some higher level of authority and a possible intervention from above. This was something many urban officials strove to avoid, and at times their strategy for dealing with urban tensions may have been guided by their desire to prevent conflicts from coming to the attention of the superior authorities.

In any case, urban politics everywhere was focused largely on the decision-making powers of the city-wide authorities. Individuals might seek redress of their grievances through patrons or other powerful intermediaries, but groups and subcommunities normally turned to the city-wide arbiters of power. Inhabitants of the city routinely expected the municipal administrators to judge their cases, settle their quarrels, and guarantee the food, water, security, and infrastructure that all town dwellers needed in order to survive. Associational groups tried to persuade, pressure, induce, or force the municipal administration to take the courses of action they favoured. However, at the same time, these associational groupings were themselves internally politicized since their members were never equal and their internal operations were never democratic. Like the city itself, the guild, neighbourhood, religious community, or caste would have its own recognized elite. The elite would struggle to maintain its authority by the effective delivery of services to the members, which might require skill both in dealing with the municipal authorities and in adjudicating the internal affairs of the association. Of course, just as city-wide authorities hoped to contain problems within the city, so it was in the interests of the associational elites to keep intracommunal conflicts "internal" rather than letting them come to the attention of the municipal authorities.

S.N. Mukherjee's classic analysis of early nineteenth-century Calcutta provides an illuminating model for the multilayered character of urban politics. As in most Indian cities before the late nineteenth century, the municipal administration in Calcutta was imposed entirely from above – in this case, by the British. But the city also had an indigenous Hindu elite whose members had become wealthy working with or for the British as bankers, merchants, or brokers. The members of this elite group shared a common political agenda posited on acceptance of British rule. They wanted more contact with European culture and more access to the lower ranks of local administration. And, in pursuing this agenda, they adopted political instruments learned from the British: public meetings, pamphlets, newspapers, and the like. Though drawn from different castes, these men openly socialized with each other – but only up to a point. For, at the same time, they belonged to traditional caste associations that adjudicated conflicts over marriage, inheritance, and ritual issues. Indeed, in order to retain influence and credibility within Hindu society, they had to assume leadership positions in these organizations. These *dals* exerted enormous power, but this second level of political activity remained largely hidden from the British, to whom the issues concerned were, after all, of no compelling interest.[69]

The hidden politics of communal organizations was also a significant theme in early modern European urban history. Wherever they were tolerated, certain religious subcommunities – Calvinists, Mennonites, Jews, and others – maintained their own communal institutions with the power to adjudicate disputes and to discipline members for deviating from group standards. All of these communities had elites whose authority was generally accepted but occasionally challenged by less privileged members. As in Calcutta, their economic value to the city as a whole was usually recognized by the municipal administration, but this rarely gave the subcommunal elites access to city-wide political power.[70] Occasionally, Calvinist leaders seized control of the municipal governments, but only rarely – as in the northern Netherlands – did they retain it for more than a few years. In most cases they soon reverted to a status closer to that of the Calcuttan *bhadralok*: an elite whose members enjoyed political influence within their own subcommunities but had only economic power in the city as a whole.

The basic thrust of my argument should by now be clear – that by looking at the political systems of cities in different and largely unconnected civilizations during the same epoch of world history we can more clearly identify not only some fundamental uniformities across cultures but also the specific structural characteristics of urban politics in any one of those cultures. However, comparative history is always fraught with risks. If we make distinctions that are too fine, we see only differences; if we make comparisons that are too imprecise, we end up with nothing more than universal truisms. The objective here is not to identify what all cities at all times had in common but, rather, to determine what cities in the highly urbanized, monetarized, commercialized, bureaucratized but still preindustrial Eurasian civilizations of the early modern era had in common with regard to how they functioned politically.

In his informative study of the Maratha capital of Poona in the eighteenth century, Balkrishna Govind Gokhale argues that "the line separating the imperial administration and Poona's urban government was always indistinct and shifting … [T]hough the concept of an urban government was not unfamiliar to Indian experience, urban government seldom developed its own distinctive corporate and judicial personality as did village government." In fact, Gokhale argues, Indian cities "failed to develop their own independent or autonomous structures of authority as did the Italian city states or the German urban centres."[71] This is a convincing observation, but it would be a mistake to expand it into a pseudo-Weberian statement about the general differences between "autonomous" European cities and "administered" Asian ones. Gokhale himself acknowledges that it was, in particular, capital cities like Poona that found it difficult to sustain a distinct corporate personality. And, of course, we know that at the same time in Europe the great capital cities were so heavily influenced by royal governments that they had few of the "independent or autonomous structures of authority" that might still be found in some German or Italian city-states. Cities across the Eurasian landmass exhibited enormous differences in early modern times, but the most important differences were not necessarily found along the Europe/Asia divide. If we can get past that assumption and think instead about the variant ways in which interests were articulated and power was exercised in cities that differed in terms of such criteria as their size, their administrative and economic function, and/or their degree of social and religious heterogeneity, then we will find new ways to think about cities of the past and new ways in which cities of the past can continue to teach us today.

NOTES

1 A preliminary sketch of some of the ideas put forward in this chapter was presented at the Center for Early Modern History at the University of Minnesota in September 2003. Portions of this chapter were subsequently presented at the University of Delhi, the University of Calcutta, the University of Hyderabad, and the University of Mumbai in the fall of 2003; at the Shelby Cullom Davis Center for Historical Studies at Princeton University in April 2004; at the University of British Columbia in November 2004; and at the University of Victoria in February 2005. A slightly shortened version of the whole chapter was presented under the title "The European City in Global Perspective, 1500–1800" as a keynote address at the conference entitled "City Limits? The European City, 1400–1900" at the University of Manitoba in October 2004. I am grateful for the comments, suggestions, and insights offered by participants and audience members at all of these occasions. I also wish to acknowledge the support of a faculty training grant from the Shastri Indo-

Canadian Institute, which made possible part of the research on which this chapter is based.

2 The literature on the political history of specific European cities is vast. Despite this – or perhaps because of this – there are relatively few works that go beyond the study of politics in specific cities to consider urban political patterns on a regional or national level. Two exemplary studies of urban political cultures in national terms are Walker, *German Home Towns*; and Halliday, *Dismembering the Body Politic*. For a first brief attempt to consider patterns of urban politics for early modern Europe as a whole, see Friedrichs, *Urban Politics*.

3 See, for example, McNeill, *World History*; and Gunn, *First Globalization*.

4 See also Coenen Snyder (this volume) on cultural exchange within Amsterdam. Eds.

5 Friedrichs, *Urban Politics*, 11.

6 A rare example is provided by McClain, Merriman, and Kaoru, *Edo and Paris*. Unfortunately, this excellent collection of studies has not yet evoked much resonance in the literature on European cities.

7 As Kenneth Pomeranz argues in his widely discussed analysis, prior to the "great divergence" that began in the late eighteenth century "the most developed parts of western Europe seem to have shared crucial economic features – commercialization, commodification of goods, lands and labor, market-driven growth, and adjustment by households of both fertility and labor allocation to economic trends – with other densely populated core areas in Eurasia." See Pomeranz, *Great Divergence*, 107.

8 McClain, *Kanazawa*, 1.

9 See also Wolfart (this volume) on the role of historiography in defining sixteenth-century German urban political culture. Eds.

10 Weber, *The City*, 80–1.

11 See, for example, the introduction to Eldem, Goffman and Masters, *Ottoman City between East and West*, 1–16; or Misra, "Some Aspects of the Self-Administering Institutions."

12 Weber, *The City*, 81.

13 Chevalier, "L'état et les bonnes villes en France."

14 Friedrichs, "Swiss and German City-States."

15 See, for example, Hansen, "95 Theses about the Greek *Polis*," esp. thesis no. 16 (261–2). Theses nos. 1–18 summarize Hansen's major arguments about city-states in general, based largely on the total of thirty-six studies presented in Hansen, *Comparative Study of Thirty City-State Cultures* and *Comparative Study of Six City-State Cultures*.

16 Cf. the discussion in Mauersberg, *Wirtschafts- und Sozialgeschichte*, 128–51.
17 Cf. the excellent overview of these debates by Bernstein, "The Benefit of the Ballot?"
18 A notable example is Goa, whose European male inhabitants voted for municipal officials in ways closely modelled on the practices of Lisbon. See de Souza, *Medieval Goa*, 132–40.
19 See also Blackstone (this volume) on overlapping jurisdiction in municipal governance in sixteenth-century Norwich. Eds.
20 Davis, "Rites of Violence."
21 Beik, *Urban Protest*.
22 See Friedrichs, "Politics or Pogrom?" and "Anti-Jewish Politics."
23 Fuma, "Late Ming Urban Reform"; von Glahn, "Municipal Reform and Urban Social Conflict." The career of the schoolteacher and political activist Ding Shiqing is vividly recounted in the records studied by Fuma and von Glahn.
24 Much has been written about the duties of the *kotwal* and *kazi* in Indian cities. The *kotwal* was the chief magistrate, or chief of police in the broad sense of the term. In cities under Muslim rule, such as those within the Mughal realm, the *kazi* (*qazi*) was the chief judge, with special responsibility for ensuring that the religious and social norms of Islam were upheld but with authority over the entire population of Muslims and non-Muslims alike.
25 Cf. Marcus, *Middle East*, 79–83.
26 Khoury, *State and Provincial Society*, 56–8, 122–6.
27 Cf. van der Sprenkel, "Urban Social Control," esp. 609.
28 Singh, *Town, Market, Mint and Port*, 42–3.
29 Ibid., 40–114 passim. The special administrative structure of Surat, where the highest officials were the governor and the commander of the fortress (both of them imperial appointees), is well explicated in Gokhale, *Surat in the Seventeenth Century*, 51–71.
30 For an overview, see Friedrichs, *Early Modern City*, 182–213. See also Cowan, *Urban Europe*, 51–58.
31 For some examples, see McClain, *Kanazawa*, 49–50.
32 Meyer-Fong, *Building Culture*, 23 and passim.
33 Finnane, *Speaking of Yangzhou*, 253–6.
34 Family-based factional conflict was a characteristic feature of Ottoman urban politics. See, for example, Schilcher, *Families in Politics*, esp. 27–40; Khoury, *State and Provincial Society*, esp.120–33, 200–9. For a

brief overview of the role of urban factions in Europe, see Friedrichs, *Urban Politics*, 35–8.

35 Gillion, *Ahmedabad*, 23.

36 Cf. Misra, "Some Aspects of Self-Administering Institutions," esp. 86–8.

37 Bayly, *Rulers, Townsmen and Bazaars*, 308–12, points out that, in theory, quasi-independent corporate bodies deriving their legitimacy from their own members were inconsistent with Islamic ideas of governance, yet this did not impede guilds or guild-like organizations, which antedated the beginnings of Muslim rule in India, from continuing to function effectively throughout the Mughal era.

38 Ramaswamy, "Artisans in Vijayanagar Society," esp. 426–35.

39 Baer, "Functions of Turkish Guilds"; Gerber, "Guilds in Seventeenth-Century Anatolian Bursa."

40 Marcus, *Middle East*, 173 and, more generally, 162–77.

41 Cf. Golas, "Early Ch'ing Guilds," esp. 575.

42 On the ejection of guilds from municipal councils in south German cities, see Naujoks, *Kaiser Karl V. und die Zunftverfassung*.

43 On this subject, see Pearl, "Change and Stability;" Boulton, *Neighbourhood and Society*, 262–8; Rappaport, *Worlds within Worlds*, 182–3.

44 McClain, *Kanazawa*, chaps. 2–3.

45 Takashi, "Governing Edo," 45–58; see also Takashi, "Edo in the Seventeenth Century."

46 For Osaka, see James L. McClain, "Space, Power, Wealth and Status in Seventeenth-Century Osaka," in McClain and Osamu, eds. *Osaka*, esp. 53; and Kusuo, "Protest and the Tactics of Direct Remonstration," esp. 87–8. For an analysis of the way in which block associations emerged in mid-sixteenth-century Kyoto, see Berry, *Culture of Civil War in Kyoto*, 210–41.

47 Nakagawa, "Approaches to the Study of 18th-Century Cities," 12. The quoted passage summarizes the views of the noted historian Naohiro Asao.

48 Gillion, *Ahmedabad*, 25.

49 Blake, *Shahjahanabad*, esp. chap. 3.

50 Cf. Friedrichs, "Jews in the Imperial Cities."

51 For a notable recent analysis of these groups and their social role, see Stuart, *Defiled Trades*.

52 The Sinti and Roma (gypsies) no doubt also constituted a caste within European society, but they were rarely found in cities.

53 McClain, *Kanazawa*, 129–32, see also 45–6.

54 Bayly, *Rulers, Townsmen and Bazaars*, 177–80.
55 The disputes between "left-hand" and "right-hand" caste associations in the European-ruled cities of south India are discussed by Mukund, "Caste Conflict in South India."
56 Cf. Johnson, *Shanghai*, chap. 3; and Naquin, *Peking*, 19–56 and passim.
57 For a useful description of such subcommunities and their stable relationships with each other in one major city, see Marcus, *Middle East*, 39–48 and passim.
58 Marcus, *Middle East*, 58–9, 87–94; Khoury, *State and Provincial Society*, 61–5, 133–7; Schilcher, *Families in Politics*, 110–14.
59 For an important case study, see Kaplan, *Calvinists and Libertines*.
60 Arasaratnam and Ray, *Masulipatnam and Cambay*, 13–20.
61 Ibid, 19.
62 For a striking example of the dynamic use of petitioning in Japanese urban politics, see Kusuo, "Protest and the Tactics of Direct Remonstration." For the role of petitions in European urban politics, see van Nierop, "Popular Participation in Politics in the Dutch Republic," esp. 284–8; and Schwerhoff, "Das Kölner Supplikenwesen."
63 Some well known examples are cited by Habib, *Peasant and Artisan Resistance*, 28–30.
64 Berry, *Culture of Civil War in Kyoto*, 106–70.
65 The literature on the Münster uprising is vast, but the study by Schilling, "Aufstandsbewegungen in der stadtbürgerlichen Gesellschaft," remains particularly significant for showing that, for many years before the situation became radicalized, events in Münster had continued to conform to the typical process by which Protestantism replaced Roman Catholicism as the official religion of many German cities.
66 Cf. Davis, "Rites of Violence."
67 See Mukund, "Caste Conflict in South India," 21–7. See also Roche, "Caste and the British Merchant Government," which emphasizes how British policy actually magnified and rigidified the social and spatial boundaries between the left-hand and right-hand caste associations.
68 Some important episodes occurred in the early eighteenth century – notably the riots of 1729 in Delhi, which began after a Hindu magnate was accidently injured near the Muslim shoe bazaar and intensified when Muslims tried to avenge the death of one of their leaders. A standard account is provided by Rizvi, *Shah Wali-Allah and His Times*, 197–202.
69 Mukherjee, "Class, Caste and Politics in Calcutta, 1815–38" and "Bhadralok and Their Dals."

70 For the exceptionally large range of religious subcommunities in early modern Hamburg and their relationship to the political authorities, see Whaley, *Religious Change and Social Toleration*; and Driedger, *Obedient Heretics*.

71 Gokhale, *Poona in the Eighteenth Century*, 87.

2

Global Yokels: Vernacular Manuscript Chronicles and Urban Identity in Early Modern Germany[1]

JOHANNES C. WOLFART

INTRODUCTION

In what follows, I argue that quite ordinary early modern German city dwellers engaged with the principles and practices of modern historiography. The import of this dynamic is likely far greater than is generally acknowledged. Conventional emphasis on humanist (i.e., Latin, elite, and [usually] published) and on secular (i.e., modern, Renaissance, and [often] courtly political) historical genres has overshadowed a very active tradition of what I call "vernacular confessional historiography" in early modern Germany. The practice of this kind of historiography apparently flourished in the many smaller cities and towns of southern Germany, especially around the turn of the sixteenth to seventeenth centuries. Proper estimation of this essentially urban historiography demands, among other things, a careful reconsideration of the precise details of its urban milieu. Such consideration, in turn, raises questions about the precise boundaries of the intellectual capabilities and cultural horizons of the early modern bourgeois, of the city dweller's limits. Such bourgeois were possessed of an emerging modern sense of time and space, of modern historical and geographical awareness. Notoriously, however, such awareness was sharply constrained by certain pieties, not all of them necessarily conventionally religious. Finally, as modern historiographers in the making, these early modern writers speak to the struggles of fully modern contemporary historians, who must pick and choose from what they know to be a limitless array – a whole world's worth, at least – of topics and data in order to satisfy the moral demands of national professional organizations, academic trends, and faculty politics. In a sense, the modern historian is still bound by the city limits that constrained the early modern writer of vernacular confessional historiography.

THE URBAN SETTING OF AN EARLY MODERN HISTORIOGRAPHY

In the late medieval and early modern periods, southern Germany was one of the most heavily urbanized regions of Europe. This fact is obscured somewhat by two recent historiographical tendencies. First, conventional histories of European urbanization deal in the categories of national historiography. Thus, "Germany" is usually considered as a whole, a practice that conceals a dramatic shift in population, wealth, and cultural influence from the south to the north of Germany over the course of the whole early modern period, say from 1500 to 1800.[2] The urban character of south Germany may be further obscured by the practice of defining urban Europe primarily in terms of "cities" of ten thousand or more inhabitants.[3] And yet, on the eve of the Reformation, southern Germany boasted no fewer than eighty-five so-called Imperial Free Cities alone.[4] Add to that a large number of ecclesiastical and territorial towns and cities, and one may easily arrive at an estimate of 100–150 urban centres in a region not much larger than the present day *Bundesland* of Baden-Württemberg. And while many of these urban centres had very small populations by modern standards, taken together these towns and small cities obviously boasted an urban population in excess of the great south German metropolises of Augsburg, Nürnberg, or Strasburg. Moreover, while the proliferation of these small cities in the landscape did encourage the development of networks of relations that linked such places, it would be wrong to conclude that distinct urban identities were subsumed by a more generalized identity of such a network.[5] Indeed, it is worth noting that contemporaries did not differentiate between larger cities and smaller towns: from the very great Augsburg to the very tiny Isny they were all simply *Städte*.[6] This means that, from the largest to the smallest, they all had citizens (*Bürger*) who conducted their lives subject to municipal law (*Stadtrecht*) and developed, through participation in public life and via a range of symbols and rituals (both avowedly secular and more overtly religious alike), strong urban identities.[7] Such identities were clearly both more extensive and more profound than that species of patriotism expressed, say, at the annual public reaffirmation of the citizens' oath (*Bürgereid*). Thus, significant differences notwithstanding, in certain regards these south German urban communities appear to have functioned much like the Venice described in Edward Muir's classic study of civic ritual.[8] It would be imprudent, however, to claim that the differences among the south German towns were purely cultural and thus largely imaginary. In some instances the inherent peculiarities born of their geographical situations alone – Lindau, for example, occupied an island on Lake Constance and was thus unusually limited – were enough to make them appear unique to contemporaries. In other instances, this or that centre developed unique manufacturing and cultural industries. Thus, Kaufbeuren achieved a reputation as a textile producer, whereas the aforementioned Isny was known, at least in humanist circles, as the home to the press of Paul Fagius, which specialized in the printing of Hebrew texts.[9] It is also the case, however, that such inherent differences as existed in terms of, say, geographic situation, provided only the most rudimentary foundations for the complex, elaborate, and distinct urban identities that developed over the course of the high-late middle ages. The superstructure, as it were, of south German urban identity in this period – widely acknowledged as the heyday of German urban culture – was the product of deliberate cultural activity and, especially, of commemorative rituals. These commemorative rituals found their most durable form, I would argue, in the scribal practices of medieval civic *Annalistik*, or *Chronistik*.

Historians have long been aware of the output of *medieval* German chroniclers.[10] For much of that time, however, estimations of these chronicles have tended towards indictments of their low factual accuracy and corresponding limited utility as sources for legal-political history.[11] In terms of literary flair or historical imagination, the chronicles have likewise generally been considered sorely wanting. Indeed, the consensus seems to be that German medieval chroniclers do not pass muster either as witnesses to the past or as narrators. That is, their long lists of – in some cases quite literally – one blessed thing after another have long been considered both unreliable and dull. In this judgment, at least, sixteenth-century humanist historians and twentieth-century scientific historians agreed: the urban chroniclers of Germany were not historians, not even primitive ones.[12] For all that, the medieval German urban chronicles have garnered some considerable scholarly attention over the years.[13]

By contrast, the so-called chronicles composed by *early modern* south German urbanites have received almost no attention as a coherent phenomenon, and certainly no positive attention. And yet, south German city dwellers of the so-called "confessional period" – roughly from the establishment of the Reformation to the Peace of Westphalia – appear to have been very busy chronicle writers. For example, a preliminary survey of municipal archives in the Allgäu/eastern Lake Constance region suggests that the practice was very common indeed. One locale alone, the small- to medium-sized city of Lindau, today boasts no fewer than three extant chronicles, all produced in the first decades of the seventeenth century. One of these in particular, the work of the brothers Ulrich and Alexius Neukomm, will serve as my primary example in what follows.[14]

The bound volume entitled *Annales Lindavienses* – and commonly known in the local historiography as the *Neukommsche Chronik*[15] – runs to about 450 half-folio-sized sides of manuscript. These include dated entries in German prose and in two distinct hands covering a period from the ninth century to 1627. The work is thus obviously one of historiography and not simply one of contemporary witness. The entries themselves cover a wide range of themes, mostly pertaining in some manner to the civic history of Lindau. These range from unique events (e.g., a key battle, an important constitutional grant, or a disastrous fire) to records of periodic data (e.g., those pertaining to the local fishery or to the price of wine set annually by the Lindau government). The Lindavian focus is broken only occasionally, most notably by a Neukomm family history at the beginning of the volume and by about one hundred doggerel verses covering events in world history. These latter appear throughout the main text in Ulrich Neukomm's hand and usually conclude longer passages of narrative coherence. Thus, they appear to function somewhat like chapter summaries. The volume is handsomely bound but otherwise largely unadorned, except for a few pages of coloured illustrations, mostly heraldic, that accompany the Neukomm genealogy and commentaries on other prominent Lindau families. Finally, the volume contains a small number of what appear to be full transcriptions of historical documents, mostly of the sort one would call eyewitness accounts. What we have here, then, the names *Annales* and *Chronik* notwithstanding, is much more than a simple diachronic record of events. In fact, the text is actually of a mixed genre, incorporating elements of several chronicle traditions with civic panegyric, genealogy, and narrative elements of universal, or world, history. Aspects of the commonplace book, the householder's journal, and the occasional newssheet or broadside are also evident. Finally, a limited number of classical and renaissance historical works, which circulated widely in print around 1600, are cited. In other words, the manuscript amounts to a multi-author text that clearly reflects exposure to a range of historiographical traditions, including to texts only available to lay urbanites via a lively market in printed works of all sorts. This interaction of manuscript and print alone makes this text remarkable as an emblem of the transition from the medieval to the modern. In terms of identification and classification of the object, it should be emphasized once more that questions of both authorship and genre are actually much more complex than the common name, especially, would imply. In that sense, *Neukommsche Chronik* is, much like "Holy Roman Empire," actually a double-misnomer.

On the other hand, one might consider this text to be a prime example of what I call "vernacular confessional historiography." The text is thus an expression of what were two primary axes of identity for early modern German urbanites: religious tension and tension surrounding the place of urban citizens in the Holy Roman Empire.

URBAN IDENTITY AND VERNACULAR HISTORIOGRAPHY: A BOURGEOIS PRACTICE?

To identify the *Annales Lindavienses* as "vernacular" obviously distinguishes the German text both from the countless Latin chronicles produced throughout medieval Europe as well as from the humanist revival of classical historiography. Significantly, it also implies something about authorship. It signals that the *Annales*, unlike their most likely medieval models, were not produced in either monastic or courtly circles. In fact, of course, they were the work of two urban commoners, both Protestants. They, in turn, borrowed heavily from other protestant Lindauers of the first generations. What vernacularity is not meant to imply, however, is that their work was naïve or that it represented "popular" or "folk" culture. Thus the term is intended, above all, to emphasize the multiple "common" aspects of such texts, especially as they were produced rather than consumed. That is, many such texts were written by more or less ordinary urbanites. The texts do not, however, have a "publication history." Moreover, it is simply not knowable if and how these manuscripts were read, if indeed they were read at all. In this sense, *vernacular* confessional historiography is fundamentally different from what is covered in a standard survey of Western historiography, even one that considers "confessional historiography" a distinct category.[16]

The principal scribes of the *Annales* were, of course, the brothers Ulrich and Alexius Neukomm. The former appears to have started writing the text in 1608. On his death in 1624, Alexius carried on until he, too, died in 1627. Annotations in his hand appear throughout the *Annales*, but it is not clear how much, if at all, he participated in the project before 1624. Since Ulrich appears to have been writing from Augsburg, some considerable distance from Lindau, it is likely that Alexius, who resided in Lindau, contributed at least in the capacity of informant.

Who were the Neukomm brothers? Unfortunately, Alexius's biography is better documented than that of Ulrich, who was actually the initiator and principal author of the project. Alexius Neukomm was the controversial pastor of Lindau who was at the centre of a citizen's revolt in 1626.[17] Like many of Lindau's native sons, he had sought higher education "abroad." Lindau had a grammar school but no *Gymnasium*, let alone a college or university.[18] Unlike his brother, Ulrich apparently did not attend university. But he obviously had an excellent grammar school education, and he did leave Lindau, eventually making a career in the service of merchants in the great city of Augsburg, where he also married and acquired citizenship.[19] In more than one sense, then, this work is an act of wistful patriotism or expatriate nostalgia. The brothers were members of an established Lindau family with traditional membership in the local tailors' guild. Since Lindau's constitution provided for quasi-representative government dominated by the city's six guilds, many Neukomms appear as office holders in Lindau throughout the fifteenth and sixteenth centuries. Their father, Georg, had served as

Obmann, or president, of that guild, an office that had also entailed a seat on the City Council. A third brother, Andreas, served as *Stadtamman*, or head of the City Court. By the early seventeenth century, however, the power of the guilds in Lindau was on the wane, as were the local Lindau cloth trade and, presumably, the fortunes of the Neukomm family. Alexius and Ulrich thus stood well outside the world of the Baroque courtier or regional professional elite. Therefore, the Neukomms documented not only the Lindau Ulrich had left but also the Lindau, now gone, in which their family had been a prominent social force.

Although as a guild family (*Zunftgeschlecht*) the Neukomms were clearly downwardly mobile, the brothers Neukomm were anything but representative of the German "common man" and his political culture as idealized by Peter Blickle. Nor can they be simply identified with the European popular culture imagined by Carlo Ginzburg.[20] Nor, indeed, can one simply consider them German "hometownsmen," to use Mack Walker's famous concept.[21] Perhaps it would do best to describe the Neukomms as they would have described themselves, albeit with a little allowance for hindsight and our knowledge that they lived on the cusp of modernity, in an age of emerging global trade and capitalism. Thus, one might simply use the redolent Anglo-French equivalent of the Neukomms' favourite term of self-description, *Bürger*: the Neukomms were bourgeois.[22]

Further, the Neukomms' position was marked by another odd tension, one with deep roots in the history of the German-speaking lands. While they were neither of the peasantry nor of the nobility or patriciate, as ordinary citizens of Lindau they were also, as has already been suggested, citizens of nowhere special. The early modern Holy Roman Empire was marked by both a striking diversity and a pronounced lack of centre. Thus, one can concur at least partially with the famous thesis of Mack Walker's *German Home Towns*. For example, Walker's basic premise that, in comparison with, say, early modern England or France, in early modern Germany there was "no there there," no London or Paris for the provincials simultaneously to emulate and to resist, is sound. One should not rush to agreement, however, with Walker's conclusion that early modern Germans therefore had *strictly* local identities and that they did not experience the ambivalent pull of both local community and emerging national society and culture.[23] Instead, the very structure of the Neukomm Chronicle is one piece of evidence that early modern Germans were indeed subject, as were their French or English counterparts, to this particularly ambivalent moment of historical geography.

Indeed, in many ways the brothers Neukomm anticipated the "national provincials" described by Celia Applegate in critique of Walker.[24] More than that, they were practically *global* provincials. At least, they possessed some awareness, albeit narrow-minded, of early modern horizons that were widening at a remarkable rate. This is evidenced by the juxtaposition in the *Annales* of the records of local events with those of world history. It is also demonstrated by the inclusion of a letter home to Germany from Venezuela, written by Titus Neukomm in 1532.[25] Applegate is on to something that seems to have eluded Walker: that his hometownspeople, strong local identities notwithstanding, also participated in the construction of regional, super-regional, national, and even international contexts for themselves. Indeed, the example of the *Annales* suggests that the ground was already well prepared for Applegate's eighteenth-century mytho-historical mediation between local identities and larger collective ones through the co-development of historical and religious identities in the confessional age. This, in turn, might ultimately permit the construction of models of Reformation and confessionalization, which, like Applegate's "provincial nationalism," satisfy both the local particularism and emerging national or imperial characteristics of German historical record. This then, in broadest terms, is the point of an investigation of early modern German vernacular confessional historiography: to account for the development of widely shared identities – and, perhaps, even of confessional thinking or religious consciousness – even in the absence of equivalent institutional structures of government, education, and state.

Under such circumstances it is hardly surprising that the vernacularity of the Neukomm Chronicle is not a straightforward attribute. As already suggested, the term should not be taken to mean naïveté or folksy simplicity. Both Neukomms appear to have been very well educated writers, after a fashion. In this they would have been fairly typical bourgeois of their generation. In Lindau, as elsewhere, the magistrates had established a so-called German school for girls and a Latin or grammar school for boys, as well as a civic library, in the first decades of the Reformation.[26] In fact, the

Annales make specific mention of the institution of the library in Lindau. Thus it was that people like Ulrich Neukomm were not only highly literate but also rudimentarily Latinate, as he strove to demonstrate repeatedly throughout his text. Nevertheless, the Neukomms' *Annales* had very little, if anything, in common with the nationally successful published histories of their own age – say, for example, Melanchthon's *Chronicon Carionis* or Johannes Sleidan's *History of the Reformation* – with which the Neukomms and their contemporaries would certainly have been familiar. Instead, it is striking that Ulrich Neukomm, in particular, deliberately considered events from a local perspective, viewed broad swaths of the past from a single vantage point, and wrote what can only be called local or provincial history, as distinct from the history of one locality. The rigid determination with which he pursued this Lindavian perspective on the world is emphasized by the absence in his work of perspective from Augsburg, which had become his adopted home, where he had married and where he had acquired citizenship. It is further expressed in his decision to write in a language heavily inflected with local Alemannic dialect, albeit decorated with Latin snippets. In sum, the Neukomms' work documents a modern bourgeois worldview in the making. Neither strictly communal nor cosmopolitan, it is the perspective of the global yokel.

To say that the Neukomms were educated does not necessarily imply that they were well or widely read. Certainly, and as already suggested, the number of sources they cited in their *Annales* was very limited. Throughout the text the most frequently cited authority was Johann Stumpf, followed by Johannes Nauclerus, Johannes Cuspinian, Sebastian Münster, Achilles Pirminus Gasser, Sebastian Franck, and Albertus Krantz.[27] Also mentioned at the outset were the Swiss historian Aegidius Tschudi and the Swabian historian Martin Crusius. Only two classical authorities were cited: Ammianus Marcellinus and Strabo. This, apparently, was the historical canon as far as the Neukomms were concerned. Moreover, it seems likely that many of the references were simply borrowed from the sixteenth-century Lindau chronicle of Oswald Kröll.[28] On reflection, however, the limited range of what we would call "secondary literature" used by the brothers is hardly surprising.

According to Uwe Neddermeyer, the advent of the printing press in the middle of the fifteenth century had actually dramatically reduced the range of texts available to readers. To minimize overhead costs, shrewd early modern print-publishers reprinted heavily and recycled texts frequently. The new medium thus soon supplanted the rich diversity of medieval manuscript transmission with reprints and multiple editions of a few outstanding bestsellers.[29] Thus Neddermeyer points out that the thirty thousand editions of German incunabula, part of Elizabeth Eisenstein's famous "print revolution," actually only contained 7,500 basic texts. Such conditions persisted throughout the sixteenth century and well into the seventeenth, and historiographical works were by no means an exception. Thus Melanchthon's methodological introduction to the *Chronicon Carionis* went through 154 editions in the year of its first appearance, 1532, and from 1558 to 1649. By comparison, Melanchthon's nearest competitor, Simon Grynaeus's *Utilitas legendae historiae*, enjoyed a mere twenty-two printings in a roughly comparable period, from 1539 to 1606. In third place was Jean Bodin's great *Methodus* of 1566, which had been through only sixteen editions by 1650.[30] Therefore, lack of selection, alone, might have prompted many a literate bourgeois to write rather than to read history. In the case of the *Annales Lindavienses*, moreover, none of the above works would have had much, if anything, to say about Lindau. Needless to say, none of them could be considered vernacular. The significance of these observations will become clearer as we now turn to a consideration of the process of confessionalization and the meaning of the term "confessional."

URBAN AND CONFESSIONAL IDENTITIES IN THE *ANNALES LINDAVIENSES*

In recent decades, most serious historians of early modern Europe have concerned themselves, in one way or another, with questions pertaining to the reception of religious change on the ground, as it were. The central problematic here concerns the mechanisms by which the sometimes sporadic and often disparate movements of pre-Reform and early Reformation established themselves in large and diverse populations over the course of only a few generations, as Zwinglianism, Lutheranism, Calvinism, post-Tridentine Catholicism, and the like. A variety of methods and theories have coincided to push this problematic to the top of the historiographical agenda. In the mid–1970s, Gerald Strauss sparked heated debate, both methodological and otherwise, with an article on the "success and failure" of the Reformation.[31] In the late 1970s, a new brand of German Peasants' War studies reinserted the study of religion into social history. By the early 1980s, the study of popular religion had emerged as a recognized subfield; then, in the mid-late 1980s, so-called "confessionalization" studies attracted widespread attention.[32] The paradigm posited the establishment of post-Reformation religious identities of considerable breadth and depth as a co-product of the processes of state-formation and the development of social control mechanisms. Confessionalization theses of this type remain hot properties.[33]

The emergence of religious identities, especially "Protestant" ones, could also be addressed rather differently, especially if one were to eschew master narratives of state formation and the emergence of German national identity. Instead of attempting to gage relative degrees of diffusion or political imposition, one might try to understand the early modern formation of new religious identities, a process that I still call confessionalization, primarily as a form of cultural production. This is certainly not to imply that the process is hermetic and untouched by the circumstances of, say, elite politics, magisterial government, or macro-economics. It does mean, however, that relatively ordinary folk can thus be seen as participants, via such creative cultural activities as vernacular historiography, in the formation of their own religious identities. In such a framework, the pursuit of confessionalism via such texts as the *Annales* actually amounts to little more than an application of some of the empirical methods of microhistorians and historians of popular religion. Nevertheless, the possible results of proceeding in this manner are quite broad, especially if one considers that one of the sites of greatest activity in this kind of confessionalization – vernacular historiography – could have lasting implications for practising historians down to the present day. This is a point – largely speculative and interpretive at this juncture – to which we shall return at the conclusion of this chapter.

As already suggested, the identity of early modern German bourgeois was determined by tension. Moreover, the tension of being a global yokel was significantly compounded, over the course of the sixteenth century, by what might reasonably be termed religious tensions.[34] These were basically threefold. First, local religious practice was frequently reconceived in tension to that of neighbours, especially those who lived on the other side of a confessional boundary. Second, local religious practice commonly developed in tension to normative broadcasts or official statements of faith. Third, the actual process of reform proceeded piecemeal over the course of decades, so that sixteenth-century people came to experience or perceive considerable variability or mutability of religious practice. In a context where *innovatio* was a species of heresy, this was obviously also a source of tension. Out of such tensions precipitated, among other things, a particular historiographical response. As long ago as 1918, Friedrich von Bezold located in the Reformation the fundamental – at least for modern historiographers – impetus to "order" the past.[35] Of course our interests, here and now, are quite far removed from those of von Bezold, then and there. Nevertheless, there is little doubt that at least one particular early modern engagement with the past, in the form of the manuscript historiography here under consideration, was inextricably linked to the post- Reformation process of confessionalization.[36]

Because the Reformation did have an immediate and isolating effect on communities like Lindau, some inhabitants actually did retreat, at least temporarily, from wider regional, territorial, or national contexts to construct, instead, more local, historical identities.[37] This accounts in the simplest manner for early modern revivals of the medieval manuscript chronicle, especially in the first half of the sixteenth century.[38] It also explains the very dynamic interplay of yokelism and globalism in the identities of early modern bourgeois like the Neukomms. And yet, the Reformation was of course also the occasion of profound tensions at the local level. It disrupted communities, it upset families, and it destabilized personal identities. Putting things back together again, as it were, was a long and difficult process, one that was not entirely distinct from the Reformation but that nevertheless appears different enough to warrant its own name: confessionalization. And while the *Annales* do indeed document many of the tensions that originated in the Reformation, on closer reading they also illuminate a very strong need to resolve these momentous ideological and institutional displacements. Thus, the text can probably tell us more about the gradual and often surprisingly subtle processes of confessionalization than it does about the cataclysm of Reformation. Another history, specifically of the Lindau Reformation, composed anonymously and probably within a decade of the completion of the *Annales*, directly challenged the Neukomm account of the Lindau

Reformation.[39] Indeed, one may consider the operation of these two histories, including an emerging historiographical dialogue, as evidence contradicting the straightforward equation of confessionalization with institutional developments, especially state-building.

So how did the *Annales Lindavienses* handle the turbinated course of reform in the Lindau church? And how did this historiographical process contribute to the construction of a new religious identity for the inhabitants of the city? As already suggested, for the crucial early decades of the Reformation the Neukomms relied almost exclusively on the account of an eyewitness, the *Bürgermeister* Oswald Kröl. Likewise, they reproduced a detailed contemporary memoir of the so-called Interim Crisis not found anywhere else. The insistence on producing eyewitness accounts serves to lend particular weight, however, to the period after 1580, following the contentious introduction of the Formula of Concord in Lindau. It is for this period, key to the process of confessionalization, that the Neukomms were themselves eyewitnesses. Thus, the *Annales* contains details – many of which, for various reasons, are not to be extracted from official government sources or church ordinances – of the practice of the Lindau church in the wake of the Reformation. For example, it is reported that, in 1613, the Lindau church reinstituted a ritual of ordination for its communally elected pastors, an act that, Ulrich Neukomm duly noted, Lindauers had not witnessed for one hundred years.[40]

The identification of this particular time frame, one century, provides a clue to the more significant function of the Neukomms' historiographical enterprise. Notoriously, Lindau had not been a signatory of the *Confessio Augustana* submitted to the Emperor Charles v in 1532; instead, the city had been one of four south German cities – the others being Memmingen, Constance, and Strasburg – that had signed the so-called *Confessio Tetrapolitana*, a careful compromise on key issues between the Lutheran/German Princes' position and the Zwinglian/Swiss/Reformed position. This circumstance largely accounts for the Neukomms' particular attention to Lindavian preparations for celebrating the Luther Jubilee of 1617. The circumstances surrounding the Tetrapolitan Confession and Lindau's self-exclusion from the Augsburg Confession were indisputable. Yet, in 1616, on the eve not only of the Luther Jubilee but also of the Thirty Years' War, the urgency of projecting an image of orthodoxy would have been great. Thus, the function of the *Annales* may be described as urban identity *formation* only in part. The *Annales* also attempted a certain amount of urban identity *laundering*.

Given the necessarily limited circulation of a manuscript such as the *Annales*, however, one must conclude that commemorative entries for 1616–17 were part of a larger conceit that also served to convince the authors themselves, and others (assuming they had an intended readership), of the thoroughgoing Lutheran rectitude of reform in Lindau. A clue to the brothers' motivation may be gleaned from an observation by the pastor Alexius, in a context other than the chronicle, to the effect that seventeenth-century Lindauers resisted the notion that their church had undergone a process of change, or had changed repeatedly, over the course of the preceding century. This idea, he claimed, was unsettling to them because it meant that their fathers and forefathers would not be saved.[41] The Neukomm chronicle therefore counteracted this sense of instability by interweaving Lindavian history with an idealized narrative of Luther's life and work. Thus, Ulrich Neukomm's versifications traced Luther's career from his birth and the dramatic inauguration of reform in 1517 through his various disputations and political battles to his glorious death. Of course, he was at great pains to lay a certain Lindavian claim to this narrative, to offset the indisputably non-Lutheran cast of the early Reformation in Lindau. For example, he slyly recorded the arrival of reform-minded preaching in Lindau in 1523 as "the advent of Lutheranism, or more precisely Zwingli's heresy in Lindau." In the same entry, Neukomm also noted the birth in Lindau of Dr Johann Marbach, who became a Doctor of Holy Writ at Strasburg and attracted 4,500 people to his funeral in 1583. Marbach, Neukomm pointed out, was "created and made a Doctor in Wittenberg in 1539 by Luther himself."[42] Indeed, throughout his work, Neukomm worked hard to establish each and every Lindavian connection to Luther. By the time of the Luther Jubilee in 1617, there was no question anymore: somehow, without undergoing any real perceptible change, the Lindau Church had become a "Lutheran Church." The centennial was celebrated fittingly in Lindau, with the expansion, in perpetuity, of the pastorage to five full-time appointments.[43] Neukomm's entries for that year were prefaced by a catalogue of Lindau clergymen, which he headed "ab instaurato Evangelio Anno Domini 1522."[44]

URBAN HISTORIOGRAPHY AND THE IDENTITY OF HISTORIANS, PAST AND PRESENT

The cultural understanding of confessionalization just outlined leads to further disagreement with the way in which most historians of historiography understand so-called "confessional historiography." This includes very serious scholars like Uwe Neddermeyer or Donald Kelley, whose survey of Western historiography actually contains a whole chapter on the Reformation with a subsection entitled "Confessional History."[45] In their view – and this is, admittedly, a very rough resumé – early modern Catholics and Protestants of various stripes wrote differing and, frequently, antagonistic accounts of the past *because* of their confessional identities. In this view, confessional historiography was simply religious apologetic. Such a view obviously proceeds from the assumption of an a priori confessional identity that existed independently of historiography and that could thus determine the act of history writing, in which it found only secondary expression. It is worth noting, as an aside, that proponents of this view generally dismiss the product of confessional historiography as fundamentally tendentious, polemical, or hyperbolic, thereby salvaging some sort of purer historiographical impulse. My own view is that the key elements of confessional historiography – religious identity and the practices of history writing – are considerably less easy to disentangle. Moreover, I would argue that, in early modern Europe, history writing was anything but a secondary act or a mere ancillary expression of confessionalism; instead, the example of the *Annales Lindavienses* suggests that it actually played a considerable part in the production of confessional identities.

Of course, this model demands that even ordinary townsfolk or vernacular writers such as the brothers Neukomm possessed some considerable historiographical ability apart from, if not prior to, the strictly apologetic or polemical sort normally called "confessional historiography." Thus, we now turn to a few more concrete observations on their working concept of history.

Easily the most widely cited work on the late medieval German urban (i.e., non-ecclesiastical or non-monastic) chronicle tradition is that of Heinrich Schmidt, which has already been mentioned. In the nineteenth and early twentieth centuries, urban chronicles had been widely condemned by historians for their unreliability as historical source, and Schmidt's primary and declared purpose was to rehabilitate them. But, writing in the 1950s, Schmidt had not the means to challenge nineteenth-century criteria of good historical writing, especially the compulsion to appear disinterested or unbiased. He was, therefore, compelled to remove the chronicles from the line of fire by arguing that theirs was an entirely unique context and tradition. Schmidt used Joachimsen's dismissive evaluation of the chronicle tradition as non-historical to this effect. Thus, according to Schmidt, the work of the chronicler had nothing to do with that of the historian and could not be evaluated by the same standard; rather, Schmidt argued, the urban chronicles derived from the amplified legal concerns of the Imperial cities. He further developed the thesis that chroniclers, and more generally all inhabitants of late medieval cities, had what amounted to synchronic imaginations.

The *Annales Lindavienses*, and Ulrich Neukomm' contribution in particular, does not fit Schmidt's model. First of all, while Ulrich referred to his work as a *Chronik* or *Annales*, he also apparently considered himself some kind of historian. For example, he referred collectively to those authors he cited, as well as to himself, as writers of histories (*Historien*). Also against an assimilation of Ulrich's work to Schmidt's thesis is his clear categorical distinction between past ages (*vor alten Zeiten*) and the historian's time (*zu unsren Zeiten*). Moreover, as Ulrich contrasted past and present, he referred to a past time that was as variegated as the present. Thus, one of his most common techniques was to locate the past origins of present things by identifying historical "firsts" with regard to topics as diverse as public health, military technology, imperial politics, and local urban fashion trends. In this way, he went well beyond the conventional identification of mythical origins;[46] in some cases, causal connections appear to be implied. For example, the same entry for 1494 notes the arrival of syphilis in Lindau and the first use of the mercenaries known as *Landsknechte*. A similar implied connection was established between the Imperial Diet held at Lindau in 1498 and a local vogue for pointed shoes.[47] Elsewhere, Neukomm explicitly attempted explanations of human actions in the past. For example, in his relation of the narrative of a rebellion that resulted in the execution of a number of citizens, Neukomm identified and distinguished both reason and cause.[48] While the explanatory formulation "on account of" (*von wegen*) is quite common, the crucial presence of historical imagination and causal narrative is best exemplified by Neukomm's use of the key term for prime cause: *Ursach*. More than a proto-thing, or *ur-Sache*, the term apparently identified key events or chains of events that led inexorably to subsequent events. This is evident, for example, in a verse linking urban manifestations of the German Peasants' War to clerical agitation.[49] Moreover, human – as opposed to divine – historical agency was identified in these terms. Thus, for example, a fire was attributed to a woman who, in her drunkenness, was careless with a taper.[50] The responsibility of causal carelessness can be contrasted, moreover, with Neukomm's identification of accidental event or coincidence.[51]

As noted at the outset, this chapter is part of a much larger and ongoing project. It is hoped that the reader now has an impression of certain historical data and is equipped with a theoretical framework within which to consider this data. In addition to this, however, every major scholarly undertaking should have a complex thesis, if only to distinguish it from an extended essay. Such a thesis generally consists of several "points" of varying magnitudes or orders of generality. Thus, one of the aims of my project is to bring particular historical data to the attention of wider audiences. As already mentioned, preliminary searches of several south German civic archives suggest that the *Annales Lindavienses* are but one example of a significant body of literature that can be designated "vernacular confessional historiography." Nevertheless, this point about the existence of urban manuscript chronicles in an age of print, or of the German baroque, is less important, in a sense, than the point about the profitability of considering such a work as "vernacular confessional historiography." Remarkably, while some chronicles have received scant attention as artefacts in German *Kulturgeschichte*, their significance as both overtly religious and self-consciously historiographical enterprises remains entirely unexplored. Finally, therefore, I would like to account for the neglect of the genre, an apparent oversight in the history of historiography, in relation to a much more general distortion in the history of historiography, a problem that, in concluding, I now address briefly.

Thus, we now leave behind early modern south German cities like Lindau – or do we? Indeed, my concluding purpose is to suggest that, in fact, "real" places like early modern Lindau have as much claim on twenty-first-century historians as any other topos, perhaps even more. In fact, what I have been arguing is that the identity of Lindauers like the brothers Neukomm was no more and no less the product of historical imagination and historiographical practice than were other conceits, like "the modern" or "the Renaissance." Further, our contemporary struggles for truer identity through better historiography look to me more like vernacular confessional historiography than humanist antiquarianism and literary art. Against the current trend, I would argue that the early modern legacy to modern and postmodern historiographies amounts to so much more than the Renaissance wordsmanship that is currently so widely admired.

It has been more than a decade now since the *American Historical Review* featured a forum and a commentary to consider the enduring influence of Renaissance historiography on the practices of contemporary professional historians. The central point of the exercise was put most succinctly by Randolph Starn, who stated: "The Renaissance is a primal scene of European historiography."[52] Carefully considered though it may be, this pronouncement raises certain difficult questions. For example, what does it mean to assert that the Renaissance is *a* primal scene, rather than *the* primal scene, of European historiography? How many primal scenes can one thing have? The answer is: really only one. Therefore, current interest in the historiography of the Renaissance is, I suspect, related to disaffection with yet another "primal scene of European historiography," the Enlightenment. This shift, however, is inherently awkward. For, while we can all now appreciate efforts to destabilize the hegemonic intellectual and political structures of the eighteenth and nineteenth centuries, many historians have also recently expressed concern – in emotional registers ranging from wistful regret to embittered rage – that the disestablishment of the Enlightenment has required an exposé of its central related claims to objective reason and, more important, *secularity*. Thus, for example, documentation of the religious biases of leading practitioners of scientific history in the nineteenth century is intended as a blow to their authority. Certainly, that is the tone of Thomas A. Brady Jr's suggestion that, at least in its personnel, the exemplary school of Leopold von Ranke was thoroughly Lutheran.[53] Under such circumstances it is highly undesirable to relocate the origins of European historiography from the modern to the early modern without safeguards against what Starn called "reenchantment."

For many historians of historiography those safeguards are available in the conception of the Renaissance as largely, if not wholly, distinct from the Reformation. I am not talking about the old chronological and geographical distinctions;[54] rather, I perceive the conceit of two coextensive and contemporaneous early modernities, one secular and the other religious, with only the former, generally identified as the Renaissance, finding a place in the history of historiography. The problem is, of course, that the data of early modern historiography cut clear across this dichotomy. A careful examination of the *Annales Lindavienses* alone warrants the following interpretative theses: (1) the process of confessionalization involved the articulation of historical arguments that did more than simply follow medieval patterns; (2) such early modern urban historiography was an important practical dimension of early Protestantism; and (3) vernacular confessional historiographers, moreover, were no less adroit or sophisticated than were late modern historians.[55]

While I am all for recognizing the importance of early modern historical writing, a responsible historian ought to acknowledge all of it, printed humanist secular and manuscript vernacular confessional historiography alike. Simply put, it is my contention – it is already more than a speculative hypothesis at this stage – that late modern historiographical theories and practices bear the deep imprint of early modern confessionalism.[56] Yet, while modern historical scholarship has become almost habitually Weberian in its identification of so-called "protestant" societies, economies, polities, and cultures, it has simultaneously endeavoured to preserve for itself a place beyond such historical influence. Thus, the scholarly neglect of early modern German vernacular confessional historiography may be seen as much more than an accidental oversight. My purpose, therefore, extends well beyond redress of balance in the scholarship of early modern historiography to a critique of late modern historiography. One might conclude, finally, that if modern historiography had any primal site it was neither the Renaissance nor the Reformation but, more properly, the early modern city, which was home to them both.

NOTES

1 My thanks to the Winnipeg Rh Foundation and SSHRC for both a development grant and ongoing support for the project "Vernacular Confes-

sional Historiography in Early Modern Germany," of which this chapter is a small part. My thanks, also, to audiences at the Centre for Reformation and Renaissance Studies, Victoria University, University of Toronto as well as at the Religion Colloquium at the University of Manitoba.

2 For an example of this tendency, see de Vries, *European Urbanization*. Strikingly, while de Vries represents Germany as a unified whole, he treats northern, central, and southern Italy separately.

3 Here again, see de Vries, *European Urbanization*.

4 Moeller, *Imperial Cities*, 41.

5 For a conceptualization of such networks as an urban landscape, see Groebner, *Liquid Assets*. For an argument that early modern German cities were nodes, whereas medieval ones were islands, see Kugler, *Vorstellung der Stadt*.

6 Classically, this lack of differentiation of urban centres according to size in early modern Germany has been remarked in Friedrichs, *Urban Society*, 288.

7 See also Blackstone (this volume) on how municipal loyalties were reflected in public life and space in sixteenth-century Norwich. Eds.

8 Muir, *Civic Ritual*; also, Muir, *Ritual in Early Modern Europe*. Muir's approach to ritual contrasts with that found in Blickle, *Fluch und Eid*.

9 Dieter, *Die Reichsstadt Kaufbeuren*; Kraus and Fischer, *Die Stadt Kaufbeuren*. In fact, the fame of Isny in this regard was probably rather limited. Indeed, one may speculate that Fagius's subsequent reputation may have been hampered by the small-town location of his press. Certainly, Jerome Friedman considers Fagius "a scholar who has been neglected to an unfortunate degree." See Friedman, *Most Ancient Testimony*, 100. Irena Backus also considers his location as a major reason for Fagius's modest reputation. See Backus, *Life Writing*, esp. xxix–xxxiii.

10 Among the great achievements of nineteenth-century German historiography and editorial entrepreneurship must be counted *Chroniken der deutschen Städte*. In the late nineteenth and early twentieth centuries, journals such as *Archiv für Kulturgeschichte* took chronicles and their writers very seriously, as did the many practitioners of German *Lokalgeschichte*.

11 Here, at least, the preoccupations of the "legal school" of German historiography clearly continue to dominate to the point where they may be considered established orthodoxy. For the early modern period, the "legal school" of historiography is associated, above all, with Günther Franz. In principle, if not always in practice, Franz has been succeeded by Peter Blickle and his students.

12 That "mere" chronicles were not "real" history was the central judgment of Paul Joachimsen's extremely influential work, *Geschichtsauffassung und Geschichtsschreibung.*
13 The most notable attempt to interpret the phenomenon of medieval urban *Chronistik* as a whole is Schmidt, *Die deutschen Städtechroniken.*
14 The provenance, authorship, basic contours, and so on of these early modern Lindau chronicles are explored in Joetze, *Chroniken der Stadt Lindau.*
15 Joetze, for example, appears actually to have preferred the German name, despite its obvious inaccuracy.
16 For example, see Kelley, *Versions of History.*
17 For a narrative of these events in English, see Wolfart, *Religion, Government.*
18 Burmeister, *Lindauer Studenten,* 63–4.
19 This *vita* is derived from comments in the *Annales* themselves. See also Joetze, *Chroniken,* 30.
20 For example, see Blickle, *Communal Reformation* and also *Kommunalismus*; Ginzburg, *Night Battles.* In any case, the political or popular cultures represented are predominantly rural.
21 Walker, *German Home Towns.*
22 This assessment is in accordance with the observation that the social profile of Augsburg's chroniclers, who, in the late fifteenth century, had been clerics, monks, and patrician laypeople, changed around the middle of the sixteenth century. See Kramer-Schlette, *Augsburger Chronisten.*
23 See also Bailey (this volume) on the transference to the wider nation of distinctly Parisian values in the nineteenth century. Eds.
24 Applegate, *Nation of Provincials.*
25 This letter has made it into the South American historiography. See Galbadon Marquez, *Descubrimiento.*
26 See Breitwieser, *Stadtbibliothek Lindau.*
27 All but the last one were clearly identified. Albertus Krantz is only mentioned by Neukomm as "Crenz."
28 The original of this has not survived. See Joetze, *Chroniken,* 6–19.
29 Neddermeyer, "Was hat man von solchen confusionibus," esp. 80: "Die Erfindung des Buchdrucks hatte eine starke Reduktion der Literaturauswahl zur Folge." See also Neddermeyer, *Von der Handschrift zum gedruckten Buch.*
30 Neddermeyer, "Was hat man von solchen confusionibus," 106.
31 Strauss, "Success and Failure."

32 For a brief survey of the paradigm's fortunes, see Boettcher, "Confessionalization."

33 For example, see volume 94 of the *Archiv für Reformationsgeschichte* (2003), which took confessionalization as its "Focal Point/Themenschwerpunkt"; See also Headley et al., *Confessionalization.*

34 See also Fisher (this volume) on religious tension within urban identities in sixteenth-century Augsburg. Eds.

35 von Bezold, "Entstehungsgeschichte."

36 As already mentioned, few historians have considered the later urban chronicles at all, and none has considered them in this way. The German Democratic Republic historians Karl Czok and Helmut Bräuer gave "religion" a wide berth. Czok, "Bürgerkämpfe und Chronistik"; Bräuer, "Geschichtsschreibung in Zwickau." Safely, in his *Matheus Miller's Memoir*, similarly reflects primarily the concerns of an economic historian.

37 This tendency is explored in Wolfart, *Religion, Government.*

38 On Melanchthon's influence, see Neddermeyer, "Was hat man von solchen confusionibus." See also, Kelley, *Versions of History*, 312.

39 Aspects of this text are considered in some detail in Wolfart, "Sex Lies and Manuscript."

40 *Annales Lindavienses*, 397. "Den 21 November [1613] war vorgemelter *M. Johann* Wilhelm Hursich, von M. Alexio Neükhum *ad Ministerium Lindaviense publicè* ordiniert, Welcher *Actus* Innerhalb hundert Jaren Inn diser Kirchen nie fürgangen."

41 Wolfart, *Religion, Government*, 157–8.

42 *Annales Lindavienses*, 248. "1523. Hatte das Lutherthum, oder vill mehr des Zwinglins Kezerei zu Lindow seinen fortgang, durch den Leßmaÿster zu den Barfußern ... Umb diße Zeit wardt geboren zu Lindow D. Johann Marbach, hernach der Hailigen schrifft Doctor unnd Professor zu Straßburg. Starb daselbst *Anno* 1581. Und giengen in die vierthalb tausent Personen mit der Leich, Er wardt von D. Luther *Anno* 1539 [1543 Joetze] zu Wittemberg zum *Doctor* creiert und gmacht."

43 *Annales Lindavienses*, 423, 424.

44 Ibid., 419.

45 Kelley, *Versions of History*, 320–46.

46 For example, the origin, or *Ursprung*, of Lindau is compared to the founding of Rome by Romulus and Remus, *Annales Lindavienses*, 338.

47 "1494. Khamen von erst an die bösen Blatren genant die Franzosen auß Italia hieher gen Lindow [...] [d]ie ersten Landtsknecht sind auffkhomen." No causality is explicitly established here. *Annales Lindavienses,* 219. "Anno 1498. In dißem Reichstag zu Lindow fiengen

zu erstes an die Fürsten die Alttväterischen geschnebleten schuch zutragen." *Annales Lindavienses*, 221.

48 This was the so-called *Rienoltaufstand* of 1396, which Neukomm explained thus: "von Ursach zwischen Rhatt und Burgershafft solle geweßt sein, wie etliche sagen, von wegen der Stüll in der Kirchen." *Annales Lindavienses*, 128.

49 "Der Bauren Krieg empörrt sich gmach / Zu Augspurg ein Auffrhur geschach/ Der Ursach war ain Ordens Mann / Der trug ain graue Kutten an." *Annales Lindavienses*, 249.

50 "Obgemelte Spitalbrunst ist von des Amptmanns, Mattheus Ecken, truneknem Weib verursacht worden. Die vergass eines brennenden Liechts in der Speckkammer." *Annales Lindavienses*, 290. It is interesting that this entry is actually a commentary in the hand of the pastor Alexius Neukomm: the moral responsibility of the *Verursacher* is therefore also being communicated loud and clear.

51 "zufalender Ursachen," *Annales Lindavienses*, 221.

52 Starn, "Renaissance Redux," 122.

53 Brady "Sacral Community." Brady relies heavily on Weber, *Priester der Clio.*

54 The work of scholars such as Heiko Oberman (who pushed the limits of the Reformation back in time) and Anthony Grafton (who has conversely stretched the Renaissance, or at lease the practices of Renaissance humanism, forward as far as possible) have effectively put paid to these. See, for example, Grafton, *Defenders of the Text*; or Oberman, *The Reformation.*

55 That "historical consciousness" could possibly predate the professional historiography shaped by Enlightenment philosophy and nationalism is suggested by Jakobi, "'Geschichtsbewußtsein.'" Nevertheless, the strict "modernist" position outlined by Koselleck in the 1970s is still regarded as something of an orthodoxy. See Koselleck, "Geschichte, Historie."

56 I am thinking here both of individual scholars as well as particular institutional contexts in which they operate. Examples of the former might include historians as diverse as Charles Austin Beard (*Written History as an Act of Faith*), Karl Löwith (*Meaning in History*), or George Marsden (*The Outrageous Idea of Christian Scholarship*). The latter include Christian seminaries and colleges, all of which teach historical courses, as well as countless "institutes," some of which enjoy the patronage of recognized universities. Such affiliation is an all-important difference, for example, between The European Institute of Protestant Studies (Belfast) and the Zentrum für Reformationsgeschichte und Lutherische Orthodoxie (Wittenberg).

3

Renaissance Venice as a Musical Model for Copenhagen

SUSAN LEWIS HAMMOND

Music has always been a vital part of a city's identity.[1] Sixteenth-century travellers to Venice identified the city with a rich and thriving musical tradition.[2] Music printing had its start there in 1501, while the Venetian firms of Girolamo Scotto and Antonio Gardane dominated the music book trade from the mid- to late sixteenth century. Makers of keyboards, organs, and wind and plucked instruments established workshops in Venice; their productions graced the concert and chamber rooms of Europe. The city's charitable confraternities (the *scuole grandi*) offered a viable patronage option for composers and contributed their own musicians to Venice's justly famous urban processions and pageantry.

The music and culture of the Danish capital of Copenhagen paled in comparison when King Christian IV took the throne in 1588.[3] Copenhagen was a capital in name only: commerce was predominantly local; the university did not attract foreign students; and the town's population numbered only fifteen thousand. In need of an urban facelift, the Danish king looked across Europe for models.[4]

Christian IV turned to Venice as a worthy musical model. My point of entry into these two seemingly disparate urban worlds is the madrigal, a genre of secular song comprised of a single poetic stanza on a serious theme. In the second half of the sixteenth century, Venice emerged as a major exporter of the Italian madrigal. Five volumes from the Venetian presses of Angelo Gardano and Ricciardo Amadino are counted in Heinrich Schwab's reconstruction of the music collections at the court of Christian IV.[5] The genre and its related forms of the strophic villanella and canzonetta circulated as a commercial product, a compositional form, a performance ideal, and an object for collection and exchange among merchants, nobility, rulers, composers, teachers, and musicians across the Continent, Scandinavia, and England.

Though scholarship has focused on Venice as the printing capital of the madrigal, studies of the genre's reception in more distant cities like Copenhagen encourage a critical assessment of traditional narratives of cultural transfer and exchange. My approach draws heavily on theories of reception formulated by Peter Burke – theories that emphasize the active, rather than the passive, role of the "recipients" of cultural influence.[6] This chapter argues that Venice and Copenhagen present a model of cultural transmission with traffic flowing in all directions.

THE STATUS OF THE MODEL

The first question to consider is what made Venice so appealing to its onlookers. What characterized the Danish experience of the city?

The contemporary discourse on early modern cities is surprisingly rich. The urban centre was a destination for travellers, a political entity, a social network, a commercial hub, a gathering place for intellectuals, and a supportive stage for culture and the arts. On all fronts, Venice presented a worthy model for emulation. Giovanni Botero, one of the most prolific writers on the comparative values of kingdoms, regions, and cities, positioned Venice as a model city in his *Della cause della grandezza delle citta* (On the Greatness of Cities), a text that enjoyed a wide circulation in Italian and translated editions. Sir Hawkins's 1635 English translation explains the allure of Venice as follows:

> for the splendour of her present Magnificence ... Venice, with the admiration of her incomparable scituation, which seemeth to be framed by Nature, to predominate over the Water, and to curbe the Ocean, enforceth no lesse wonder. The greatnesse besides of the inestimable Arsenall; the multitude of Shippes of Warre, Trade, and Passengers; the incredible number of Engines, Ordnance, Munition, and of all Navall preparations; the height of the Turrets, the riches of Churches, the magnificence of

> Pallaces, the fairenesse of Market-places, the varietie of Arts, the order of Government; the handsomenesse of Men, and beautie of Women, dazeleth the eyes of all beholders.[7]

The visual beauty of the city and its inhabitants gave seeming proof of an internal political, social, and civil order.[8]

Venice presented a worthy and timely model for Copenhagen as the Danish capital developed a strategy for entering the world stage. Copenhagen's reputation prior to Christian IV's ascent to the throne in 1588 was only regional for, as Botero complained, "there is growing no merchandise of value (excepting seafish) neither is there any famous Mart towne, which is able to draw, or long to maintaine traffique with other nations."[9] In the first half of his reign, Christian IV embarked on a construction program to build a capital of European stature. Drawing inspiration from French architectural models, construction on a new castle, Rosenborg, was begun just outside the city walls; the spires were refurbished and made higher on city churches; a new city hall was built in 1610; and an elaborate stock exchange was constructed between 1619 and 1622.[10] The new image of the Danish capital reached European audiences in Jan Dircksen van Campen's engraving *Hafnia Metropolis et Portvs Celeberrimvs Daniae* (Copenhagen Metropolis and Celebrated Danish Port) of 1611. The prospect formed the basis for images of the city throughout the century. An engraving by Rombout van den Hoeye from around 1640 adheres closely to its model (figure 3.1).

The Latin inscription at the bottom of the original engraving of 1611 supplied textual commentary for the visual glorification of the city and its leader above:

> Copenhagen, you, rising from the Baltic waves of Thetes. You, who from a small provincial town became a great harbour, now you thrive in the twentieth Danish King's time to stretch your high spire to the sky. The great blessings, which you boast, are owed to Christian the Fourth, who takes his name from Christ – Christ, thus announces here the quite true law, the King thus encloses the walls with a Daedalian work.[11]

The king based his commercial reforms on the Dutch mercantile system of regulated companies, trade monopolies, and large-scale

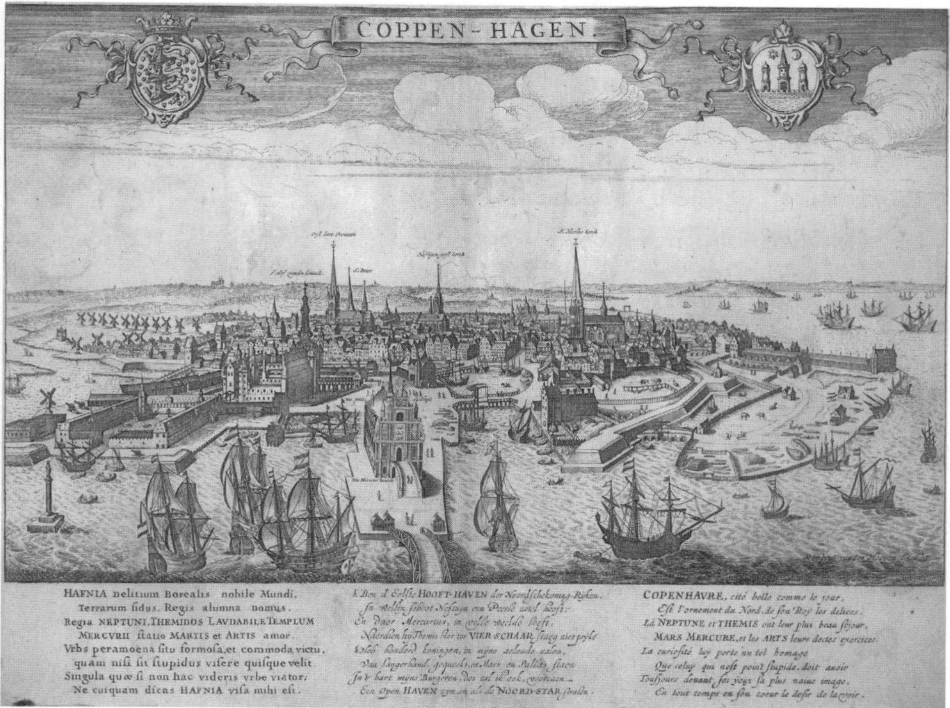

Figure 3.1
Rombout van den Hoeye, Prospect of Copenhagen, ca. 1640. With permission from Det kongelige Bibliotek, Müllers Pinakotek 17, 7, II. FOL.

trade organizations, such as the East India Company, which was established in 1616.[12] The university structure of Protestant German-speaking lands was transplanted to the University of Copenhagen and other centres of learning in the Danish kingdom. Christian IV's extensive travels to Protestant courts and cities of northern Germany in the impressionable early years of his reign left him with models for urban court and civic culture.[13]

Christian IV recognized the value of having sophisticated, well educated, and worldly personnel to manage the affairs of the city, court, and kingdom. In 1600, he instituted stipends of four hundred daler yearly to fund four foreign study trips as a means of preparing Danes for future administrative, academic, and religious careers.[14] Though many studied in German-speaking lands, Danish students travelled in great numbers to the universities and cities of Roman Catholic Italy. Between 1581 and 1620, a total of 150 Danes matriculated at the universities of Siena and Padua.[15] Many later served the Danish government as councilmen, advisors, and diplomats.[16] The country's top ecclesiastical post, that of Bishop of Sjælland, went to Hans Poulsen Resen (1561–1638), who had made extensive contacts with Italians during his studies in Padua in the 1580s.[17] The choice of Venice as a destination for musical training was a mark of the city's reputation as a European centre for music-printing, instrument-making, virtuoso performance, and training. The tradition of musical excellence at the basilica of St Mark's and the fame of its *Maestri di Capella* – an illustrious group that included the earlier northern masters Adrian Willaert and Cipriano de Rore – solidified the city's reputation for performance and training.[18] The Englishman Thomas Coryate spread the fame of Venice far and wide in his published travelogue, in which he described "Musicke, which was both vocall and instrumentall, so good, so delectable, so rare, so admirable, so super excellent, that it did even ravish and stupifie all those strangers that never heard the like."[19] The secularization of the Republic and its outright anti-Papist attitude made Venice an appealing and safe destination for Lutherans who were inspired by Venetian triumph over the pope in the interdict of 1606–07.[20]

But the reputation of Venice reached even greater numbers in the writings of Venetian publicists who constructed a mythic vision of the city that would take hold across Europe. The writings of Francesco Sansovino, Gasparo Contarini, Giovanni Botero (as we read above), Paolo Sarpi, and others conveyed a sense for a well-nigh legendary Venice and were published in both Italian and foreign editions. Even the Venetian Constitution became a subject of international wonder and debate. In his *De magistratibus* (Venice, 1543) Gasparo Contarini praised the Venetian Constitution for its balance of aristocratic, monarchic, and democratic elements: "Such moderation and proportion characterize this Republic and such a mixture of all suitable estates, that this city by itself incorporates at once a princely sovereignty, a governance of the nobility, and a rule of citizens."[21]

The Venetian notion of balanced government with shared power bears a striking resemblance to the Danish concept of *Adelsvælen* (noble rule), whereby the state was administered as a limited monarchy with power shared by the king and an independent body known as the Council of the Realm. Danish sovereignty rested with

Danmarks krone (the Crown of Denmark), a concept that embraced the monarch, the aristocratic Council, and the citizens as represented by the Council. This shared constitutional outlook, if it heightened Danish interest in Venice as a political entity, also legitimized the city as a destination for Danish court musicians.

VENICE AND COPENHAGEN: TRANSALPINE MUSICAL EXCHANGE

The link between Venice and Copenhagen was largely forged by individual musicians from both sides of the Alps. Gregorius Trehou, a Netherlander by birth, assumed the post of chapel master at the Danish court in 1590. His earlier studies in Venice, possibly under Andrea Gabrieli at St Mark's, may have paved the way for the Danish study trips that followed.[22] Melchior Borchgrevinck, Andreas Aagesen, Wilhelm Egbertsen, Hans Nielsen, and Mogens Pedersøn made the first trip from Copenhagen to Venice to study with Giovanni Gabrieli in 1599. Christian IV sent an unnamed student to Venice in 1601, while Borchgrevinck returned there for the winter of 1601–02. It is worth speculating that Borchgrevinck came into contact with Netherlands composer Joannes Tollius, then active in Padua, who joined the Danish chapel as a singer in 1601.[23] Another group of Danes made the trip to Venice in 1602: Hans Nielsen for his second time, Hans Brachrogge and Niels Mortensøn Kolding for their first. Christian IV penned a letter of 3 April 1605 to Giovanni Gabrieli to introduce Pedersøn, who studied under the Venetian master for the next four years.[24] The 1610s saw a decline in foreign travel on account of the outbreak of the Kalmar War against Sweden in 1611 and renewed religious intolerance occasioned by the jubilee of the Lutheran Reformation in 1617.[25] Hans Brachrogge and Niels Mortensen Kolding left for Venice in 1619. Kolding's return from Venice in the spring of 1622 marked the end of over two decades of cultural travel.[26]

But the cultural learning was by no means one way. There is much evidence that Italian composers were inspired by contact with the Danish court musicians. During his service to Emperor Rudolf II at Prague (from just before 1580 to 1613), Italian composer and instrumentalist Alessandro Orologio developed associations with courts at Dresden, Wolfenbüttel, Kassel, and, quite possibly, Copenhagen under Christian IV, whom Orologio named dedicatee of his instrumental *Intradae* (Helmstaedt, 1597).[27] Orazio Vecchi broadcast his high esteem for the Danish court musicians in the preface to his madrigal comedy *Le veglie di Siena* (Venice, 1604). His dedication – "To the most honourable and magnificent Prince Christian IV" – ended with a warning regarding the complexity of the music that followed, which he described as "difficult to perform ... but easy for Christian IV's musical establishment under [the direction of] Signor Melchior Borchgrevinck ... [whose excellence] is confirmed by the authority of Giovanni Gabrieli."[28] Here Vecchi singled out the Danish musical establishment as a model performance ensemble, superior even to native Italians.

Most significant, Venetian printer and publisher Angelo Gardano recognized a market for the music of Hans Nielsen and Mogens Pedersøn, whose first books of madrigals appeared from his presses in 1606 and 1608, respectively. The title pages offer a striking example of the merging of Danish and Italian musical culture. Gardano used the stylizations "Giovanni Fonteo Danese" (Hans Nielsen) and "Magno Petreo Dano" (Mogens Pedersøn) to Italianize Nielsen and Pedersøn, whose names must have had little recognition value. Yet, Gardano highlighted their Danish origins and service to Christian IV, perhaps in an effort to advertise their perceived exoticism (figure 3.2).

Nielsen and Pedersøn dedicated their books to Christian IV. Listings for the volumes appear in catalogues of books available at the semi-annual Frankfurt fair, which confirms that Gardano's commercial ambition for the madrigals extended beyond Venice and Copenhagen.[29] Musically, Nielsen and Pedersøn combine a traditional harmonic language with more progressive approaches to text expression evident in their respective settings of Guarini's "T'amo mia vita" (I Love You, My Life).[30] The fusion of Danish authorship and patronage with Italian production and musical style offers a fruitful example of a two-way cultural exchange.

While Gardano capitalized on the allure of Danish madrigalists, madrigal printing in Copenhagen was dominated by the music of Italians. Soon after his return from Venice, Danish court musician Melchoir Borchgrevinck assembled two anthologies of madrigals printed under the title *Giardino novo i–ii* (Copenhagen, 1605–06). Their contents and earliest printed concordances are given in table 3.1 and table 3.2.

BASSO

DI GIOVANNI
FONTEIIO DANESE
MVSICO DELLAMAESTA
DEL RE DI DANIA.
IL PRIMO LIBRO
DE MADRIGALI
A Cinque Voci.
Nouamente Composto & dato in Luce.

IN VENETIA.
Appresso Angelo Gardano.
M D C. V. I.

K

Figure 3.2
Title page from Giovanni Fonteiio Danese (Hans Nielsen), *Il primo libro de madrigali a cinque voci* (Venice, 1606), fol. 1r, Herzog August Bibliothek Wolfenbüttel: 1.3.5 (6) Musica

While one might expect to find madrigals by Danish composers, given that so many had gone to great lengths to study in Venice, Borchgrevinck included only five of a total fifty-two settings by Danish composers: two by Borchgrevinck himself (placed, rather modestly, at the end of each anthology), a setting (in two parts) by the singer Nicholas Gistou positioned towards the end of *Giardino*

Table 3.1 *Giardino novo I*: Contents and Earliest Printed Concordances

Composer	*Text Incipit*	*Folio*	*Earliest Printed Concordance* RISM	*Place, Date*
Claudio Monteverdi	Io mi son giovinetta	2v	M3467	Venice, 1603
Leone Leoni	Come viver poss'io	3r	L1992	Venice, 1595
Girolamo Casati	Dubbij fra duo mi vivo	3v	unknown	
Grisostomo Rubiconi	Ami Tirsi e me'el nieghi	4v	R3033	Venice, 1599
Salomone Rossi	Pur venisti cor mio	5r	R2748	Venice, 1600
Marsilio Santini	Questa che dolce canta	5v	S896	Venice, 1602
Leone Leoni	Dimmi, Clori gentil	6v	L1996	Venice, 1602
Salomone Rossi	Che non fai che non pensi7r	R2748		Venice, 1600
Leone Leoni	Vorei scoprire il premio	7v	L1995	Venice, 1598
Leone Leoni	In questo fior ascoso	8r	L1992	Venice, 1595
Leone Leoni	Se la vita ch'amor	8v	L1992	Venice, 1595
Girolamo Casati	Scherzava e poi fuggia	9r	unknown	
Claudio Monteverdi	Quel augellin che canta	9v	M3467	Venice, 1603
Simone Molinaro	Baci amorosi e cari	10v	M2931	Milan, 1599
Giaches de Wert	Io non sono pero morto	11r	W885	Venice, 1586
Giovanni Croce	Qual di voi scende	11v	C4465	Venice, 1585
Giovanni Colombi	Leggiadro mio Pastor	12r	C3433	Venice, 1603
Marsilio Santini	Anima del cor mio	12v	S896	Venice, 1602
Gabriel Fattorini	Rondinella loquace	13r	F137	Venice, 1604
Giaches de Wert	Fra le dorate chiome	13v	W885	Venice, 1586
Simone Molinaro	Cantiam, Muse, cantiamo	14r	M2931	Milan, 1599
Claudio Monteverdi	Non più guerra	14v	M3467	Venice, 1603
Francesco Bianciardi	Del vago Roscignuolo	15r	B2605	Venice, 1597
Claudio Monteverdi	Ah dolente partita	15v	M3467	Venice, 1603
Melchior Borchgrevinck	Amatemi ben mio	16r	unknown	

Source: Tables 3.1–3.2 are compiled from Henrik Glahn, ed., *20 Italienske Madrigaler fra Melchior Borchgrevinck* "Giardino novo I-II" København 1605/06 (Copenhagen: Egtved, 1983), 29–47. RISM numbers are given for both single-author publications and anthologies. See Karlheinz Schlager (ed.), *Einzeldrucke vor 1800*, Répertoire international des sources musicales, ser. AI, vols. 1–9, 11–13 (Kassel: Bärenreiter, 1971–) and François Lesure (ed.), *Recueils imprimés XVIe–XVIIe siècles*, Répertoire international des sources musicales, ser. B (Munich: G. Henle, 1960).

Table 3.2 *Giardino novo II:* Contents and Earliest Printed Concordances

Composer	Text Incipit	Folio	*Earliest Printed Concordance* RISM	*Place, Date*
Giovanni Le Sueur	La mia Leggiadr'e vaga	2v	unknown	
Benedetto Pallavicino	Leuò con la sua mano	3r	P789	Venice, 1593
Francesco Bianciardi	Ardemmo insieme	3v	B2605	Venice, 1597
Giovanni Vincenzo Palma	Ero cosi dicea	4r	unknown	
D. Pietro Marsolo	Mi dona la mia Donna	4v	M751	Venice, 1604
Leone Leoni	Combattean dolcemente	5r	L1992	Venice, 1595
Leone Leoni	Hor a mercè d'amor	5v	L1992	Venice, 1595
Claudio Monteverdi	Cruda Amarilli	6r	M3475	Venice, 1605
Curtio Valcampi	Ohime doue è l mio cor	6v	unknown	
Benedetto Pallavicino	Amor i parto	7r	P793	Venice, 1600
Benedetto Pallavicino	A poco a poco io sento	7v	P793	Venice, 1600
Giovanni Paolo Nodari	Parlo misero taccio	8r	unknown	
Claudio Monteverdi	Cor mio mentre vi miro	8v	M3467	Venice, 1603
Hans Nielsen	Corr' al suo fin mia vita	9r	N687	Venice, 1606
Agostino Agresta	Caro dolce ben mio	9v	unknown	
Francesco Spongia Usper	O se torn'il mio sole	10r	U115	Venice, 1604
Giovanni Le Sueur	Femisi inanzi amor	10v	unknown	
Pietro Quartieri	La bella Flor	11r	Q36	Rome, 1592
Ippolito Sabino	La pastorella mia	11v	S53	Venice, 1589
Curtio Valcampi	I tuoi capelli ò Fili	12r	unknown	
Nicolo Gistou	Quel augellin che canta	12v	unknown	
Nicolo Gistou	Ma ben arde nel core	13r	unknown	
Curtio Mancini	Già riebamaua	13v	M294	Venice, 1605
Curtio Mancini	Quando altro Sol	14r	M294	Venice, 1605
Giovanni Pietro Gallo	Miracolo non fù	14v	G265	Venice, 1597
Leone Leoni	Dolci bacì e soaui	15v	L1996	Venice, 1602
Melchior Borchgrevinck	Baci amorosi e cari	16r	unknown	

novo II, and Hans Nielsen's "Corre al suo fin mia vita" (My Life Is Running towards Its End), which appeared in the composer's first book of madrigals printed in Venice that same year.

Instead, Borchgrevinck drew the bulk of settings from twenty-two Venetian madrigal books printed between 1595 and 1605 by the houses of Giacomo Vincenti, Ricciardo Amadino, and Angelo Gardano. Borchgrevinck may have acquired the source books during his travels to Venice in 1599 and 1601–02 or from colleagues returning from the Serenissima. The Venetian travels improved Borchgrevinck's access to the most up-to-date music, a feature that distinguished the *Giardini novi* from anthologies issued by the printer and editor Pierre Phalèse in Antwerp.[31] Borchgrevinck took only three madrigals from non-Venetian sources: two by Simone Molinaro from his first book of madrigals (Milan: Tini & Besozzi, 1599) and one by Pietro Quartiero from his first book issued in Rome (Coattini, 1592). He must have had a handful of other music books available as well: Borchgrevinck likely drew the single setting by Nodari from a lost music edition dated ca. 1605; the Tregian manuscript (Egerton 3665) included twenty-one madrigals by Nodari (nr. 677–91), which were likely copied from such a source.

As a compiler, Borchgrevinck's work depended not only on his knowledge of and access to Italian repertory but also on his personal taste. Borchgrevinck favoured the music of Leone Leoni, the chapel master at the cathedral in Vicenza, who is represented by eight settings. The high number of settings can best be explained by their availability in Venice: four volumes of Leoni's five-voice madrigals were published there between 1588 and 1602, along with numerous settings in anthologies. Borchgrevinck showed a distinct preference for a nexus of composers active at the Mantuan court whose madrigals account for a total of sixteen settings. Of these, Monteverdi and Pallavicino were especially prominent, with six and three madrigals each. Wert, Rossi, and Casati (who may be identified in the Mantuan register of musicians from 1600) each contributed two pieces.[32] To this list can be added Ippolito Sabino, whose madrigal "La pastorella mia" Borchgrevinck selected from a book of madrigals Sabino had dedicated to the Gonzagan prince Ferrante in 1589. Borchgrevinck's inclusion of a single madrigal by Giovanni Croce likely stems from their acquaintance in Venice: Croce served as vice-chapelmaster at the cathedral of St Mark's since the early 1590s and was promoted by Doge Marino Grimani to succeed Gabrieli as chapelmaster in 1603. Borchgrevinck filled the rest of the volumes with a string of lesser known composers: music by Le Sueur, Casati, Palma, Valcampi, Colombi, Rubiconi, and Agresta may not have been printed before.

Borchgrevinck's travels to Venice likely influenced what he excluded from *Giardino novo I-II* as well. There are no madrigals by Luca Marenzio, which is a striking omission since foreign anthologies traditionally favoured Marenzio's lighter, villanella style madrigals.[33] Marenzio was also the favoured composer for single-author volumes. Pierre Phalèse printed all of Marenzio's five-voice madrigals in a single volume in 1593 and followed it with a collection of his six-voice madrigals the next year. Both publications were part of the Danish court repertory, which may account for Marenzio's absence from the Copenhagen anthologies: his music was readily available, making its Danish reprinting unnecessary from a repertory standpoint.

Borchgrevinck's Italian travels exposed him to stylistically progressive, even provocative music. This is most strongly shown by his inclusion of Claudio Monteverdi's setting of Guarini's "Cruda Amarilli" (Cruel Amaryllis). The madrigal took centre stage in a controversy between the composer and the staunch conservative theorist Giovanni Battista Artusi that heated up in the Venetian presses in the mid-1590s and culminated with an exchange of pamphlets and prefatory letters.[34] Artusi took issue with unprepared or unresolved dissonant notes, an error of part-writing that Monteverdi justified by the expressive claims of the verbal texts. Borchgrevinck's was the first printing of "Cruda Amarilli" outside Italy, appearing only one year after the madrigal's debut in Monteverdi's fifth book of madrigals for five voices (Venice, 1605). Considering the close proximity of the Italian and Danish printings of "Cruda Amarilli," it seems likely that Borchgrevinck knew the madrigal in manuscript form as it had circulated since the mid-1590s. Such an early interest in what Monteverdi defended as the *seconda prattica* (second practice) was unique to Denmark.

Borchgrevinck's poetic tastes mirrored the times, with nine settings of texts by Giovanni Battista Guarini, whose drama *Il pastor fido* (The Faithful Sheppard) inspired more than 550 madrigals by 125 different composers that survive in printed sources alone.[35] With the exception of Sannazaro, the remaining identified poets are now rather obscure: Celiano, Casone, Cavaletto, Gradenico, A.

Guarini, and Martinengo. Two texts appear twice across the *Giardini novi*: Molinaro and Borchgrevinck each set "Baci amorosi e cari," and Guarini's "Quel angellin" inspired both Monteverdi (volume 1) and Gistou (volume 2). The prevailing themes of "baci" (kisses), sweet embraces, and the miracle of love ("Miracolo non fù d'Amore") and its denial ("Cruda Amarilli") infuse the *Giardini novi* with a sensuality typical of the reception of pastoral poetry across Europe.

Borchgrevinck selected music with the abilities of northern audiences and performers in mind. The lighter poetic structures of the texts in Borchgrevinck's anthologies lent themselves to conservative musical settings, with expressive moments of text setting but few daring harmonic feats. Gistou's setting of "Quel augellin, che canta" (The Little Bird That Sings) from Guarini's *Il pastor fido* uses common textural devices such as the silencing of the two lower voices for the opening bird song and the flowing melisma on the word "canta" (singing) to convey textual meaning. Nodari exploits hard and soft hexachord shifts in his setting of Guarini's opening text, "Parlo, miser, o taccio?" (Should I, poor wretch, speak or hold my tongue?), an instance of poignant text expression that is recalled in the modulatory passage to the soft hexachord on text "Chiusa fiamma tal' hor da chi l'accende" (A smothered flame is clear indeed to he who lit the fire). By erring on the side of caution in terms of the difficulty and sophistication of the settings, Borchgrevinck assured their performance and transfer across northern Europe.

In terms of technical and artistic achievement, the anthologies aspire to Venice's fame as a printing centre. They are the first instance of polyphonic part-books printed in Denmark and the first Italian-texted publication of any kind. With the *Giardini novi* we also have the first printing of an international repertory intended to circulate beyond Danish borders, as indicated by their listing in the Frankfurt bookfair catalogues and the dedication (in French) of the second volume to King James I of England, brother-in-law to Christian IV.[36] Prior to their appearance, music printing in Copenhagen was limited to a few occasional pieces and a handful of sacred music books intended for Lutheran church services.[37] The novelty and technical mastery of the anthologies is captured on their title pages, which are among the finest examples of copper engravings from the period. The title page of *Giardino novo II* illustrates a banquet hall, complete with courtiers, guests, and attendants that pay

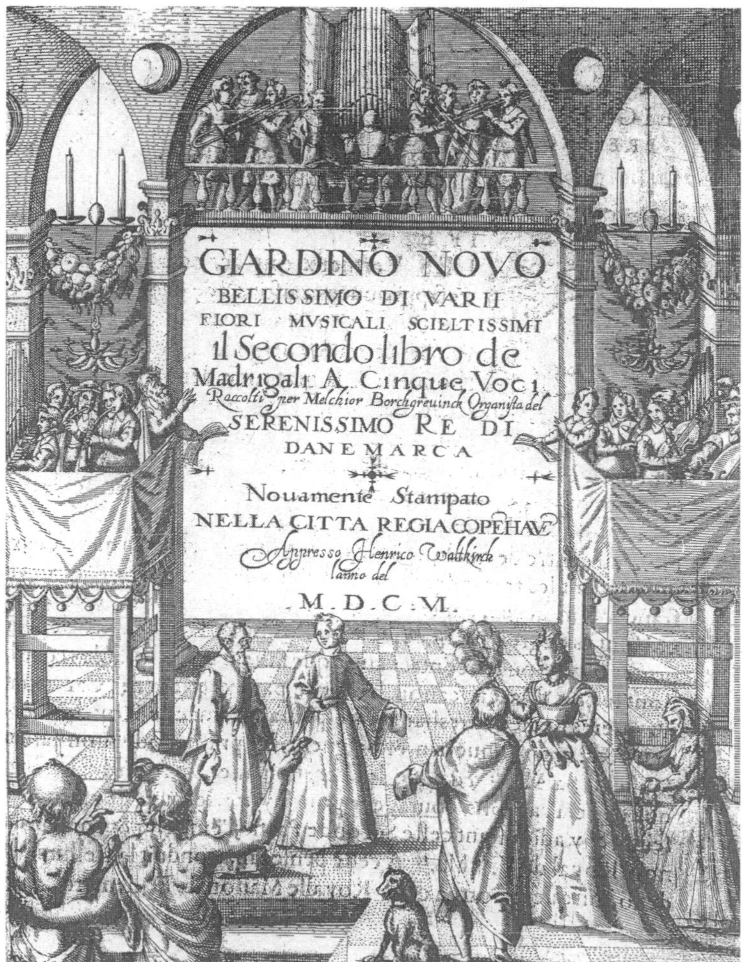

GIARDINO NOVO
BELLISSIMO DI VARII
FIORI MVSICALI SCIELTISSIMI
il Secondo libro de
Madrigali A Cinque Voci
Raccolti per Melchior Borchgreuinck Organista del
SERENISSIMO RE DI
DANEMARCA
Nouamente Stampato
NELLA CITTA REGIA COPEHAVE
Appresso Henrico Waltkirch
l'anno del
M.D.C.VI.

Figure 3.3
Title page from Melchior Borchgrevinck (compiler), *Giardino novo II* (Copenhagen, 1606), fol. 1r, Herzog August Bibliothek Wolfenbüttel: 1.3.5 (11) Musica

tribute to the SERENISSIMO RE DI DANEMARCA (the Most Serene King of Denmark) and his CITTA REGIA COPENHAVE (Royal City of Copenhagen). Consorts of brass, woodwind, and string players, coupled with singers, flank the central organ gallery, an arrangement that alludes to the polychoral tradition of performance associated with St Mark's at the time of Giovanni Gabrieli (figure 3.3).

The style and overall artistic merit of the title pages reflect the Venetian-inspired modernity of the city in which they were printed.

CONCLUSION

As case studies, Venice and Copenhagen present a model of cultural transmission with traffic flowing in all directions. Italian composers sought out the Danish king as a patron and praised his musical establishment for its skill and refinement. Gardano's printing of madrigals by Nielsen and Pedersøn attest to the commercial viability of Danish madrigalists in European markets. The Danish reception of the madrigal was part of a broader engaged interest in Venice as a city of culture, physical beauty, and good governance. The Danes proved themselves talented students who transformed what they learned in Venice into music that served a distinct, northern purpose. The Copenhagen anthologies are a remarkable polyglot example of the selection and adaptation embedded in bricolage: Italian madrigals, with a French dedication (of the second volume) from a Danish king to an English one, compiled by a Dutch-born organist from sources gathered in Venice. The title, *Giardino novo* (New Garden), captures the impulse to domesticate the madrigal by breeding it with other foreign influences to create a new, unique "Danish" hybrid. The title evokes flora rising from the (Danish) earth. The image can be interpreted as a growth metaphor for the almost instantaneous creation of a symbolic capital, the foundational rhetoric attached to Christian IV's act of literally raising Copenhagen from the ground up.

NOTES

1 Scholarly interest in music and cities has spawned its own subfield of urban musicology. See the special issue of *Urban History* 29, "Music and the City" (2002), esp. Carter, "The Sound of Silence," 8–18.
2 See also Fisher (this volume) on the role of music in constructing civic identities in sixteenth-century Augsburg; and Bailey (this volume) for another view of relationships between the arts and civic, even national, identity. Eds.
3 The most useful English-language study of the court is Bergsagel, "Foreign Music and Musicians in Denmark," 19–24.

4 The conference "Cultural Traffic and Cultural Transformation around the Baltic Sea, 1450–1720" (Carlsberg Academy, Copenhagen, 21–22 March 2003) offers examples from architecture, commerce, news media, court ceremony, and the visual arts of the active import and transfer of foreign cultural goods and expertise in the Scandinavian region. Revised versions of ten of the papers appear in a special issue of *Scandinavian Journal of History* 28 (2003). Articles in *Scandinavian Studies* 77, 3 (2005) by Erik Thomson, Daniel Riches, and the present author, respectively, broaden the dialogue to include economic, military, and musical exchange between Scandinavia and Continental Europe.

5 Schwab, "*Italianità in Danimarca*," 142–5. Schwab's table lists a total of twenty-seven madrigal books from Antwerp (16), Copenhagen (3), Hamburg (1), Nuremberg (2), and Venice (5).

6 Burke, *European Renaissance*.

7 Botero, *Delle cause della grandezza delle cittá*, quoted from the English translation by Hawkins, *The Cause of the Greatnesse of Cities*, 17–19.

8 Muir, "Images of Power," 16–52. See also Hoople (this volume) on the relationship between architecture and civic values; and Perkins (this volume) on how architecture registers the sometimes incoherent relationships between past and present. Eds.

9 Botero, *Le relazioni universali*, quoted from the English translation of Johnson, *Historical Description*, 125.

10 Christian IV's construction and renovation of Frederiksborg, Rosenborg, and Kronborg castles drew inspiration from the *Livre d'Architecture* (1559) by Jacques Androuet du Cerceau (Burke, "The Uses of Italy," 12).

11 My English translation of the Danish "Kiøbenhavn, Du, som stiger op af den baltiske Thetis' Bølger, Du, som fra en ringe Landsby er begyndt at blive en stor Havn, nu vokser Du i den tyvende danske Konges Tid og strækker Dine høje Spir op imod Skyerne. De store Goder, hvoraf Du praler, skyldes Christus og den Fjerde, der bærer Navn efter Christus – Christus, thi her forkyndes det sande Ords Lov, Kongen, thi han omgiver Murene med et dædalisk Væerk," quoted in Lindberg, *Sirenernes Stad København*, 1:311.

12 Knowledge of the Dutch mercantile system came from several diplomatic missions to Holland. The most important was the tour of Christian Friis, Jacob Ulfeldt, and Jonas Charisius (then senior advisor on foreign policy and secretary of the German Chancery) from November 1607 through August 1608.

13 For a fascinating account of the interaction of the Danish and German courts during this time period, see Wade, *Triumphus Nuptialis Danicus*.

14 Carøe, "Stipendium Regium og dets Stipendiarier," 139–53.
15 Helk, *Dansk-norske studierejser*, 43.
16 Silvert Grubbe (1566–1636) and Jacob Ulfeldt (1567–1630) travelled extensively through Italy and later had careers in the Chancery. Grubbe went on to become governor at Malmøhus in 1610, while Ulfeldt advanced to Chancellor of the Realm (Gamrath, *Christian IV-tidens Danmark*, 47, 49).
17 See Kornerup, *Biskop Hans Poulsen Resen*.
18 On St Mark's, see Rosand, "Music in the Myth of Venice"; Bryant, "The *cori spezzati* of St Mark's"; and Ongaro, "The Chapel of St Mark's."
19 Quoted in Arnold, *Giovanni Gabrieli*, 203–4.
20 Bouwsma, "Venice and the Political Education of Europe," 274.
21 Quoted in ibid, 270.
22 Kongsted, *Motets by G. Trehou, J. Tollius and V. Bertholusius*, vii.
23 On his biography, see Rasch, "Tollius, Joannes," 554.
24 The letter survives at the Danish National Archives (Foreign Department of the German Chancery General Part 1, Until 1676, Latina Registrant, vol. 9, 1600–15, fol. 121v–122r) and is transcribed in Hammerich, *Musiken ved Christian den Fjerdes Hof*, 188.
25 Adherents to the Papist religion were expelled from the Danish kingdom by a decree of 19 June 1613 (Rørdam, *Danske Kirkelove*, 3:38–9). On 4 July 1616, Christian IV issued a decree requiring all guides accompanying youths abroad to be examined and subjected to a religious test administered by the bishop of the diocese from whence the trip originated (The Royal Library, three-page pamphlet, cited in Heiberg, *Christian IV and Europe*, no. 1411, 409–10). On the jubilee, see Kornerup, "Reformationsjubilæet i Danmark 1617," 33–83.
26 Payments for Kolding's return from Venice are dated 29 March 1622 and 22 May 1622 (Hammerich, *Musiken ved Christian den Fjerdes Hof*, 66–7).
27 Polk, "Orologio, Alessandro," 18:748.
28 "AL SERENTISSIMO ET POTENT.MO PRENCIPE CHRISTIANO IV ... difficile rapresentarsele per gustar compitamente di questi nostri Italici concenti, le serà facili tato dal Signor Melchior Borchgrevinck in vero degno Musico della Maesta vostra per esser'egli nella professione singulare, e per tale confirmato dall'auttorità del Signor Gio. Gabrieli frà quegli del la prima schiera de virtuosi stimatissimo frà noi," fol. 1v of Vecchi, *Le veglie di Siena* (Venice 1604), exemplar at the Murhardsche Bibliothek, Kassel. English translation from Jacobsen, *Madrigaler fra Christian IV's tid*, XIV n. 15.

29 Nielsen's *Il primo libro de madrigali* is listed in Lutz's fall and spring catalogues of 1606, while Pedersøn's volume is listed in Lutz's spring catalogue of 1608 (Göhler, *Verzeichnis der in den Frankfurter und Leipziger Messkatalogen*, 2:27 and 58).

30 For a discussion of their music, see Arnold, *Giovanni Gabrieli*, 216–23. For modern editions, see Jacobsen, *Madrigaler fra Christian IV's tid*, Dania sonans 2 (Nielsen) and 3 (Pedersøn).

31 Phalèse's *Musica divina* (Antwerp, 1583) included repertory stretching back forty years. Cipriano de Rore's "Anchor che col partire," for instance, dates back to Venice 1547.

32 Glahn, *20 Italienske Madrigaler*, 31.

33 Marenzio is well represented in Antwerp anthologies *Musica divina* (1583), *Harmonia celeste* (1583), *Symphonia angelica* (1585), and *Melodia olympica* (1591) as well as in the first two volumes of *Gemmæ Musicæ* (Nuremberg 1588–89). Thomas Watson's *Italian Madrigals Englished* (London, 1590) opens with two Latin hexameter poems in honour of Marenzio, then presents twenty-three of his madrigals.

34 For a summary of the debate, see Carter, "Artusi, Monteverdi, and the Poetics of Modern Music," 171–94.

35 Hanning, "Guarini, Battista," available at <http://www.grovemusic.com>.

36 The volumes appear in catalogues from 1605–07. For details, see Göhler, *Verzeichnis der in den Frankfurter und Leipziger Messkatalogen*, 2:8. On the dedications, see my "Danish Diplomacy and the Dedication of *Giardino novo* II (1606)," 9–18.

37 All music printed in Denmark between 1535 and 1749 that survives at the Danish Royal Library is listed in Davidsson, *Danskt Musiktryck intill 1700-Talets Mitt*, 81–93. All twenty-five of the books that predate *Giardino novo* consist of music for the evangelical mass, church ordinances, psalm books, and altar books.

4

Walking The City Limits: The Performance of Authority and Identity in Mary Tudor's Norwich

MARY A. BLACKSTONE

City dwellers participated in an intense evolution of civic identity and social cohesion in mid-Tudor England. Between 1520 and 1600, the population of London mushroomed from as low as fifty thousand to as high as 200,000, and although English provincial centres remained very much smaller, they, too, experienced significant increases in population and wealth during the sixteenth century. As England's second city throughout this period, Norwich's population doubled from approximately ten thousand to over twenty thousand.[1] London's increased size and resulting wealth and power generated anxieties and tensions within its boundaries as well as without. Both the provinces and the Crown regarded this emerging giant with anxiety,[2] but more moderate increases in population and wealth in provincial urban centres also posed potential difficulties for the Crown and local officials responsible for maintaining control and authority. The Tudors, however, came to see the increasing importance of provincial urban centres as something they could control and turn to their advantage in effecting a shift from medieval to modern power structures. As magnets for increased population and generation of wealth, then, provincial centres also became critical loci for power negotiations in Tudor England.[3]

When surveying the evolution of relations between English civic government and the Crown, Robert Tittler has observed that, "after only 13 borough incorporations in the first 55 years of the Tudor dynasty, we find eight in the last seven years of Henry VIII, 12 in the nearly seven years of Edward VI, and a striking 24 in the slightly shorter reign of Mary."[4] Indicative of a much broader restructuring that was under way in the country's power base, these statistics foreground efforts not only by newly incorporated boroughs but also by long established cities (like Norwich) to push their "limits" both literally and figuratively. In 1556, Norwich renegotiated its 1404 charter to extend the territory under its jurisdiction beyond the city walls to specific suburbs. This charter confirms the city's debt to the Crown, but the Crown stood to benefit from the city's dominant economic and cultural position in East Anglia as much as Norwich would benefit from its charter. Throughout this period, then, the city carefully negotiated between its responsibilities and allegiance to the Crown, on the one hand, and independent, and sometimes divergent, local practices and policies intended to strengthen its own authority, civic identity, and social cohesion, on the other.

Because of the range of extant materials, Norwich affords a particularly good opportunity to study the negotiation of such competing allegiances in the provinces during the intense period of Counter-Reformation in Mary's reign. Rather than focusing exclusively on the intentionality of authorities and official policies, however, this examination considers the highly intertextual process whereby men and women in the streets (some of whom were themselves local officials) actually constructed collective meaning and a sense of belonging from the conflicting, public performances of authority all around them.

A perspective of the city of Norwich created by one of its residents at the end of our period provides an insightful point of departure. In his book *The Cosmographical Glasse,* William Cuningham views much of the universe and the world, not to mention England, from his vantage point in Norwich, and he includes a 1558 bird's-eye-view map of his city. The earliest surviving printed map of an English provincial city, it tells us much regarding the way in which such cities and their residents saw themselves (figures 4.1, 4.2).

Cuningham features himself and his instruments centred in the foreground of the map and situated on a hill just outside St Giles Gate. Not unlike Michel de Certeau's "voyeur-god," he points to the city as he sees it – and as he would have us see it. From his vista on the margins, Cuningham represents the city as neatly contained partly by its medieval walls and partly by the river Wensum "coming from Yermouth ... thorow the City" and "into the countrye."[5]

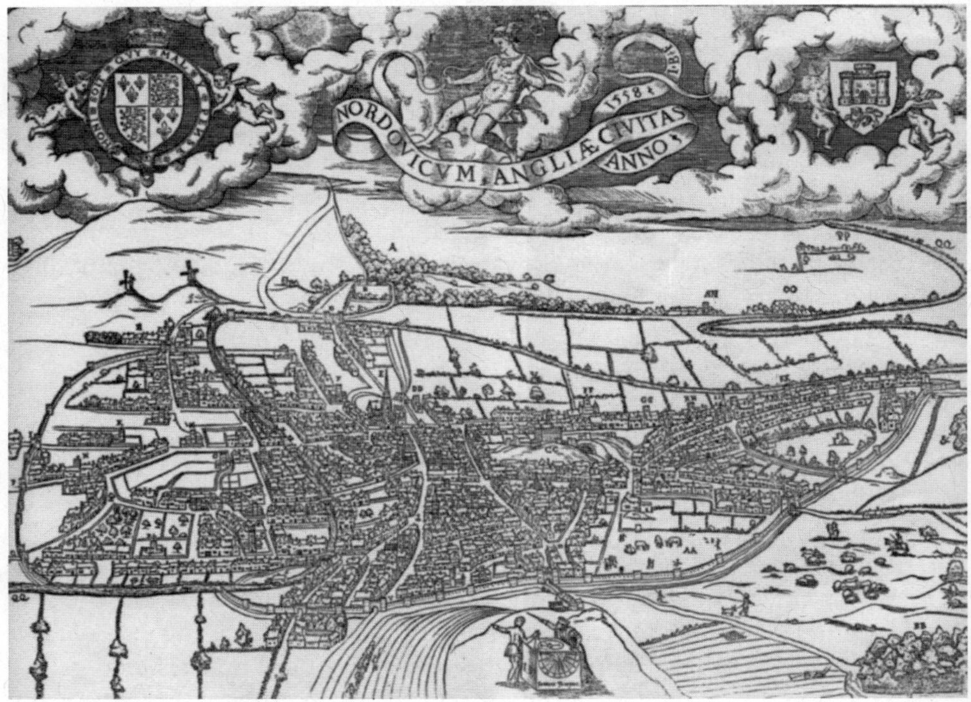

Figure 4.1
A Map of Norwich by William Cuningham, 1558.
With the Permission of the Trustees of the Bodleian Library.

Having temporarily left the "walkers" of the city, whom de Certeau credits with writing the urban text "without being able to read it,"[6] Cuningham represents the topography of the city in detail, including people and animals as well as architectural features and the landscape; however, in constructing his text he is unapologetically selecting and bending those details to put the best face of the city forward. Although we view the city from the northwest, he turns the facade of the cathedral around so that we see its south face.[7]

Cuningham's position relative to the city limits underscores the element of fluidity crucial to the city's presented integrity. Just as the river connects the city with what lies beyond, so too the walls of the city facilitate exits and entrances through numerous clearly delineated gates and bridges leading out to the suburbs. The walls may divide the substantial green spaces within the city from those outside its boundaries, but Cuningham enjoys his position of voyeur from the margins because the city "limits" in fact facilitate con-

THE DECLARATION OF THE PRINCIPAL places in the Citie, after th'order of th'Alphabete.

A	Thorpe VVoode.	X.	S.Stephens Gates.
B	S.Leonardes.	Y.	Brasen dore.
C.	The place where men are customablie burnt.	Z.	S.Iohns gates.
D.	Bisshoppes Gate.	&.	Lakenam VVoode.
E.	The Cathedrall church, called Christes Churche.	AA	Chappell in the fielde.
F.	S.Martins at the Pallis Gate.	BB	Eaten VVoode.
G	Pokethorpe Gates.	CC	The Castell.
H.	The Suburbs called Pokthorpe.	DD	The hospitall.
I.	Magdalene gates	EE	The market place.
K	S.Butholdes.	FF	S.Peters permantigate.
M	S.Clementes.	GG	S.Martines on the hill.
N	S.Augustines.	HH	S.Iohns on the hill.
P.	S,Augustines Gates.	II	S.Michaels.
Q.	S.Martines Gates.	LL	S.Iohns at the gates.
R.	S Martines at th'Ooke.	MM	S.Stephens.
S.	The new milles..	NN	Thorpe.
T.	Hellgates, the Suburbs ioyning to it, called Heibam.	QQ	In the righthand is that part of the riuer Yerus coming from Yermouth, and renneth thorow the City.
V.	S.Benets Gates.	QQ	The left hand th'other part of the forsaid riuer going hier into the countrye.
VV	S.Giles Gates.		

This Picture must be placed before the 9.leafe.

Figure 4.2
"The Declaration of the Principal Places in the Citie, after th'order of th'Alphabete." A key to the landmarks and locations identified in Cunningham's map of Norwich, published in 1559.

nections. They not only enable him to represent the city as a whole but also allow him to place it within a larger context. This includes the East Anglian countryside that fed the market town as well as the immediately surrounding areas such as Thorpe Wood, Mousehold Heath, and Carrow, home of Sir John Shelton, Mary's former guardian and later her privy councillor. The former St Leonard's Priory, known locally as "Mount Surrey" after the dissolution, also figures prominently as the sumptuous home built by Sir Henry Howard, Earl of Surrey and son of the Duke of Norfolk. Connections with local magnates had spatial implications within the city walls as well. For instance, as the profile of the church declined in the city at the dissolution, the profile of the Howards as Dukes of

Norfolk increased through the acquisition of properties such as those belonging to the Grey Friars and the Austin Friars.[8]

Of course, the royal jurisdiction of Norwich castle dominates the city as a reminder of its most powerful patron, a relationship acknowledged in Cuningham's depiction of Elizabeth's arms counter-balancing the city's arms at the top of the map. In the same way, the cathedral precinct, a historical focus of hotly debated jurisdictional battles with the city,[9] represents another competing source of authority that bridged boundaries. The presence of the cathedral gave Norwich its claim to city status, but some unpopular activities associated with the church were relegated to territory outside city walls. Cuningham's identification of "the place where men are customablie burnt"[10] outside the Bishop's Gate reminds us of the recent Marian persecution of local protestants and the then Bishop of Norwich's role in such matters.[11]

These allusions to connections with entities beyond the city's medieval walls, the visible markers of its "limits," highlight one of the increasingly serious challenges facing city authorities during this period. After the dissolution, the city substantially extended its jurisdiction and property within its walls, but this was more than matched by the expansion of its boundaries outside its walls. Under its 1556 charter, the city extended its authority to include Mousehold Heath and Thorpe Wood as well as the parishes of Carrow, Lakenham, Eaton, Earlham, and Heigham.[12] Much less of the open space surrounding the city walls in Cuningham's map is, therefore, actually outside the city limits, but his lack of detail regarding these spaces highlights a practical challenge facing not only the cartographer but also other residents and the many individuals travelling into and out of the city every day: How do you know where the actual city limits are? Are these discrete or are there overlapping relationships with other jurisdictions? How do you identify those who belong and those who do not? What are the particular identifying features of the city and its citizens? How are those features related to or distinct from those places and people outside its literal and figurative limits?

Cuningham's map may be read as one resident's response to some of these questions. Although in producing this map Cuningham may have "disentangled himself from the murky intertwining daily behaviors" of de Certeau's walkers, his basis for transforming "urban *fact*" into a "readable concept" of the city cannot be divorced from his own daily experience in the streets of Marian Norwich. De Certeau argues that the everyday practices of walkers "in organizing a bustling city were characterized by their blindness. The networks of these moving, intersecting writings compose a manifold story that has neither author nor spectator, shaped out of fragments of trajectories and alterations of spaces: in relation to representations, it remains daily and indefinitely other."[13]

But the self-conscious nature of Cuningham's performative appearance centre stage in a map that becomes a "theatre," a place for seeing both the "the pictural figurations of the practices that produce it" and the "historical operations" that formed and continued to form the city, suggests that we should question the relative blindness of walkers in sixteenth-century Norwich.[14] A number of surviving materials from the period suggest that other walkers were also encouraged to share the impetus behind his map – to order, capture, and fix civic identity as a unified whole delineated by readable limits and bounds. A walk down the streets of Marian Norwich, in fact, provides insights into the self-consciously performative and intertextual production of space in which walkers could publicly negotiate, synthesize, and articulate their story, their collective identity, and their allegiances. However, not unlike Cuningham's individual effort at a fixed representation, which, in the end, betrays shifting and permeable boundaries, the walkers' performative process appears to have been energized by a fascination with "limits," which highlights the dynamic mobility and fluidity of social cohesion in the period.

Out of several performative ceremonies through which limits helped to inform civic identity[15] in Marian Norwich, the pageants prepared for the Lord Mayor's inauguration in 1556 are perhaps the most interesting because of the substantial surviving texts. As the first such extant texts in England, they predate the first surviving text for London Lord Mayor's shows and carry comparative significance beyond the city of Norwich. Devised in honour of the last of three terms served by Augustine Steward, these three pageants display many of the characteristics of later London Lord Mayor's shows, whose texts have received considerably more attention from scholars.[16] As in London, the Norwich pageants function as a catalyst for the negotiation of civic identity; however, despite many similarities, they also differ in some respects in their approach to such negotiations and the nature of the projected collective identity.

First of all, despite the processional character of the overall event, not unlike what we have come to associate with London shows, the pageants did not process. The first pageant was erected at the church of St Peter's Hungate (Steward's parish church), the second in the parish of St John Maddermarket, and the third in the parish of St Andrew's. The surviving texts describe the pageants, associated speeches, and interactions with the mayor, but determining the full processional performance text, including the route from the beginning to the end of the event, requires interpolation. This textual ambiguity regarding the official route followed by the mayor and his entourage may derive from a recognition that citizens and, according to David Galloway, "the large crowds from the surrounding countryside,"[17] may have found their way from one pageant to another by various routes. The pageant descriptions assume the point of view of a walker retracing and reflecting upon a trajectory that further illuminates de Certeau's connection of speech acts to the practice of walking, and the gaps exemplify how "a migrational, or metaphorical city ... slips into the clear text of the planned and readable city." Both the text and the procession it describes provide a "space of enunciation": selective in its focus on specific spaces, discrete in deriving literal and figurative "limits" and meaning out of the spatial elements peculiar to each separate pageant, and emphatic in implying a "mobile organicity," a sense of direction that emerges upon closer examination of the implied route.[18]

As the chief spectator and the chief actor in this pageant, Steward would certainly have displayed a "mobile organicity" as he progressed from his home across from Erpingham Gate (leading into the cathedral precinct)[19] via his parish church of St Peter Hungate, past St Andrews Hall (the former Blackfriars Convent, which he had been instrumental in securing for the city from the Crown), and other parish churches, such as St John's Maddermarket and St Andrew's (whose substantial renovations he had helped initiate) most likely to arrive at the Guildhall, the chief seat of civic government overlooking the market (which was spread out below the Castle hill, the dominant reminder of royal authority).[20] Although the description of Steward's progress and pageants stops short of this destination, we know that inauguration festivities customarily concluded there with a civic feast. Situated in the premier symbol of commerce to which he as mercer owed his position in the community, the Guildhall had recently been enhanced by renovations partly due to Steward's efforts and his gift of a rock crystal mace as well as the book in which the pageant descriptions came to be recorded.[21] Apart, then, from the three pageants for which we have descriptions and speeches, the overall performance text for the procession sets Steward's literal and figurative "place" in the community within the context of architectural references to his accomplishments, the wealth and stature of the community, and the competing levels of authority vying for the allegiance of its citizens.[22]

Steward's progress, like the London Lord Mayor's shows, functions somewhat like royal progresses. As Clifford Geertz has observed, they "locate the society's center and affirm its connection with transcendent things by stamping a territory with ritual signs of dominance."[23] Walking through the wealthy core of the city, Steward symbolically establishes his authority at the centre of civic power and situates himself on a continuum between church and state authority. The progressive nature of the event appropriately reflects his own economic and social mobility at the climax of his achievement as third time mayor while also symbolically inviting the community to join in – to guide and direct him and share the sense of order and direction that the pageants suggest he will bring to the office. The Norwich pageants in fact anticipate the orientation of Elizabeth's coronation pageant described by Susan Frye as "a show of [London's] wealth and wisdom" from "the perspective of civic groups whose primary concern was to establish the values they considered conducive to social stability and financial gain ... on their own ground in their own terms."[24] In a manner linked to the tradition of the *speculum principis,* the tone and substance of the Norwich pageants situate the pageant performers as representative of the assembled community in their efforts to guide and instruct the mayor with respect to the direction in which he should take the city. While projecting a concept of civic identity as emerging out of the community, the pageants also present Steward as one "whome ye elect do call / this yere to be yo*u*r guyd,"[25] someone who has emerged out of the community to lead it for a year before returning to the everyday practices of another walker in the city.[26]

Unlike the coronation pageants featuring a monarch, then, the Norwich pageants only temporarily elevate Steward above other members of the community. On a literal as well as a figurative level, he remains on the ground walking the streets of his own neighbourhood with other citizens. Although the size of the crowd gathered in

Norwich for these celebrations may have limited access to some degree, spectators could have moved with him from pageant to pageant and therefore assumed a more participatory and less passive role in the ceremony. At the very least, he would almost certainly have been accompanied by the city's two sheriffs and four bailiffs as well as the twenty-four aldermen and sixty members of the Common Council annually elected by the freemen of the city. After having performed in the first pageant, the five city waits could also have joined the procession, wearing their livery and badges with the city coat of arms. Unlike the London pageants, which were borne before the mayor in an increasingly elaborate procession, the Norwich processional would have focused clearly on the mayor and on those who accompanied him from place to place. While the procession enabled a member of the wealthy elite in Norwich to establish his authority over the core of the city, it also served as a magnet to attract people from elsewhere inside and outside the city limits into its core and, if only for a day, establish their ownership of its mayor and the geographical and economic centre.

All three pageants produce an image of Steward as an "open" figure to be moulded and defined by members of "the commo*n*n wealthe" of the city, to stand as a symbol for those qualities that characterize the community and that citizens should strive to achieve. The first pageant associates him with numerous "vertewes." He seeks "the peoples heallthe" and employs "goodwill and wisdoom*m*e" "To Awgmennt the commo*n*n wealthe." His

> ... treuthe assurethe hym so
> that neither Loue nor enveous might
> his faith ca*n*n make forgoe.

He is characterized as a "faithfull frennd at neede" for the city with particular reference to how "hys Lyberall porte hathe bene yo*u*r stay/In Somme Adversetye."[27] This couplet probably alludes to actual incidents of adversity in which Steward played a prominent role. During Kett's rebellion, Steward stood in as mayor and helped restore order after rebels breached the city's walls and carried the current mayor off to Mousehold Heath.[28] This theme foreshadows similar motifs in later London Lord Mayor's shows, in which David Bergeron identified a "pervasive ... concern for the preservation of the unity of the state against those forces that would destroy it;

hence, the great concern for the commonwealth, both national and local."[29] Lawrence Manley also notes the frequent reliance on the spectre of chaos in the London shows. In both London and Norwich, the public spectacle of an orderly, annual succession of mayors, let alone a mayor who had mustered fortitude when faced with disorder in the not too distant past, must have been reassuring when set against the backdrop of past and potential "Adversetye."

The first Norwich pageant also alludes to another point of civic crisis in which Steward figured prominently. In his opening lines, the allegorical speaker, Time, refers to "My dawghter trewth."[30] Mary had chosen as her motto "Truth the daughter of Time," an emblematic reference that also appears frequently in pageantry in Elizabethan London because Elizabeth took the same motto (but with an obvious difference in meaning). In the Norwich pageant, however, the motto served not only as a standard allegorical nod to the reigning monarch but also as a reminder of the close connection between Mary, Steward, and Norwich very early in her reign. Norwich emerged as one of the first and strongest supporters of Mary's claim to the throne, and Steward actually stored her plate and valuables in his own home during those uncertain times.[31] Given this connection, though, the lack of a more overt reference to the monarch from whom derived the mayor's authority and civic stature is surprising. London pageants usually name and praise the monarch much more explicitly and at some length, but coming three years after the hopefulness of Mary's accession, this oblique and passing reference may arise from unease due to developments such as the Spanish marriage, the execution of Protestants, and proposals to reclaim church property acquired by the city and many others after the dissolution.

Apart from this subdued allusion to Mary and the authority derived from her, then, the first pageant creates a historical frame for Steward's mayoralty with reference to "his ded*e*s his gift*e*s his vertews riffe," which "declare his famous name." Time begins by placing this practice of praising and reverencing "all soche wourthie men / As dyd ther weallthe vpphollde" within the humanistic context of ancient Rome, thereby simultaneously elevating both Steward and Norwich by comparison. However, he is neither a stranger nor aloof from his fellow citizens. Ostensibly, the five city waits who performed in this pageant were introducing the mayor with whom they would be working (and with whom they had worked twice before) to the rest of the community.[32] However, given the community's familiarity with Steward's past accomplishments, which not only establish his credentials for office but also connect him with the mythology constructed around the city, they deem it unnecessary to specifically recount the stories associated with the city's mythology or "boste his worthi lieffe / or counte from whens he camme."[33]

Having acknowledged the temporal limits derived from personal and civic history as well as the figurative bounds established by external authority and personal allegiances, Steward and his procession move on to the second pageant, which focuses on negotiating the characteristics of a well governed "commo*n*n wealthe." John Buck, headmaster at Norwich grammar school and composer of the speeches in the first pageant, may have delivered the second pageant speech.

Certainly, with its overt objective of instructing the mayor and his council on their responsibilities to the community, the voice of a schoolmaster would serve the speech well. As a spokesperson for the community, however, Buck also simultaneously articulates the essential elements of Norwich civic identity and produces the architectural and geographical space that realizes, signifies, and encompasses this identity. Much like Cuningham with his map and Augustine Steward with his enhancement of civic architecture and territory, Buck functioned as a walker in the city until he emerged out of the community to produce his perspective, his vision of social cohesion. Of course, as an employee of the city, Buck, in his final stanza, not surprisingly transforms anything that authorities might perceive as criticism into a compliment: "To Councell the wise, to folley yt soundethe / for whatt nedethe councell where wisdome abou*n*deth." Still, his previous utopian itemization of the characteristics of a "commo*n*n wealthe" outlines a vision of social order in some respects ahead of its time elsewhere in England, albeit a fairly accurate vision of the panoptic community that would be realized to an increasing extent in Elizabethan and Stuart Norwich.[34]

Also like Cuningham and Steward (who lived on the city boundary with the cathedral precinct), Buck produces and performs his vision from the margins. Although constructed at the heart of the city, the pageant consists of a set of city gates leading to "a greate Castell w*i*th towers made for Armes of the Cyttye & ye lyonn being cowched vnd*er* the gate & vppon eu*ery* tower a Morrian w*i*th his darte & his targett." Buck speaks to the mayor, the aldermen and council, and the people standing with them, apparently on the ground outside the pageant gates. He takes them outside the city in order for them to see it as a whole and to embrace what it can and should be. By giving the mayor a copy of his speech and "so passinge throwghe the Gate all ye greate orden*n*ans with a grete nombre of chambers wer shott offe," he invites the mayor and the rest of the community to metaphorically enter and realize that vision.

The overall experience of the pageant, with the mayor and other officials presumably standing at the gate and the rest of the community around them, would have for the moment realized the sense of social cohesion, shared values, and order to which Buck's message aspires. The walls and castle – the two dominant features of the city in its arms – protect the community (underscored by the shooting of ordinance); they enclose and define it as a social whole, and they order and control it. Characterized by inclusivity, Buck's genuine "commo*n*n wealthe" encompasses youth and age, rich and poor; insists on shared values ("fere god and serue hym") as well as "quiet and con*n*corde;" and assumes a wide range of responsibilities under the aegis of the mandate of city authorities "to gouerne to Rule and protecte." He ascribes a moral value to order when admonishing the "wourthey Counsull condin*n*glie Electe" to maintain the city "In suche coomlye order as doethe Appertaine / All visse to abanndon*n* and vertewe maintayne."[35]

Order and good government begin with the individual official who must personally serve as a lantern shining "suche Lighte for to make / As others of yow good Exaumple maye take." They must be godly and "Cawsse others do the same," and this godliness must manifest itself in the parameters of government. They must "Prouyde for the poore" and "Cause yoothe to be trayned and seasoned in Tyme / In vertew and Labour from synne vice and Cryme" (not surprising coming from the headmaster of Norwich School). These two expectations lead logically to his next expectation for the maintenance of law and order: "Cause eu*e*ry man walke according to his callinge / In quiet and con*n*corde withowte strieffe or brawlinge." With allusion to the Mayor's Court, he then devotes two whole stanzas to the importance of impartial, fair, and reasoned justice by charging officials not to give "yo*u*r sentence, for mede or for feare / when wisdome hathe tryed Lette Iustice appere."[36]

Such a listing of civic duties frequently appears in the later surviving London shows, but, from several perspectives, the earlier date and particular emphasis of this pageant make it interesting as a construction of Norwich citizens and their community. First of all, through allusion, the enumeration of responsibilities extends the literal production of civic space accomplished by the procession and the three pageant stops to other spaces either on or outside the processional route – for example, the Guildhall (which housed both the Mayor's Court and the recently refurbished jail) and Norwich School (within the cathedral precincts). The position of care for the poor in the listing (second only to godliness) also conjures up a whole network of almshouses, hospitals, and tenements maintained by the city. With the dissolution, the responsibility for this network of facilities had shifted from primarily the church to civic government, which consolidated and maintained it through a poor relief tax.[37] The first of its kind in England when introduced in 1549, the compulsory tax supported the refoundation of St Giles's hospital, located between the river and the cathedral precinct. Surveys actually reveal that many aldermen and councillors, including Steward, also housed the poor, and civic government apparently took Buck's admonition seriously by further extending poor relief through the stockpiling of corn in 1557. Simultaneously, they also issued regulations excluding any more poor people without the means to support themselves from settling in the city. This, in fact, laid the groundwork for more innovative and substantial actions in 1570, which set Norwich up as a "disciplined" and panoptic community taken as a model by the rest of the country. These measures included a formal census of the poor; a Book of Orders for their management; a broader system of jails, workhouses, and hospitals; and a doubling of the poor rate.[38]

This transfer of social responsibilities from the church to civic government corresponds with a similar transfer of religious and medieval tropes in the pageant itself into a secular and early modern context. From the first stanza the orator situates his vision within the diabolical struggle of the morality plays. He urges councillors to abandon all vice and "vertewe maintayne." In reminding them of the rewards of virtuous behaviour, he paraphrases scripture: "for who so the hungrie and thirstie shall feede / God will rewarde him, seven follde for his deede." Neglect of good government will result in chaos such that "The Cyttie ys plaged in wreke of soche eavelle" and great accomplishments "by discorde & mallise shall seace." Despite the appropriateness of allusions to the morality play tradition within the context of Counter-Reformation culture, the resulting effect makes the city and its councillors rather than the church responsible for the "soul" of the community. As in the first pageant, allusion to the Crown remains oblique, with an ambiguous suggestion that the exercise of wisdom shall cause "this wealle pieblicke" (possibly national as well as local) to "florisshe as A Rose." Of course the castle, the local seat of royal authority, dominates the pageant, and the exit of the "Richelie app*ar*reilled" orator through its gates could identify him with that authority's right to instruct and confirm elected civic officials.[39] The description, however, interprets the gate as "a Cytte gate." Buck is a civic not a royal employee, and this castle has actually been constructed by the city (most likely paid for by Steward's Mercers Guild, although the records do not survive) and stamped with its own coat of arms. When the orator invites the mayor, other officials, and the assembled public to enter this vision of civic utopia, he not only transforms the spectacular effects of the royal entry in order to elevate civic authority but also displaces royal authority and transforms the feudalism from which it derived.

The overall direction of these pageants places the mayor and chief performer at the centre of orations that take an increasingly focused audience from a concern with the past to a concern with the future. The first pageant derives its veneration of Steward from the past and addresses it to the entire community. The second envisions what the city is and/or could be through a lesson on responsibilities directed to the mayor and other officials. The third extends and rechannels allusions to the medieval morality play to provide guidance and assistance directed specifically to the mayor. Here citizens of high and low degree set Steward up as the ideal leader of the community and assume his openness to collective determination of his character and approach. He must listen to and incorporate good counsel. In anticipation of the challenges that will face him, an orator introduces the four cardinal virtues (Prudence, Justice, Fortitude, and Temperance) who argue for the supremacy of their virtue much as do the four daughters of God (Mercy, Truth, Justice, and Peace) during the judgment of "humanum genus" in the *Castle of Perseverence*. If fully developed within the context of this tradition of dramatic debate, then, the female characters who become the mayor's counsellors at the end of the play would have included Truth, a direct allusion to the first pageant and Mary. If, as Janssen has argued, the mayor's pageants drew from the play *Respublica*, which the Chapel Royal most likely performed for Mary early in her reign,[40] the choice of the cardinal virtues becomes even more curious as that play also ends with counsel from the four daughters of God, including Truth. While the royal entertainment may have served as a model for elevating an incoming mayor and the city itself, its emulation stopped short of further reference to Mary.

In absorbing and adapting the morality play form, though, the pageant invests the mid-sixteenth-century relationship between mayor and commonwealth with neo-feudal allegiances related to those identified by Lawrence Manley in later London shows.[41] The orator sets the allegorical stage by introducing the "Carnall vertews" and attributing their coming to Fame, who had announced "to all Estates" that Steward had "of hyghe and Lowe ... wonne the voysse / To haue the seate and rulinge Chaire." Whereas allusion to Fame in the first pageant directed attention to the past, now it directs attention forward to Steward's term of office. Upon hearing of his election "of theire [the people's] cawsse as Iudge to sytte," the virtues felt "bounde / to seeke him owte" and "presente them selves on yow too waighte" as his counsellors:

> thay shalbe Allwaie at yowre hannde
> and guyde yow safe in wayes full straighte
> yf you keepe them no kinde of power
> can*n* dommaige at annye owre.

Presenting themselves as clients suing a patron, the virtues underscore the importance of their service in helping this lord-like mayor not to "miskarrye." Prudentia says, "Refuse me not for I am shee / thatt will yow serue bothe nighte and daie," and Justitia means "for good and Ill / at all assaies to serue yow styll." Fortitudo asks that he receive her "nowe I hvmmblie praye / and I will sarue as I best maye," and Temperantia concludes the development of the client/patron relationship with the traditional gift-giving ritual, which is like that which concluded the previous pageant and like that which marked the visits of local magnates such as the Dukes of Norfolk to the city.[42] The performance of such allegiance to the mayor on the part of local performers playing the virtues cultivates by example a broader civic allegiance.

Collectively, these pageants display many characteristics in common with London Lord Mayor's shows, such as their "'imaginative refeudalization' of culture"[43] and the blending of elements from religious ritual and drama with a secular context. These particular preoccupations situate the participants in a liminal space where they can negotiate the limits of competing levels of authority: city and sovereign, secular and religious. However, the resulting ritually induced "communitas" may have produced somewhat different conceptions of civic identity and its position relative to cultural hegemony.[44] Manley has argued that the shows of Elizabethan and Stuart London foreground the neo-feudal connection between city and monarch and the city's central role in the development of the nation-state, but the pageants of Marian Norwich acknowledge the monarch only indirectly and foreground a local conception of commonwealth, which produces and performs the mayor as neo-feudal lord. Mary's uncompromising and incendiary approach to religious policy, in fact, contrasts sharply with the prominence given to Temperance in the pageants. As "the best" of the virtues, she gets the last word and promises "for good svccese or greate mischaunce / for pleasannte Caullme or stormie winde" to "bannishe quite the Raging will / and keepe always my vertew styll."[45]

Although "beating the bounds" of civic identity, the Norwich pageants also blur the boundaries in favour of fluidity, permeability, and mobility. De Certeau has argued that processional and narrative activity "*authorize* the establishment, displacement or transcendence of limits, and as a consequence, … set in opposition, within the closed field of discourse, two movements that intersect (setting and transgressing limits)."[46] The walls, bridges, and gates that figured in Cuningham's depiction of the city figure literally and metaphorically in the pageants. Both visions of order depend upon a conception of commonwealth that facilitates a measure of openness and inclusion.[47]

In their blending of medieval morality play traditions within early modern secular ceremony,[48] the pageants lead to further understanding of how blurring the boundaries of authority and identity contributed to the local conception of commonwealth. The climate during the Marian Counter-Reformation encouraged the continuation of the Norwich Grocers' Corpus Christi pageant (not suppressed until 1559), which would have preceded the mid-summer inauguration by fewer than three weeks in 1556, and related allegorical, processional, and musical elements in religious rituals.[49] We know, however, that the city also continued the practice of hiring preachers, which it began after the Reformation, and that its common council encompassed a range of Protestant and Catholic religious allegiances throughout Mary's reign.[50] Mathew Reynolds has linked Steward with the emergence of Protestantism in Norwich,[51] and we know the succeeding mayor, Henry Bacon, a staunch Puritan, led the city to replace the image of the Trinity on its seal with the city arms.[52] Although the Bishop of Norwich clearly pursued Mary's religious agenda, comparatively few Norwich citizens suffered execution for Protestant beliefs, and scholars are debating the extent to which Norwich authorities actively participated in and supported Mary's persecution of Protestants.[53] As was the case in early Elizabethan London,[54] many citizens, including common councillors, may have developed a flexible approach to religious practice like that of the city waits who performed not only in secular ceremonies like these pageants but also in religious services at Norwich Cathedral under revolving religious regimes.[55]

In the face of such diversity and conflicting allegiances, the pageants develop a conception of civic order and identity by downplaying allegiances to Mary's policies and promoting a religiously informed but non-denominational level of authority, a secular alternative in the context of religious turmoil. Mervyn James has argued that "the theme of Corpus Christi is society seen in terms of body; and that the concept of body provided urban societies with a mythology and ritual in terms of which the opposites of social wholeness and social differentiation could be both affirmed, and also brought into a creative tension, one with the other. The final intention of the cult was, then, to express the social bond and to contribute to social integration."[56] To some degree, the Norwich mayor's pageants adopt the secular agenda of the older biblical drama. Similar to the recently revived Grocers' Guild Corpus Christi entertainments in its processive spectacle,[57] the mayor's pageants would have contributed to collective pride as an expression of civic wealth and status, second only to London and its emerging tradition of mayor's shows.[58] The first pageant focuses on social differentiation – establishing Steward's exceptional credentials to be mayor – and the final pageant frames him as the god-like judge. Coming just after the Grocers' Corpus Christi entertainment, this Mercers' Guild celebration of its distinguished member could have contributed to the guild rivalry that arose in mounting biblical drama. If mounted by the incoming mayor's trade guild, over time such pageants would also highlight on their own the differentiated guild structure and project what James has identified as "a symbolism of temporal mutation within the urban body."[59] The status achieved by men like Steward spoke to a degree of social and economic mobility, while the content, the processional and stylistic features of the pageants, underscored a continuum of social and political structure and order. The collective instruction of council and mayor in their responsibilities, with emphasis on the need to seek good counsel, contributed to an affirmation of social wholeness to some degree vested in the construction of the mayor as an everyman figure.

Like the Corpus Christi entertainments, the occasion of presenting the new mayor functioned as "an occasion on which the urban community could effectively present and define itself in relation to the outside world."[60] Taking as a comparative point of departure the explicit humanist allusion to Rome and oblique allusion to Mary in the first pageant, processing literally and figuratively in the second past architectural features that construct the city's "limits" and its character, the entertainments conclude with an exemplary model of the social mobility facilitated by the economy of this early modern urban centre set within the context of traditional feudal relationships and the judgmental conclusions found in medieval biblical plays and the psychomachia of the moralities.

The processive and performative frame brings the mayor, the council, and the community together to perform its social wholeness by invoking the "limits" that differentiate it – political, geographical, temporal, topographical, social, cultural, and spiritual.

James's identification of social cohesion and social differentiation as fundamental to civic pageantry betrays a fundamental tension similar to that found in the process of setting and transgressing boundaries as articulated by de Certeau. In drawing together those who "belong" around a shared heritage, identity, and values, the pageants construct an urban vision of communality that stands as an alternative to the cohesive and differentiating bonds of lineage and lordship in an earlier, primarily agricultural and rural society.

At the same time, however, the fusion of god, magistrate, and feudal lord that elevates Steward above other walkers in the city points to a position of privilege derived not simply from his sense of responsibility to the community or his particular vision and insight but also from a position of economic privilege. Like many other Tudor mayors in Norwich, his position derived from physical and social mobility. As a mercer, Steward's involvement in the city's cloth trade connected him with international as well as English markets and with the sheep farming countryside that supplied and fed his market town. He used the financial success of his international ventures to invest not only in urban real estate and gifts to the city but also in rural pieces of the feudal past, such as the manors of Welborne and Gowthorpe in Swardeston. Social and financial mobility enabled him, like Cuningham, to achieve multiple perspectives of the city by moving outside its walls as well as walking its streets. Manley has argued that later London pageants sought to stabilize such urban mobility and fluidity by constructing a cohesive neo-feudal order. Reflecting upon the "'incorporative rituals of the past,'" Manley argues that, "as London came to play an increasingly important role in the national economy and polity, communal identification developed side by side with social differentiation, so that 'community in the sense of people of different status doing things together was ... eroded' even while mythology and pageantry became more prominent."[61]

Despite the intentions of social cohesion behind the pageantry, then, its received meaning, its impact on everyday practices and citizens' concepts of identity, evolved within the fluid intertextuality of differentiating social practices, competing claims to authority, and visions of "commo*n*n wealthe." The pageants construct a "fiction of knowledge" within an ongoing, intertextual negotiation of boundaries characterized by divergence, difference, and disagreement:

> The city is left prey to contradictory movements that counterbalance and combine themselves outside the reach of panoptic power. The city becomes the dominant theme in political legends, but it is no longer a field of programmed and regulated operations. Beneath the discourses that ideologize the city, the ruses and combinations of powers that have no readable identity proliferate; without points where one can take hold of them, without rational transparency, they are impossible to administer.[62]

A fascination with limits and boundaries reflects the fact that the city identified many of its most challenging threats to cohesive order and stability as "other," as coming from outside.[63] Cuningham's map and Kett's rebellion provide two extreme examples of collective identity performed from the margins of the community, but those who did not belong also had an important performative role to play in blurring, extending, and reconfiguring city limits from within. Whereas individuals like Cuningham, who belong, often need to step out of the city to see it as a whole, those who do not belong can serve as catalysts in making the bounds visible from within and prompting a reconsideration of them by those who do belong. For example, an overtly performative class of "others," touring players created additional texts for the negotiation of allegiance and identity.

Like the mayor's pageants, their performances provided a public environment for the collective exploration of limits and boundaries on the part of Norwich residents and visitors alike. During Steward's mayoral year the Chamberlains provided rewards to players whose patrons were the Queen, the Duke of Norfolk, and the Earl of Oxford.[64] Their touring network spatially linked the different communities they visited in cultural neighbourhoods in much the same way as the mayor's procession linked different neighbourhoods in Norwich. In walking the country they bridged boundaries and projected the interests of their patron into the popular construction of local and national commonwealth.[65] In the early days of Mary's reign, the city examined the Lord Russell's Minstrels and found that they possessed "vnfitting songes" reflecting their patron's Protestant opposition to Catholicism. As a result, two other minstrels connected with devising the songs endured enforced performances in the pillory – one "w*ith* a paper vppon his hedd" and another with his ear nailed to the pillory.[66] In this climate, the Queen's Men responded with an intensive and extensive touring circuit stretching from the Court to Kent to Beverley to Exeter that could bring Mary, her government, and her vision of England into communities around the country.[67]

Few of these touring performers' plays survive to inform our understanding of this vision or of how it might have influenced Norwich citizens, but one play possibly in the Queen's players' touring repertoire in 1556 has survived. *The Interlude of Wealth and Health* concludes with specific praise for Mary, and the central allegorical characters called Wealth, Health, and Liberty embody the country as a whole when they are misguided and abused by three false counsellors (a clear allusion to members of Edward's government). These counsellors receive their comeuppance from Remedy, a character who generates fear because he is "not fraide to do right punishment" and "Willing to fulfil his soueraines commaundement."[68] Given the explanation that he dwelled "not heare" (l. 621) and that his costume included a red cap (l. 834) and elegant gown (l. 625), Remedy probably represents Cardinal Pole, who had returned from long exile in 1554 to become both the spiritual and secular head of Mary's government:

> That none of you shall diminishe, nor amisse be tane
> I good remedy therfore may & will speake w*ith*out bla*m*e
> For the comen welth, & helth both of the soule & body
> yt is mi office & power, & therfore I haue my actoritie.
>
> (ll. 588–91)

Rather than foregrounding Mary, then, the play focuses on introducing Pole – his policies and points of view – and establishing his "actoritie" to rule. The agenda, then, behind this play has similarities with that of the mayor's pageant, although its approach, substance, and ultimate effect differ significantly.

For instance, the spatial dynamics of the performance text for play and pageant would have differed to a very high degree. Records for Steward's tenure do not provide details as to where players performed, but in previous years the city hosted players in St Andrew's Hall and paid for the construction of scaffolding, charcoal, drink, and "ij men y*a*t kept the dores."[69] Although it is possible that the players also played in the city at other times and in other venues, performance indoors before the mayor created a more contained and controlled audience-actor dynamic. The central performer of the pageants – the mayor – walked the streets deriving his authority from his connection with the citizens and his openness to facilitating and standing proxy for their conception of a commonwealth. Although the pageant characters appeared on fixed, sometimes elevated staging, they interacted freely – sometimes on an even footing – with their chief audience, the mayor. If staging for the play evolved as in the past, Remedy would have appeared on enclosed, elevated, fixed staging affording little opportunity for physical interaction with the audience. Unlike the earlier court interlude, *Respublica*,[70] in which the character People urges moderation and fosters a close and affectionate relationship with the central title character, *Wealth and Health* presents Remedy as asserting and commanding in preachy dialogue that makes little attempt to disguise his lack of respect for his audience. He complains about the difficulty of maintaining Wealth, Health, and Liberty because "the people be so variable / And many be so wilfull, they will not be reformable" (ll. 539–40). Later he warns that "Craft wyll out and disceite wyll haue a fall" (l. 937) and "god wyl punish the people when they be detelt" (l. 798). Scholars have noted the general failure of Mary and Pole to recognize the merits of passionate persuasion over assertions of "actoritie," and Remedy's character seems to confirm this observation.[71] Certainly his vengeful, judgmental approach to authority stands in stark contrast to the more temperate magistrate constructed by counsel in the final pageant. The anticipation of Remedy with fear and his association with punishment and suspicion could only have highlighted rather than counteracted the more inflammatory performance propaganda of public burnings, which had begun in Norwich in 1555 with the execution of three Protestants.[72]

Whereas Steward's procession effectively decentred the source of power as he symbolically stepped outside the city limits in the second pageant in order to be invited into the city and then drew the city to its geographical centre with his acceptance of their counsel in the third pageant, Remedy's judgmental assertions of authority and the literal and figurative boundaries constructed in performance negated any decentring effect of the Queen's Men's "progress," or tour, around the country. In their capacity to inspire a sense of belonging, the ordered inclusion (high and low, rich and poor) emphasized in Steward's pageants contrasts sharply with the enforced exclusion radiating from Remedy's pronouncements. David Loades has noted the mistaken emphasis that Mary and Pole placed on assertions of authority over passionate persuasion, and Remedy's repeated recourse to "actoritie" would appear to bear this out.

This interlude clearly delineates those who belong and those who do not, using a time honoured technique of fostering social cohesion through characterization of the "other." Apparently injected simply for effect, Hance Beerpot has no essential connection to the plot when he enters as a drunk singing a "dutche songe." Connected with war and credited with trying "tiget englishme*n*s welth away," Beerpot associates with the vice figures (ll. 389, 399, 400, 766). Remedy rebukes him by declaring that "there is to mainy allaunts in this reale, but now I good remedy haue so prouided that English men shall lyue the better dayly (ll.760–2)." The play positions two other vices less overtly. Shrewd Wit's first lines are in French, and Ill Will begins speaking Spanish to avoid Remedy's wrath.

Remarkably, the play appears oblivious to the instability of boundaries performed in this manner. John Pound has observed that "Norwich merchants ... had long experience of trading with the Dutch, a number of them being members of either the Old or New Hanse, that is the Company of Merchant Adventurers." In the 1540s and 1550s, Norwich had begun to attract Dutch and Walloon "incomers" because of the textile industry and because of the friendlier environment for their Protestant beliefs. At the onset of a much larger immigration in 1565, forty-two such families already called the city home. At this point, the players' sentiments could have found sympathetic resonance with Norwich audiences (they certainly would have after 1565) despite the aliens' expertise and trading connections, which contributed significantly to Norwich's long-term "welth and helth."[73]

Such tactics could have backfired, however. Susan Frye's observations regarding the transaction of social business in Elizabethan pageantry applies equally to the earlier entertainments discussed here: "It is in the unstable space between signifier and signified that change occurs. It is the instability of language that perpetually undermines its authoritative use. The instability of signs allows not only representation to map conflicting and overlapping discourses, but also the evolution of those discourses as signs – created in part from only sign systems and in part from emergent codes – to alter the distinctions and categories that constitute meaning."[74]

Remedy's identification as a stranger highlights Pole's long exile and association with Rome, and the sound of Spanish could have raised the spectre of the aliens most disliked by the English ever since Mary's marriage to Philip II. As Mary's closest allies, Philip and his Spanish entourage were hated and feared by members of the nobility as well as by common labourers. A Norwich carpenter who fought in Wyatt's rebellion expressed his animosity and fears about the Spanish liaison most articulately: "we should lie in swine sties in caves and the Spaniards should have our houses, and we should live like slaves."[75]

The play reveals little sensitivity to what might or might not play well in the provinces and foster a shared sense of identity and social cohesion around popular allegiance to Mary's government. In the face of Remedy's preference for preachy demands and assertions, Norwich audiences might recall Fortitude's advice in the third pageant, where she urges the Mayor to have a "hardie mynde / to doo thos things that righte allowe / thoughe might gainsaie with frowninge browe." Justice anticipates the need for such independence in judging cases involving "doubtfull Lawes," while Temperentia urges a "staed mynde" to banish "the Raging will."[76] Remedy's character contrasts sharply with this ideal of moderation while potentially cultivating a spirit of civic independence, most especially in its model citizen, the mayor.

Remedy alludes to Pole's argument behind the return of church lands (l. 569, 584) – something high on his agenda in reuniting Rome and England and already a well known if unpopular item on the Privy Council agenda. Having paid £81 of his own money to procure St Andrew's Hall and worked hard to effect the assimilation of this and other dissolution properties as symbols of civic identity, Augustine Steward could not have sympathetically contemplated relinquishing the probable place of the Queen's Men's performance or other church property.[77]

While injecting a contrasting element of dissonance into the intertextual performative mix, the Queen's Men demonstrate the role of "others" who transgress boundaries: "This actor, by virtue of the very fact that he is the mouthpiece of the limit, creates communication as well as separation; more than that, he establishes a border only by saying what crosses it, having come from the other side. He articulates it. He is *also* a passing through or over."[78]

The crossing of limits by walkers who "belong" also figured in the "readable" utopian texts constructed in the pageants and the early city map. Similar crossings of boundaries by local or travelling priests and preachers (regularly paid by the city) would have contributed to the construction of civic identity through performance texts also characterized by moral didacticism and contrast.[79] The complex performance texts of Protestant executions took place in the margins outside the city gates.[80] Once again, "incomers" breach the limits of authority to precipitate local negotiations of identity. Coming all the way from his home in King's Lynn in 1557, Simon Miller performed his opposition to Catholicism for Norwich people leaving a church service by demanding to know where he could attend Mass administered under the Book of Common Prayer. Although whisked away to the Bishop of Norwich's prison, then initially released, he soon returned from King's Lynn for a repeat performance and was then burned along with Elizabeth Cooper, the wife of a Norwich pewterer, who had made a similarly performative denouncement of Catholicism during Mass. Their collective performance while dying at the stake inspired another woman, Cicely Ormes, the wife of a Norwich weaver, to publicly declare her own opposition to Catholicism, and she was burned in the same place just over two months later.[81]

Here we have a glimpse of walkers in Marian Norwich – both citizens and "others" – synthesizing official and divergent performance texts and not only developing but also performing independent allegiances and a sense of community that transcended the official "limits" of authority. With places of performance outside the city walls and at its geographical centre, walkers could traverse both literal and figurative limits, literal bridges and gates or symbolic spaces transformed by circumstances to simultaneously embody multiple demands for allegiance. These spaces of performance became liminal spaces of overlap and negotiation, places where boundaries, different levels of authority, different concepts of identity could be blurred and reconstituted in shifting and popular expressions of communitas. Such performances embody de Certeau's concept of the spatial story, "a sort of delinquency in reserve, maintained, but itself displaced and consistent, in traditional societies … with an order that is firmly established but flexible enough to allow the proliferation of this challenging mobility that does not respect places, is alternately playful and threatening, and extends from the microbe-like forms of everyday narration to the carnivalesque celebrations of earlier days."[82]

The civic identity emerging from the collective, intertextual vigour of spatial performances in Marian Norwich constructs an urban commonwealth indebted to but far more moderate, cohesive, and forward thinking than Mary's conception of the nation-state.

NOTES

1 Corfield, "Urban Development in England," 39, 44–5.

2 Standard discussions of internal tensions include Beier, "Social Problems in Elizabethan London"; and Pearl, "Change and Stability in Seventeenth Century London." However, the extent to which these tensions reflected or caused genuine instability has since been seriously questioned by scholars such as Ward, *Metropolitan Communities*. For anxieties expressed by the Crown, see, for example, Hughes and Larkin, *Tudor Royal Proclamations*, 2:46–8, 466–8. For similar concerns expressed by the provinces and in current literature, see Manley, *Literature and Culture in Early Modern London* passim, but esp. 130–1, 196–8.

3 See Coenen Snyder (this volume) on the importance of the capital, Amsterdam, to the development of the economic and social values of Dutch republic. Eds.

4 Tittler, "The Incorporation of Boroughs," 24.

5 Cuningham, *The Cosmographical Glasse*, from the key to the Norwich map inserted between fols. 8 and 9.

6 de Certeau, *Practice of Everyday Life*, 92–3.

7 See also Perkins (this volume) on constructed vistas of Edinburgh in the late eighteenth century. Eds.

8 Cox, "Religious Houses," 329, 354, 431, 433.

9 The cathedral authorities and city officials were in and out of conflict from the first city charter in 1404 until 1538. See Atherton, *Norwich Cathedral*; Simkins, "Ecclesiastical History," 258; Blomefield, *Essay towards a Topographical History of the County of Norfolk*, 211.

10 Cuningham, map between fols. 8–9.

11 Simkins, "Ecclesiastical History," 260–1. Acknowledgment of local patrons takes another form in Cuningham's book. With Elizabeth's recent accession in 1558, Cuningham and the city had to consider other less overtly Catholic patronage connections. His entire book, let alone this map, was dedicated to Robert Dudley, whose marriage into a prominent Norfolk family and recent rise to prominence under Elizabeth made him an obvious choice.

12 Barringer, "The Changing Face of Norwich," 1.

13 de Certeau, *Practice of Everyday Life*, 92–4.

14 Ibid., 121. These figures help to define and contextualize the commons just inside the walls at St Giles Gate, through which Cuningham would have passed on his way to the hill from which he observed the city. The

combination of grazing cattle and archers no doubt represented the activities that went on there, although presumably not simultaneously. People ploughing their fields and shepherds with their sheep also help to define the bucolic suburbs surrounding Cuningham's vista. Despite the overall drift of his book towards a more "scientific" approach to spatial delineation, his Norwich map clearly represents the city with what de Certeau characterizes as the earlier type of "'narrative' figures," pictorial references to the operations – both historical and contemporary – that produced it.

15 Another obvious ceremony revolving around "limits" was perambulation day. A ceremony whose origins stretched back into the Middle Ages, "beating the bounds" was practised in numerous communities well into the modern era. In Norwich the mayor, along with the waits and other officials, traversed the bounds of the city in late May. The ceremony symbolically confirmed their authority at the margins of the city while also marking out a particular segment of geography and its inhabitants as having something in common and distinct from those outside its bounds. Unfortunately, the ceremony does not assume a high profile in surviving mid-Tudor records. They are silent as to the details of the ceremony or any interactions that may have involved the citizens. Nor do the records tell us whether, in fact, the citizens enclosed within these bounds – particularly those in the newly acquired suburbs – actually felt a sense of belonging and a common connection with those inside the city walls. See, for example, Galloway, *Norwich 1540–1642*, 50, 61, 351.

16 See, for example, Manley, *Literature and Culture in Early Modern London*; Lancashire, *London Civic Theatre*; Bergeron, *English Civic Pageantry*; and Withington, *English Pageantry*.

17 Galloway, *Norwich 1540–1642*, xxi.

18 de Certeau, *Practice of Everyday Life*, 93, 98–9. One could argue that, collectively, these pageant texts provide another example of the connection identified by de Certeau between walking, itineraries, and early maps. "The chain of spatialising operations seems to be marked by references to what it produces (a representation of places) or to what it implies (a local order). We thus have the structure of the travel story: stories of journeys and actions are marked out by the 'citation' of the places that result from them or authorize them" (120).

19 Steward had been instrumental in resolving the hotly contested issue of authority over the precinct in the city's favour in 1539. See Bindoff, *History of Parliament*, 384.

20 For fuller biographical details relating to Steward, see Bindoff, *History of Parliament,* 383–5.

21 Throughout the Tudor period, Norwich invested significantly in symbols of its power and authority that could serve as symbolic foci for civic identity and allegiance. This included the waits and other officials who attended the mayor with liveries featuring the city arms. It also included building projects encompassing its walls and bridges, its churches, and its civic buildings, such as the Norwich Grammar School, St Andrew's Hall (at 125 feet by 70 inches still cited as the best example of friar architecture in England) and the Guildhall. The latter was much smaller than St Andrew's Hall, but it was extensively renovated with a new privy, new paving, elaborate painting and writing on the walls, a window with the arms of the city, new furniture in the treasury, hangings in the mayor's chamber, painted alter cloths, and a new mass book for the chapel. See Norwich Chamberlains Accounts 1554–5, Norfolk Record Office (NRO), 18a, fols. 67v–68r, 73v; 1556–7, fol. 91v. See also Tittler, *The Architecture of Power,* 19, 23, 40, 54, 92, 112–3, 126–7, 144–9, 154–5.

22 See Coenen Snyder (this volume) on how architectural space registers the presence of seventeenth- and early eighteenth-century Amsterdam's Jewish community. Eds.

23 Geertz, *Local Knowledge,* 125

24 Frye, *Elizabeth I,* 26.

25 Galloway, *Norwich 1540–1642,* 39.

26 Of course, Steward's social and economic status as well as his ongoing position as an alderman up to his death in 1571 mean that he would never be just "an ordinary" citizen, but these factors would not have affected his participation in the "practice of everyday life" as conceived by de Certeau to the same degree as would the role of mayor, with its high visibility and ceremonial functions.

27 Galloway, *Norwich 1540–1642,* 38–9.

28 Bindoff, *History of Parliament,* 384. For a full description of Kett's rebellion from the perspective of local history, see Rawcliffe, *Medieval Norwich,* 277–99.

29 Bergeron, *English Civic Pageantry,* 138.

30 Galloway, *Norwich 1540–1642,* 38.

31 Great Britain, *Acts,* ed. J.R. Dasent, 4: 294–295, 298–299; Cozens-Hardy and Kent, *Mayors of Norwich,* 48.

32 It is unclear as to what the waits did in the performance. Both the description and the text for the first pageant seem to suggest only one

actor and one speaking part. The "morien" at the top of the pavilion was most likely a decorative feature and not an actual actor. Of course, the topic of "Time" would have made the introduction of music a suitable accompaniment, and we know from the early Lord Mayor's Shows in London that music was certainly an important feature of these performances. However, apart from the marginal gloss noting the participation of the waits, there is no reference to music in the description or the speech given by Time. For a discussion of the waits' participation in this pageant, see Janssen, "The Waites of Norwich," 57–64.

33 Galloway, *Norwich 1540–1642*, 38–9.

34 Ibid., 38, 40.

35 Ibid., 40.

36 Ibid.

37 See Warne (this volume) for an analysis of relations between civic authorities and the poor in nineteenth-century London. Eds.

38 Pound, "Government to 1660," 49–55.

39 This could also be an allusion to the important precondition for the London Lord Mayor's shows: his approval by the sovereign and his trip to Westminster or the Tower for his oath of fealty to the Crown.

40 Janssen, "The Waites of Norwich," 61. She cites similarities in their references to Truth, the use of four female virtues/daughters of God as counsellors, and the reliance on musicians for performance. The waits also performed in the cathedral. Janssen does not note a possible local connection with the play. John Hopton, who had been Mary's private chaplain and confessor, was appointed Bishop of Norwich in 1554 (Simkins, "Ecclesiastical History," 260). The provenance of the extant Macro manuscript can be traced back to a sixteenth-century Norfolk antiquary, Henry Spelman. See Greg, *Respublica*, vii.

41 See, for example, Manley, *Literature and Culture in Early Modern London*, 13–14, 212–21 passim.

42 Galloway, *Norwich 1540–1642*, 41–3. For examples of gifts given to the Dukes of Norfolk as well as gifts given to the city by the Dukes of Norfolk, see Norwich Chamberlains' Accounts, NRO 18a, fols 57v, 72v, 73v, 129r.

43 Manley, *Literature and Culture in Early Modern London*, 212.

44 Here, I am alluding to the concepts of "liminality" and "communitas" as developed by Victor Turner in *From Ritual to Theatre*, 20–59.

45 Galloway, *Norwich 1540–1642*, 43.

46 de Certeau, *Practice of Everyday Life*, 123.

47 The Marian Norwich concept of commonwealth implies a role for all "degrees" of social class, a concern for the poor on the part of the rich, a "laissez-faire" attitude towards religious practice, and an openness to "incomers" (be they English or foreign) who could enhance the civic economy (not, however, towards idle vagabonds). When placed in the context of postmodern standards and the early tendency towards "enforced inclusion" in a civic panopticon, this may not seem like an inclusive society, but by mid-Tudor standards it was certainly ahead of its time.

48 For a discussion of the allegorical, processional, and musical elements adapted by the pageants from the morality play tradition, see Janssen, "The Waites of Norwich," 61–2.

49 See Fisher (this volume) on the importance of processions to confessional allegiance in early modern Augsburg. Eds.

50 See, for example, in 1554–55 and 1556–57, Norwich Chamberlains' Accounts, NRO 18a, fols. 72r, 97r; McClendon, *The Quiet Reformation*, 194–9.

51 Reynolds, *Godly Reformers*, 45.

52 Cozens-Hardy and Kent, *Mayors of Norwich*, 55.

53 For instance, McClendon argues that, from the beginning of public executions in 1555, "religious conflict all but disappeared from the mayor's court. The magistrates neither heard cases involving religious controversy, nor assisted local church authorities in the apprehension of religious nonconformists." She argues that "Norwich stands in marked contrast to the experience of many other communities" at this time because only two of its residents ever went to the stake – and these only because they actually incriminated themselves publicly. "City magistrates were disinclined to become involved in the deadly persecution of religious dissidents and in effect shielded them from execution" (102–4). Reynolds points to McClendon's exclusive focus on civic documents and the importance of parochial evidence. His book refutes her thesis.

54 Frye, *Elizabeth I*, 45–6.

55 Alexander Cowan has, for instance, remarked on the tolerance towards dissenters in Norwich (Cowan, *Urban Europe*, 113); Galloway, *Norwich 1540–1642*, xl–xli.

56 James, "Ritual, Drama and Social Body," 4.

57 Galloway, *Norwich 1540–1642*, 37, 43, 44.

58 These pageants may have emerged out of civic rivalry between England's first and second city. Anne Lancashire has recently drawn attention to

the fact that only in 1553 do we have "the first definite evidence ... of a substantial, constructed pageant being used on land" in London to mark a mayoral inauguration. Similar documentary uncertainties cloud the origins of inaugural pageants in Norwich (as well as its establishment as a regular tradition); however, regardless of how long such traditions had been in place in Norwich and London before 1556, it is likely that the Norwich entertainments were seen at least in part as a response to the London shows. Given the general importance placed on urban centres by Mary's government, as demonstrated earlier by Tittler, it would not be surprising to find expressions of civic pride and identity emerging during her reign. See Lancashire, *London Civic Theatre*, 183–4.

59 Galloway, *Norwich 1540–1642*, 44, 50; James, "Ritual, Drama and Social Body," 18.

60 James, "Ritual, Drama and Social Body," 12.

61 Manley, *Literature and Culture in Early Modern London*, 130; see also Archer, *The Pursuit of Stability*, 93, 99.

62 de Certeau, *The Practice of Everyday Life*, 92, 95.

63 Griffiths, "Inhabitants," 63–88.

64 Galloway, *Norwich 1540–1642*, 37.

65 The geographical "limits" of Oxford's players included not only locations in Norfolk, Suffolk, and Kent (not far from Oxford's seat in Essex) but also Somerset, Oxfordshire, and Gloucestershire. Norfolk's players were more intensively focused in the East Anglia area – Norfolk, Suffolk, and Cambridgeshire – but in the Marian period they also travelled in Sussex and Devon. Not surprisingly, given the family's status as a long-time patron of the city and a major property owner there, Norfolk's players received as much as the Queen's players in rewards from the city, while Oxford's players received only two-thirds that amount. We know, as well, that, in contrast with Norfolk's Catholicism, Oxford was one of several privy councillors regarded with suspicion because of his Protestant faith, and in 1556 he was under active investigation for conspiracy. What we do not know is what these players performed. It is tempting to speculate that Reformation and Counter-Reformation perspectives could have vied for the allegiances of Norwich citizens. We know that the Earl of Oxford's father had been a patron of players who performed plays with a distinctly Protestant perspective – including the work of John Bale. His works were proclaimed heretical and ordered to be burned in 1555, so it is unlikely that the earl's players were performing his work the next year in Norwich. See White, *Theatre and Reforma-*

tion, 15, 17–18, 21, 53, 68; Hughes and Larkin, *Tudor Royal Proclamations*, 57–60.

66 Galloway, *Norwich 1540–1642*, pp. 33–4.

67 For a sampling of this touring circuit, see Lancashire, *Dramatic Texts and Records of Britain*, 396–7. For details drawn from documentary sources so far published, see volumes published in the Records of Early English Drama series.

68 Greg, *Interlude of Wealth and Health*, ll.454–5; all further references will be to the text of this edition.

69 Galloway, *Norwich 1540–1642*, 25.

70 It was probably intended for performance not long after her accession as it seems to focus on providing good counsel to a new queen on how the country can best be managed. Because this play required a large cast drawn from the Royal Chapel choir it is unlikely that it would ever have toured.

71 Loades, *Oxford Martyrs*, 258–9.

72 As the public face of Mary's government, Pole and the character Remedy displayed little understanding or appreciation of how to present a consultative image or publicly negotiate a relationship between sovereign and city in a manner that Susan Frye has suggested Elizabeth refined throughout her reign.

73 Pound, "Government to 1660," 40–3.

74 Frye, *Elizabeth I*, 35.

75 Rye, *Depositions Taken before the Mayor and Aldermen of Norwich*, 56.

76 Galloway, *Norwich 1540–1642*, 42–3.

77 Bindoff, *History of Parliament*, 384. The semiotics of Steward and the aldermen seated at one end of St Andrew's Hall while the Queen's Men, and Remedy in particular, appropriated the other end to chastize the perpetrators of the Reformation and preach Counter-Reformation could have created a stand-off involving three levels of authority (city, church, and state) that could potentially blur the lines between reality and fictional performance and contribute unanticipated entertainment for the larger audience assembled from the community at large.

78 de Certeau, *Practice of Everyday Life*, 127.

79 See, for example, Norwich Chamberlains Accounts, NRO 18a, fols 28v, 36r, 57r, 66v, 72r, 97r, 128v, 129v. In equally even-handed fashion, the city also purchased a new lectern for the Guildhall chapel in 1556–57 (ibid., fol. 94r) as well as a new mass book in 1554–55 (ibid., fol. 73v).

80 The burnings took place under the auspices of the Bishop of Norwich, so no mention of them appears in city records, and only three of the victims

actually came from Norwich. This grim form of pageantry took place in Norwich in 1555 (with three executions), 1557 (with four), and 1558 (with three). See Ridley, *Bloody Mary's Martyrs,* 164–6.

81 These instances also demonstrate the capacity of ordinary individuals to publicly assert their disagreement with the official policies of church, state, or city. At the level of city policy, for instance, in 1554 a Norwich cobbler took issue with recently imposed sumptuary laws applying to journeymen and labourers. He saw it as an example of the ruling elite picking "quarrels with poor men. But poor men will speak one day." Clark, *English Towns in Transition*, 125.

82 de Certeau, *Practice of Everyday Life*, 130.

5

Rational Luxuries and Civilized Pleasures: Nationalizing Elite Parisian Values, 1848–49

MELANIE A. BAILEY

Théophile Gautier lived through some anxious moments as he made his way back to Paris from Spain in 1849.[1] He subsequently articulated his fears to readers of *La Presse*, the daily newspaper for which he had been theatre and music critic for several years.[2] He had been in Paris during those glorious February days of 1848, when the Second Republic had come into existence, betokening the realization of equality as well as true liberty and possibly even fraternity. He had lived through the June Days a few months later, when workers and other protestors had been killed in the streets by a government desperate to restore order, to restrain radical demands, and to regain the confidence of businesspeople and bankers. However, he had not witnessed the most recent public demonstrations, which had attempted to compel the government to withdraw French troops from Rome in 1849. As if all of these political, economic, and social problems were not enough, Paris experienced a cholera outbreak.[3]

Gautier had lived through the Revolution of 1830 and the Revolution of 1848, and he had certainly heard stories of the "great" Revolution of 1789. He understood their effects. Based solely on the information given to him in Spain, though, he could not determine whether yet another revolution had occurred in 1849 or whether people should use a different term to describe the events. He worried that he would not be able to return to his familiar routines, such as going to the opera and participating in the other activities essential to the civilized society of Paris.

He expected to find that the recent crises had shattered life in the city. He anticipated finding the Tuilleries once again filled "with cannons and soldiers, the red cortège of revolt crossed by the black cortège of cholera; the Vandals of order having sacked the printers, those sacred instruments of human thought; the theaters closed, the state of siege having delivered Paris up to the arbitrary." Having thus prepared himself for a situation with features of both the Black Death and the Revolutionary Terror of the mid-1790s, he delighted to find that a far different mood prevailed. He gathered evidence of scientific and operatic activity in the districts of the city frequented by Parisian social, intellectual, and creative elites. He could therefore boast that the life of "ideas cannot die in this fine and interesting city, the brain of the world, whatever may be the wrongs of governments [or] of the governed." Obviously, he concluded, Parisians had not lost their spirit. Nothing could resist the force of their determination to spread civilization throughout the country and all of Europe.[4]

Yet, even while Parisian elites were "decimated by the plague, saddened by political calamities," they nonetheless happily flocked to the Champs-Elysées exhibition of the "marvels of industry" and to the four theatres that had all premiered operas or plays in the same week. He avowed that this "so just, so *spirituel*, so reasonable, so wise, being that is called 'everybody' is there to repair the wrongs of individuals" by showing collective mettle and supporting civilization. Gautier also praised those theatre directors who "exhausted their supreme resources to surround a work of thought with some splendor, despite the epidemic, the revolt, the state of siege and the general misery." Together, artists and their public supporters formed a "noble intellectual tribunal that shows that France is not yet a barbarous country and that the beautiful keeps some worshippers there."[5]

The turmoil of the past year and a half had taught or reminded Gautier and other commentators that Parisians knew how to adapt to circumstances while preserving the essence of their civilization.[6] They believed that the entire nation should acquire Parisian attitudes and resilience. Thus, they would welcome the Second Republic to the extent that its leaders pursued equality and nationalized reason, discernment, and a certain degree of tolerance. If all went as planned, then the entire citizenry would eventually appreciate the arts, understand the sciences, and have the faculties necessary to participate in the public life of a rejuvenated, united nation.

Gautier, akin to other Parisian journalists who identified personally with their city, believed that its inhabitants ought to remember their shared history; they needed to preserve those values and customs that enabled them to overcome trials and tribulations that would have reduced any other people to barbarity. By involving themselves in the intellectual and cultural life of the city (such as going to the opera or reading newspaper coverage of the latest debates at the *Académie des sciences*), elite Parisians defended the liberty for which the revolutionaries of 1789 had struggled.[7] *Revolutionary* liberty encompassed more than the basic freedom to work and the civic rights that the Second Republic extended by granting universal manhood suffrage and (at least temporarily) creating workshops and jobs for the unemployed. The revolutionary liberty sought by French republicans of 1848 included the right of each individual to become civically, economically, *and* intellectually independent. Each citizen had the right to become fully sovereign over himself.[8]

By (re)activating their will to realize the promises of equality and fraternity, as well as to effect the liberation of minds and spirits sought by French *philosophes* of the Enlightenment, influential Parisians could support the Second Republic and the revolutionary aspirations of 1848. Gautier, Hector Berlioz, and Léon Foucault all assumed that Paris had both the right and the means to lead the effort to nationalize and democratize the possession of rational luxuries and civilized pleasures. They suggested that prevailing elite Parisian notions of enlightenment and discernment already served as the foundation for French republican ideology and should form the core of French identity.

Throughout this chapter, I consider the manner in which three of the music and science commentators for two different daily newspapers established connections between the capital city, the values of its cultural and/or social elites, and the formation of the French national identity.[9] By the late nineteenth century and the establishment of the Third Republic, these connections had become central to national self-understanding, especially in official discourse, and have endured even to the present. Gautier wrote explicitly and repeatedly about Paris's association with enlightenment and civilization, as did his journalistic peers Hector Berlioz and Leon Foucault. Through their analyses of key intellectual or cultural institutions, such as the *Théâtre de la Nation* or the *Académie des sciences*, they strived to demonstrate that Parisian performers, intellectuals, and audiences together reflected and created attitudes that ought to become national values under the Second Republic. Through their reflections on Parisians' reactions to revolution, they indicated the ideal way to cope with dramatic changes. Through their descriptions of their own feelings about their city, their fellow Parisians, and France, these commentators offered a model of national identity that, implicitly and in effect, drew primarily on the intellectual currents of the Enlightenment while admitting some Romantic effervescence.[10]

As the new regime asserted republican virtues, instituted universal manhood suffrage, and disdained aristocratic privilege, journalists worried that the government would attempt to eliminate the glitter and luxury from the operas produced at the national theatres. In the face of the budgetary crises that persisted throughout the Second Republic and eventually brought about the regime's demise, the government began to make significant cuts in State spending on culture. Theatres periodically closed as entrepreneurs could not always meet the challenge of operating them in the midst of conflict and without government subventions. Perhaps posing a worse threat to opera and the sophisticated civilization in Paris than basic financial difficulties, many republicans maintained that democratizing access to theatres would necessarily entail fewer fascinating stage effects, lower-quality performers, and less interesting scripts and scores.

Meanwhile, critics such as Gautier argued that Parisian theatres would serve as republican "schools" for the citizenry,[11] vehicles for nationalizing discernment, and international proof that a republic could democratize luxury rather than penury. Given these crucial functions, he believed, the government should provide levels of funding necessary to enable Parisian theatres to attain even greater heights of artistry. To make them genuinely *republican*, the administration would have to improve accessibility without compromising quality. They had to enable all citizens to become more fully human, civilized, and French.

In this vein, Gautier urged his fellow citizens to consider the model of the arts-loving Athenian Republic, rather than militaristic

Sparta, if they genuinely wished to close the material and cultural gap between the workers and the elites. Since every human being, whether rich or poor, aspired to experience beauty, they should encourage all women to "perfume themselves with flowers, to sparkle with diamonds, to shine in satin," and to appear "beautiful and smiling." The government and society should not require "black broth and coats" nor enact "stupid" sumptuary laws. Gautier and other commentators suggested that the personal hygiene, social etiquette, and intelligent forms of cultural pleasure found in Paris would enable republican virtue and should define French identity.[12]

Not surprisingly, the First Revolution – the Revolution of 1789 – served as a reference point for most political, social, and cultural prescriptions. Yet, pro-republican journalists recommended that every citizen think more about the future than the past. Gautier warned that they would trip and fall if they tried to move forward while looking behind to the past for guidance. They could and should maintain the life of the city while ensuring that every national institution oriented itself towards the future and in light of republican values. The nation's elected and self-appointed leaders should choose new symbols. Gautier suggested less use of red: "not that red be not a beautiful color, the color of the flame of life and of wine; but in the modern heraldry, it is blood and not sovereign dignity that it represents, and the young republic that has proposed to abolish the death penalty has a horror of blood." The French citizens of the new republic should also leave aside fasces and other "reminiscences of badly understood antiquity." The generation of 1848 should create its revolution as the first of its kind.[13]

Perhaps, instead of feeling that events controlled them, the citizenry could actively contribute to the definition of their revolution. Gautier explained that "our revolution" had to invent "its usages, its songs, its terminology, its emblems, its wardrobes" before it could fulfill its liberating promise and serve as a force for civilization. He asked his readers to consider the impression that they would make upon the archaeologists of the year 4949, who would discover traces of mid-nineteenth-century Paris. He wanted those people to conclude: "That is from the great era of French art, from the epoch of the Second Republic, artists were numerous; they wrote, sang, painted, sculpted new works for a new world." Gautier believed that *Parisian* achievements ought to represent the *national* spirit and signify the state of the nation in its entirety.[14]

Given that creative people had such a crucial role to play in establishing the identity that Paris would have in their own time, as well as three thousand years into the future, they incurred a duty to observe certain general rules. Not surprisingly, given the fact that Gautier was well educated and a wordsmith by vocation, he emphasized the need to defend the French language – in the form spoken and written by Parisian elites. He averred that writers should "respect the beautiful national idiom of that language of reason and of liberty, that modern Word whose indefinable life dissipates, wherever it penetrates, shadows and barbarity." Writers – and, indeed, all citizens – could demonstrate their patriotism simply by "knowing our language." Only by retaining some continuity in language could the French express the particularities of their experience while conveying fundamental truths about the human condition. If all citizens throughout the nation came to speak the Parisian version of the French language, then France's culture would become both democratic and truly national without compromising quality.[15]

Gautier anticipated that "true" artists and writers would hasten to use their (particularly Parisian and eventually national) rationality, sensibility, and discretion to represent beauty, goodness, and liberty in modes that would resonate with every citizen.[16] They intuitively understood that they had the responsibility and capacity to express the pure, lofty, enlightened ideals that the new regime aspired to realize. The integration of the best of tradition with the spirit of innovation had long characterized the cosmopolitan culture of Paris with which Gautier personally identified.[17]

Gautier particularly endorsed the proposal to democratize the "elegant pleasure" of opera-going because lyric theatre could engender a unifying, *uncommon* culture. Everyone could develop the values embraced by elite Parisians if they, too, attended the opera on a regular basis. He expected that partaking of the "collective pleasures" of opera would endow the "masses of spectators" who currently knew nothing of great music or ballet with "new feelings and an entirely fresh fancy." By awaking dormant, laudable enthusiasms, impresarios would not only discover an "artesian well" of revenue but also perform a vital service to the nation. Gautier firmly believed that all people wanted to sample the beauties and delights that filled the lives of Parisian elites and distinguished the capital from all other cities in the world. Everyone would want to become civilized *à la français* if only they had the opportunity.[18]

Republicans who hoped to spread a common sense of enlightenment and an appreciation of refined culture as the basis for the national identity – in other words, to nationalize the attributes and attitudes possessed by a narrow segment of Parisian society – would have to expend money and energy to achieve that goal. On the other hand, since the poor were "innumerable like drops of the sea," according to Gautier's calculations, the sum of their sous might fund a "refinement and a splendor of which no aristocracy, however golden it might be, could cover the cost." Leaders could ascertain the price level at which they might simultaneously maximize quality and accessibility. Thus, the Second Republic could respond to the democratic "spirit of the century" and the existential "needs of the time" by pursuing cultural policies designed to make it possible for everyone to become virtual Parisians. Perhaps they could never become *true* Parisians without living there and helping to generate the city's aura of civilized excitement, but they could certainly become Parisians once removed.[19]

Until elected leaders made irrevocable decisions about "our political future," Gautier averred that he would continue to "dream the most beautiful of all" possible dreams for himself, for Paris, and for France. Although human ingenuity had permitted enormous technological and scientific advances by the mid-nineteenth century, he did not believe that Parisians could enjoy existential peace and true liberty if the national culture enshrined materialistic values.[20] He worried that the French would abandon the humanist ideals of Voltaire in favour of vulgar (English) utilitarianism. People who wilfully neglected the old, trusted, and benevolent muses honoured by Parisian elites would spread confusion and intensify conflict. If the republicans wanted to cure the malaise among the populace and save the French soul, they would promote reconciliation between "purified intellect and powerful matter" as elite Parisians could already claim to have done.[21]

Inspired by a similar conviction that the future of the nation depended upon nationalizing reason and taste, as well as upon improving the accessibility and democratic image of public cultural institutions, the new regime renamed the erstwhile *Académie royale de musique* (more familiarly known as the *Opéra*) as the *Théâtre de la Nation*. Upon his return to revolutionary Paris in July 1848 after a sojourn in England, Hector Berlioz[22] incurred what he obviously considered an unfortunate obligation: to attend – and write about – the reopening of the *Opéra* under its new name. Such name changes caused Berlioz to worry about the state of his city and the nation even more than usual. When a political or cultural leader seemed overly preoccupied with hat styles, fashion (whether in clothing, in music, or in other domains of cultural life), and names, Berlioz feared that he had decided to elide more substantial questions about what people, institutions, and nations ought to do. He wanted Parisians and the French to aspire towards lofty ends. However, if the republicans of 1848/49 failed to address the real shortcomings in Parisian artistic life, which Berlioz had witnessed over the past several decades, then the city would undoubtedly lose its claim to be the capital of civilization. At the same time, France would lose its starting point for effecting the desired transformation into a true republic in which each citizen would boast enlightened taste and cultured reason.[23]

Reflecting on the problems experienced by many Frenchmen in the era of the Second Republic, which ranged from unemployment to problems ascertaining how best to change hearts and minds in favour of republican ideals, Berlioz observed that even a normally serene worldly Parisian man of the day found himself worrying about whether he could continue to claim both a hat and a head. As even basic social proprieties and good sense alike went in short supply during the revolution, the critic thought that, "in the theaters, as elsewhere, [many people] do not have a hat to put on their heads, and heads, even in certain places wherein they are of a prime necessity, may seem still rarer than hats." If so fortunate as to have the basic human requirement (a head, which would confer the capacity for critical reflection and, thus, freedom) and a basic exigency of mid-nineteenth-century Parisian society (a hat, which might signify discernment in the matter of appearance), a man could proceed to concern himself with how to occupy himself. Without the deployment of good sense and taste, republicans could not succeed in restoring Parisian pre-eminence and, hence, making Parisian and national institutions once again worthy of their patrons. He believed that the revolutionaries had to make far more than simple, superficial changes if republicans were to nationalize reason and taste.[24]

Berlioz had come to Paris from the provinces as a university student twenty years earlier, at which time he had enthusiastically thrown himself into a routine of opera-going and concert-attending (to the chagrin of his father, who hoped that his son would dedicate himself to his medical studies). Thus, he, as much as Gautier, had personal reasons both for wanting the city to retain a lively public musical life and for the new regime to educate the populace to appreciate truly great art. He enjoyed the operas played in French theatres in the late eighteenth century more than most contemporary compositions; he believed that French culture had fallen away from the high standards achieved in the seventeenth and eighteenth centuries. Although still sceptical about whether they could actually succeed, he supported republican schemes for reinforcing French civilization by nationalizing the best activities and practices common in the capital. Berlioz appreciated the potential usefulness of a well directed revolution as a catalyst for a national rededication to the causes for which the *philosophes* and creators of French "classical" culture had fought.

Berlioz repeatedly reiterated that the government and all Frenchmen of character would have to work hard if they hoped to restore Parisian pre-eminence among European cultural capitals. The *Académie royale* had not declined simply because of a lack of attendance during the revolution. Its degeneration as the embodiment of national civilization and artistry long predated 1848. The erstwhile medical student Berlioz reported that it had "succumbed to a paralysis of heart; due to that, a weakness of pulse, that torpor, that malaise, that general catatonic state that one noticed in it for so long and that gave it all the appearance of decrepitude." Along with a loss of "vigor" and "elasticity" in the limbs and gangrene of the feet, the institution's brain had shrunk to a size hardly worth measuring.[25]

Having undertaken an arduous autopsy and having optimistically predicted that the musical soul of the nation might yet spring to life, the minister of the interior urged the theatre's administration to attempt the "interesting and difficult experiment of galvanization." The seemingly moribund operatic body jolted to life following the shock of having additional money allocated and a new group of directors appointed. It remained to be seen whether these directors would consult musical experts and begin to make the kinds of permanent changes in the life of the theatre that would help it remain alive and even thrive in years to come. Berlioz and the other members of the largely Parisian audience that had gathered to witness the opening of the new *Théâtre de la Nation* had the first chance to judge. The keenness of his hopes for Parisian music and the future of France as a leader in European music made Berlioz particularly anxious that the revival of the lyric stage go well.[26]

Although his fellow Parisians generally seemed quite blasé, as if they "had lived all their lives in the [college] amphitheater and Volta's pile was their favorite instrument," the commentator had not become inured to traumatic episodes of urban and national (re)definition. He knew that he always invested far too much of himself in the fortunes of the city and the nation. Even though he readily admitted that he, too, had *almost* become habituated to these sicknesses, deaths, autopsies, and attempted galvanizations that followed regime changes, "of which we have seen a considerable number in France," he nonetheless found it "impossible to maintain the sang-froid necessary for the deep study" of the repercussions of the operation that occurred at the *Opéra* in 1848.[27]

The tension of the reopening had caused him to feel "tormented" by an "intimate and profound suffering," characterized chiefly by "buzzing in [his] head, twinges in [his] eardrum, in [his] heart above all; muscular and nervous twitchings, an extreme disquiet, an impossibility of keeping still." He yielded to his desire to flee the concert hall early, falling "prey to an access of fever that dissipated only twelve hours later." At the end of his column, he recommended that his readers consult those in the audience who, unlike their reviewer, had managed to maintain the "lucidity of mind" needed for reasoned analysis. Berlioz assumed that the precarious health of the *Opéra* and the overall status of the cultural life in the capital city had implications for the future of the nation and for all people who like to imagine themselves civilized. He did not hesitate to indicate that he associated personal well-being not only with the welfare of the musical institutions in Paris but also with the attitude of the government towards the non-material dimensions of existence, such as those afforded by the *Opéra*. His assumption that the future of the nation, indeed of civilized people, was threatened by the weakened *Opéra* and diminished cultural life in Paris was both categorical and unquestioning.[28]

Berlioz feared that the Republicans would throw out the enlightened cultural baby with the materialistic, monarchist bathwater. They must not allow the romantic passions of revolution to dominate good sense and lessons garnered from experience. He unhappily observed that "the French … who play the game of revolutions with so much grace, who set their country and Europe upside down over a word or a line, who, in order to have a great occasion to raise an immense noise," would want "light fulminating in bursts on the remotest parts of their horizon." As they adored change in itself, they typically failed to evaluate the likely effects of each change. Berlioz claimed that, whereas the French would "turn away all social and religious dogmas in derision, and attack family and property," they would treat artistic banalities as sacred objects of "blind and unmovable faith, enthusiasm, love, devotion." As a result of its proclivity for revolution, France was wasting its human resources and losing its cultural prestige among Europeans. To succeed in their civilizing mission, Parisians and, in time, all of the French needed to better balance reason and emotion.[29]

Given that he wanted to consider himself a patriot and a true Parisian, Berlioz happily spotted other citizens of the capital who apparently agreed. Many Parisians, in fact, seemed to share his penchant for rational luxuries and civilized pleasures. The manifest existence of these cosmopolitan Parisians in the theatres of the city, all of whom shared a love for "great and noble ideas, poetic passions, reveries wherein the human soul is exalted and is deified," gave him hope that his country might prosper once again. When united spiritually and physically in the concert hall, these worthy individuals became a "multiple human being who, carried on the wings of music, discovered a world of new sensations and ideas and added an existence of luxury and poetry onto the necessary and prosaic aspects of existence, and enjoyed it with an immense joy, unknown to other men." By means of well chosen and well performed music that would permeate the body and generate a range of intense emotions, the Second Republic could prompt everyone to become aware of what it meant to be human and civilized. It would promote a French national identity that truly aspired towards the universal.[30]

In the name of democracy, the government should compel directors to stop "shielding" the public from enlightenment. In search of an easy profit and operating under the assumption that citizens needed to be cosseted, directors had taken to staging bland, populist operas designed to elicit cries of enthusiasm rather than to arouse deeper, more profoundly human sentiments. Berlioz avowed that, in his capacity as citizen-critic, he would continue to demand the realization of the ideals that supposedly reigned supreme in this "time of humanity, of morality, of sensibility, and of fraternity." He would reiterate the associations between great thought and prosperity so that politicians and utilitarians might feel compelled to embrace the cause of culture and a national identity based upon enlightened taste and reason.[31]

A true Parisian in spirit and a Frenchman by birth, Berlioz had "such a horror of oppressive and absurd things" that he could not make himself "guilty of egoism nor dryness of heart." He beseeched his fellow citizens to oppose "injustice, inequality, abuse, oppression, spoliation" wherever and however they appeared. At the moment, the patron goddess of French music and cultural life had her face painted blue, white, and red to disguise her sickly pallor and wrinkles. Even worse, she seemed inclined to start wearing nose rings. Hopefully, if all citizens endeavoured to make themselves fully Parisian in their tastes and demeanour, then they might halt the national slide down the slippery slope that ended in barbarism.[32]

Gautier and Berlioz turned to music and the arts as potential resources in the citizenry's quest to become more genuinely human and civilized – by which they meant tasteful, discreet, and enlightened. Other intellectual and cultural endeavours might likewise contribute to the creation of an admirable, unifying French national identity that drew upon the traits supposedly cultivated by elite Parisians. Physicist and newspaper commentator Léon Foucault, for example, frequently promoted the advancement of theoretical science as vital to the republican cause.[33] Both through their admirable personalities and through their intellectual pursuits, the nation's leading scientists modelled the virtuous, civilized conduct that every citizen should emulate.

Foucault clearly hoped to join the celebrated company that formed the *Académie des sciences*, which had convened in Paris for almost two centuries.[34] He appreciatively described their meetings as hours when friends of enlightenment found kindred spirits who listened sympathetically, spoke temperately, and revealed essential truths about nature. These men demonstrated the value of republican – and potentially national – virtues such as rationality, critical open-mindedness, hard work, and fraternal sociability. Scientific knowledge, Foucault believed, furthered the cause of civilization by giving citizens the means to place the turmoil of the streets, the Assembly, and their own minds into perspective. Under a genuine republic, France might enjoy a true, lasting prosperity that neither democracy nor wealth alone could afford. By propagating the insights of France's great scientists (most of whom resided in Paris), the political and social leaders of the new regime could help each citizen to become more aware of the human condition and of the rationally determinable laws that governed the universe.[35]

Just after the *Académie* reconvened for the first time after the February Revolution, Foucault evoked the warm, egalitarian fellowship of the scientists and their supporters with delight. He knew that all present had been profoundly affected by the fact that, "in less than a week, a revolution was accomplished," yet "the irresistible movement that swept us all up did not disunite us." The congregation of leading French scientists seemed determined to make their contributions to the nation under the Second Republic. They put aside their personal concerns and inner turmoil to help France and to promote enlightenment. If publicized, the cosmopolitan sophistication and civilized conduct of the elite Parisian, which Foucault recognized in the demeanour of France's greatest scientists, would provide the entire citizenry with inspiration in their own quests to become more civilized.[36]

Despite the ephemeral nature of everything in the human world, "science, friend of all governments," remained constant and a source of pleasure for those who lived in accord with its discoveries. Foucault averred that, in the aftermath of the Revolution, *académiciens* could best serve the nation by demonstrating rationality, civility, and discretion, whether at work or in their gatherings before a public. Along with cultivated taste and a concern for the well-being of humankind, these traits should become general throughout the nation since they enabled human happiness.[37]

Some thought that the scientists showed an inappropriate coldness and lack of interest in politics when they decided not to suspend their meetings because of the Revolution. Foucault did not believe that a resolution to cease scientific activities would have served the republican cause. Why, he wondered, should "the members of the Company have abandoned their chairs? why should the public have been missing? why should the journalists have neglected to occupy their reserved places?" During periods of political and social unrest, science and scientific knowledge allowed mature people to preserve their equilibrium and to remember their place in the cosmic order. If the identity and well-being of the nation depended on rational thought and the kinds of work undertaken by scientists, then it would have been unpatriotic for the *académiciens* to do anything other than to continue their intellectual efforts.[38]

The columnist confidently asserted that the "commotions that disturb empires can modify nothing of the great laws of nature, the discovery and confirmation of which form, after love of country, the first care of true scientists." Since no patriot would want France to lose its prestige as a home for great minds or for Paris to lose its status as the home of the world's finest academies in science, the arts, and language, then the public would expect its talented representatives to continue their contributions to the development of knowledge and the progress of civilization throughout Europe and the world. Foucault applauded *académiciens* for not worrying about terrestrial matters they could not control and for instead dedicating themselves to the reasoned pursuit of knowledge. Along with other elite Parisians, they found ways to adapt to circumstances while defending the essential elements of civilized life.[39]

Foucault argued that genuinely patriotic scientists ought to dedicate themselves to educating everyone about the interconnections between knowledge, social harmony, material prosperity, personal happiness, and national greatness. He worried that they would become distracted from their true purpose if they attempted to win applause from the "multitude," especially before the multitude had adopted elite Parisian attitudes and taste; rather, scientific creators were obliged to serve as leaders of the citizenry as the French continued down the path towards enlightenment and complete liberty. He acknowledged that the "material results that strike the multitude and make it love the source from which they emanate would not suffice to preserve all of science's dignity." As a consequence, scientists would need to publicize that reason and imagination advanced the common good as much as, if not more than, manual labour and commerce. Indeed, the "discovery of a new relationship, of a harmony that charms the mind is ... an inquiry that, even in the time which we are in, must be greeted with the same favor as the most direct and most immediately industrially applicable uses." Those who desired the efflorescence and democratization of Paris-based civilization in France but who depreciated theorists were as foolish as those who would disdain the sun because it could not exert its power instantaneously from millions of miles away.[40]

On the basis of his own understanding of French history, human nature, and the universe, Foucault concluded that "the more one observes and the more one meditates, the more one believes in the incessant mobility of the parts, in the inalterability and in the stability of the whole." Elite Parisians had modified their habits and mores gradually over time, yet their delight in rational pleasures and civilized luxuries remained constant. They retained their ability to cope with change by applying reason and discretion. Even though he repudiated the political contestation and social conflict that often characterized life in the capital, particularly during revolutionary eras, Foucault knew himself to be profoundly Parisian because he sought enlightenment and wanted to nationalize Parisian attitudes. He accepted the necessity of change while personally identifying with atemporal rationality. He maintained that the French as a whole would do well to follow the example of the nations' greatest scientists, all of whom lived in or spent much time in Paris, if they wished their nation to return to the path laid out by Enlightenment philosophers of the eighteenth century.[41]

In the mid-nineteenth century, French national identity and nationalism remained protean. The revolutionaries of 1848 and contemporary chroniclers interpreted the nation's mission as one of leading the progress of civilization within European culture. The French were to deploy a human universal (reason) in order to propagate something particular to them (taste); their cultural particularity would result from the influence of history in addition to encounters with manifestations of human creativity produced by citizens of France *and* other (especially European) nations. They recognized the right of other nations to exist and to compete for pre-eminence, though patriots certainly anticipated French supremacy in each encounter after the republicans had successfully democratized and nationalized elite Parisian sensibilities. Moreover, they believed that humans would not achieve full autonomy as individuals or as a species without diversity among national cultures.

Belgian political philosopher Jean-Marc Ferry has characterized the mid-nineteenth century as a moment prior to the "radicalization" of nationalisms that fed the conflicts of the twentieth century. The geographical, cultural, and juridical patriotisms of this period permitted individual European countries to make particular contributions to civilization within the broader context of European civilization. Prior to the turn of the century, the idea of a European intellectual and cultural space could exist along with notions of national cultural spaces.[42]

The inclination of French commentators during the Second Republic to temper Romantic particularism with Enlightenment universalism indicates their desire to construct a national identity that would unify the French without necessitating the defeat of other European nations. They could take pride in French creators and the would-be national values that elite Parisians personified above all others, yet their expressions of patriotism did not refer to a specific "other" or specific "others" against whom the French would have to define themselves. Paris, the intellectual and cultural capital, served as the positive reference point as French journalists and commentators elaborated their ideas about what qualities their nation as a whole should represent in its encounters with fellow Europeans and fellow humans.

Berlioz, Gautier, Foucault, and other commentators interpreted the French dilemma under the Second Republic in similar fashion. They believed that previous leaders had failed to recognize that true personal and collective happiness on earth was contingent upon the successful democratization of certain qualities, such as reason and discretion. Although politicians and rhetoricians repeatedly associated those attributes with the French national character, such journalists realized that only a small slice of the Parisian elite and, perhaps, some elites in provincial capitals actually possessed them. Commentators urged revolutionary leaders of 1848–49 to alter that situation by increasing the level of enlightenment throughout the population. The Second Republic ought to occasion the advent of a shared, truly *national* perspective based on Parisian values and the traditions of the Enlightenment.

Foucault, Gautier, and Berlioz all believed that the French could create a useful common sense of enlightenment by democratizing access to knowledge and opportunities to develop cultural sensibility. When they accepted the national mission to extend and expand civilization as defined by the great minds and elite souls of Paris, they would find it possible to meet any challenge, to assimilate any new invention or idea, and to provide sources of confidence in the midst of change. In time, they hoped, all citizens would fulfill their collective responsibility to spread Parisian civilization as France's gift to the world.

NOTES

1 I developed the following narrative based upon Théophile Gautier, "Théâtres," *La Presse*, 2 July 1849, 1.

2 Tulard, "Gautier, Théophile," in Tulard, *Dictionnaire du second empire*, 562–4, provides an excellent, concise overview of the novelist, poet, and critic's life. Snell, *Théophile Gautier*, offers a thoughtful, astute analysis of Gautier's aesthetics and his historical context. The more recent biography by Abersfeld, *Théophile Gautier*, gives an overview of his personal life. Extant scholarship on Gautier ignores his opera criticism and his observations of life in Paris during and after the 1848 Revolution.

3 For a basic but effective discussion of the events that transpired in the period, including a consideration of the significance of the Second Republic in the history of Paris, France, and French Republicanism, see Agulhon, *1848*. Benjamin, *The Arcades Project*, 698–739, includes interesting quotes and reflections about mid-nineteenth-century French social movements, particularly around 1848. For comments about Paris as the centre of revolution in 1848, see Harvey, *Paris, Capital of Modernity*, 59–89.

4 Théophile Gautier, "Théâtres," *La Presse*, 2 July 1849, 1.

5 Ibid.

6 See also Saklofske (this volume) on the less optimistic responses to revolution of the English romantic poets. Eds.

7 See also Warne (this volume) on journalistic interventions in plebeian life in nineteenth-century London. Eds.

8 Kristeva, in *Sens et non-sens de la révolte*, has explicated the differences between these two conceptions of freedom, traces the lineage of revolutionary freedom to 1789, and suggests that the French pursued this kind of psychological and intellectual freedom through each successive revolution. Kristeva's description of this specifically French version of the ancient Greek/Socratic freedom to "know thyself" seems similar to the characterization of French national and republican identity that newspaper columnists of 1848–49 would have offered. The revolutionaries of 1848 did not extend such freedoms to women, though some feminists

used this opportunity to make claims for the recognition of women as citizens. See Riot-Sarcey, *La démocratie à l'épreuve des femmes*.

9 See also Blackstone, Hammond, Perkins, and Wolfart (this volume) on the relationships between civic and national identities. Eds.

10 The French national identity and form of nationalism described in this chapter derives from the original 1789 concept of a French nation based on acceptance of certain principles (such as the Rights of Man and Citizen). The journalists did not articulate a version of the "blood and soil" nationalism more common among German nationalists. The French nationalism manifested and advocated by republican writers drew primarily on the Enlightenment, though with a greater emphasis than German nationalism upon the importance of creating a "spiritual" connection among citizens, which one might attribute to the influence of Romanticism. After all, both Gautier and Berlioz were leading figures in the French Romantic movement, but French Romanticism never rejected the Enlightenment in quite the same way as did other European interpretations of Romanticism.

For a comparison of various European nationalisms in the nineteenth century (and a good, concise discussion of approaches to understanding nationalism during the period), see Kramer, *Nationalism*. Other useful books on nationalism that have influenced my interpretation include Anderson, *Imagined Communities*; and Boudon, "L'essor des nationalisms français," 343–63 (see particularly the section on Michelet and his "Romantic" version of French nationalism, which held that the French had a mission to spread civilization).

11 Not only were all citizens to have affordable tickets available, but the activities of the Parisian theatres would also serve as a model for provincial theatres.

12 Théophile Gautier, "Théâtres," *La Presse*, 6 March 1848, 1.

13 Ibid. Gautier characterized the revolution of 1848 as "our [our generation's] revolution."

14 Ibid.

15 Ibid. Many scholars and intellectuals have considered the specifically linguistic basis for French national identity. Clark, *Literary France*, makes this argument from the perspective of a literary critic/historian of literature. For contemporary French commentaries on the theme, see Kristeva, *Au risque de la pensée* and *Etrangers à nous-mêmes*.

16 See also Johnson (this volume) on women artists who found it more problematic to represent the civic values of fin-de-siècle Paris. Eds.

17 Ibid. For comments on the cosmopolitan spirit of Paris, see works such as Higonnet, *Paris*; Seigel, *Bohemian Paris*; Metzner, *Crescendo of the Virtuoso*; and Martin-Fugier, *La vie elégante*.
18 Théophile Gautier, "Théâtres," *La Presse*, 20 March 1848, 1.
19 Ibid.
20 For a summary of the kinds of changes apparent in France by the time of the Second Republic, see Pinkney, *Decisive Years in France, 1840–1870*. It has a sequel in Plessis's *Rise and Fall of the Second Empire, 1852–1871*, esp. 58–131.
21 Théophile Gautier, "Théâtres," *La Presse*, 24 April 1848, 1.
22 Jacques Barzun's two-volume *Berlioz and the Romantic Century* initiated serious historical scholarship on Berlioz's life and work. The almost equally lengthy *Berlioz*, by David Cairns, is accessible but offers less context for the composer, conductor, and critic. For an excellent short biographical appreciation, see Bloom, *The Life of Berlioz*.
23 Hector Berlioz, "Ouverture du *Théâtre de la Nation, où du Théâtre National, où de l'Opéra* (vieux style)," *Journal des Débats*, 26 July 1848, 1.
24 Ibid.
25 Ibid.
26 Ibid.
27 Ibid.
28 Ibid.
29 Hector Berlioz, "Du Droit des Pauvres: Sur les Spectacles, Bals et Concerts," *Journal des Débats*, 24 September 1848, 1.
30 Hector Berlioz, "Société des Concerts du Conservatoire," *Journal des Débats*, 7 March 1849, 1.
31 Berlioz, "Du Droit des Pauvres."
32 Hector Berlioz, "Quelques mots sur l'état présent de la musique; ses défauts, ses malheurs et ses chagrins," *Journal des Débats*, 28 September 1849, 1.
33 For biographical information on Foucault, see: Gillespie, *Dictionary of Scientific Biography*, 84–7; Tobin, *The Life and Science of Léon Foucault*; and an excellent overview of his life and significance in Tobin, "Léon Foucault." Amir D. Aczel, *Pendulum,* sets Foucault in the context of the major scientific and social trends of the time.
34 Foucault was elected to the *Académie* in 1865, three years before his death.

35 Léon Foucault, "Académie des Sciences," *Journal des Débats*, 12 March 1848, 1.
36 Ibid.
37 Ibid.
38 Ibid.
39 Ibid.
40 Léon Foucault, "Académie des Sciences," *Journal des Débats*, 30 March 1848, 1.
41 Ibid.
42 Ferry, "Cultures et Civilisations," 1–7 ; and Ferry, *De la civilisation.*

6

The "Divine Little City" and the "Terrible Town": Henry James on Florence and New York

ROBIN P. HOOPLE[1]

Henry James was the quintessential city dweller. In the opening paragraph of *The American Scene* (hereafter *AS* with page number), he declares his affiliation to the city of his birth: "One's ... youth had been full of New York" (*AS* 1). Over the course of his peripatetic youth and expatriate adulthood, James also lived in Boston, London, Paris, Venice, Florence, and Rome, and though many of his later years unfolded in the village of Rye, he remained a creature of the city in both his fiction and in his travel writing. James was an eager critic of city life, and his travel records, like his novels, focus sharp eyes on its contours, seeking significance in the urban aesthetic. He looked to the cities of the Italian Renaissance to set a standard of spiritual beauty, and he assessed New York by that standard. Though Florence served as his primary benchmark, Venice added accents to his views, and figures from the Italian *campagna* illustrated the subtle shift from Italian to American settings with concomitant losses of natural grace.[2] This contrast signals a principal issue in James's indictment of the commercial hegemony he encountered on his 1904–05 American tour, and it informs his exaltation of Florence's indigenous urban aesthetic as set against the expressive barrenness of his native city.

James's registration of his aesthetic project is rooted in his changing views of John Ruskin's attitude towards Renaissance art. Initially enthusiastic about *Stones of Venice*, he ultimately rejects Ruskin's imperious demands for a landscape of uncompromised aesthetic virtue. James's quarrel with Ruskin sets the terms – however ambivalent their application might prove – for his later critique of New York. Ruskin's contention prompts James to cavil that "it savours of arrogance to demand of any people, as a right of one's own, that they shall be artistic" (*Italian Hours*, 177 [hereafter *IH* with page number]). In reply, James proposes that:

> Art is the one corner of human life in which we may take our ease. To justify our presence there the only thing demanded of us is that we shall have felt the representational impulse. In other connections our impulses are conditioned and embarrassed; we are allowed to have only so many as are consistent with those of our neighbours; ... with their convictions and prejudices, their rules and regulations. Art means an escape from all this. Wherever her shining standard floats the need for apology and compromise is over; there it is enough simply that we please or are pleased. There the tree is judged only by its fruits. If these are sweet the tree is justified – and not less so the consumer. (*IH* 181–2)

Art, then, is the ease and luxury of pure response. Such a conception might well complicate James's view of New York since relinquishing the demand that a people be artistic might excuse Americans, and New Yorkers in particular, for their lack of an aesthetic of which he could approve. But even if James's leisurely prescription is liberating, some canons for judging a people's aesthetic aspirations and accomplishments need apply. James must, then, negotiate between Ruskin's stern strictures on Venice and Florence and the outcroppings of the American urban aesthetic. Rigorous and unbending judgment is Ruskin's requisite of aesthetic response: "Instead of a garden of delight, he finds a sort of assize court in perpetual session" (*IH* 182). Some might claim that, when James assesses New York in *The American Scene*, he is as much given to judgment as he here accuses Ruskin of being. But James's critique arises from his anguished sense both of a banished American aesthetic and an abandoned American spirituality, evident to him everywhere in the urban setting.[3] He yearns to be borne along by the fast-moving American current, to allow the "fluidity of apprehension" to break over him in a "mild warm wave" (*AS* 3); however, despite his own prescription for open-minded response to the unfolding modern ethos, the sourness of its urban fruits ultimately fails to please and elicits his stern judgment.

Florence offered James an ideal site for the appreciation of urban cultural refinement. From early on, it had held James in its thrall. Writing to his father in 1870, he describes Florence as "the divine little city … alone in the great earth with nothing but a lover – and that lover moi! … no mere account of Florence … can bring you to a knowledge of her benignant influence. It isn't this that or the other thing … it's the lovely genius of the place" (*Henry James Letters* I, 188 [hereafter *LE* with volume and page number). Above all else, it was Florence's aesthetic unity that gave force to his famous contention that "It is art that *makes* life, makes interest, makes importance … and I know of no substitute for the force and beauty of its process" (*LE* IV, 770, emphasis in original). As home to many of the great paintings of Tintoretto, Titian, Fra Angelico, and other Renaissance masters, Florence nourished James's sense of a cultural feast. Viola Hopkins Winner tells us that Tintoretto composed by fusion – "neither the single figures nor objects are detachable" – thereby "creating a feeling of aesthetic completeness" (41–2).[4] This quality James prized above all others; and it serves as an analogue for the aesthetic unity of Florence as a city. W.R. Martin suggests that Titian, with his introspective dramas, was the painter closer to James's own practice (113),[5] but the dynamic juxtaposition of the two painters reached a climax in James's inspection of their work in Florence and promoted his sense of the city's immense and invigorating cultural achievement. The Florentine "heritage of beauty," says James, "forms a clear intellectual atmosphere into which you may turn aside from the modern world and fill your lungs as with the breath of a forgotten creed" (*IH* 381). Art does indeed make life, James asserts, and its appreciation breathes life into the urban soul.

Florence furnished James not only with a profound artistic record but also with a model architectural text.[6] The Pitti Palace with its Boboli Gardens – the Florentine address of the Medici – articulated a cultural continuity enriched by a vital historical consciousness. The Palace's painting collection embodied that continuity with its record of the public face, while across the Arno, the Uffizi Gallery and the Academy offered the spiritual heart of the Renaissance. But the Duomo, with its magnificent bell tower, signified for James the architectural sublime.[7] Celebrating Florence for its immersed aesthetic sense, he declares that "its colours *sing*" and illustrates with the campanile:

> But perhaps the best image of the absence of stale melancholy or wasted splendour, of the positive presence of what I have called temperate joy, in the Florentine impression and genius, is the bell-tower of Giotto, which rises beside the Cathedral. No beholder of it will have forgotten how straight and slender it stands there, how strangely rich in the common street, plated with coloured marble patterns, and yet so far from simple or severe in design that we easily wonder how its author, the painter of exclusively and portentously grave little pictures, should have fashioned a building which in the way of elaborate elegance, of the true play of taste, leaves a jealous modern criticism nothing to miss. Nothing can be imagined at once more lightly and more pointedly fanciful; it might have been handed to the city, as it stands, by some Oriental genie tired of too much detail. Yet for all that suggestion it seems of no particular time ... you come at last to regard it simply as the graceful, indestructible soul of the place made visible. (*IH* 382–3)

James's rapturous description is essential to his treatment of New York in *The American Scene* as he finds it not merely a satisfying aesthetic object but also an exemplar of what Marianna Torgovnick calls "spiritual form," the notion that an object can carry the power of the spiritual in the illumination of its presentation.[8] The campanile evinces such spiritual form in its attenuation, achieved without loss of detail; its testimony to the "strangely rich"; and its forceful imposition of the qualities of the painterly. His praise of its aesthetic impact points to spiritual form in its "friendly radiance," which emits "the graceful, indestructible soul of the place made visible." When James explores New York in search of a comparable aesthetic, he finds in the skyscrapers a parody of the campanile's architectural apotheosis. Wistfully, in the same paragraph that denounces the towers, he recalls its serenely disinterested beauty: "You don't feel it to have risen by the breath of an interested passion that ... is for ever seeking more pliable forms. Beauty has been the object of its creator's idea, and, having found beauty, it has found the form in which it splendidly rests" (*AS* 77–8). Though Ruskin deplores the intrusive presence of the cab-stand at its base, James finds in the campanile an expression of spiritual form that is not diminished by such modern trappings.[9]

In the bare fact that it could boast of towers, New York held some promise of an architectural text that might illuminate the great experiment in democracy with a comparable experiment in the urban aesthetic, an experiment that would in time yield its own exemplars of spiritual form. But James failed to find it. Instead, everywhere he looked, he found an imposed symbolism, and, as Sheila Teahan points out, however earnest the creators of the symbols, this imposition embodies a radical disjunct between outward object and intended meaning.[10] Trinity Church, which might have given the New York skyline a structure as graceful as the Florentine Duomo, was "cruelly overtopped" by the skyscrapers and, thereby, stripped not only of its former "noble pre-eminence" (*AS* 78) but also of its potential as a redemptive spiritual presence. To be sure, the towers constituted a kind of aesthetic, but although James is willing to grant them "a fleeting distinction" (*AS* 81), he likens them to "American beauty" roses: "Crowned not only with no history, but with no credible possibility of time for history, and consecrated by no uses save the commercial at any cost," and he concludes that "they are simply the most piercing notes in that concert of the expensively provisional into which your supreme sense of New York resolves itself" (*AS* 77). When Daniel Boorstin decries that "planning the future without a sense of history was like planting cut flowers,"[11] he is echoing James's sense of a doomed America, severed from its cultural roots. For these urban blooms – emblematic as they are of an ersatz, showy beauty in contrast to the subtle time-steeped charms of Florence – are "the last word of economic ingenuity only until another word might be written ... possibly a word of still uglier meaning." Their lease is short for they are destined "to be 'picked' ... with a shears ... by waiting fate, as soon as 'science,' applied to gain, has put upon the table, from far up its sleeve, some more winning card" (*AS* 77). That the life of buildings should depend on a hope of "gain," in an analogy to the card sharp's sleight-of-hand in producing winning cards by reaching up his sleeve, is a manifestation of the "absence of forms" (*AS* 25) that everywhere prevails in the American architectural text.[12]

Rather than contributing to aesthetic harmony, the skyscrapers as urban icons stick out as the sharp sterile points of a bristling "pincushion" (*AS* 76), attesting that, though the flowers may be artificial, their thorns are real. The towers are "monsters of the mere market" (*AS* 80) peering out on the world with "glassy eyes" (*AS* 77), and, in James's personifying extension, with supercilious sneers. James concludes that, for every potential source of a redemptive urban aesthetic, New York has substituted the regalia of the "triumphant payers of dividends" (*AS* 76). The "bitterness of history [has] dropped the acid into the cup" (*AS* 79) of James's remembrance, leaving him with a horrified sense of "the new landmarks crushing the old quite as violent children stamp on snails and caterpillars" (*AS* 81). David McWhirter can argue that the provisional quality of the New York skyline held an ambivalent appeal to James as a manifestation of his own radical "openness to many stories, rather than an exclusive commitment to one,"[13] but after considering the totality of James's comments, it is difficult to interpret his response to the skyscrapers as anything other than an indictment of all that they represent. As Peter Buitenhuis points out, James, along with Louis Sullivan and Frank Lloyd Wright, "recognized in the skyscraper a peculiarly American form and strove to evaluate it in terms of their vision of American life."[14] Denouncing their aesthetic impact as revelatory of their commercial origins, James declares that "the last word of the mercenary monsters should not be their address to our sense of formal beauty" (*AS* 96).

When James viewed other examples of urban architecture, domestic and civic, he found a deplorable dearth of native aesthetic integrity. He visits Tiffany's on upper Fifth Avenue and expresses a modicum of pleasure in its not being twenty-five stories high. But, like the New York Public Library further down Fifth Avenue, it has the dubious distinction of being a borrowed architectural form. James responds with muted praise despite the pretense: "to whatever air Palladian piles might have been native, they can nowhere tell their great cold calculated story, in measured chapter and verse, better than to the strong sea-light of New York" (*AS* 186). And, however kindly James might give with one hand, he is ready to take away with the other. For this artistic borrowing has the effect of "the abundance of some ample childless mother who consoles herself for her sterility by an unbridled course of adoption" (*AS* 186). In concert with the feminine images James employs elsewhere in *The American Scene* – images that entail a derogation of maternal duties in a society in which the youth have been allowed too much unfettered rein – this image bespeaks a misguided appropriation of styles lacking cultural continuity with the American architectural vernacular.

Florence everywhere testified to culture generated in depth, triumphing in both its achievement and in its respect for its origins. Instead of raising cut flowers, Florence cultivated its historical roots. In this Renaissance city, James says, the great have secured the union between history and beauty. The Boboli Gardens illustrate James's sense of serene aesthetic unity, expressed not in the architectural text but in the landscape. And if his first sight of New York in 1904 makes him gasp, the Boboli Gardens emit a profound "sense of *history* that takes away [his] breath" (*IH* 427, emphasis in original). On a "soft Sunday afternoon, the deep stillness" pervades and evinces an "insidious irresistible mixture of nature and art, nothing too much of either, only a supreme happy resultant, a divine *tertium quid*," so that "the revelation invoked descends upon you" (*IH* 306–7). The peace of the gardens breeds a redemptory aesthetic that raises life above mere organic process and combines nature and art in perfect equilibrium. The resulting "divine *tertium quid*" is the harmonious registration of this aesthetic, a third term glimpsing the urban soul. The Boboli Gardens, then, constitute further evidence of spiritual form to James: an emerging, ennobling sense arising from an achieved harmony between natural forms and sensitive human intervention in the landscape.

New York's Central Park might have reprised the Boboli's higher harmonies. A product of the ingenuity of William Cullen Bryant, poet and editor of the New York *Evening Post*, and the talents of landscape architect Frederick Law Olmsted, Central Park, above all else, gave New York a garden.[15] James goes to the park to satisfy the aesthetic appetite, and though he finds it "inordinately amiable" (*AS* 174), he is met with disappointment and a pervasive sense of doom. Instead of being imbued with history, Central Park expressed itself in memorials of malign events and the more garish aspects of the emerging American culture. A host of feminine images convey James's sense of the exasperated helplessness of the park to stand up to the many pressures imposed upon it; it is like "the cheerful, capable, bustling, even if overworked, hostess of the one inn, somewhere, who has to take all the travel, who is often at her wits' end to know how to deal with it, but who ... has, for the honour of the house, never once failed of hospitality" (*AS* 174–5). In contrast with the Boboli's graceful ease, Central Park is "too self-conscious, being afraid to be just vague and frank and quiet"; it is like "an actress in a company destitute ... of all other feminine talent; so that she assumes on successive nights the most dissimilar parts" (*AS* 176). James grants that the park is a laudatory example of municipal good will but finds it fraught with the pressures of serving too many people with too gross a set of needs. Its artificial polyglot nature may be "New York at its best" (*AS* 177), but it is also New York at its most turbulent. Its virtues may represent an attempt at social form, but none of them suggests spiritual form, to say nothing of serenity.

If Giotto's bell tower and the Boboli Gardens take pride of place in James's analysis, the rows of Florentine domestic piles reinforce the idea of a life-enhancing urban aesthetic. James sees from his room "a line of sallow houses" (*IH* 171), antique and eroded, across the Arno. In parentheses, he describes "their shabby backs," a comment that would seem to disparage but to which he adds: "All this brightness and yellowness was a perpetual delight; it was part of that indefinable charming colour which Florence always seems to wear ... a kind of grave radiance – a harmony of high tints – that I scarce know how to describe." But James *does* describe it: it is the essence of "a delightful composition" (*IH* 172), and, as he will soon say in the preface to *The Ambassadors*, "composition alone is positive beauty."[16] While appreciating their aesthetic virtues, James was not blind to the economic realities behind the genteelly decaying house fronts, which evoke melancholy in the "sensitive stranger":[17] "Lovely, lovely, but it makes me 'blue'" (*IH* 176). The aging Florentine houses have surrendered some of their original dignity en route to their decline into "economical winter residence[s] to English and American families" (*IH* 175) with enough money to travel – an ironic reversal of the pattern of Old World immigration to America. But, although the buildings are old and have outlived their original purpose, they still survive and contribute their "harmony of high tints" to the "delightful composition" of the city.

In a curious twist, some features of the domestic buildings in the two cities shared a pattern, of which two are noteworthy for the echoes they will receive in James's treatment of New York. As well as the descent to rental properties, "which seemed so doubly conscious of a change of manners, that threw a tinge of melancholy over the general prospect," James describes the "enormous windows, the iron cages fastened to the lower ones" (*IH* 175). The cages seem mere filigreed attachments to the Florentine dwellings; and the change of manners offers a mere melancholy reflection on the passage of time, a reflection that registers emphatically for James because of his acute awareness of history and its importance to place. These images recur in New York, but with the American "defeat of history" (*AS* 113) they fail to carry any sense of elegance and grace, any sense of the flow of life that might express some reverence for age. James locates the cages of the New York dwellings in the ghetto of the lower East Side, where the crowded district's susceptibility to fire led to the construction of fire escapes. James ironically dubs the ghetto "the city of redemption" (*AS* 133), where, instead of a mere change of manners as in Florence, he finds an unhappy change of masters. The fire escapes capture James's eye for their reductive effects in providing "the spaciously organized cage for the nimble class of animals ... a little world of bars and perches and swings for human squirrels and monkeys" (*AS* 134).[18] Not only do the fire escapes belie the notion of redemption but they also transform the cage into a prison for animals, human though they be, and create an "irresistible" urge to reduce the inhabitants to the status of lesser species. In America, the prevailing lack of respect for old buildings is paralleled by the denigration of the poorer citizens relegated to inhabit them.

And whereas Florence sees its older buildings revert to rental properties, New York sees its buildings – by no means as old – eradicated to make way for new edifices in a mania for change that James deplores.[19] For every time one asks the value of a piece of property prior to sale in Europe, "we indulge in the question twenty times in the United States" (*AS* 160). This dominating ethos of all things marked for sale, and many marked for quick sale, sounds the essential note of modern America for James and is particularly evident to him in New York: "nowhere else does pecuniary power so beat its wings in the void" (*AS* 159). In this brave new America, this "vast crude democracy of trade" (*AS* 67), money is touted as a short-cut to civilization: "Here was the expensive as a power by itself, a power unguided, undirected ... exerting itself in a void that could make it no response, that had nothing – poor gentle, patient, rueful, but altogether helpless, void! – to offer in return" (*AS* 9). Driven by what James, in "The Jolly Corner," dubs the "money-passion," the inevitable descent into turbulent economic flux generates "the note of loneliness on the part of these loose values – deep as the look in the eyes of dogs who plead against a change of masters" (*AS* 160). But James's indignation goes beyond the pathos of the dog for he sees the waste of relatively new structures "marked for removal, for extinction, in their prime" not only as the eradication of any historical continuity but also as analogous to the guillotining of the young in the French Revolution: "the youths and maidens, all bewildered and stainless, lately born into a world decked for them socially with flowers, and for whom, none the less suddenly, the horror of horrors uprose" (*AS* 158). What makes their fate all the sadder for James is that American society aspires to build "some coherent sense *of* itself, and [is] literally putting forth interrogative feelers ... into the ambient air" (*AS* 159, emphasis in original), while undermining the very means by which such a sense could be nurtured. The variant social attitudes to domestic buildings between the Old World and the New World, then, adumbrate James's views of the importance of architecture as a cultural, social, and historic text.

At both the public scale and the private scale, then, his New York experience imbues James with a deep awareness of cultural deprivation, of spiritual want. In *Henry James and the Art of Power*, Mark Seltzer draws attention to James's depiction of "the blankness of the American street-page" and its impact on the "starved story-seeker" (*AS* 244).[20] The aesthetic deprivation of the New York street-page resonates with the blankness James notes in his earnest search for spiritual meaning in the nation's capital.[21] There, the "fine blank space" where there should be a spiritual sign is the cultural void where "the aesthetic appetite in you – long richly fed elsewhere – ... goes unassuaged" (*AS* 381). It is in the Italian cities that James's aesthetic appetite was "richly fed," whereas in the "hustling, bustling desert ... one too often [had] to tighten one's aesthetic waistband" (*AS* 67). And while he early on insists on calling this an "apparent void" (*AS* 12), entertaining the possibility that his inability to apprehend a spiritual core is a failure on the part of the restless analyst, he becomes increasingly convinced that, in a culturally impoverished America, the outcome of the national quest is not the satisfaction of noble aspirations but, rather, the starvation of the spiritual and aesthetic strivings of its citizenry.

For James, the negative effects of a deprived aesthetic appetite are exacerbated by New York's unrelenting assault on the senses, an assault that continually reminds the "shuddering pilgrim" (*AS* 94) of the city's paucity of quiet charms. Lacking the "saving complexity" (*AS* 10) of a city that builds a rich present on the foundations of its past, New York "told me more of her story at once, then and there, that she was again and elsewhere to tell ... she was in fact fairly shrieking it into one's ears" (*AS* 100). Dispossessed of "any happy accident or surprise, any fortunate nook or casual corner, any deviation, in fine, into the liberal or the charming," she offers no reprieve from the "assault of the street" (*AS* 111). The resulting "fury of sound ... acted on your nerves as so much wanton provocation, so much conscious cynicism ... [and] it might ... have struck you as brazen that the horrible place should, in such confessed collapse, still be swaggering and shouting" (*AS* 109). The harmony of Florence has been drowned out by the cacophony of New York, but it is the city's lack of manners that James finds most shocking: "It might have struck you that great cities, with the eyes of the world on them ... should be capable either of a proper form or (failing this) of a proper compunction; which tributes to propriety were, on the part of New York, equally wanting." That such rudeness should be accompanied by "the most blatant of ... pretensions ... that she is one of those to whom everything is always forgiven" (*AS* 109) compounds the insult to James's refined sense of urban decorum.

And yet New York, which by the time of James's visit had emerged as the great American metropolis, might well have evolved into the showcase city for a society founded on the tenets of Washington and Jefferson. When James visits Ellis Island to trace the great American dream as exemplified by immigration, he bumps up against one of the great American myths – the errand into the wilderness – which arms and informs his immigrant metaphor. The errand embodies the search for the lost Garden Paradise, for which the engine of temptation is figured by the "tree of knowledge" (*AS* 85), as evinced by Ellis Island. This immigrant portal, which opened for business in 1892, could not avoid anticipating an American version of "mean streets," a concept Arthur Morrison had popularized in the notion of malign thoroughfares in his stories about London's East End in 1896. The idea of places inimical to civilized passage has since expanded to suggest the hard and grinding qualities of life in cities everywhere. But for James, New York is a notable source of data on mean streets. The jostling pavements where the "aliens" prevail serve as prelude to James's visit to Ellis

Island, whose administration building is a portal where the hopeful masses are "marshaled, herded, divided, subdivided, sorted, sifted, searched, fumigated" (*AS* 84). Instead of entering a city embodying the ideals of the nation's founding, the immigrants will find themselves thrust into the bosom of the city James describes as a "poor dear bad bold beauty" (*AS* 109). In this most corrupt of the feminine images James deploys for New York, the city as prostitute to its commercial interests consummates the infamy of its fall from grace, even as the "voice of the air" reminds him that " 'you distinctly take an interest and are the victim of your interest ... You *care* for the terrible town' " (*AS* 108, emphasis in original).[22]

The dehumanizing atmosphere of Ellis Island stands in poignant contrast to James's depiction of Italians in situ as the Italian landscape had everywhere suggested to him the quiet and even idyllic nature of the Italian underclass in all its configurations. Using diction that echoes his notion of art as graceful ease, he extols their natural dignity: "The poorest Venetian is a natural man of the world. He is better company than persons of his class are apt to be among the nations of industry and virtue – where people are also sometimes perceived to lie and steal and otherwise misconduct themselves. He has a great desire to please and to be pleased" (*IH* 17).[23] It is not as though Italian cities lack their hustlers and their cynical merchants – as James describes variously – or that their cultural glories weren't also founded on trade. The Medici were, after all, the Rockefellers of their time. Rather, there is a sense of the harmonious deportment of the Italian people in their own environment. Perhaps the urchin he encounters on Torcello best illustrates James's sense of their innate grace:

> One small urchin – framed ... to be the joy of an aristocratic mamma – was the most expressively beautiful creature I had ever looked upon. He had a smile to make Coreggio sigh in his grave; and yet here he was running wild among the sea-stunted bushes, on the lonely margin of a decaying world, in prelude to how blank or to how dark a destiny? Verily nature is still at odds with propriety; though indeed if they ever really pull together I fear nature will lose her distinction. An infant citizen of our own republic, straighthaired, pale-eyed and freckled, duly darned and catechized, marching into a New England schoolhouse, is an object often seen and soon forgotten; but I

think I shall always remember with infinite tender conjecture ... this little unlettered Eros of the Adriatic strand. (*IH* 77)

The children of Torcello "suggested forcibly that the best assurance of happiness in this world is to be found in the maximum of innocence and the minimum of wealth" (*IH* 76–7). James's observation makes a telling counterpoint to America, where the maximum of temptation is coupled to the minimum of fulfillment. As James describes immigrant life, such sunny creatures would soon be crushed by the "pushing male crowd" (*AS* 83) of the great metropolis. The only freedom they are likely to experience is the "freedom to grow up to be blighted," severed by the "great shears of Fate" (*AS* 137) in a reprisal of his image of the doomed American Beauty roses. For, while the urchin might thrive unfettered on the decaying Island of Torcello, James suggests he would only contribute to the "feeding of the mill" (*AS* 84) – the dark Satanic mill of industry – were he to pass through the gates of Ellis Island and become yet another victim of the "visible act of ingurgitation on the part of our body politic" (*AS* 84). The milling of the immigrants, rendering them grist for the "vast money-making structure" (*AS* 83), fits James's vision of a society in which people are reduced to commodities ground to fit the specifications of a system in which everything is for sale.[24] The visitor to this portal, says James in a continuation of the ingestion metaphor, "has tasted of the tree of knowledge," adding that "the taste will be forever in his mouth" (*AS* 85). However intent the Puritan fathers in their errand into the wilderness to subdue the natural man and to produce the saints of the original American covenant, James forecasts the expulsion from the New World Eden in the fact and the usufruct of the European immigrants.[25]

In "The Question of Our Speech," his June 1905 address at Bryn Mawr College, delivered late in his travels when his hopes for discovering a redeeming aesthetic had long since been dashed, James argued that American women were charged with the responsibility of transmitting culture. The deeper concern for this transmission was manners, which had emerged for James as the crucial test of civilization: "I was infatuated ... with the question of manners, in their largest sense – to the finer essence of which tallness [of buildings] had already defined itself to me as positively abhorrent" (*AS* 317). Like the tall buildings, the new technologies promoted the commercial enterprise while being inimical to social form: "Free existence and good manners, in New York, are too much brought down to a bare rigour of marginal relation to the endless electric coil, the monstrous chain that winds round the general neck and body, the general middle and legs, very much as the boa-constrictor winds around the group of the Laocoon" (*AS* 88–9).[26] James figures urban electrification under a Trojan metaphor, visualizing the boa-constrictor cord – prelude to an even more horrific ingestion – as the force that not only catapults the masters to the upper floors of the towers but also rockets drones and consumers alike through the bowels of New York in the subway system that opened during James's visit and that he likens to a "projectile in the bore of a gun" (*AS* 101). The violence of James's description is chillingly prescient: "It appeared ... all one with every other element and note ... all the signs of the heaped industrial battle-field, all the sounds and silences, grim, pushing, trudging silences too, of the universal will to move – to move, move, move, as an end in itself, an appetite at any price" (*AS* 84). This frenzied rush to nowhere in a city devoid of a spiritual core is perhaps James's grimmest reflection on the American scene, in light of which his appeal to the young women of the nation seems little more than a final and futile gesture.

If James ultimately recoils at the aesthetic void, perhaps it is as aesthete that James must be seen in his evaluation of the two contrasting civilizations. Shortly after James's death, Stuart Pratt Sherman declared that his "controlling principle is a sense of style, under which vice, to adapt Burke's words, loses half its evil by losing all its grossness. In the noble society *noblesse oblige*, and nothing else obliges ... He is not an historian of manners; he is a trenchant idealistic critic of life from the aesthetic point of view."[27]

However, as Jonathan Freedman points out, James's aestheticism is not at odds with his modernity but is, instead, a vital link; and Freedman's perspective of James poised between the two can account for much of James's assessment of New York. This is because James was not viewing his native city as a hoary conservative, suspicious of all change. He came to America as a "repatriated absentee," longing to find evidence of the fulfillment of the American promise. But he found his every hope thwarted, and, as his frequent reprisals of the Italian ideal in *The American Scene* attest, he came to see New York and Florence as opposed exemplars of their civilizations. Florence proclaimed to James the virtues of a fulfilled culture: the gardens, the palaces, the churches, the galleries all insist on the continuity of their human history. While Giotto's bell tower is the timeless embodiment of beauty, New York's skyscrapers are cut flowers that defy the sense of history, becoming instead the principal exhibits in the "expensively provisional." The Duomo, depicted as "some mighty hillside enameled with blooming flowers" (*IH* 422), fits James's ideal of art as easy serenity; the Boboli Gardens make a reverential and restful bow to the city's history; the Uffizi Gallery bespeaks a passion irradiating its realm. New York attracted immigrants from the European underclass to promote the commercial enterprise, promising riches for their children but in the end reducing them to pawns whom advertising torments into machines of consumption and seducing them from their legitimate roles as illuminated citizenry. From hence the vanishing church; from hence the transitory forms and the disjunctive symbols; from hence the suppression of history. James derogates the American metropolis for its antagonism to those features of the European city that grace it with soul.

At the close of "Florentine Notes," James expresses his understanding of the organic well-spring of the spiritual form he found everywhere flourishing in Florence and nowhere encouraged in New York:

> Call it much or call it little, the ineffaceability of this deep stain of experience, it is the interest of old places and the bribe to the brooding analyst ... We can "lay out" parks on virgin soil, and cause them to bristle with the most expensive importations, but we unfortunately can't scatter abroad again the seed of the eventual human soul of a place – that comes but in its time and takes too long to grow. There is nothing like it when it *has* come. (*IH* 427; emphasis in original)

Cities have souls, a presence that lingers as a "faint sigh in the breeze" (*IH* 427); and, in Florence, James explores a city that makes joyous witness to life as a great aesthetic adventure linking its past and present. At the outset of *The American Scene*, he declares that the drama of his American adventure will be an investigation of the modern short-cut to nurturing the "human soul of a place": "Never would be such a chance to see how the short-cut works, and if there be really any substitute for roundabout experience, for troublesome history, for the long, the immitigable process of time" (*AS* 12–13).

When he visits the Presbyterian Hospital, where "the genius of the terrible city seemed to filter in with its energy ... softened" (*AS* 188), James catches the glimmer of such a possibility for New York. He hasn't forsaken the hope of finding a "human soil" in which cultural growth can be nurtured, and such exceptions, possessing the "note of mildness and the sense of manners" lacking elsewhere, hold out a tantalizing promise. But there is a blighting force that threatens the hospital's potential to act as a "saving presence": "It carries with it an aftersense ... the image of some garden of the finest flowers ... masked by an enormous bristling hedge of defensive and aggressive vegetation, lacerating, defiant, not to be touched without blood" (*AS* 188–9). Despite his openness to possibilities, James comes to a sad sense that a spiritual flowering on the Florentine model was not in New York's future, stamped out by the rank growth of the "money-passion."

NOTES

1 This article was revised by Isobel Waters after the author's death.

2 It is reasonable to ask whether one is justified in using James's perspective on Florence, first published in serial form in 1874, as a benchmark for his views on New York, written thirty years later. If James had made no explicit mention of Florence in *The American Scene* such a criticism would be telling; but since James reprises elements of the Florentine aesthetic in *The American Scene* with specific and pointed reference, it is appropriate to employ the contrast. The fact that all the essays in *Italian Hours*, including "The Autumn in Florence" and "Florentine Notes," were extensively revised by James prior to publication in 1909 further validates the comparison.

3 In the Richmond chapter, James describes Washington, DC, as another setting illustrative of the flawed American ethos. He casts about for a figure expressive of his sense of the American void:

> But something is absent more than even these masses are present – till it at last occurs to you that the existence of a religious faith on the part of the people is not even remotely suggested. Not a Federal dome, not a spire nor a cornice pretends to any such symbolism, and though your attention is thus concerned with a mere negative, the negative presently becomes its sharp obsession. You reach out perhaps in vain for something to which you may familiarly compare your unsatisfied sense. You

liken it perhaps not so much to a meal made savourless by the failure of some usual, some central dish, as to a picture, nominally finished, say, where the canvas shows, in the very middle, with all originality, a fine blank space. (*AS* 380–1)

If the quest for spiritual form becomes the urgent subject of James's inquiry, this void is central to his sense of cultural malaise. Pippin's parenthesis, in *Henry James and Modern Moral Life*, is insightful: "In James's mythic landscape, the name for such a collapse of the reliability of traditional form, such uncertainty and new vacancy as well as radical possibility, is simply 'America'" (5).

4 See also Perkins (this volume) on the very different aesthetic effects of eighteenth-century Edinburgh. Eds.

5 While this may be, it doesn't alter the fact that James describes Tintoretto – whose works he was impressed by in Venice as well as Florence – as "an immense perpetual moral presence ... the greatest of painters" in a 1869 letter to William James (*LE* I, 137); and, in 1871, he writes to Charles Norton that "the emotions wrought by his pictures had worked themselves into the permanent substance of *my* mind more than I can feel it of any other painter" (*LE* I, 260, emphasis in original).

6 Speaking of Boston in "Twice-Told Trails: Hawthorne's Boston," at a Hawthorne Society Conference in 2000, Andrew Grobman referred to "the architectural text of the city," with the implication that such a text incorporates a record of the city's growth, development, history, and aspirations. This concept is essential to my chapter, and I am happy to credit Professor Grobman with its use and illustration.

7 Although the campanile received its marble cladding shortly after completion in the fourteenth century, the Duomo's facade was not similarly sheathed until 1887. James was living in Florence at the time, and participated – decked out in full Renaissance regalia – in the city's celebrations. Not uncharacteristically, he prevaricates on his degree of involvement; writing to William, he claims that "I give them [the street celebrations] a wideish birth" (*LE* III, 183), but several weeks later he writes to Fanny Kemble, providing a gleeful description of his part in a fancy dress ball and other festivities: "I wish you could have seen me – I was lovely" (*LE* III, 184). Witnessing this event may have confirmed James's sense that Florence was not a city mired in its past but, rather, a city blessed with a dynamic cultural present.

8 This concept of spiritual form is implicit in Torgovnick's *Primitive Passions*, especially in the sections where she treats ecstatic consciousness (14–15). She used the term in a paper entitled "Spirituality: Modernism's

Other?" presented to the Modern Language Association in Washington, DC, in 1996. Her defining properties included concepts of ecstasy and irradiation of the person/artefact/natural event.

9 See also Coenen Snyder (this volume) and Saklofske (this volume) on the built environment as an index to forms of cultural, spiritual, and economic life. Eds.

10 Teahan, "Engendering Culture," 54.

11 Cited in Dowd, "Clash of Civilizations."

12 The towers not only cheated the church of its spiritual testimony but were mandated by the churchwardens. That they were complicit in the "extinction of Trinity" for monetary gain added another charge to his indictment of the American enterprise:

> The interest in this case being above all, as I learned to my stupefaction ... that the very creators of the extinguisher are the churchwardens themselves, or at least the trustees of the church property. What was the case but magnificent for pitiless ferocity? – that inexorable law of the growing invisibility of churches, their everywhere reduced or abolished *presence*, which is nine-tenths of their virtue, receiving thus ... its supreme consecration. (*AS* 83, emphasis in original)

12 McWhirther, *Construction of Authorship*, 19.

14 Buitenhuis, "Aesthetics of the Skyscraper," 324. Buitenhaus's study is an insightful exploration of the views of these three great Americans on the aesthetics of the skyscraper. He, too, recognizes James's use of Giotto's bell tower as an analogous structure and claims that James was prescient in highlighting the need to see the skyscrapers as part of the overall urban profile. Wright, Buitenhuis tells us, came to similar conclusions thirty years later, though he differed from James in his belief that the "commercial motive ... was a force for good" (323) and most definitely decried any efforts at ornamentation along the lines of the marble-clad campanile.

15 The Central Park historians, Elizabeth Blackmar and Roy Rosenzweig, claim that the pressure to create the park came from affluent Americans who, having taken the Grand Tour, returned impressed by the graceful public spaces in European landscapes and determined that New York should have a similar amenity. The state legislature gave the city the right of eminent domain and some fifteen hundred squatters were cleared off the seven hundred-acre space to enable the park commission to begin its work. The controversy over their displacement underscored the troubled history of the park, which has included quarrels over jurisdiction, use, and policing from the outset. James's representation of the park offers

some insight into its character as public space and as an emanation of the republic.

16 James, *Art of the Novel*, 329.

17 The "sensitive stranger" is just one of many narrative voices in *Italian Hours*, of which "aching alien" and "infatuated alien" are important examples, given the focus on "aliens" in *The American Scene*. Much has been made by Ross Posnock and others of the "restless analyst" as the most prominent of the plethora of narrators in the travel record, of which other examples are the "repatriated absentee," the "fond critic," the "restored absentee," and so on. But multiple voices are no less important in the Italian travel book and deserve more attention.

18 James's treatment of race has been a vexed question ever since he published *The American Scene*. Among others, Maxwell Geismar excoriates James as an inexcusable racist in *Henry James and the Jacobites* (1963). Recent scholars have been less inclined to find fault with James over images such as the reductive animal images presented here. Ross Posnock, in *The Trial of Curiosity* (1991), Sara Blair in *Writing of Race and Nation* (1996), and Beverly Haviland in *Henry James's Last Romance* (1997) all find accommodations for what earlier scholars had assessed as racist, each contending that James's intense sense of culture offset his apparently unkind remarks about particular racial and religious communities. Gert Buelens treats this controversy in two important works, "James's 'Aliens'" (1999), and *Henry James and the Aliens* (2002). The article summarizes commentary on the significance of the aliens to *The American Scene*, showing in some detail James's acute comprehension of the relation between the consuming society and the presence of large numbers of unassimilated communities in American society; the book treats the relations between James's homoerotic penchant and the immigrant population he discovered on his return visit in 1904–05.

19 A particularly grievous loss was that of his own birth-home: "the effect for me ... was of having been amputated of half my history" (*AS* 91). How much James's reactions to his changed homeland were affected by nostalgia is a difficult question, and it is reflected in the title he originally proposed for the book but had to give up when it was claimed by Thomas Hardy: *The Return of the Native*. His next working title, *The Return of the Novelist*, suggested a less subjective stance, while his final title stressed his observer status even more pointedly. The impact of nostalgia is equally relevant to James's response to Florence and, indeed, to Italy; he frequently plays the lover, "overwhelmed with the pitifulness of this absurd want of reciprocity between Italy itself and all my rhapsodies

about it" (*LE* I, 428). But whereas his undeniable interest in the "bad bold beauty" of New York is tinged with bitterness, his passion for Florence remains unblemished – even if unrequited – as this 1884 comment to J.A. Symonds suggests: "I nourish for the said Italy an unspeakably tender passion" (*LE* III, 30).

20 Seltzer, *Art of Power*, chap. 3, esp. 108.

21 In Washington, DC, the blankness looms in the buildings that suggest the very heart of the nation. I discuss the symbolic implications of the Washington skyline, particularly the Washington monument, for James's quest to decipher the American cultural code in "Henry James's Alphabet of Impressions: the Example of the Obelisk."

22 As Robert Pippin contends in *Henry James and Modern Moral Life*, James had profoundly mixed feelings for his native city, even in the state in which he found it on his 1904–05 visit. The multiple perspectives of the narrators express and reinforce James's deep ambivalence and, as Pippin points out, cannot be interpreted as "observations with a straightforward claim to truth or verisimilitude" but must, instead, be seen as "objects of interrogation ... occasions for often critical self-interrogation and not as straight statements of 'criticism'" (41). James is indeed having a conversation with himself (or selves) wherein he assumes many voices. But despite the undeniable state of commingled apprehension and interest (tantamount to titillation) that New York elicits in him, and notwithstanding the fact that, for James, "nothing is my *last word* on anything" (*LE* II, 221, emphasis in original), the quality and quantity of his negative comments ultimately outweigh the positive. Pippin contends that James is reassured by the radical possibilities entailed in the cultural emptiness of which he is so acutely aware. In my reading, while James acknowledges occasional glimmers in the darkness, he is far from finding, in Pippin's words, "ample positive evidence of the emergence, perhaps the reemergence out of the chaos of the long American founding, of the human and so humane scale" (44). Rather, James's negative comments build in intensity after the excited awareness of possibilities he expresses earlier.

23 This link between the notion of art as easy serenity, with a sensual as well as a spiritual dimension, and the mentality of the Italian people is an integral one for James. In reference to the Florentine carnival, he speaks of their capacity for a

> sweet staring idleness. The faculty of making much of common things and converting small occasions into great pleasures is, to a son of communities strenuous as ours are strenuous, the most salient characteristic

> of the so-called Latin civilisations. It charms him and vexes him, according to his mood; and for the most part it represents a moral gulf between his own temperamental and indeed spiritual sense of race, and that of Frenchmen and Italians, far wider than the watery leagues that a steamer may annihilate. But I think his mood is wisest when he accepts the "foreign" easy surrender to *all* the senses as the sign of an unconscious philosophy of life, instilled by the experience of centuries – the philosophy of people who have lived long and much, who have discovered no short cuts to happiness and no effective circumvention of effort. (*IH* 393)

Even though this "unconscious philosophy of life" involving "easy surrender to *all* the senses" vexes him at the same time that it elicits his admiration, his positive responses outweigh the negative, when "his mood is wisest." Just as I argue that, for all his ambivalence, his ultimate "take" on New York is an indictment, so, too, James's prevailing perspective on Florence is celebratory.

24 While the male immigrants, as potential workers in the American underclass, were enthusiastically invited into this new world without much screening, the women were carefully scrutinized, as an editorial in the *New Orleans Times-Democrat* describes, under the headline "Keeping Watch on Immigration" and subtitle "A Woman the Guardian of the Moral Wicket of the East" (8 July 1905, 3:13). The woman in question is Mrs John Stucklen of New York, who appears in the article as "The Only Woman in the United States Sitting upon a Board of Inquiry" with the adjunct "Ellis Island Where Are Bared the Past Life and the Future of Woman and Girls from the Old World." The year is 1905, and though Mrs Stucklen can't vote in any American election, she is permitted to sit in judgment on moral questions concerning immigration, where the morals of woman are of the greatest interest. At least one implication of the stringent morality involved in admitting women to the United States imposed a kind of exogamy in the immigrant populations, which might lead towards a fragmentation of social life beyond the rigours of the grinding commercial system into which they were entering.

25 It must be acknowledged that James's twenty-one-year absence from the United States prior to his arrival in 1904 put him in an uneasy position in relation to the populations he referred to as "aliens." He acknowledged that discriminating the aliens from other sectors was a difficult if not impossible task; and he was prepared to number himself among them, both in his own homeland and in the Italian landscape. But he drew the line at seeing himself altered as he found the "aliens" altered. The

peasant aliens had had the most gentle and affecting manners in the Italian *campagna*; in America they had joined the masses of aggressive and questing seekers after the golden American dream.

26 See also Saklofske (this volume) on the responses of English romantic poets to technology and industry. Eds.

27 Sherman, "Aesthetic Idealism," 399.

PART TWO

Gender, Mobility, and the City

PREFACE

Gender, Mobility, and the City

ARLENE YOUNG

The chapters in part 2 span the period from the end of the eighteenth century to the beginning of the twentieth century, a period when industrialization was driving unprecedented urban expansion throughout Europe. Although the cities that figure in these chapters – Edinburgh, London, and Paris – were not directly dependent on industrial development for their growth, they were the political, cultural, and commercial centres of nations whose populations were increasingly urban and whose futures would be materially shaped by the vagaries of urban growth and development. In the nineteenth century, the thriving capital cities of Europe were emblematic of progress and of the promise of the future; they were the testing grounds for the great potential and the great pitfalls of urban life and urban development. Drawing on current cultural analyses that posit the city variously as a specialized landscape to be observed or otherwise consumed, as a commercial and/or performative space, or as a contested terrain, the chapters in this part demonstrate that the burgeoning city was a locus of cultural contradictions that encompass violence and order, misery and prosperity, and that both enable and disable mobility. The paradigmatic figure of the nineteenth-century European city, the *flaneur*, the disengaged middle-class male observer who dominates most historical analyses, has been largely marginalized in the chapters that comprise "Gender, Mobility, and the City." The focus is, rather, on those groups whose perspectives and interests are more typically overlooked – women, the poor, and the physically impaired.

The city emerges as a consumable, if somewhat incongruous, product of history and modern urban design in Pam Perkins's

"Exploring Edinburgh: Urban Tourism in Late Eighteenth-Century Britain." Perkins posits Edinburgh as the site of an early version of urban tourism, as a destination outside the circuit of the traditional European Grand Tour that fascinated visitors with its sometimes jarring juxtaposition of the "picturesque insalubrity" of the Old Town and the "airy, elegant regularity" of the new city. Drawing on visitors' accounts of their experiences of Edinburgh, and, to a lesser extent, on more consciously constructed responses in fiction, Perkins demonstrates that the ancient/modern dichotomy that obtains with regard to the architecture and layout of the city similarly organizes travellers' reactions to its culture, especially with regard to the manners and mores of women. Edinburgh's women, like the city itself, are simultaneously perceived to be "quaintly, delightfully old-fashioned" and "breathtakingly – perhaps even alarmingly – modern," especially in their overt enthusiasm for public entertainments such as theatre. The apparent discordance of the local colour of a violent past and the intellectual sophistication of Enlightenment thought encompassed by the city and its culture is in fact what gives late eighteenth-century Edinburgh its unique appeal. "It was precisely the indivisibility of old and new," Perkins perceptively argues, "that gave the city as a whole so much interest both architecturally and aesthetically."

In Vanessa Warne's "Clearing the Streets: Blindness and Begging in Henry Mayhew's *London Labour and the London Poor*," the object of the tourist gaze shifts from the historic city to the terra incognita of the areas of London inhabited by the poor. The "tourist" remains in the comfort and safety of his or her middle-class home, reading accounts of "the traveler in the undiscovered country of the poor," that is, Mayhew's interviews of London's street people. Using both Mayhew and other contemporary observers of London street life, Warne focuses on the experience of the city's blind poor to explore charity, community, and mobility within the city. She further sets out to reveal "disability and the city as interdependent and mutually constituted cultural constructs," an interdependence Warne illustrates with the example of a blind street-seller's right to ply her trade being undermined by the police's perception of her as a beggar. The blind street-seller's mobility is here cast as vagrancy, limiting her legitimate rights to have free access to urban spaces. The aesthetic sensibilities of affluent, able-bodied Londoners are accordingly pitted against the rights of the disabled poor to use the city streets in order to work and interact with each other in the only form of community available to them. Philanthropic efforts to provide for the indigent blind through institutionalized charity have the added benefit (in the eyes of the philanthropists) of "clearing the streets" of blind beggars. Implicit in this chapter is what was explicit in Perkins's treatment of Edinburgh: a tension between the "picturesque insalubrity" of traditional urban spaces, in this case the local colour of the street-life of the poor, and the contemporary vision of the modern city. The move to clear the streets of beggars, Warne points out, "would declutter, modernize, and homogenize street life, transforming streets into traffic arteries and facilitating the circulation of pedestrians, passengers, and goods."

Julie Johnson's "A Contested City: Gwen John, Suzanne Valadon, and Women Artists in Fin-de-Siècle Paris" moves the focus of analysis from Great Britain to the Continent. Taking as her point of reference the dominant historical perception of Paris at the turn of the century as a "city of dualities" comprising all the excitement, turmoil, and contradictions inherent in modernity, Johnson considers the effects of "this complex urban landscape" on the experience of women artists trying to forge identities and careers "in the contested urban spaces of fin-de-siècle Paris." By examining the careers of Montmarte resident Suzanne Valadon and Welsh artist Gwen John, who resided in Paris during this period, Johnson considers "what it meant to be an artist and a woman in a modern metropolis on the eve of the twentieth century." Valadon's "powerful and blunt realism" registers her experience of urban life as deeply contradictory at the most intimate levels of response. The challenges she faced as a woman, mother, and artist find expression in her unconventional, "aggressive," even "notorious," depictions of female nudes, and in her unconventional yet "powerfully intimate" portraits of children, including her son. The material and personal precariousness of urban life for women at the end of the nineteenth century is reflected in the statutes of a cooperative organization for women artists, set up to provide financial aid to members temporarily incapacitated by illness, aid that would be denied to those "recovering from an attempted suicide." Though John was not driven to such desperation, poverty forced her, as it did many female artists, to work as a model for other artists. John accordingly represents the conflicted figure of the woman whose autonomous agency in a male dominated field is simultaneously underwritten and undermined by her adoption of a conventionally feminine role, in this case that of muse. As Johnson notes, John's independence "was thus intertwined with her status as a model and muse, which ... both assisted and yet detracted from her development as an artist." While modelling absorbed her time, it also brought her into contact with Rodin and influenced the development of a uniquely female artistic sensibility. Johnson evaluates this sensibility in a perceptive analysis of two of Johnson's paintings that embody "a woman artist's exploration of [the complexities] of her life in the city."

In the chapters that comprise "Gender, Mobility, and the City," the proto-modern European city emerges as a centre of consumerism and spectacle, where the old and the new are uneasily balanced in a state of sometimes contradictory co-existence. Perkins, Warne, and Johnson perceptively explore issues of fraught gender and class relations in the urban milieu, issues such as the place of women, the poor, and the disabled in the contested spaces of the city on the verge of modernity. All three chapters provide insight into the complex and sometimes perplexing process that three European capital cities underwent in their evolution from traditional seats of government and commercial enterprise into fully modern international urban centres.

7

Exploring Edinburgh: Urban Tourism in Late Eighteenth-Century Britain

PAM PERKINS

When Samuel Johnson wrote about his famous journey to Scotland in 1773, he had little to say about Edinburgh; the city was, he explained, "too well-known to admit description."[1] Many of Johnson's contemporaries might have found that assertion rather surprising. Edinburgh was, after all, then undergoing one of the era's most ambitious attempts to reinvent a major urban centre – the planning and building of the neo-classical New Town.[2] In the words of R.A. Houston, "by the end of the eighteenth century," Edinburgh "had already become a new town" not just in "its physical appearance" but also in its "attitudes" and "society."[3] Nor were those changes in attitude limited to those who lived in Edinburgh. A city that had led Daniel Defoe, in 1726, to reflect sadly on the damage done by the "infinite disadvantages" and "scandalous inconveniences" of its geographic location had become, less than a century later, a "romantic town" whose "strangely varied prospect of antique grandeur and modern regularity" enthralled its many visitors.[4] The obvious appeal of the Highlands to eighteenth- and early nineteenth-century travellers has, perhaps inevitably, influenced much of the subsequent critical writing on Scottish travels of this period, with Enlightenment and Romantic-era constructions of rural Scotland as the wild "other" to refined, modern England attracting considerable attention in recent analyses of literature and national identities.[5] Yet, during the last decades of the eighteenth century and the early years of the nineteenth, as Scotland in general became an increasingly popular tourist destination and as Edinburgh was transformed by the development of the New Town, one can also find a lively and extensive literature produced by visitors – actual and fictional – to the city. Rather than finding Edinburgh too familiar to merit comment, many of these travellers constructed it as a sublimely disorienting locale, with the city's unusual architecture, striking geographic setting, dark, often tragic history, and, perhaps most important, its urbanely sociable women all working together to shape what presented itself as a fascinatingly strange urban space. What one finds in many of the surviving travellers' accounts of Edinburgh from the final quarter of the eighteenth century up through the era of Scott is a vision of the city as a space that, far from being a mere stepping-off point on the road to the Highlands, combines in itself aspects of both the cultivated and cultured metropolitan world of Enlightenment Europe and of the supposedly strange, exotically unfamiliar lands to the north.

While it is true that many of the travellers who came to Edinburgh in the decades between Johnson's famous journey and the early nineteenth-century tourist craze sparked by Scott did use the city as a staging post for journeys north, Edinburgh also attracted interest in its own right, perhaps in part because it did not fit entirely comfortably with late Enlightenment ideas of the city as either a monument of past grandeur or as the site of cosmopolitan modernity.[6] While there was nothing unusual about what might be called urban tourism during that period, the most familiar versions of such tourism in contemporary British literature were either accounts of provincials travelling to London or of men and women of the gentry and aristocracy visiting the great cultural centres of Continental Europe, with the Grand Tour as both the epitome and the pinnacle of such travels. Yet Edinburgh, a city possessing neither a court at which to polish aristocratic manners nor monuments of classical grandeur to refine an educated taste, could not serve the same purposes for tourists or be represented in the same terms as such standard Grand Tour destinations as Paris, Vienna, or Rome, even if it did end up serving as a *faute de mieux* destination for young English people during the years that the Continent was more or less closed to them by the Napoleonic wars. Rather, what one finds in many of the descriptions of Edinburgh from this period are attempts to convey an idea of a city that is simultaneously British and un-English, ancient and new, poised somewhere between ultramodern rational urban design and primitive unplanned sublimity in its built environment, and between dour Puritanism and dazzling, disturbing intellectual sophistication in its cultural manners.[7]

This is not to say that Edinburgh lacked any approximation of the sorts of monuments and tourist sites that attracted attention in other major cities: there was a standard cluster of visitor attractions, with Holyrood Palace and the Edinburgh Castle at the top of the list. Yet the discourse around these sites in the writing left by travellers from this period suggests that what fascinated them was not the sort of aesthetic experience supposedly offered by the churches, palaces, and galleries of the great Continental cities or by the British country houses that were also increasingly popular destinations at this time but,[8] rather, a visceral glimpse of a darkly violent past, the effect of which was heightened by juxtaposition with the comfortable familiarity of a modern British city. Highland society, as Johnson and many others made very clear, was seen at the time as offering a glimpse of the fading remnants of a culture long since extinct in the more settled and urban parts of Britain. Yet, even if Edinburgh was part of that modern, urban British world that emphasized, by contrast, the exoticism of the Highlands, it, too, visitors agreed, was strongly and ineradicably marked by its history. As a result, it suggested not, as the Highlands did, that modern culture was spreading out to even the wildest outreaches of Britain but almost the reverse: that modernity was inescapably shaped by the remote past. Even as Edinburgh was celebrated for its rapid strides towards modernity – one late eighteenth-century observer boasted that the "remarkable" changes made in the city over a mere two decades were "not perhaps to be equalled, in so short a period, in any city of Europe; nor in the same city for two centuries, taking all the alterations together"[9] – what numerous visitors of this period saw was a place in which traces of the past inescapably haunted and marked the rational Enlightenment city.

In at least one notorious case, this sense of the past leaving its mark on the Edinburgh present was exemplified in a very literal manner, as tourist after tourist was shown what was supposed to be the blood of David Rizzio staining the boards of the floor at Holyrood Palace. Most were frankly sceptical: a Miss Lucy Elizabeth Sherwood, who visited in the 1820s, admitted seeing "some dusky spots but wither [sic] they can be proved to be blood or not I think nobody would assert";[10] one A.L., visiting in 1785, was even more dubious. Shown by the "Keeper of the Rooms [what she] said was the blood of Riccio [sic], and which she herself could not wash out tho' she had frequently attempted to do so," he commented that "I had not credulity enough to believe it, but the Story has gained faith with many."[11] Yet others, whether they believed or not, found the sight a powerful evocation of the past. According to Mary Ann Grant, who visited Edinburgh in 1803, when "we passed the spot, where poor Rizzio was assassinated, and where the stain of his blood is shewn as indelible, I involuntarily shuddered; what a scene of horror for poor Mary!"[12] Nor were questionable stains the only tangible remnants of past tragedy over which tourists could have shuddered at Holyrood in the later eighteenth century: a number of travellers mention being shown what were supposedly the thigh bones of Lord Darnley and a mummified corpse that was said to be that of a countess of Roxborough. Thomas Newte, who received a corpse-and-all tour of Holyrood in 1785, was disapproving: he thought "[t]his exhibition was the most indelicate I ever beheld: and it ought not to be suffered,"[13] but he described it in some detail nonetheless. The schoolgirl Eliza Dawson (later Fletcher), who was in Edinburgh the following year, was similarly both appalled and fascinated by the spectacle, which she wrote about with measured distaste, even as she reveals that she observed the corpse of the supposed countess closely enough to note the condition of its nails and teeth.[14] While the bones and mummy seem to have ceased being a part of the Holyrood tour by the nineteenth century, memories of them persisted. In 1813, the diplomat Nathaniel Wraxell was shown Holyrood Chapel by an old woman who, much to his disgust, claimed to have "seen [the bones] a hundred Times."[15] Yet, however much visitors professed revulsion, the fascination with these gruesome displays, and the sense that they were part of the cultural character of Edinburgh, is testified to by their appearance, over more than half a century, in almost every traveller's description of the city. Clearly enough, they resonated in some way with the later eighteenth-century conception of Edinburgh as a place steeped in its own past and suggest the difficulty of drawing any clear, conceptual distinction between "modern" urban Scotland and the remnants of the past supposedly embodied in the Highlands. Even the sceptical Miss Sherwood noted, after her tour of Holyrood: "Persons to feel the Effect of time in the world should visit such places as these."[16] As this comment makes plain, what she found in Edinburgh, even as late as the mid-1820s, was not the modern, commercial city so proudly envisioned by William Creech in 1793 but, rather, a living evocation of a dark and tragically irrational past.

From roughly the last quarter of the eighteenth century onwards, this sense of Edinburgh as a place that straddled the ancient and the modern was of course reinforced in a very literal – and a very visually impressive – manner by the geographical and physical divide between the old city and the new. The old city had of course been notorious throughout the eighteenth century for its picturesque insalubrity; while early travellers tended to be impressed by the "stately" breadth of the High Street and the height of the Old Town buildings,[17] visitors from Defoe onwards seemed more overwhelmed by the filth and smells of the city than by its streets and its buildings, and they implicitly or explicitly measured Edinburgh against what was presumed to be the greater cleanliness and healthfulness of English metropolitan life. It would be wrong, Defoe wrote earnestly, to assume that the inhabitants of Edinburgh "delight" in "stench and nastiness" any more than do those of Bristol or London; it is merely that the cramped locale requires them to live unhygenically.[18] Defoe's comments were echoed (indeed, plagiarized) a generation later, in 1746, by an anonymous visitor who extended his disgust to the people, particularly the women, and described Scotswomen's plaids as "very good cover-sluts [that] serve to hide the nastiness of their undress."[19] Johnson's "grumbled" complaint to Boswell, as they picked their way up the High Street in 1773, that "I smell you in the dark"[20] has been frequently quoted. And, as late as 1822, an American visitor to Edinburgh was claiming that he had undergone what had become the archetypically Edinburgh experience of being dowsed by a chamber pot emptied from the upper storey of a Cowgate flat.[21] The new city, in contrast, delighted visitors with its airy, elegant regularity. Thomas Newte, whose travels took place in the mid-1780s, found the New Town already remarkable for its "beauty, elegance, and commodious as well as salubrious disposition and situation."[22] His contemporary Henry Skrine, who first visited Edinburgh in 1787, was even more effusive, proclaiming the New Town "the most regular and superb city that any country can boast: the streets all intersect each other at right angles, and the buildings are of the finest white stone, constructed in the most perfect uniformity." He even went so far as to announce that "St. Andrew's square would vie with most of the

London squares in extent, and exceed them in regularity."[23] In its New Town, Edinburgh thus embodied far better than London what Richard Sennett has described as the "breathing" city of the late Enlightenment, in which open, sweeping spaces encouraged health and circulation.[24]

Yet such contrasts between the admirable "regularity" and "uniformity" of the New Town and the dank jumble of the Old Town do not imply that visitors saw Edinburgh as admirable mainly for its embrace of either contemporary urban design or its more or less successful attempts to revivify classical rationality and order. On the contrary, just as tourists thrilled to being brought into proximity with the violent past as they strolled through the orderly rooms of eighteenth-century Holyrood, numerous visitors insisted that it was precisely the indivisibility of old and new that gave the city as a whole so much interest both architecturally and aesthetically. Rather than seeing Edinburgh as being divided by geography and architecture, most travellers of this period were inclined to represent it as a unified prospect in which apparently incongruous parts worked together to form a sublime urban whole. One J. Lettice, for example, who was travelling in 1792, singled out for praise the effect created by the "long line of modern houses, built of white stone, upon an elegant and uniform plan, facing the old castle and the town ... and thus, at once, giving and receiving the happiest effect of contrast."[25] Even more rapturously, a self-described Commercial Traveller, who visited Edinburgh in 1815, sums up this perspective on the city in his account of the view from Calton Hill. Despite his predictable complaints about the "combinations of villainous smells" he is forced to endure during his walk through the Old Town, he is overwhelmed once he ascends the hill itself: "I gazed around me with astonishment! I felt as if I had been translated into another world: every unpleasant feature of the picture was thrown into shade. The city lay below us in all the pride of ancient grandeur and modern elegance. Anything I had ever imagined of superlative magnificence, shrunk into poverty and meanness when my eye fell on this wonderful place."[26] This image of an Edinburgh that is composed for the viewer like a painting suggests the degree to which the city occupies a somewhat anomalous place in the sort of Enlightenment urbanism that produced the rationally ordered New Town. Rather than being of interest strictly as a built, human environment, the city is aestheticized and admired in much the same way as a natural landscape would be, with what ought to be discordant architectural elements softened into harmony by the observer's artistic eye.

It was, of course, entirely usual in the eighteenth-century arts to incorporate a city into a picturesque landscape. Views of Rome from the campagna were frequent in both visual and literary art, for example, while Jane Austen's Catherine Morland famously demonstrates her newly honed aesthetic taste by turning up her nose at the prospect formed by the city of Bath as viewed from a nearby hill. The unusual point here is not just that the Commercial Traveller is suggesting the aesthetic harmony of a potentially jarring architectural juxtaposition but, more important, that he is doing so in a manner that implies the city surpasses, rather than harmonizes with, the beauties of the natural world. *Anything* that he has been able to imagine falls short of this view, he writes, and while it is easy enough to dismiss this as the vague hyperbole of an unpractised writer – as did *Blackwood's Magazine* in a review professing amused disdain at the idea of a commercial traveller presuming to write about culture and taste[27] – it nonetheless suggests that Edinburgh is, in some way, unrepresentable and, thus, perhaps aligned more closely with the indescribable sublimity of the natural world than it is with more conventional urban environments. This idea, admittedly latent at best in the work of the Commercial Traveller, was developed more clearly in the writing of some of his contemporaries. The American "Franklin James," for example, claimed (somewhat hyperbolically) that the "amazing height" of the Old Town houses meant that, on a cloudy day, "the tops of the houses appear at a distance to be confounded with the firmament, and the clouds are seen rolling over their roofs." Similarly, when walking along the Nor Loch by night, he reports, his "imagination sometimes transports [him] into those gloomy forests described in the Arabian Tales."[28] James's implicit comparison of the Old Town buildings to cloud-covered mountains is anticipated in the travels of Henry Skrine, who also uses language as appropriate to mountains as it is to architecture to describe the Old Town buildings: they are "singularly lofty," he reports, and "irregular[ly]" scattered in "several ranges."[29]

What one finds in many of these representations of Edinburgh is thus an implicit or explicit sense that, far from being exciting either because it embodies the new, rational principles of urban design, or because of its antique splendour, it is a city built around a series of paradoxes. The Old Town, an intensely crowded, confusing warren of people and buildings, evokes lyrical descriptions that link it with the sublimity of cloud-capped mountains; the ultra-modernity of the New Town invites observers to look back to the distant, golden past of classical Greek culture at its height.[30] Yet, such paradoxes went beyond either tourist sites or the built environment and extended to accounts of the cultural and social life of the city as well. One finds numerous travellers of this period reporting themselves variously charmed, alarmed, or bewildered by a culture that seemed to hover somewhere between stereotypes of Scots dourness and something that English travellers, at least, tended to see as French frivolity, or between old-fashioned, sober religious devotion and the extremes of modern intellectual daring. This sense of a split within the Scottish national character is, of course, a familiar trope in Scottish literature, although the division is usually expressed in terms of a rural/urban or Highland/Lowland divide, or even as a split between the characters of the two major cities. Charles Dibdin, travelling in the early 1800s, insisted that "[t]he solid and the substantial seem to describe GLASGOW, which give but little idea of the gaiety and fashion of EDINBURGH. They are in their way the Lacedemonians and the Spartans, and so indeed they seem to consider themselves. EDINBURGH laughs at the plainness of GLASGOW and GLASGOW pities the frivolity of EDINBURGH."[31] Despite Dibdin's decidedly shaky grasp of classical geography and culture, the insistence that the Scottish urban character incorporates two very different styles of life remains plain enough, but many of Dibdin's forerunners and contemporaries were quite prepared to see these differences inscribed within the urban culture of Edinburgh itself or, even more specifically, on the characters of the city's women.

Of course, the idea that a large, disparate group of people will have a single, definable cultural identity is, at best, a myth, and many of the studies of eighteenth-century British travel writing from the 1990s on have analyzed the limitations of such "manners and customs" when writing about groups that differ from the writers' own and the distorting impact of the "ethnographic gaze."[32] Yet, however much one might critique the limitations of what travellers reported about the cultural and social life of Edinburgh during the last quarter of the eighteenth century and the first decades of the nineteenth, such observations, particularly when focused on the women, are more or less continuous with the attitudes expressed towards the more tangible aspects of the city, such as its architecture and its tourist sites. Like the city itself, the women are seen as being both quaintly, delightfully old-fashioned when looked at from one vantage point, or breathtakingly – perhaps even alarmingly – modern when viewed from another. One finds this doubleness in female roles worked through most fully in accounts of the city's public amusements – or the relative lack of them – as Edinburgh is represented as a city that is at once intensely social and dourly withdrawn into its own domestic life. It is shown as being, in effect, an urban world in which the contrasts and links between past and present inscribed on its physical appearance are both echoed and reinforced by the pull between modern manners and old-fashioned reserve exemplified in the cultural practices of its women.

Such comments on the social life of Edinburgh by late eighteenth-century travellers are less in agreement with each other than are the descriptions of tourist sites or the built environment, perhaps, in part, because a number of writers were using accounts of Edinburgh manners to point satiric or polemical arguments rather than necessarily attempting anything like ethnographic observation. At least two Scottish writers of this period, for example, showed fictitious visitors to Edinburgh being surprised by the extent and style of social life that they encounter there; however, in doing so, the writers in question were saying rather more about English or British society in general than about the specifics of Edinburgh female manners. In Tobias Smollett's *Humphry Clinker*, the Anglo-Welsh traveller Jery Melford is agreeably impressed with the elegance and quiet good taste of both the Edinburgh parties he attends and the Edinburgh ladies he meets; here, Smollett implicitly makes Edinburgh into an idealized contrast to the decadence and excess of London life as Edinburgh offers his travellers polite sociability without snobbish pretension or excess. Smollett's picture of sedate but sociable late eighteenth-century Edinburgh life is supported by Stana Nenadic's account of the attractions drawing late eighteenth-century Highland women to Edinburgh. According to Nenadic, "Social visiting, supper parties and musical evenings, in and out of the home, were the bedrock of gentry leisure in Edinburgh by the later decades of the eighteenth century."[33] Yet, even such relatively innocent pleasures could evoke dismay, as one can see by turning to the later novelist Mary Brunton. Brunton's Ellen Percy, who arrives in Edinburgh a generation after Smollett's characters, finds a city whose inhabitants gradually reveal themselves as being no less frivolous, selfish, and pleasure-seeking than are those of the London that she is fleeing, despite surface differences in manner. In this case, Brunton, an evangelical moralist, is obviously more concerned with what she saw as the distressing failings of contemporary British women in general than about Edinburgh in particular. Even so, the shared underlying need, in two such different novels, to insist upon the fact that Edinburgh does indeed have a culture built around public pleasures points to the ingrained contemporary perception that Edinburgh culture was simultaneously both more old-fashioned and more intellectually advanced than was that of London – a difference represented in large part through the behaviour of the cities' women.

Not all commentators, of course, would have agreed that, even if there had been a distinctive Scottish urban life in the past, it remained that way by the end of the century. In a much reprinted series of letters to Sir John Sinclair, the printer William Creech outlined what he saw as the major changes in Edinburgh in the years between 1763 and 1783, tracing in the process "by what imperceptible degrees society may advance to refinement, and in some points to corruption, whilst matters of real utility may be neglected."[34] In particular, Creech singles out for comment what he implies is the distressing increase in popularity of the theatre, noting with considerable dismay the shifting practice of young women, who (he implies) are becoming increasingly more interested in public entertainment, at the expense of private piety. In 1763, he writes, Saturday night was a deeply improper night for theatre going, while in 1783, "the morality of stage-plays, or their effects on society was not thought of. The most crowded houses were always on Saturday-night. The boxes for the Saturday-night's play were generally taken for the season, so that strangers often on that night could not get a place. The custom of taking a box for the Saturday-night through the season, was much practised by boarding mistresses, so that there could be no choice of the play, but the young ladies could only take what was set before them by the manager."[35] What is at stake here is the creeping infringement on the Scottish Sunday, assumed to begin on Saturday at midnight, which was noted by visitors to Edinburgh as a particularly decorous, solemn day. Creech might have been worried in 1783 that churchgoing was falling off (he thought it a gloomily telling detail that, by then, hairdressers' "busiest day was Sunday,"[36] something that again implies that women's decadent interest in their public appearance was interfering with proper devotional attitudes), but, as late as 1824, at least some travellers found that "no where is the Lord's day kept with such strict attention as in Scotland." There is, one observer reported with enthusiastic approbation: "no going to gardens as there exist no such a thing – no servants going out on Sundays except to their places of worship – no bakers baking dinners or cakes or fruit sold & if any one [sing?] on a Sunday the Police Officer wd request him to cease – the streets are solemnly still as there are no carriages on that day nor no Stages & the streets look deserted only at going & returning from places of worship when you may discern long trains of people. What a contrast with the same day at Paris!"[37] Despite the familiar Dickensian insistence upon the English Sunday as the ultimate embodiment of gloom and restraint, at least some English visitors of the previous generation seem to have found Edinburgh public practice even more enviably strict than their own.

That said, the point here is not whether or not Edinburgh was more or less pious than London or whether its citizens – the women in particular – were more or less observant in the early years of the nineteenth century than they had been in the middle of the eighteenth but, rather, that the city was, by the last years of the eighteenth century, being represented as a place in which domestic piety and order were being undercut by a rage for public pleasure, a change embodied in the practice of the supposedly increasingly frivolous Edinburgh women. There is nothing unusual in this in itself: as Creech, for one, makes clear, the fear that the "gradual progress of commerce and luxury" might lead to a destructive "effect upon manners"[38] haunted the eighteenth-century mind. In many ways, Creech's gloomy worries about the impact of the theatre on piety echo the more familiar rhetoric of an English polemicist such as Hannah More, who, around the same time, was thundering out warnings about the taste for Sunday concerts and other such modern corruptions. What is different about Edinburgh is that the parameters of the debate – modern decadence versus old-fashioned decorum – aren't as easily fixed as they can be in the work of a writer such as More. What one finds in many descriptions of Edinburgh, Creech notwithstanding, is a sense that its urban culture is one in which the social, the intellectual, and the devotional lives of its women offer – again, like its cultural sites and its architecture – an odd, perhaps intriguing, mixture of the old and the new rather than a straightforward replacement of respectable old ways with the decadent new.

Women were, of course, the focus of much of the wider British debate about changing manners and the decadence of public life, and so it is unsurprising that they should also be central to travellers' representations of Edinburgh. What was perceived as the feminine intrusion into the public sphere and their improper pursuit of public pleasure was one of the major sources of anxiety of conservative British polemicists into the early years of the nineteenth century. Yet, even if there were some writers on Scotland, such as Brunton and Creech, who gloomily insisted upon the growing similarities between social life in London and Edinburgh, most travellers who commented on Scottish women seemed to find them relatively little interested in the dissipations of public life and to be noteworthy for their virtuously modest demeanour. Even Edward Topham, who was so shocked by the Edinburgh ladies' habit of kissing men in greeting that he worried about the impact on Scottish marriage ("the young ladies become so habituated to salutes ... that their sensations are perfectly hebetated and dull ... how languid and insipid must be the marriage bed, when incapable of deriving pleasure from this source?") commented as well on their dislike of "routs" and "large sets of company" and their cultivation of a taste for domestic pursuits.[39] Likewise, Sir John Carr, visiting the city a generation later, was impressed by the combination of "frankness of character" and modest decorum of the women he met there. A Scotswoman's manner, he writes, "seems impregnated with friendship, and is guarded by a natural modesty, which gives a purity to her conversation, and fills the person to whom she addresses herself, with equal esteem and respect for her."[40] The picture created by both accounts is of a society in which sociable exchanges between men and women are sober, rational, and, above all, conversational – that is, such socializing seems to occur mainly in the private or quasi-private space of a drawing room rather than at a dance, a play, or a concert.

Yet, not all visitors to Edinburgh were equally charmed by this vision of an old-fashioned sociable world of polite conversation.

On the contrary, if politely conversable Edinburgh women seemed to offer some English visitors a glimpse back to a more sober, domestic-minded age and, thereby, to evade one late eighteenth-century British cliché of modern, wayward femininity – the dissipated woman of fashion – they risked tumbling straight into another: the bluestocking. Admittedly, Edinburgh lacked any direct equivalent of the French *salonnières* or of such English literary hostesses as Elizabeth Montague; indeed, as Alexander Murdoch and Richard B. Sher have noted, "women rarely participated in the world of the Scottish Enlightenment."[41] Yet, even if Edinburgh women had few formal outlets for intellectual debate, they seem to have made the most of the informal opportunities open to them. Almost all visitors to Edinburgh during this period commented on the intellectuality of the private, and usually mixed, social gatherings to which they were invited, with many, especially those from overseas, coming to the city in specific hopes of making social contact with the great men of the day, whether the men in question were figures such as Smith, Hutton, and Cullen in the later years of the eighteenth century or Scott and Jeffrey in the opening decades of the nineteenth.[42] Like the architecturally open, orderly New Town, the open, frank debates of late Enlightenment Edinburgh private society apparently offered interested visitors a vision of a new, rational order. The presence of women at such intellectual gatherings evoked rather less enthusiasm, however. The American visitor Franklin James proclaimed his distaste for the conversation of Edinburgh women at considerable length: "Instead of talking on those subjects which it is so becoming and graceful in a woman to know," he complains,

> they prose away on mineralogy, politics, borough reform, and the *corn*-bill: "they are certainly the very *flour* of the sex," says *Peter*, in his excellent "Letters to his Kinsfolk." Mrs. Kyndear is at the head of the *Femmes Savantes* of this order: she bores me to death with learned harangues about geology, pebbles, and the botanical names of plants, which she *ecorche's* in the most ridiculous manner. She knows more about Dr. Hope's laboratory, than what is going on in her own family, and can analyze a fossil, although she cannot tell the component parts of a pudding![43]

John Gibson Lockhart is even harsher in his quasi-fictional *Peter's Letters*, which James so enthusiastically takes as his model, as he imagines an Edinburgh *converzatione* that features Francis Jeffrey finding himself "ambush[ed]" and "entrap[ped]" by a party of half-a-dozen bluestockings who, with Jeffrey safely "pinioned up against a wall," proceed to bombard him with lectures and questions.[44]

There is nothing unusual, of course, in early nineteenth-century attacks on the pretensions of learned women, but at least some observers were prepared to see such women as peculiarly a reflection of Edinburgh culture. As Lockhart explains, the Scottish educational system ensures that "the kinds of information most in request here" are equally accessible to both men and women:

> To be able to talk with fluency about the Politics and Belles Lettres of the day, is all that is required of an accomplished man in Edinburgh, and these are the accomplishments which the ladies, modest as they are, would require more modesty than is either natural or proper to suppose themselves incapable of acquiring. That ignorance of the learned languages and ancient literature, which the men have not the assurance to attempt disguising, has broken down effectually the first and most insurmountable barrier which separates the intellectual pretensions of the two sexes in England.[45]

The Balliol-educated Lockhart is, of course, directing his satire here as much against men as women, but the point remains that his alter ego Peter is suggesting that one of the defining characteristics of Edinburgh society is that the men and women converse more or less as intellectual equals. The result is that the supposedly old-fashioned feminine preference for polite conversation over public dissipation that was noted by earlier observers of Edinburgh society becomes not a facet of women's rejection of contemporary decadence but, rather, an indication of a troublesomely modern breakdown of conventional gender roles. For Lockhart, at least, Edinburgh's supposed suspicion of the new fashions for and in public dissipation is not so much a welcome glance back to the past as it is an unsettling glimpse of an emerging world in which intellectual order and discipline is being cast to the winds.[46]

A vision of an urban social world in which intellectually pretentious women bear down and overpower "men of high literary character"[47] might seem far removed from the Edinburgh of late eighteenth-century tourists such as Eliza (Dawson) Fletcher and Thomas Newte, shuddering over the mummified corpse of a long-dead supposed countess. What links the satire of Lockhart and James with the earlier, more straightforward tourist accounts of Fletcher and Newte is the sense of Edinburgh as a city that embodies both Enlightenment rationality and unsettlingly irrational disorder – a disorder that encompasses not only the traces of the city's violent, tragic past but also the sublimely jarring effect of its architectural disunity and its cultural divides between piety and pleasure, old-fashioned feminine modesty and modern female self-assertion. As many critics have argued, Highland Scotland served, in the late eighteenth-century and Romantic British imagination, as a source of domestic alterity and as a site for the location of values and aspirations that were supposedly foreign to the metropolitan concept of modern British identity.[48] Yet, as so much of the writing on Edinburgh from this period indicates, aspects of British urban life could also be inflected with the sublime and the disconcertingly unfamiliar, making the city – Samuel Johnson notwithstanding – as much a strange and exciting subject for exploration and observation as were the remoter hinterlands that seemed so much more obvious a site for the tourist gaze.

NOTES

1 Johnson, *A Journey to the Western Islands of Scotland*, 35. But contrast Edward Topham, *Letters from Edinburgh*, who published his account of a 1774–75 trip to Scotland a few years after Johnson's *Journal* appeared. Topham writes – perhaps somewhat mischievously – in his introduction that one might think it "unnecessary, that any further accounts of Scotland be given" and that even he would have thought any "account of the Highlands or western islands" redundant, so he has instead focused on what he implies is the less familiar territory of Edinburgh (vii).

2 For a very detailed account of the process and timing of the building of the New Town, see Youngson, *The Making of Classical Edinburgh*; compare the comment of Topham, *Letters from Edinburgh*, writing a year after Johnson's visit: "Great part of this plan [of the New Town] as yet remains to be executed, tho' they proceed as fast as their supplies of money will allow them" (5–6).

3 Houston, *Social Change*, 378.
4 Defoe, *Tour*, 577; Brunton, *Discipline*, 224, 235.
5 The fullest recent discussion of tourism in Scotland during this period mentions Edinburgh only in passing, focusing mainly on reports of the notoriously foul smells of the Old Town. See Glendening, *The High Road*, esp. 43, 165.
6 See Buzard, "Translation and Tourism," for a discussion of Scott and Romantic-era tourism.
7 See also Bailey (this volume) on the importance of Enlightenment values in certain civic visions; Coenen Snyder (this volume) on travellers' reactions to Amsterdam; and Johnson (this volume) on how fin-de-siècle Paris faced modernity. Eds.
8 See Fabricant, "Literature of Domestic Tourism," for an analysis of the cultural meanings of county house tourism in this period. Hamilton Palace, in Lanarkshire, seems to have been the main destination for later eighteenth-century visitors to Scotland who were interested in this sort of travel; many of the Edinburgh tourists mentioned in this chapter also visited it and commented on its most famous work, Rubens' "Daniel in the Lions' Den." Edinburgh itself lacked any comparable public or quasi-public art collection – although Raeburn's studio attracted some nineteenth-century tourists – and the well known paintings of Scottish kings at Holyrood were the subject of more amusement than admiration.
9 [Creech], *Letters*, 6. Houston, *Social Change*, 10–11, notes that, even though a number of Creech's specific points were "probably incorrect," his "general picture of significant social change is surely correct."
10 [Sherwood], *Diary*, 29 January 1827.
11 [A.L.], *Journey*, fol. lv.
12 Grant, *Sketches*, 2:42.
13 Newte, *Prospects and Observations*, 310.
14 Fletcher, *Tour*, 20.
15 Wraxall, *Diary*, fol. 44.
16 [Sherwood], *Diary*, 29 January 1827.
17 See, for example, Macky, *Journey through Scotland*, 65.
18 Defoe, *Tour*, 577.
19 *The Contrast*, 46–7, 60.
20 Boswell, *Tour to the Hebrides*, 167.
21 [James], *Franklin's Letters*, 7–8. The name of the author does not appear on the title page, although "by Franklin James" is pencilled in on the fly leaf of the copy in the National Library of Scotland. The writer was, judging by internal evidence, an American medical student; however, given that he openly proclaims that he is modelling his work on John

Gibson Lockhart's semi-fictional collection *Peter's Letters*, there is a good chance that many of the specific details about his encounters are fictionalized to some degree.

22 Newte, *Prospects and Observations*, 325.

23 Skrine, *Three Successive Tours*, 65.

24 Sennett, *Flesh and Stone*, 261–70. While Sennett focuses his discussion of this sort of city on Paris, he also glances at Washington DC, which, like Edinburgh's New Town, was a late eighteenth-century creation designed on neo-classical principles.

25 Lettice, *Letters on a Tour*, 511.

26 *Letters from Scotland*, 72.

27 "Miss Spence and the Bagman," 428.

28 [James], *Franklin's Letters* 3, 2.

29 Skrine, *Three Successive Tours*, 65–6.

30 Comparisons between Edinburgh and Athens were commonplace by the 1820s. See, for example, the raptures of an aristocratic Pole, who was obviously quite happy to accept Scottish attempts to map ancient Athens onto modern Edinburgh: "the Firth of Forth," he wrote, "is certainly worth the Aegean sea; Leith is good enough to take the place of the Piraeus; the castle on the rock that of the Acropolis" (McLeod, *From Charlotte Square to Fingal's Cave*, 8). Compare, as well, the somewhat brisker summary of a French traveller of the same period: "Edinburgh, in proudly proclaiming herself the Athens of Great Britain, does not alone refer to the analogies of her site, to her Piraêus (Leith), her Acropolis, with its citadel (the castle), to her future Parthenon (the projected temple on Calton Hill), &c. Edinburgh is still more proud of aspiring to the designation, on the score of her philosophers, orators, critics, and poets ([Pichot], *Historical and Literary Tour*, 2:290). Pichot, however, goes on to make plain his scepticism about the intellectual accomplishments of the "modern Athenians," mocking in particular the literary pretensions of the women.

31 Dibdin, *Observations on a Tour*, 337 (misnumbered as 387).

32 See, for example, Pratt, *Imperial Eyes*; Hunt, "Racism, Imperialism, and the Traveler's Gaze"; Chard, *Pleasure and Guilt on the Grand Tour*; and Tobin, *Picturing Imperial Power*.

33 Nenadic, *Lairds and Luxury*, 203.

34 [Creech], *Letters*, 44. Substantial passages or key details from these letters appear in, for example, the tour of I. Lettice (by permission, he stresses); the introduction of an 1825 collection of letters on Scotland; *The Contrast*; and a tourist's guidebook, *The New Picture of Edinburgh*.

35 [Creech], *Letters*, 42.

36 Ibid., 17.
37 [Beecroft], *Journal of a Tour to Scotland*, 56v–57 ff.
38 [Creech], *Letters*, 44.
39 Topham, *Letters from Edinburgh*, 17, 38.
40 Carr, *Caledonian Sketches*, 129.
41 Murdoch and Sher, "Literacy and Learned Culture," 131.
42 See Saint-Fond's *Travels* for an account of late eighteenth-century intellectual tourism in Edinburgh: he describes visits to Hutton, Black, Cullen (who cures Saint-Fond's depression by prescribing a daily dose of rum punch), Aiken, and Adam Smith – who escorts the horrified Saint-Fond to a Highland piping competition (2:225–50). Pichot, a generation later, reported on Scott and Jeffrey, as did the Pole, Krystyn Lach-Szyrma, and the American professor Garscombe, whose letters were reprinted in *The Contrast*. It was not only distinguished foreigners who engaged in such celebrity-hunting, however; the Beecrofts managed to find an excuse to call on Scott at Abbotsford and to introduce themselves to other literary figures in Edinburgh and Glasgow.
43 [James], *Franklin's Letters*, 31–2.
44 Lockhart, *Peter's Letters*, 58–9.
45 Ibid., 54.
46 See also Johnson's (this volume) discussion of the inequalities faced by women artists in fin-de-siècle Paris; and Bailey (this volume) on journalistic optimism that Enlightenment values will prevail in the face of change. Eds.
47 Lockhart, *Peter's Letters*, 55.
48 Compare Malcolm Chapman's comments, which, for the *Waverley* generation, seem almost as appropriate to Britain as a whole as to Scotland: "Since the eighteenth century … the Scottish people have increasingly looked to the Highlands to provide a location for an autonomy in which they could lodge their own political, literary and historical aspirations (quoted in Simpson, *The Protean Scot*, 45).

8

Clearing the Streets: Blindness and Begging in Henry Mayhew's *London Labour and the London Poor*

VANESSA WARNE

Henry Mayhew's *London Labour and the London Poor* (1851–62) is an ambitious and wide-ranging study of mid-Victorian London and of the lives of its lower-class citizens. In a typical passage from the first of the series' four volumes, Mayhew describes a Saturday night street market and the boisterous nature of the trade conducted there:

> One man stands with his red-edged mats hanging over his back and chest, like a herald's coat; and the girl with her basket of walnuts lifts her brown-stained fingers to her mouth, as she screams, "Fine warnuts! sixteen a penny, fine war-r-nuts." A bootmaker, to "ensure custom," has illuminated his shopfront with a line of gas, and in its full glare stands a blind beggar, his eyes turned up as to show only "the whites," and mumbling some begging rhymes, that are drowned in the shrill notes of the bamboo-flute player next to him. The boy's sharp cry, the woman's cracked voice, the gruff, hoarse shout of the man, are all mingled together.[1]

Images of red-edged mats and brown-stained fingers set the scene, but Mayhew's central visual spectacle is the blind man, an overly illuminated figure fixed by the "full glare" of the blazing gaslight. A beggar in a space defined by commerce, the blind man is singled out by his exclusion from trade. Easily seen but not easily heard, he is also isolated by his ineffectual voice. The man is, however, most obviously separated from those around him by his inability to view his surroundings. A grim portrait of a visually disabled person's life in the city, Mayhew's street scene identifies blindness with both social isolation and economic dependence.

Nineteenth-century poems featuring blind beggars make similar links, frequently portraying blind people as solitary figures in busy crowds. In Book VII of his posthumously published autobiographical poem *The Prelude* (1805, 1850), William Wordsworth describes a blind man as a motionless anomaly in an otherwise kinetic urban scene:

lost
Amid the moving pageant, 'twas my chance
Abruptly to be smitten with the view
Of a blind Beggar, who, with upright face,
Stood propp'd against a Wall, upon his Chest
Wearing a written paper, to explain
The story of the Man, and who he was.
My mind did at this spectacle turn round
As with the might of waters, and it seem'd
To me that in this Label was a type
Or emblem, of the utmost that we know,
Both of ourselves and of the universe;
And, on the shape of the unmoving man,
His fixed face and sightless eyes, I look'd
As if admonish'd from another world.[2]

The blind beggar, the "unmoving man" in the "moving pageant," is, for Wordsworth, an instructive and poignant "spectacle." Throughout Book VII, Wordsworth characterizes London as a "mighty place"[3] notable for its "endless stream of men, and moving things."[4] The city is also, for Wordsworth, a space that makes the lack of personal connections between individuals in urban settings painfully clear. "How often in the overflowing Streets," Wordsworth laments, "Have I gone forward with the Crowd, and said / Unto myself, the face of every one / That passes by me is a mystery."[5] Wordsworth understands the blind man as an exemplum of the limited knowledge individuals have of both each other and themselves, a form of ignorance typified by the inability of a blind man to read the sign that tells the story of his own life.

Wordsworth's construction of the blind man as an embodiment of a universally experienced metaphoric blindness gestures towards the similitude of poet and blind beggar; however, the passage containing this suggestion ultimately foregrounds differences between Wordsworth and the blind man, highlighting both the mobility Wordsworth enjoys as he moves around the city and the intensely visual nature of his experience of London.[6]

At the end of the nineteenth century, a similar encounter inspired an equally pessimistic portrait of a blind urban dweller. Arthur Symons's 1892 sonnet "The Blind Beggar" stresses the immobility and isolation of a blind man he observed in the street:

He stands, a patient figure, where the crowd
Heaves to and fro; a sound is in his ears
As of a vexed sea roaring, and he hears
In darkness, as a dead man in his shroud.
Patient he stands, with age and sorrow bowed,
And holds a piteous hat of ancient years;
And in his face and gesture there appears
The desperate humbleness of poor men proud.

What thoughts are his, as, with the inward sight,
He sees the glad unheeding Fair go by?
Is the long darkness darker for that light
And sorrow nearer when such mirth is nigh?
Patient, alone, he stands from morn to night,
Pleading in his reproachful misery.[7]

While the octave's description of the blind man as one who "hears in darkness" enacts a synaesthetic blurring of blindness with deafness, constructing the blind subject as doubly disabled, the sestet imagines ways in which the man's suffering might be increased by his proximity to able-bodied city dwellers. Symons's simile comparing a blind person to a dead man in his shroud is particularly noteworthy: identifying disability not simply with social isolation and economic dependence but with death, Symons takes the ineffectuality of Mayhew's mumbling beggar and the immobility of Wordsworth's unmoving man to a new extreme.

The bleak assessment of the experience of blindness and, more generally, of urban life common to these three portraits can be attributed in part, if not wholly, to the fact that these passages characterize blind people on city streets as spectacles rather than as human subjects. The decision to speak about, rather than with, blind people informs the messages these authors produce about both disability and the city, messages that are significantly complicated by a series of interviews Mayhew conducted with blind subjects for *London Labour and the London Poor.*[8] These interviews, which constitute a complex and detailed history of visually disabled, working-class Victorians, have led one of Mayhew's most recent and most astute critics, Martha Stoddard Holmes, to explore the relationship between the autobiographical narratives of blind street people and Mayhew's "utter fascination with blindness."[9] Adding to Holmes's work on Mayhew and blindness, this chapter uses interviews from *London Labour and the London Poor* to examine the lives of blind Londoners and to investigate the relationship between blindness and both social and spatial aspects of the nineteenth-century city. Focused on the experiences of visually disabled people, it explores three aspects of urban life: charity, community, and mobility. Paying particular attention to the development of social institutions aimed at regulating mendicity, and to the contemporaneous emergence of a new set of values about streets and street life, I examine the interaction of disabled and able-bodied urbanites in London's public spaces. I suggest that Mayhew's interviews with blind people promote the rights of blind citizens while simultaneously resisting the transformation of crowded streets into swift-moving, uncluttered urban thoroughfares. In the process, I attempt to advance a geography of Victorian London that acknowledges the presence of disabled people and that recognizes disability and the city as interdependent and mutually constituted cultural constructs.[10]

MENDICITY IN THE METROPOLIS

Mayhew began writing about London's poor areas in 1849 in a series of articles for the *Morning Chronicle*. The success of this series prompted him to create *London Labour and the London Poor,* serialized in 1851 and 1852 and published in book form in 1861 and 1862. Mayhew originally hoped to create "a cyclopaedia of the industry, the want, and the vice of the great Metropolis."[11] The completed series is, however, a less than comprehensive study of London's working classes, its primary focus being "street-folk," people who survived by selling, scavenging, begging, or performing in the streets. Combining transcripts of interviews with tables of statistics and commentary on such issues as rat infestation, street cleaning, and the sewer system, Mayhew's study of the different groups working in London's streets is largely a study of urban life.

The project was premised on the belief that middle-class readers knew little about London's poor and were unfamiliar with areas of the city occupied by them. In a preface, Mayhew praised the first volume for "supplying information concerning a large body of persons, of whom the public had less knowledge than of the most distant tribes of the earth."[12] Referring to eighteenth-century explorer James Bruce, whose reports of Ethiopia were received with scepticism, Mayhew explains: "the traveller in the undiscovered country of the poor must, like Bruce, until his stories are corroborated by after investigators, be content to lie under the imputation of telling such tales, as travellers are generally supposed to delight in."[13] When Mayhew compares the poor with "distant tribes," himself with a world traveller, and the city with a world that has been inadequately explored, he advertises and heightens the significance and allure of the series. As recent scholarship on Mayhew has shown, his characterization of the poor parts of London as an "undiscovered country" also lends his work an unmistakably ethnographic quality.[14]

Reviewers of *London Labour and the London Poor* appear to have shared Mayhew's view of the city's poor areas as terra incognita. William Makepeace Thackeray, writing for *Punch*, reflected that London's poor will remain unknown to the middle classes until "some clear-sighted, energetic man like the writer of the *Chronicle* travels into the poor man's country for us, and comes back with his tale of terror and wonder."[15] The *Eclectic Review* also praised Mayhew, explaining that "[h]e has travelled through the unknown regions of our metropolis, and returned with full reports concerning the strange tribes of men which he may be said to have discovered."[16] While the identification of the poor with "strange tribes of men" or, in Mayhew's case, with "distant tribes" is a logical extension of the "undiscovered country" image pattern, it is considerably less credible. Upper- and middle-class Londoners could steer clear of poor parts of the city, but avoiding poor urbanites would have been a far more difficult undertaking.[17] The presence of the working poor and of beggars embodying extreme poverty on streets used by upper- and middle-class pedestrians and passengers has been widely documented and was viewed by many Victorian commentators as a nuisance, if not as a threat.[18]

One such commentator was the author of an 1848 *Fraser's Magazine* article entitled "The Plague of Beggars." In it, he asks: "What greater nuisance can there be conceived than to have one's footsteps tracked, one's path beset, one's door besieged, by these ubiquitous masqueraders! We take a solitary walk, occupied by our own thoughts. At every crossing an impudent urchin trails a dirty broom before us ... At the short intervals we must encounter the whining interruption of the sturdy Irishman who is always starving ... Before our walk is half finished we have run the gauntlet of almost every form of pretended distress, and bourne, as best we may, the fretting interruptions of every variety of ragged and dirty falsehood."[19] Interrupting his thoughts, cluttering his path, blocking his door, the city's poor are anything but a mystery to this author. Characterizing the street as a gauntlet and London's poor as a plague, these complaints are paradigmatic of nineteenth-century rhetoric against mendicity. Equally conventional is the author's assertion that beggars are "masqueraders." More than merely a nuisance or an obstacle, a limit on the ease of the middle classes' movement around town, they are sturdy people who pretend to be starving and are, as such, objects not only of derision but also of suspicion.

Similar views on London's beggars were expressed by the *Quarterly Review* in 1815. Responding to an 1815 House of Commons committee on "Mendicity and Vagrancy in the Metropolis," the *Quarterly Review* argued that "the most deserving objects of real and deep distress are the last to court attention to their unhappy situation in the public streets and highways".[20] Committed to the view that "no worthy people, however distressed, have been known to have recourse to street-begging,"[21] the author expressed a desire to put an end to indiscriminate alms-giving and to prevent "the sons and daughters of mendicity and vagrancy" from "infesting the streets" of London."[22] The *Quarterly Review*'s correspondent paid particular attention to the committee's records related to London's blind beggars, a group who were not immune to accusations of being both undeserving and dishonest. Eagerly documenting the existence of individuals who "affected blindness," the article repeats the committee's account of a beggar who claimed to be blind but "who could see so well by night he wrote letters for his brother beggars."[23] There is also testimony about a blind child being hired out to different adult beggars who pretended to be the child's parents in order to manipulate passers-by. Perhaps most damning of all, the article makes reference to two blind men who found begging so profitable that they were able to leave large legacies to family and friends when they died.

Both this essay and the House of Commons Inquiry that prompted it document contemporary attitudes towards mendicity and disability; however, neither leads to palpable changes in social practices: a decade later, blind beggars continued to occupy London streets and the government continued to ponder their eradication. An 1823 parliamentary committee investigating charitable institutions continued the work of its predecessors; one of its reports was discussed at some length in the *Westminster Review* in 1824. Examining the committee's interest in "the good and bad distribution of the means of happiness,"[24] the author of this article appears to view blind vagrants with less suspicion and more sympathy than did his *Quarterly Review* colleague. Praising the founding of "hospitals for the indigent blind" and arguing that "the good produced by these is unalloyed,"[25] he identified visually disabled people as deserving objects of charity. Promoting the institutionalization of impoverished blind people in hospitals, he was, however, no less eager to see city streets cleared of blind beggars than were his predecessors. While the existence of these two parliamentary commissions demonstrates the endurance both of mendicity and of public interest in it, differences in the tone and the conclusions reached by commentators hint at the fact that nineteenth-century British culture became gradually more compassionate towards disabled people while remaining largely intolerant of begging.

A more conclusive barometer of this trend is the history of charitable practices and institutions – a history that charts both a pattern of increased compassion for the disabled and the persistence of staunch opposition to mendicity. From the 1820s onward, London witnessed a notable increase in institutionalized forms of charity and a consequent decrease in the number of blind men and women begging on urban streets. David Owen, commenting on the development of institutions and private charities for the urban poor, has described the years 1820 to 1860 as an era that "saw the energies of the philanthropist reach a high, almost a frenetic pitch."[26] A growing number of philanthropic organizations catered specifically to the blind. Prominent among them was Day's Charity, founded in 1836 in London and commonly known as the Blind Man's Friend. Having lost his sight, Charles Day left a legacy of 100,000 pounds to be distributed to blind Londoners in the form of small pensions. By 1861, there were at least sixteen different metropolitan charities and funds devoted to lower-class blind and deaf people. These included the London Society for Teaching the Blind to Read (founded 1839), the Home Teaching Society for the Blind (founded 1855), and the Association for Promoting the General Welfare of the Blind (founded 1856). By the end of the 1880s, there were thirty-two different charities for blind people located in London.[27]

The founding of these types of charities was laudable but was not an unambiguous expression of compassion for lower-class disabled people. As M.J.D. Roberts has shown, the growth in the number of charities in operation in the nineteenth century was paired with, and perhaps even prompted by, strong opposition to mendicity and by growing suspicion about the legitimacy of the poor's claim to charity. Choosing to give to institutions instead of to individuals, middle-class Victorians sought assurances that their donations would go to deserving recipients and that the money they gave would be well managed. A key participant in the movement towards more cautious and less direct forms of charitable giving was the London Mendicity Society, or LMS, founded in 1818 to address what its members viewed as "the alarming prevalence of Mendicity in the Metropolis."[28] Dissatisfied with the administration of the Poor Laws and with what they perceived as the lax enforcement of laws against vagrancy, founders of the LMS hoped to mediate between beggars, civil authorities, and charitably minded individuals.

To be more specific, the LMS, characterized by its opposition to what Roberts terms "individually bargained 'gift relationships,'"[29] tried to ensure that those who gave to London's needy had adequate information about who was and who was not a deserving recipient of charitable support. To achieve this goal, it developed a system in which subscribers to the LMS gave printed tickets to beggars in lieu of coins. These tickets could be exchanged for meals, but candidates first had to answer a set of questions about their history and habits and be deemed deserving. The society also employed officers who approached and investigated people they suspected of begging on the streets. Those who were judged undeserving or dishonest were reported to the police. The police and the courts were, in turn, encouraged to do what the LMS could not, namely, charge and incarcerate vagrants. The society appears to have had considerable success in this arena: its records show that "one third of all metropolitan police office committals for vagrancy – some 10,000 cases – were instituted by society officers between 1818 and 1830."[30] Forcibly removing some beggars from the street while encouraging others to receive charity from private institutions instead of appealing for it in public spaces, the LMS paired the seemingly antagonistic but ultimately contiguous activities of doling out charity and suppressing begging.[31]

Reflecting on the support that the LMS received from middle-class citizens of metropolitan London, Roberts concludes: "Torn between emotions of suspicion, annoyance, unease and pity, they sought a way out and found it in the volunteer professionalization of the gift relationship."[32] The professionalization of the gift relationship, the push for the state to play a greater role in policing mendicity, and the increase in the number of charitable institutions for the blind: these developments reflect a growing desire for a clearer definition of middle-class social responsibility but are, first and foremost, expressions of strong opposition to street beggars. Motivated in some cases by compassion and in others by disgust, characterized by different degrees of tolerance, sympathy, and mistrust, the individuals writing about, thinking about, and participating in these developments share a common goal – namely, the removal of both able-bodied and disabled beggars from London's streets.

MAYHEW'S BLIND BEGGARS

Given the cultural climate in which Mayhew interviewed London's poorest citizens, it is not at all surprising that his subjects repeatedly comment on social opposition to street begging. For instance, several blind sellers of shoelaces tell Mayhew that "The officers of the Mendicity Society ... are their worst enemies."[33] According to a blind woman Mayhew interviewed for volume 1, the police were equally antagonistic. Mayhew, who typically gives the trade but not the name of his subjects, identifies this interviewee as the woman who "may be seen nearly every fine day, selling what is technically termed 'small-ware,' in Leatherlane, Holborn."[34] She tells Mayhew that, because she wears a sign that reads "PLEASE TO BUY OF THE POOR BLIND," she is accused of begging instead of street selling: "I'm afraid of the police; they're so arbitry. (Her word). It's not very long since one of them – and I was told afterwards he was a sergeant, too – ordered me to move on. 'I can't move on, sir, said I, 'I wish I could, but I must stand still, for I'm blind.' 'I know that,' says he, 'but you're begging.' 'No, I'm not,' says I, 'I'm only trying to sell a few little things, to keep me out of the work'us.' 'Then what's that thing you have tied over your breast?' says he. 'If you give me any more of your nonsense, I'll lock you up'; and then he went away. I'm terrified to think of being taken to the station."[35] More than simply a record of an unsurprisingly antagonistic encounter between a representative of the law and a poor Londoner, this interview chronicles an able-bodied officer's interaction with a disabled citizen. Doubtful about both her ability and her willingness to support herself through trade, the police sergeant contemplates clearing the street of a seller he perceives to be a beggar. The sign she wears, advertising her poverty and bodily impairment and encouraging passers-by to buy her goods, is understood by the sergeant as an unambiguous request for charity. Requests for charity made on the street are not legal nor are they, in his opinion, justified. Perceiving the disabled woman's decision to publicize her disability as inappropriate and her involvement in trade as illegitimate, the sergeant discourages her from supporting herself, threatens her with incarceration, and insists she move continuously through the streets instead of remaining in one place.

This incident and others like it from *London Labour and the London Poor* offer significant insight into the daily lives of blind lower-class Londoners. Giving otherwise marginalized individuals an opportunity to share their experiences of urban life, poverty, and disability, the series also allows for the relatively uncensored expression of lower-class animosity towards civil authorities and class inequalities. Towards the end of Mayhew's interview with the small-ware seller, a fellow street seller joins in and reflects on injustices suffered by the poor. She objects, "any shopkeeper can put what notice he likes in his window, that *he* can, if it's ever such a lie, and nothing's said if he collects a crowd; oh dear, no. But we mus'n't say our lives is our own."[36] Mayhew adds that these sentiments are expressed with "a bitterness not uncommon on the part of street-sellers."[37]

Mayhew responds to complaints of this kind by promoting blind people's right to sell items in the streets and to occupy the metropolis's public spaces without being harassed. When he shares the small-ware seller's story with the reading public, he draws attention to challenges faced by the disabled poor and allows the seller a voice in ongoing debates concerning poverty and mendicity. Mayhew also encourages his readers to treat street-folk charitably. When he introduces an interview with a blind tailor turned street seller, he notes, "the following biography is given to teach us to look with a kindly eye upon the many who are forced to become street-sellers as the sole means of saving themselves from the degradation of pauperism or beggary."[38] Forced into the street by disability, the blind, Mayhew argues, sell items in public spaces by necessity, not by choice.

Mayhew's role as an advocate of blind street sellers is, however, compromised by his insistence on the inability of blind people to be financially self-sufficient. He proposes that "of all misfortunes, blindness is one which, to those who have their sight, appears not only the greatest of human privations, but a privation which wholly precludes the possibility of self-help, and so gives the sufferer the strongest claim on our charity."[39] He echoes these sentiments when he describes the blind as among those "individuals who, from some privations or affliction that rendered them utterly incompetent to labour for their living, had a just claim on our sympathies and assistance."[40] Striking a similar note, he argues: "There must be some mitigating plea, if not a full justification, in the conduct of those who beg directly or indirectly, because they cannot and perhaps never could labour for their daily bread – I allude to those afflicted with blindness, whether 'from their youth up' or from the calamity being inflicted upon them in maturer years."[41]

Describing blind street sellers as unable to "labour for their daily bread," grouping them with "those who beg directly," Mayhew blurs the distinction between disabled traders and disabled beggars. For him, all lower-class blind people are, ultimately and necessarily, blind beggars.

Mayhew's understanding of blind sellers as beggars aligns him with the "arbitry" police sergeant. Whereas, in the case of the police officer, his belief in the dependency of lower-class blind people on charity justifies their imprisonment, Mayhew's conviction that the blind are incapable of supporting themselves through trade prompts him to criticize current laws against mendicity. Particularly concerned with the practice of imprisoning beggars, he characterizes the jailing of blind people as unusually cruel: "By the present law, for a blind man to beg is to be amenable to punishment, and to be subjected perhaps to the bitterest punishment which can be put upon him – imprisonment; to a deprivation of what may be his chief solace – the enjoyment of the fresh air; and to the rupture of the feeling which cannot but be comforting to such a man, that under his infirmity he still has the sympathies of his fellow-creatures."[42] Mayhew argues that the imprisonment of blind beggars unjustifiably adds to their deprivation, denying them both the comfort of charitable gestures and the pleasures of outdoor life. Charity is figured as highly valuable to blind people: it not only provides necessary financial support but creates and solidifies bonds between able-bodied and disabled citizens of London and between those with financial resources and those without.

When he explains that charity assures the blind man that "he still has the sympathies of his fellow-creatures," Mayhew echoes Charles Lamb's 1822 essay "A Complaint of the Decay of Beggars in the Metropolis." In it, Lamb describes a contemporary campaign to remove beggars from London's streets: "the old blind Tobits that used to line the wall of Lincoln's Inn Garden, before modern fastidiousness had expelled them, casting up their ruined orbs to catch a ray of pity, and (if possible) of light, with their faithful Dog Guide at their feet – whither are they fled? Or into what corners, blind as themselves, have they been driven, out of the wholesome air and sun-warmth? Immersed between four walls, in what withering poor-house do they endure the penalty of double darkness, where the chink of the dropt half-penny no more consoles ... Was daily spectacle like this to be deemed a nuisance, which called for legal interference to remove?"[43] Lamb's comments, published more than three decades before Mayhew's, are further proof of the longevity of public debate about the presence of blind beggars in London's streets. Like Mayhew, Lamb sees charity as both a necessary form of financial support and a source of social consolation. He also figures freedom of movement and contact with the wider community as indispensable facets of blind people's well-being.

Charity, mobility, community: Mayhew and Lamb are united in the belief that these are the blind beggars' rights. They are also united in their belief that the city street is the place where these rights can be most fully experienced and enjoyed. Whereas Lamb waxes poetic about blind Tobits and blind corners to make this point, Mayhew relies primarily on statements made by blind people. His interviewees repeatedly identify the street as a valued and important social space for lower-class blind people. For instance, a blind bootlace-seller tells Mayhew about meeting other blind people in London's streets:

> The blind people in the streets mostly know one another; they say they have all a feeling of brotherly love for another, owing to their being similarly afflicted. If I was going along the street, and had a guide with me that could see, they would say, "Here's a blind man or blind woman coming"; I would say, "Put me up to them so as I'll speak to them"; then I should say, as I laid my hand upon them, "Holloa, who's this?" they'd say, "I'm blind." I should answer, "So am I." "What's your name?" would be the next question. "Oh I have heard tell of you," most like, I would say. "Do you know so and so?" I would say, "Yes, he's coming to see me," or perhaps, "I'm going to see him on Sunday": then we say, "So you belong to any of the Institutions?" that's the most particular question of all; and if he's not a traveller, and we never heard tell of each one another, the first thing we would ask would be, "How did you lose your sight?" You see, the way in which the blind people in the streets gets to know one another so well, is by meeting at the houses of gentlemen when we goes for our pensions.[44]

Conversations of this kind, made possible by the presence of blind people in public spaces, demonstrate the extent to which the street accommodated the development and sustenance of communities of lower-class blind urbanites.[45]

Blind interviewees also comment on the pleasure they derive from travelling London's streets. In an interview conducted by Andrew Halliday, one of Mayhew's collaborators, a blind beggar discusses his mobility and his detailed knowledge of the city's geography: "'I don't often come down this way (Gower-street), only once a month. I always keep on this side of Tottenham Court-road; I never go over the road; my dog knows that. I am going down there,' (pointing); 'that's Chenies-street. Oh, I know where I am: next turning to the right is Alfred-street, the next to the left is Francis-street, and when

I get to the end of that the dog will stop; but I know as well as him.'"[46] Far from being a terra incognita, London, for this blind beggar, is a knowable and known space, fully accessible to and fully understood by blind individuals.

The mobility of blind people in the city is also the focus of an interview Mayhew conducts with a "blind informant" whose occupation is not given. Because it offers detailed evidence of the experiences of a blind Londoner and of contemporary cultural conceptions of blindness, I quote from this interview at length. Mayhew's subject, displaying a showmanship shared by several of Mayhew's most memorable interviewees, explains:

> Do you know, I can hear any substance in the street as I pass it by, even the lamp-post or a dead wall – anything that's the height of my head, let it be ever so small, just as well, and tell what it is as well as you can see. One night I was coming home – you'll be surprised to hear this – along Burlington-gardens, between twelve and one o'clock, and a gentleman was following me. I knew it was not a poor man by his walk, but I didn't consider he was watching me. I just heerd when I got between Sackville-street and Burlington-street. Oh, I knows every inch of the street, and I can go as quick as you can, and walk four mile an hour; know where I am all the while. I can tell the difference of the streets by the sound of my ear – a wide street and a narrow street – I can't tell a long street till I get to the bottom of it. I can tell when I come to an opening or a turning just by the click on the ear, without either my touching with hand or stick.[47]

The interviewee's knowledge of London's public spaces, his reference to his rapid pace, and his insistence on his possession of a knowledge of the city that is comparable to that of sighted individuals are all noteworthy. When he continues his story, he elaborates on his own skills and on the curiosity of the gentleman who follows him:

> Well, as I was saying, this gentleman was noticing me, and just as I come to turn up Cork-street, which, you know, is my road to go into Bond-street, on my way home; just as I come into Cork-street, and was going to turn round the corner, the ser-

geant of police was coming from Bond-street, at the opposite corner of Cork-street, I heerd him, and he just stopped to notice me, but I didn't know the gentleman was noticing me too. I whipped around the corner as quick as any man, that had his sight, and said, "Good night, policeman." I can tell a policeman's foot anywhere, when he comes straight along in his regular way while on his beat, and they all know it too. I can't tell it where there's a noise, but in the stillness of the night nothing could beat me. I can't hear the lamp-posts when there's a noise. When I said, "Good night, policeman," the gentleman whipped across to him, and says, "Is that man really blind?" and by this time I was half way up Cork-street, when the gentleman hallooed to me to stop; and he comes up, and says, says he 'Are you really blind?" The sergeant of the police was with him, and he says, "Yes, he is really blind, sir"; and then he says, "How is it that you go so cleverly along the street if you're blind?" Well, I didn't want to stop bothering with him, so I merely says, "I do far cleverer things than that. I can hear the lamp-post as well as you can see it." He says, "Yes, because you know the distance from one to another." The sergeant stood there all the time. And he says, "No, that can't be, for they're not a regular distance one from another." Then the gentleman says, "Now, could you tell if I was standing in the street when you passed me by?" I said, "Yes; but you mustn't stand behind the lamp-post to deceive me with the sound of the substance." Then he went away to try me, and a fine try we had … I had agreed to touch every substance as I went along and round the street to look for him; we always call it looking though we are blind. Well, when he had stood still the sergeant told me to go; … and on I went at the rate of about three mile an hour, and touched every lamp-post without feeling for them, but just struck them with my stick as I went by, without stopping, and cried out, "There's a substance." At last I come to him. There's a mews, you know, just by the hotel in Cork-street, and the gentleman stood between the mews and Clifford-street, in Cork-street; and when I come up to him, I stopped quite suddenly, and cried out "there's a substance." As I was offering to touch him with my stick, he drew back very softly, just to deceive me. Then he would have another try, but I picked him out again, but that

> wouldn't satisfy him, and he would try me a third time; and then, when I come up to him, he kept drawing back, right into the middle of the road. I could hear the stones scrunch under his feet; so I says, "Oh, that's not fair"; and he says, "well, I'm beat." Then he made me a present, and said that he would like to spend an hour some night with me again.[48]

Blindness, in this passage, is simultaneously a spectacle for upper-class consumption and a state that, far from being obvious or self-evident, requires close observation, repeated testing, and a police officer's corroboration. While the interviewee's pleasure in his mobility is evident, the fact that he is followed, questioned, and tested is difficult to view positively, primarily because it identifies him as a figure suspected either of faking disability or of misrepresenting his abilities.

Of course, the blind man's failure to conform to cultural expectations about the limited mobility of blind people attracts the inquisitive gaze not only of the unnamed gentleman but also of Mayhew. Although contributing to *London Labour and the London Poor*'s efforts to draw attention to the experiences of London's blind people, the interview necessarily reifies the cultural construction of disabled people as appropriate objects of public curiosity. Mayhew prefaces this interview with the declaration that "the blind are remarkable for the quickness of their hearing,"[49] a generalization that recalls his understanding of all lower-class blind people as unable to support themselves. On a more positive note, this interview allows a blind lower-class man to reflect at length on his experiences of disability in the city and on attitudes towards blindness, and also to share these reflections and experiences with a sighted and primarily middle-class reading public. By devoting significant space to the story of a blind man's skilled negotiation of city streets, Mayhew is also able to complicate conventional views of the blind beggar by suggesting that the challenges encountered by blind urbanites in their daily lives are social, rather than physical, in nature. The obstacles the blind face can take the relatively benign form of a gentleman's curiosity as well as the more threatening form of police-enforced laws against mendicity. To put this another way, lampposts and laneways do not impede a blind man's movement around the city but social values related to disability and mendicity can and do.

DISABILITY AND THE CITY

When Mayhew records and relates experiences lower-class blind people had in London's streets, he communicates messages not only about disability but also about the ideal attributes of urban culture. Mayhew expressed his passion for the cluttered streets of London in 1856 in *The Criminal Prisons of London*, a book he described as a "literary Atlas of the World of London."[50] In a section entitled "Of the London Streets, Their Traffic, Names and Character," Mayhew writes: "The thoroughfares of London constitute, assuredly, the finest and most remarkable of all the sights that London contains ... The same thoroughfares are, simply, the finest of all sights – in the world, we may say – on account of the never-ending and infinite variety of life to be seen in them."[51] Imagining streets filled with pedestrians and conveyances, "jammed as compactly together as the stones on the paving beneath," he asks, "Is there any sight in the Metropolis, moreover, so thoroughly *Londonesque* as this in its character?"[52] The "variety of life" found in streets is particularly central to Mayhew's celebration of them. Both his interest in street life and his passion for variety are apparent throughout *London Labour and the London Poor.* His enthusiasm for streets filled with the sights and sounds of diverse groups of people is, for instance, readily apparent in the description of the street market I quote at the beginning of this chapter. It is also something he shares with his subjects. For both Mayhew and his blind interviewees, the street is a site of economic production and exchange: of working, selling, and buying as well as travelling. Similarly, Mayhew and his subjects portray streets as places of social exchange both within various social groups and between them. Finally, and perhaps most important, they consider streets appropriate locales for begging and for charitable giving. Revealing the extent to which attitudes towards disabled urbanites are bound up in and informed by opinions about the appropriate uses and character of urban spaces, Mayhew and his interviewees are united both by their support of the rights of the disabled and their shared vision of what cities are and should continue to be.

A correspondence between opinions concerning blind beggars and views on the ideal character of urban life also exists among opponents to street begging, including, somewhat surprisingly, one of Mayhew's collaborators on *London Labour and the London*

Poor, the above-mentioned Andrew Halliday. The link between opposition to blind beggars and support for urban reform is apparent in a section from volume 4 on different forms of begging. In it, Halliday commends the London Mendicity Society for decreasing the number of street beggars but urges the police to increase their efforts: "The officers of the Mendicity Society have cleared the streets of nearly all the impostors, and the few who remain are blind men and cripples ... I cannot think, however, that the police exercise a wise discretion in permitting some of the more hideous of these beggars to infest the streets."[53] Comments like this one demonstrate the inextricability of ideas about disability, mendicity, and urban life. When Halliday expresses his aversion to disabled beggars and promotes a tightening of the campaign against mendicity, he implicitly envisions a new kind of city. If the changes Halliday desires were to take place, forms of social, economic, and charitable exchange associated with "blind men and cripples" would necessarily go with them, and the street, formerly associated with meeting, buying, and giving as well as travelling, would become a more definitively middle-class space and would take on the more narrow function of thoroughfare. In other words, the clearing of the "more hideous" disabled people from London's crowded streets would do more than remove groups of people Halliday deems unsightly from public spaces: it would also declutter, modernize, and homogenize street life, transforming streets into traffic arteries and facilitating the circulation of pedestrians, passengers, and goods.

Exemplifying the inextricability of ideas about disability and ideas about the city, *London Labour and the London Poor* is of value to historians, geographers, and disability theorists alike. The relationship between the city and disability has been the focus of recent scholarship by a number of geographers and disability theorists interested in the relationship between urban culture and bodily difference. Prominent among them is Brendan Gleeson.[54] In his 1999 book *Geographies of Disability*, Gleeson surveys the history of Western cities and examines the ways in which the conception and creation of urban spaces have shaped disabled people's daily lives. Gleeson, who sees the street as one of the most important arenas of disabled experience, explains that "much of the surviving evidence about disabled people in industrialism located them in street settings, usually as displaced figures marginalized from formal public spaces and domestic realms."[55] In an earlier article entitled "A

Geography for Disabled People?" Gleeson takes a less historical and more theoretical approach, arguing that "urban environments reinforce, rather than cause, the social marginalization experienced by physically impaired people."[56] Arguing that there is "no necessary correspondence between impairment and disability," he proposes that "far from being a natural human experience, disability is what may become of impairment as each society produces itself socio-spatially."[57]

London Labour and the London Poor corroborates Gleeson's vision of disability as a socio-spatial phenomenon. The blind people in Mayhew's study are visually impaired, but they are disabled by the culture in which they live. Neither disability nor the city are naturally occurring, nor are they independent of one another: ideas about the city shape ideas about disability and vice versa. They are, in other words, mutually constituted, historically specific products of cultural values and social practices. Born of and shaped by a society's valuation of certain types of bodies and certain modes of communal living, both disability and the city are cultural rather than natural. When blind beggars, central figures in Mayhew's portrait of London, are threatened with removal from the public spaces of the city it is not because their physical impairment prevents their survival in the material city; rather, it is because the society in which they live privileges and favours a certain kind of body and a certain formulation of public space.

Speaking out against efforts to remove blind lower-class people from London's public spaces, *London Labour and the London Poor* resists the marginalization of the blind in cities by increasing the visibility of the blind in the public press. Opposed to contemporary efforts to institutionalize impoverished disabled people, Mayhew asks his readers to look, and to look compassionately, at the visually impaired people with whom they share their streets. Similarly opposed to the creation of a new kind of street life, Mayhew celebrates the street's capacity to function as a site of charitable exchange, as meeting place and as market place. While his treatment of blind people as spectacles and his characterization of blind people as incapable of earning a living are problematic, Mayhew's advocacy of blind people's right to occupy urban spaces is compelling. It is, however, the combination of his voice and the voices of his subjects that makes the series' messages about disability and the city meaningful. A collaboration between an able-bodied, middle-class interviewer and his disabled, lower-class subjects, *London Labour and the London Poor* gains persuasiveness and credibility from its form. Providing impoverished blind subjects with a space in which to share their experiences and opinions with middle-class readers, Mayhew's interviews are a textual parallel to his vision of a charitable urban community, a community characterized by diversity and by the sharing of the city's public spaces between the rich and poor and between able-bodied and disabled urbanites.

NOTES

1 Mayhew, *London Labour and the London Poor*, 1:9–10.
2 Wordsworth, *The Prelude: A Parallel Text*, bk. 7, lines 608–22.
3 Ibid., bk. 7, line 74.
4 Ibid., bk. 7, line 158.
5 Ibid., bk. 7, lines 594–7.
6 See also Saklofske (this volume) on Wordsworth's reactions to the city. Eds.
7 Symons, "The Blind Beggar," lines 1–14.
8 See also Bailey (this volume) on journalists' purveying of elite cultural values. Eds.
9 Holmes, "Working (with) the Rhetoric of Affliction," 37. In this article, Holmes discusses ways in which Mayhew's interviews with blind people reveal "his utter fascination with blindness" (37). The article, which focuses on autobiographical narratives of disability and the telling of stories about disability, is largely reproduced in Holmes's book, *Fictions of Affliction*. In it, Holmes discusses Mayhew's "eager questions about blindness" (35) and the relationship between *London Labour* and "the cultural history of discrimination" (42). For a treatment of disability and Mayhew that focuses on narrative techniques and rhetoric, see Holmes. For a reading of Mayhew that focuses on utilitarian economics, see Gallagher, "The Body Versus the Social Body in the Works of Thomas Malthus and Henry Mayhew." For a discussion of Mayhew's "obsession with the streets" (89), see Maxwell, "Henry Mayhew and the Life of the Streets."
10 See also Fisher (this volume) and Land (this volume) on other kinds of appropriations of city spaces and streets. Eds.
11 Mayhew, *London Labour and the London Poor*, 1:xv.

12 Ibid.
13 Ibid.
14 The ethnographic dimensions of Mayhew's work have been discussed by, among others, Yeo, "Mayhew as a Social Investigator"; Prasch, "Photography and the Image of the Poor"; and Green, "Learning from Henry Mayhew."
15 Thackeray, quoted in Humpherys, *Travels into the Poor Man's Country*, ix.
16 *Eclectic Review*, quoted in Himmelfarb, "The Culture of Poverty," 715.
17 Mayhew's designation of poor areas as foreign lands may not accurately reflect the relationship between upper- and lower-class people, but it does accurately reflect the fact that housing in mid-Victorian London was geographically divided between rich areas and poor areas. Urban historian Gareth Stedman Jones has commented on the development of rich and poor neighbourhoods, noting that "nowhere had the process of segregation been carried further than in London. By 1861 it was practically complete" (*Outcast London,* 247).
18 Evidence of the presence of the poor and of beggars on streets used by the upper- and middle-classes can be found throughout the journalism, literature, and visual art of the Victorian period. See John Hollingshead's *Ragged London in 1861* and a collection of four volumes of facsimiled articles from Victorian magazines entitled *Poverty in the Victorian Age*. For discussions of the interaction between London's classes, see Himmelfarb, "Culture of Poverty"; Himmelfarb, *Idea of Poverty*; Jones, *Outcast London*; and Dyos and Reader, "Slums and Suburbs."
19 "The Plague of Beggars," *Fraser's Magazine*, 37 (1848): 395–402 at 395.
20 "Mendicity," *Quarterly Review*, 14 (1815): 120–45 at 140.
21 Ibid.
22 Ibid., 120.
23 Ibid., 131
24 "Charitable Institutions," *Westminster Review*, 2 (1824): 97–121 at 120.
25 Ibid., 119.
26 Owen, *English Philanthropy, 1660–1960*, 170.
27 For more information on charities for the blind, see Owen's seminal study *English Philanthropy, 1660–1960* and Lees and Ralph's "Charitable Provision to the Blind and Deaf People in Late Nineteenth-Century London."
28 Roberts, "Reshaping the Gift Relationship," 208.
29 Ibid., 204.
30 Ibid., 218.

31 See also Johnson (this volume) on aid societies for destitute women artists in late nineteenth-century Paris. Eds.
32 Roberts, "Reshaping the Gift Relationship," 231.
33 Mayhew, *London Labour and the London Poor*, 1.398.
34 Ibid., 393.
35 Ibid., 394.
36 Ibid.
37 Ibid.
38 Ibid., 342.
39 Ibid., 407.
40 Ibid., 322.
41 Ibid., 395.
42 Ibid.
43 Lamb, "A Complaint," 136–7.
44 Mayhew, *London Labour and the London Poor*, 1:398.
45 Holmes, who also discusses this passage, groups it with other evidence from *London Labour* of "what we might now call blind culture." See Holmes, "Rhetoric of Affliction," 37.
46 Mayhew, *London Labour and the London Poor*, 4:434.
47 Ibid., 1:403.
48 Ibid.
49 Ibid., 402.
50 Mayhew and Binny, *Criminal Prisons of London*, 64.
51 Ibid., 53.
52 Ibid., 54.
53 Halliday, *London Labour and the London Poor*, 4:431–3.
54 For different perspectives on disability and the discipline of geography, see Hahn, "Disability and the Urban Environment"; Butler and Parr, *Mind and Body Spaces*; and Chouinard and Grant, "On Being Not Even Anywhere Near 'The Project.'"
55 Gleeson, *Geographies of Disability*, 99.
56 Gleeson, "A Geography for Disabled People?" 393.
57 Ibid., 391.

9

A Contested City: Gwen John, Suzanne Valadon, and Women Artists in Fin-de-Siècle Paris[1]

JULIE JOHNSON

In a memoir recounting his years as an art student in Paris during the 1880s, John Shirley-Fox described the excitement of watching receiving day at the art galleries.[2] Standing with a crowd of students and those on "a mischief and 'ragging' bent," Shirley-Fox watched from the street as artists who had been accepted for exhibition at the Salon arrived with their submissions. What provoked the strongest reaction from the crowd was not an illustrious French painter, however, but the "appearance of some attractive-looking woman artist."[3] As Shirley-Fox noted, the woman involved in these encounters often found herself at the centre of a dangerous altercation: "She was at once surrounded by a group of the more enterprising onlookers ... Attempts were even made to secure by force whatever she might be carrying, and she had to put up with many jests and rather risky compliments before reaching the security of the interior of the building. Sometimes, when things got a bit too rowdy, the police would make a charge, and a general scuffle would ensue. Two or three people generally got arrested in these encounters."[4]

Perhaps it is unsurprising that a young woman's arrival at the gallery would be met with such aggressive enthusiasm by a group of predominantly young men. However, when viewed from the perspective of the aspiring woman artist, this scene presents us with a vivid example of conflict. The artist's work had been accepted to the Salon, an achievement that marked her official acceptance into the public world of art. However, as Shirley-Fox points out, this particular artist arrived on the steps of the gallery only to be met with tumultuous disrespect. She may have been a formal part of the art world, but her presence at the gallery was enough to cause a small riot on the streets of Paris.[5]

An example such as this underscores the connections between women artists and experiences of heightened tension as they emerged with increasing force into public life at the turn of the twentieth century. The art world at this time was undoubtedly entering a critical and momentous stage for women, and scholars have appropriately called them part of a generation that, as Sîan Reynolds has noted, "broke many taboos, crossed some literal and symbolic frontiers, and had benefited from the fairly sudden removal of the obstacles of the past."[6] However, historians have also noted that these developments did not often translate into critical or long-term success for women due to domestic responsibilities and ongoing institutional impediments that upheld the primacy of men in art.[7]

This chapter explores some of the ways in which women artists living in Paris at the fin de siècle faced a profession of contradictions, an unstable environment of difficulty and disappointment mixed with excitement and groundbreaking achievement. By examining the careers and work of two prominent artists at this time, Gwen John and Suzanne Valadon, I argue that their unstable entries into the public world of art found expression in the images they created. Both women captured the inconsistencies of female agency in the city not with depictions of urban landscapes or boulevard cafés but, rather, by reworking traditional themes of privateness – interior spaces and images of children. Their ambiguous portrayal of these domestic scenes was not part of the traditional oeuvre for women artists, however, but a way of re-evaluating the shifting and uncertain nature of female identity and selfhood at the fin-de-siècle. Poised at the intersection of opportunity and constraint, Gwen John and Suzanne Valadon were in a unique position to explore the elusive and highly changeable nature of their experience, and their artistic legacies shed new light onto not only the pathos but also the triumphs of life for women in a modern Paris on the eve of the twentieth century.

WOMEN ARTISTS IN THE CITY

Scholars of fin-de-siècle Paris often describe the city in terms of duality, and historians have long supported this view by examining its past through the lens of failure or fortune, as a series of crises or a tale of burgeoning optimism and opportunity.[8] The approach is part of a tendency, according to Jean-Pierre Bernard, to define "*les deux Paris*" by its "two inseparable dimensions" – "its materiality, walls, life, and organs, and its immateriality, its symbolic charge, and aura,"[9] and has resulted in a sizable body of literature that frequently characterizes the city's history as "beleaguered" or "belle."[10] Key proponents of Paris as a historical city of crisis, particularly during the second half of the nineteenth century, note the increased cultural obsession with crime and criminality and have argued that urban dangers of every variety, from homicide and arson to shoplifting and acid throwing, received frenzied attention from a proliferated mass press that aimed to increase its readership by reporting the shocking details of these stories.[11] Historians sympathetic to this approach also point to the political scandals and intrigues of the Boulanger Affair and the Dreyfus Affair, as well as to the painful legacy of the Franco-Prussian War, and argue that these crises created a sense of unease and disquiet among Parisians, who felt that their city and country were in a state of disrepair, and that they were suffering from a moral and intellectual decline – a *dégénérescence*, which doctors and medical experts diagnosed with increasing frequency.[12] Conversely, those who emphasize the pleasure and splendour of Paris at the turn of the twentieth century discuss the Universal Expositions, the Eiffel Tower, and the city's exciting boulevard culture of spectacle and consumerism, which were fundamental to the culture of the belle époque.[13] These accounts describe Paris as the vibrant and innovative cultural centre of Europe that attracted artists and writers from all over the world to join in its labyrinth of cafés, cabarets, and art salons and that stood as Europe's model of modernity as it faced the new century.[14]

Despite the richness these studies have brought to the field, some historians have noted the limitations of this dualistic approach. Mary Louise Roberts, for example, has cogently asked how historians of fin-de-siècle France might move beyond the dichotomy of "cultural crisis or belle époque" in order to explore new avenues of interpretation.[15] In her study about French women at the fin de siècle, Roberts examines the intersections between these two modes of analysis and shows how the forces of crisis, pleasure, and spectacle actually coalesced at the end of the nineteenth century and created a space in which Parisians, particularly women, could strike out in new and creative ways.[16] By examining the interrelated nature of *les deux Paris,* Roberts has demonstrated how the combination of impulses, both positive and negative, created a dynamic public and urban space in which women could reimagine and rearticulate their sense of self in the late nineteenth century. While this approach illuminates the unique possibilities that existed for women in a complex urban landscape, it also indicates that fin-de-siècle Paris was a contested city, one fraught with challenges for women living in the French capital. If the mingling of danger and pleasure, crisis and belle époque culture, had stimulating results for women's emergence into urban spaces, it had confusing and ambiguous effects as well.

Fin-de-siècle Paris undoubtedly played a crucial role in the professionalization of women artists, and, as art historians have demonstrated, it became a leading centre of art and the principal destination for women interested in an art education.[17] According to some scholars, the late nineteenth and early twentieth centuries were akin to the "glory days" for women artists in France, who received artistic training and education and possessed an "optimism" about their potential for careers as artists.[18] Despite the fact that conditions at the most traditional and institutionalized levels of art education were slow to improve during this period – the École des Beaux-Arts did not permit women to enter until 1897 – this did not mean that young women in the arts were not publicly active in Paris. They emerged through a considerable, and ever-increasing number of ateliers and academies, such as the Académie Julian, which, as art historians have argued, stressed "competitiveness and innovation" in its arts program and provided women with an art education that was comparable to that of men.[19] Many women's art associations also emerged at this time and functioned as venues through which artists could gain important professional exposure at exhibits and salons. Some, like the Union des femmes peintres et sculpteurs, combined this practical assistance with a wider, more politicized agenda and played an active role in the fight to gain access to the École des Beaux-Arts.[20] They helped women advance their careers and expand their professional circle, and they provided much needed emotional and artistic support.[21] By 1900, both through women's art associations and other venues, such as the Paris Salon and the Société nationale des Beaux-Arts, women began to exhibit their work with increasing frequency.[22] Numerous booklets and articles described the opportunities for women artists in the city, with titles such as "Lady Art Student's Life in Paris" and *A Woman's Guide to Paris*, which the author noted had been written "in response to the ever-increasing tide of women visiting the French capital alone or with other women, in order to provide them with practical advice on independent life in the city."[23]

These factors indicate that women encountered an art world of increasing optimism, dynamism, and opportunity in fin-de-siècle Paris. It was a centre of artistic training, study, and travel, where women could enjoy some of the same privileges as their male counterparts. However, there were other women's art societies in the city that had a decidedly different focus and that illuminate some of the difficulties women artists often faced as they fought to survive in Paris.[24] One such group was the Association mutuelle des femmes artistes de Paris, a cooperative organization created in 1894 by women painters, sculptors, engravers, writers, and musicians living in Paris, who, according to their statutes, formed in order to "allocate a financial allowance to participating members of the Association who, due to illness, find it absolutely, but temporarily, impossible to carry out their profession."[25] Their statutes extensively outline the payment of dues and the method by which artists who became ill could then draw assistance for a period of up to six months.[26] The group limited its active membership to five hundred women, who were required to be residents of Paris, under fifty years old, and of good health at the time of enrolment.[27] Unlike the lofty goals of the Union des femmes peintres et sculpteurs, there is nothing in the statutes of the Association mutuelle that describe a vision for expanding the influence of women artists in Paris or for providing crucial professional support through exhibitions. Instead, like other cooperative organizations of the time, they joined together to defend themselves against the pitfalls of life in the city and the financial uncertainty connected with their profession. Articles from their statutes reveal the dismal lives some of these women led. Members were prohibited from collecting assistance if they were late with their dues or if they were recovering from an attempted suicide.[28]

This organization is striking in several ways. First, the Parisian women of the Association mutuelle described themselves as working professionals who relied on their artistic livelihoods for financial support and economic survival: this was not a social club.

Félicien Fagus, writing for *La Revue Blanche* in 1901, described the artists of the Association mutuelle in this way: "They are little hands; people who ... show themselves unashamed of being craftsmen, hands working to live, that need to live from this work ... labourers: professionals."[29] Fagus described these artists as proud and independent workers struggling to make a livelihood for themselves, not women of leisure engaged in a hobby or artists dedicated to the cause of women in art. However, it is also clear from the Association mutuelle's statutes and from its existence as a cooperative that there were women artists in the city who suffered from depression, illness, and financial uncertainty: that they found it necessary to include an article that excluded attempted suicide cases from collecting benefits speaks to the prevalence of this plight among its members. Its statutes indicate that the women of the Association mutuelle did not explicitly come together in order to advance their careers but, rather, to provide themselves and each other with enough financial stability to make working possible. The Association mutuelle and its emphasis on providing aid speaks at once to the hardships faced by women who struggled to be artists in Paris, yet also to their independence and determination to create solutions for survival in the city.

Indeed, Paris could be a difficult and trying city to live in as a woman, a fact that was not lost on women journalists of the day. Marguerite Durand's paper *La Fronde* included many articles that underscored the complex atmosphere of opportunity and defeat that faced women professionals living in Paris.[30] Their reports often emphasized the struggles of work, motherhood, and independent life for women as well as the decidedly difficult nature of trying to do these things in Paris. They argued that living in the city was a trial for many women: relationships were harder to find and sustain, work was more difficult to secure, families were harder to raise, and basic survival was simply more challenging.[31] They also devoted articles to the "suicide problem," which, in the late nineteenth century, had become a growing concern discussed by medical professionals and those in the developing field of sociology, most notably by Emile Durkheim.[32] Theorists argued that suicide was a modern scourge upon France, particularly in the large cities of the nation, where life was often intense and challenging and resulted in an increased number of nervous conditions and neurasthenia.[33] The journalists at *La Fronde* believed that suicide was an increasing problem for Parisian women in particular, one they described as an "epidemic:"[34] "It is a sinister sign of the times: the constant spread and growth of suicides. It is not only men who find in the void an escape from their fruitless efforts and their dashed hopes; it is not only the elderly weary from poverty; it is women, young women."[35] These reports about the difficulties of life for Parisian women appeared alongside articles dedicated to the successes and triumphs of the burgeoning feminist movement in France, and they paint an interesting yet ambiguous image of life for women in the capital. By reading reports on the pitfalls, drawbacks, and dangers of urban life, Parisian women could see their city through the eyes of fellow Parisiennes, in all of its complexity. Undoubtedly, articles of this nature were part of a larger project as women fought for parity in the workforce and control over their professional lives.[36] However, these issues also reveal that Parisian women had and expressed concerns that were urban in focus and that they utilized their expanding public voices to convey these concerns to a growing audience.

GWEN JOHN, SUZANNE VALADON, AND THE REARTICULATION OF PRIVATE LIFE

Gwen John and Suzanne Valadon were two artists who lived and worked in late nineteenth-century Paris and traversed the unsettling and conflicted path of urban life in distinctive ways. They came from different socio-economic and educational backgrounds, had different nationalities, and did not travel in the same social circles, but both experienced the difficulties of life as a professional artist and as a woman in Paris. Gwen John (1876–1939), the daughter of a Welsh solicitor, successfully studied at the progressive Slade School of Fine Art in London from 1895 to 1898.[37] After graduation, she travelled through Europe with her women friends and eventually took up residence in Paris, where she lived and worked for the rest of her life. Suzanne Valadon (1865–1938) was the illegitimate daughter of a working-class charwoman who grew up and lived in bohemian Montmartre.[38] She became a single mother at eighteen and worked as a model for artists in order to support her son. It was partly through these connections that her artistic career flourished, and, although she did not have the luxuries of an art education, she became a successful and well known artist.

Both women became professional artists who exhibited their work in galleries and art societies in Paris and other urban centres but also relied on their jobs as artist models to make extra money.

Gwen John became the muse for Rodin, and Suzanne Valadon famously sat for Renoir and Toulouse-Lautrec. This was a common source of employment for struggling women artists at the fin de siècle and, as art historians have noted, captures the tension and conflict within their profession during these years: in order to maintain their independence as professional artists, some had to depend not only on their talents as creators of art but also on their ability to act as muses for other, usually male, artists.[39] Paris, particularly Montmartre, had become the centre of a bustling model industry in the late nineteenth century, and at the Place Pigalle "would-be models draped themselves around the fountain dressed up in brightly coloured rags as nymphs, cherubs, and Greek Gods."[40] These "model markets" emerged in any quarter of Paris that was frequented by artists. Modelling was not just a rite of passage for would-be artists but was also a serious profession for many Parisian women.[41] The woman artist-as-model became a pervasive and provocative cultural image in the late nineteenth century, one that was discussed and described in the popular literature and fiction of the day. Zola's *L'Oeuvre* showcased the seedy underworld of Parisian artists and their models, and in books such as Georges Montorgueil's *La parisienne peinte par elle-même*, the model was described as "art's humble servant" and catalogued in all her various "types" – the young debutant, the chatter-box, and the "inconsiderate" and "sentimental" poser.[42]

John's work as a model was necessary, in part, to help pay for her rented rooms and studio apartments in Paris, which formed a fundamental part of her urban and independent life.[43] John's brother, the successful artist Augustus John, remembered his sister's city dwellings as "slums" and "dungeons ... into which no ray of light could ever penetrate," but he also noted that "Gwen was delighted with her new quarters and would not listen to my arguments. She never did."[44] While it is not surprising that John would perhaps be proud of her meagre lodgings when dealing with her brother, these apartments were a considerable financial responsibility.[45] During the early years of the twentieth century, John became increasingly known for her work with small, intimate interiors, which, according to the art historian Alicia Foster, was part of a larger stylistic art movement at this time. Foster has argued that John's images of her studio apartments should be read not only as "the sign for her individual life, [but placed] in relation to, or in conversation with, the work of her contemporaries."[46] These contemporaries included both Scandinavian artists and the French *peintres d'intérieurs*, whose work with the Symbolist interior influenced John's own art.[47] John's professional motivations for choosing to paint interior spaces have been overshadowed by some art historians who argue that she was a recluse, and who have supported this claim by relying upon a heavily quoted passage from a letter she wrote to her friend: "As to whether I have anything worth expressing, that is apart from the question. I may never have anything to express, except this desire for a more interior life."[48] Although her paintings of private, domestic spaces do emphasize themes of interiority, John's apartments were also a busy public and professional space, where she hosted patrons and potential customers to view and purchase her art, and where she eventually had models sit for her. Her relationship to the interior was multifaceted and much more complex – professionally, it was an artistic style that demonstrated her knowledge of and connection to the art world of the fin de siècle; as an artistic theme, it was a way for John to explore the nature of interiority and privacy in the midst of an urban setting; and, practically, the interior of her home was also her office and studio, a place where she hosted and conducted her work but that was difficult to maintain. John's images of interior spaces, therefore, are compelling examples of a woman's shifting relationship with both public and private life and demonstrate the ambiguities of her urban existence.

In *A Corner of the Artist's Room in Paris* (1907), for example, the studio is at once a pleasing, feminine, and cheerful private space as well as a vacant place of work. The colours are warm and inviting and create a feeling of peace and tranquility, but the empty chair and sparse furnishings highlight the solitude and frugality of John's home. An umbrella and a jacket rest against a chair as artistic props but also serve as the sole signs that the room is inhabited, which creates a feeling of both presence and absence. A prominent window is closed to the city outside, and although it brings light into the room, it also creates an atmosphere of separation, detachment, and stuffiness. This interior was John's home and workspace, her refuge and retreat, and also her subject matter. It represented not only her financial independence and freedom as an artist in Paris but also the hardships inherent in that struggle. In *Woman Dressing* (1907), John articulates the theme of isolation more explicitly. Again, John depicts one corner of her room, with a window and a few pieces of furniture. In this sketch there is also a female figure, who is nude, seated on a chair, and facing the window. Her back is to the viewer and her head is hung, which allows us to gaze upon her unchallenged. It is impossible to determine whether she is merely dressing, as the title indicates, or lost in a moment of quiet reflection or even sadness. The figure's identity is also unclear – it could be the artist herself, or a model – and her nudity adds to the feeling of vulnerability and intimacy. Her posture and static position next to the table suggest that they are somehow similar, a pair of inanimate objects. In this image, John captures the privacy of an interior space but also communicates a powerful sense of longing, loneliness, and isolation. The presence of the female figure adds an elusive element: she is dressing herself, but this action is at odds with the ominous and alienating atmosphere of the interior.

Both of these images demonstrate John's use of interior spaces to convey several themes at ones – freedom and isolation, independence and hardship, public life and private life. In a review of a Gwen John exhibit at the Tate in London, David Boyd Haydock notes: "Some have seen Gwen John ... as a feminist icon: an embodiment of sadness, loneliness, incipient madness. Perhaps it was the lack of real recognition in her lifetime, or the fact of having worked in the shadow of great men, but the truth is that her work remains enigmatic, curious, and out of reach."[49] I would suggest that the curious and elusive nature of John's early images of interiors are connected to the complex ways in which she traversed professional and urban life as a woman artist in fin-de-siècle Paris, specifically the trials and ambiguities of this journey. John worked as a paid model for Rodin and, through him, made important contacts and artistic strides, but, ultimately, she was abandoned and suffered from his patronage.[50] She was able to exhibit and sell some of her work, which brought her joy and professional credibility, but it was rarely enough to truly support her life in Paris. John's images of her rented rooms and studio apartments are compelling examples of these early years in the city, specifically, the ways in which she simultaneously invested images of privateness and interiority with a sense of alienation and vacancy, on the one hand, and with a powerful sense of intimacy, self-possession, and self-knowledge, on the other. In this way, her depictions of intimate spaces represent more than feminine themes of domestic interiority or even feminist themes of struggle: they do both simultaneously, and through this process, depict profound ambiguity.

In a similar way, Valadon infused her work with the contradictions and ambiguities of a woman artist. Unlike John, who maintained a tentative relationship with Paris, Valadon was deeply entrenched in the bohemian world of Montmartre at the fin de siècle, and it was here that she fuelled her artistic training and style by interacting with the innovative French artists of the late nineteenth century.[51] She became famous, some said notorious, for her unique and unusual approach to painting the female body, a subject that had been the traditional domain of male artists. Contemporary art critics wrote that she "tortured" the academy with her nudes: their "ugly anatomy" possessed a sense of "fiendish sensual pleasure."[52] As one critic wrote: "[Valadon] always paints with the same intense talent ... but with such rage!"[53] Indeed, art historians have noted the brazen and unforgiving nudity in Valadon's representations of the female body, an effect she achieved with an aggressive incorporation of line and colour.[54] She created a sense of heaviness by tracing limbs, hands, and breasts in thick black lines, and she often depicted her subjects in awkward positions, which gave them a decidedly masculine nakedness.

Valadon also applied this style to the image of the child, which, unlike the female nude, had traditionally been a popular subject for women artists. Unlike typical images of children, such as those of Elizabeth Vigée-Lebrun or Mary Cassatt, who depicted them at robust play or in loving embrace with their mothers, Valadon's portraits of children challenged the traditional, warm gaze of a mother. Her son Maurice's "skinny body and air of suffering" evoked empathy in her,[55] and her sketches of him demonstrated her interest in capturing the body's unique individuality and identity. In sketches such as *Maurice Utrillo enfant, nu, debout, jouant du pied avec une cuvette* (1894), (figure 9.1), Valadon draws her son isolated, alone, and naked. He is placed in a cold, empty, and lonely room, and his body is thin and frail. He looks neglected as he plays forlornly with a pot on the ground and is removed from the cozy domestic scene that typically acted as the backdrop for children in paintings. His arms and legs appear particularly thin, set in stark contrast to his over-sized and awkward-looking hands. In images such as this, art historians have noted that Valadon explored the physical dejection, despair, and poor health of the child's body, which was more profound because she placed this relentless gaze upon her own child.[56] As a single parent, Valadon had to provide for her son while trying to develop her artistic career, and her images of Maurice captures the rigours and trials of their lives in Montmartre. As Thérèse Rosinsky has commented: "Valadon's art and work are inseparable ... It was her daily life – the familiar faces of her family and friends, the gardens and landscapes of her neighbourhood – that she retraced for her viewers."[57] Valadon used a powerful and blunt realism to show things as they were. As she noted: "One should never put suffering in drawings, but all the same one has nothing without pain. Art (is here) to eternalize this life that we hate."[58]

Like her images of the female nude, Valadon's sketches of children combine powerful and yet contradictory themes – a mother with the strength and conviction to depict her child and their life together in all its grim reality but also with the tenderness to reveal his intimate and private identity. In her sketch of Maurice, Valadon captures this intimacy in his face, which appears gentle and soft against his oddly misshapen body. Valadon's sparse but deliberate use of line is capable of capturing Maurice's delicacy, awkwardness, and air of introspection. As with Valadon's images of the female nude, however, looking upon this young, frail body also creates a sense of uneasiness and tension for the viewer: his naked vulnerability and awkward pose, as well as his downcast glance, all combine to create an effect that is almost heart-breaking in its loneliness and yet powerfully touching in its ability to communicate emotion. In Valadon's nude sketches of children, she was able to demonstrate some of the trials of childhood and motherhood in late nineteenth-century Paris. Thérèse Rosinsky has argued that, in her sketches of Maurice, Valadon never placed herself at his side, "choosing her role as artist over that of mother."[59] Indeed, her portrayal of children is unconventional in terms of arrangement and composition, which made her unique among artists at this time, but her love and affection for Maurice still resonate in her art. In addition to the stark sense of realism, her sad sketch of Maurice is also a powerfully intimate and honest depiction of a son, seen through the eyes of a mother who was not afraid to explore her child's humanity and individuality. In this way, Valadon's early images of children demonstrate both the difficulties of single motherhood in Paris and the liberating ability to portray the truths of this experience through

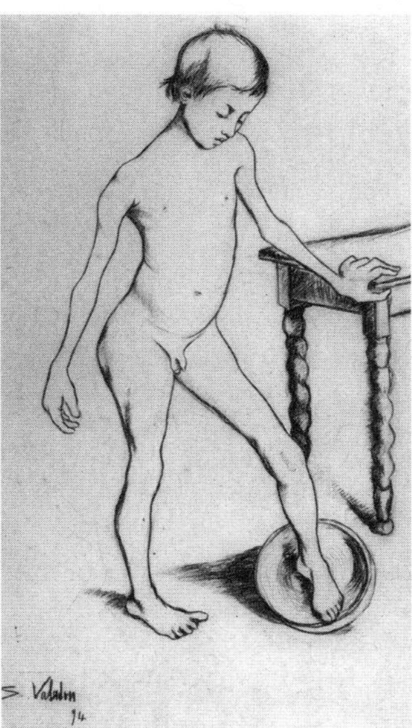

Figure 9.1
Suzanne Valadon, *Maurice Utrillo enfant, nu, debout, jouant du pied avec une cuvette*, 1894. Pencil on paper.

art. By casting her harsh and honest gaze upon the body of her son, and depicting his individuality, Valadon was able to rearticulate the traditional and private role of motherhood and examine the challenges she experienced as both a mother and an artist.

CONCLUSION

Women artists at the fin de siècle were often grouped within the larger cultural phenomenon of the "new woman," a late nineteenth-century model of womanhood that represented independence, education, and professional opportunities.[60] Reynolds has called for historians to explore this "wider 1900 generation of French women … in order to see what there was about them that was truly 'new.'"[61] What was "new" for women artists living in Paris at this time was not simply that they could fight for work and an independent life in the fin-de-siècle city but that this process was often profoundly contradictory and ambiguous. Although historians and art scholars have carefully articulated the various ways in which women attempted and eventually succeeded at entering a male-dominated art realm, they have paid less attention to the ways in which life for Parisian women artists at the end of the nineteenth century was not just a hard-won struggle for professional independence and equality. Life for women in *les deux Paris* could also be ambiguous, filled with anxiety and a sense of imperilled and confused identity.

Harold Mah defines these aspects of identity in terms of multiplicity, complexity, and "phantasy," and he argues that, throughout the modern era in France, concepts of selfhood were caught up in contradiction and "intense cultural and political conflict."[62] Historians concerned with questions of gender can benefit from this model of an ambivalent and multifaceted understanding of identity, particularly in its application to the ways in which women saw themselves and responded to their surroundings in the contested urban spaces of fin-de-siècle Paris. This is not to negate their significant achievements in an expanding and increasingly modern city at the turn of the twentieth century but, rather, to demonstrate the inherent instability and uncertainty involved in this process. For women artists, these complexities appeared in some of the institutions and practices of the Parisian art world, such as women's art cooperatives and their jobs as models for other artists, which were encouraging and yet limiting experiences. Themes of ambiguity also appeared in the art they produced. Although Gwen John and Suzanne Valadon did not often paint typical pictures of the urban landscape – its streets, markets, or cafés – their images of interior spaces and children also represented their complex lives as urban professionals in fin-de-siècle Paris. Both of these artists infused their images with themes of self-knowledge and intimacy as well as alienation and uncertainty, and, in the process, they cast their traditional experiences of private life in a decidedly new and ambiguous light.

NOTES

1 Early drafts and portions of this chapter were first presented at the "City Limits" conference at the University of Manitoba and at the Society for French Historical Studies' fifty-third conference in Houston. The author would like to thank the editors of "City Limits" for their valuable sug-

gestions and comments, and her panel participants at the SFHS conference. Karen Offen, Kristen Stromberg Childers, Geoff Read, and Daniella Sarnoff all provided helpful feedback and commentary. The author is also grateful to her doctoral thesis advisor, Harold Mah, for his many years of guidance. The Social Sciences and Humanities Research Council of Canada, the Ontario Graduate Scholarship Program, and Queen's University have provided generous research support.

2 Shirley-Fox, *Art Student's Reminiscences*, 153–4.

3 Ibid.

4 Ibid.

5 See also Perkins (this volume) on the smoother assimilation of women into the cultural and intellectual life of Edinburgh. Eds.

6 Reynolds, "Running Away to Paris," 340.

7 Chadwick, *Women, Art, and Society*; Borzello, *A World of Our Own*; Harris and Nochlin, *Women Artists, 1550–1950*; Tufts, *Our Hidden Heritage*.

8 Charles Rearick has commented on this continuing trend in "Introduction: Paris Revisited."

9 Bernard, *Les deux Paris*, 12.

10 Barrows, *Distorting Mirrors*, 2.

11 Weber, *France*, 107; Kalifa, *L'encre et le sang*, and *Crime et culture au XIXe siècle;* Chevalier, *Laboring Classes and Dangerous Classes*; Shapiro, *Breaking the Codes*. See also Schorske, *Fin-de-Siècle Vienna*; and, for the case of London, Walkowitz, *City of Dreadful Delight*. [See also Bailey (this volume) on other mid-nineteenth-century journalistic responses to the perception of crises in Paris. Eds.]

12 Shapiro, *Breaking the Codes*, 2. See also Goldstein, *Console and Classify;* Nye, *Crime, Madness, and Politics in Modern France*; Cahm, *The Dreyfus Affair*; Forth, *The Dreyfus Affair and the Crisis of French Manhood*.

13 Rearick, *Pleasures of the Belle Époque*; Seigel, *Bohemian Paris*.

14 See also Perkins (this volume) on Edinburgh's face of modernity. Eds.

15 Roberts, *Disruptive Acts*, 2.

16 She emphasizes the ties between "the era's cultural crisis and its penchant for performance" and demonstrates the ways in which theatricality was not merely part of the splendour and entertainment of the *belle époque* but was also an act of "subversion" and disruption, used by women journalists as a means of articulating female identity. See Roberts, *Disruptive Acts*, 1–17.

17 Garb, *Sisters of the Brush*; Benstock, *Women of the Left Bank*; Weisberg and Becker, *Overcoming All Obstacles*; Sauer, *L'entrée des femmes*;

Fehrer, *The Julian Academy, Paris, 1868–1939*; Cherry, *Painting Women*; Campbell Orr, *Women in the Victorian Art World*; Swinth, *Painting Professionals*; Reynolds, *Paris-Edinburgh*.

18 Borzello, *A World of Our Own*, 128 and chap 4.

19 Weisberg, "Women of the Académie Julian," in Weisberg and Becker, *Overcoming All Obstacles*, 13.

20 Garb, *Sisters of the Brush*, 4.

21 Ibid., 6. For the statutes of the Union, which include these points, see *Journal des femmes artistes*, 3–4.

22 Charlotte Yeldham has compiled a collection of statistics and tables on women's art exhibits in her two-volume study of women artists in France and Britain during the nineteenth century. See *Women Artists in Nineteenth-Century France and England*, 2:201–8.

23 Quoted in Foster, *Gwen John*, 19. See also Holland, "Lady Art Student's Life in Paris"; Alcott-Nieriker, *Studying Art Abroad*; Belloc, "Lady Artists in Paris," 378.

24 See also Warne (this volume) on charitable institutions for the disabled in nineteenth-century London. Eds.

25 Article 2, *Association mutuelle des femmes artistes de Paris: Statuts*, 5.

26 Article 23, ibid., 10.

27 Article 6, ibid., 6.

28 Article 13, ibid., 8.

29 Fagus, "Association Mutuelle des Femmes Artistes de Paris," 144–5.

30 Studies of *La Fronde* include Roberts, *Disruptive Acts*; Rabaut, *"La Fronde" féministe*.

31 Some of the issues they discussed revolved around the nature of personal relationships in Paris. In one article, a reporter noted the growing disparity in the marriage rate between couples in Paris and the rest of France, and commented that, out of one thousand marriages, approximately one-eighth survived beyond their silver wedding anniversary in Paris, while one-quarter of the nation's couples surpassed the same milestone. The reporter expressed concern over this gap and argued that reasons for the divide included the weak moral fibre of Parisians and their shorter life expectancy. See "Ce que dure le Mariage," *La Fronde*, 18 December 1898, 2. Writers at *La Fronde* also discussed the insufficiency of women's wages and the hardships involved in making ends meet in the city. As Aline Valette noted in her column "Le Travail des Femmes," many of the city's women worked for "starvation wages," which provided them with hardly enough money to pay bills and have sufficient left over to feed themselves and their families. Valette indicated that an average yearly

salary for many working-class women in 1898 was about 900 francs, and, after deducting rent and basic utilities, which cost approximately 435 francs in Paris, she calculated that "1 franc 27" was left for food each day. Elsewhere, however, she estimated that basic food costs would have been about "1 franc 80" per day, thus demonstrating the inability for some to keep themselves afloat. She also noted that this was the best scenario and did not account for unexpected expenses, such as illness or other emergencies. See Aline Valette, "Le travail des femmes – les 'tireuses d'aiguelle,'" *La Fronde*, 19 December 1897, and "Le travail des demmes – salaires de famine" *La Fronde*, 3 February 1898.

32 Durkheim, *Suicide*.

33 Studies such as these depicted Paris as an urban centre that threatened all social classes: the poor were faced with the struggles of basic survival, while the wealthy and leisured had to deal with an excess of excitement, indulgence, and luxury. Theorists believed that these "dangers" were responsible for agitating and unnerving urban dwellers to the point of causing them to harm themselves or others. See Proal, *Le crime et le suicide passionnels*, 304. For other contemporary accounts of suicide, see Garrison, *Le suicide dans l'antiquité;* Sarty, *Le suicide*.

34 Marie-Louise Néron, "Epidémie de suicides," *La Fronde*, 3 May 1898.

35 Marcelle Tinayre, "La nostalgie de la mort," *La Fronde*, 23 January 1898.

36 Coffin, *The Politics of Women's Work*; Stewart, *Women, Work, and the French State*; Zylberberg-Hocquard and Diebolt, *Femmes et travail au dix-neuvième siècle*.

37 Foster, *Gwen John*, 77. Other studies of Gwen John include Langdale, *Gwen John*; Roe, *Gwen John*; Thomas, *Portraits of Women*; Langdale and Jenkins, *Gwen John*; Chitty, *Gwen John, 1876–1939*.

38 Studies of Suzanne Valadon include Rose, *Mistress of Montmartre*; Fondation Pierre Gianadda, *Suzanne Valadon*; Rosinsky, *Suzanne Valadon*; Storm, *The Valadon Drama;* Rey, *Suzanne Valadon*; Mathews, *Passionate Discontent*; Betterton, *Looking On*.

39 Dawkins, *The Nude in French Art and Culture*; Lathers, *Bodies of Art*.

40 Rose, *Mistress of Montmartre*, 39–41.

41 Lathers, *Bodies of Art*, 42. See also Walker, *The Invention of the Model*.

42 Zola, *L'Oeuvre*; Montorgueil, *La parisienne peinte par elle-même*, 123–32.

43 For a detailed description of the different addresses and places where Gwen John lived between 1898 and 1911, see Foster, *Gwen John*, 19–29.

44 John, "Gwendolen John," 236–40.

45 In Clive Holland's article "Lady Art Students' Life in Paris," (233) he breaks down the average costs for a few years' art study in Paris in 1903: "cost of painting materials, etc., 125 francs (£5); furnished rooms, 750 francs (£30); attendance, 100 francs (£4); cost of living, 625 francs (£25). And to this can be added at least the sum of 250 francs (£10) for incidentals. This amounts to a total of 1,850 francs (£94) per annum."

46 Foster, *Gwen John*, 42.

47 Ibid., 46–50.

48 McEwen, "A Room of Her Own," 111–14.

49 David Boyd Haydock, "The Troubled Genius of Augustus John (and His More Talented Sister): People Are Like Shadows." *Times Literary Supplement*, 22 October 2004, 18.

50 Chitty, *Gwen John*, 71.

51 Rosinsky, *Suzanne Valadon*, 28.

52 Basler, *Suzanne Valadon*, 11.

53 André Salmon, *Montjoie*, décembre 1913, cited in Robert Rey, *Suzanne Valadon*, 14–15.

54 Rosinsky, *Suzanne Valadon*, 77–9.

55 Florent Fels, *L'Art vivant de 1900 à nos jours*, vol. 2, (Geneva: Pierre Cailler, 1950), cited in Rose, *Mistress of Montmartre*, 87.

56 Rosinsky, *Suzanne Valadon*, 13.

57 Ibid., 12.

58 *Suzanne Valadon ou l'Absolu*, Archives of the Musée National d'Art Moderne, CNAC Georges Pompidou, Paris, cited in Rosinsky, *Suzanne Valadon*, 25.

59 Rosinsky, *Suzanne Valadon*, 33.

60 Studies of the new woman as a cultural phenomenon include Holmes and Tarr, *A Belle Epoque?*; Elliott, "New and Not so 'New Women' on the London Stage," 33–57; Showalter, *Sexual Anarchy*; Stansell, *American Moderns*; Roberts, *Disruptive Acts*.

61 Siân Reynolds, review of *Disruptive Acts*, by Mary Louise Roberts, *H-France Review* 3, 61 (June 2003). Available at http://www.h-france.net/vol3reviews/reynolds.html (viewed 17 February 2009).

62 Mah, *Enlightenment Phantasies*, 12.

PART THREE

Redressing Boundaries

PREFACE

Redressing Boundaries

BERNARD DOV COOPERMAN

Students of the urban, whether backwards-facing historians or future-oriented planners, have recognized and often celebrated diversity as inherent in the city environment. But urban heterogeneity is not a simple or univalent phenomenon. Diversity of function, a necessary by-product of urban specialization, leads inevitably to unequal economic status.[1] Both specialization and inequality are then often linked to complex patterns of identity: ethnicity and religion are reinforced by, and in turn themselves strengthen, functional, social, and economic distinctions. Indeed, identity and vocation are often confused in observers' minds; cause and effect become hopelessly entangled; and ascribed status comes to be seen as immutable. Members of certain groups are assumed, by their very nature, to be suited to specific social roles. Finally, this diversity will be expressed spatially and fixed in the city's very contours. Market streets and ghettos, industrial zones and ethnic neighbourhoods: considerations of functional efficiency and of status combine to shape the city as space as well as concept. Diversity draws the urban map, and the city dweller must learn to discriminate carefully in order to find his or her way, and sometimes even to survive.

The lines drawn by heterogeneity and difference cannot, however, be absolute. If they remain permanently uncrossable, the city will die. In the energized and crowded urban environment, communities inevitably interact – peacefully for the most part, but at times of crisis in tense and even violent confrontation.[2] Though municipal government can be co-opted by one or another powerful faction, it must ultimately seek to control violence and help the civic organism to achieve equilibrium. The communal elements in a living city cannot live in total isolation one from the other. Interaction between neighbourhoods and populations is the necessary result of the city's inherent diversity. The inherent tension between specialized difference and necessary interdependence is what energizes the urban environment, holding crowds in check while promoting dynamic and constantly shifting patterns.

The chapters in this section examine both boundary establishment and boundary crossing, the twin processes so central to the urban dynamic, during Europe's early modern period. Between the sixteenth and the eighteenth centuries, marked urban growth created new problems of city governance and strained traditional solutions to the breaking point. Whether or not we accept that this was a period in which organs of government sought to impose greater control on the individual, there was clearly a need for increasingly sophisticated mechanisms of control in the more and more crowded urban environment. The needed new forms of equilibrium were both imposed from above and created from below, as these chapters demonstrate.

Perhaps the most basic boundary issue was the required definition of the city itself. This was not a simple matter of geographical markers. It also necessitated rulings about who might, and who might not, lay claim to the rights and privileges of the collective. Population growth and military technology gradually made the medieval wall obsolete, but the issue of jurisdiction remained crucial to urban privilege and functioning.[3] Who belonged within the municipality's purview? Which burghers had special rights in matters of tax and trade? And who among the rising numbers of indigents could lay claim to the welfare services of the city? For this last category, municipal authorities sought clear-cut and expert medical diagnoses on which to base their decisions. Contemporary doctors, however, found themselves caught between such official demands and the shifting terminologies within which they themselves understood specific conditions.

From even before the days of Malthus, scholars have thought of cities, and early modern cities in particular, as population drains – the "graves of mankind."[4] Though there has been scholarly debate for some time now over this "urban graveyard effect," it is clear that the increasing incidence of syphilis, the "French pox," after 1496 led to a growing health care crisis. English readers are familiar with how, by the end of the eighteenth century, William Blake powerfully linked venereal disease with urban suffering and morbidity ("the youthful harlot's curse / Blasts the new-born infant's tear, / And blights with plagues the marriage hearse"). But in the sixteenth century doctors were not yet certain of the aetiology of this new disease, much less how to distinguish it from the more familiar, if declining, threat of leprosy. The urban experience of disease would force scientific thought and urban sensibilities together, gradually introducing new themes into medical discourse. Thus, the administrative demands of urban public health policy served to create simultaneously two different sets of borders: applied distinctions between insiders and outsiders among the poor, and intellectual lines between modern and older approaches to disease.[5]

Religion was creating its own borders: very real boundary lines within cities that had once been homogenously devoted to a single saint and governed by a single liturgical calendar. Of course, even medieval cities had had small numbers of religious outsiders – most notably Jews. But it had been relatively easy to pass rules that kept Jews out of the public space on Holy Days and that forbade them from sounding their prayers in voices loud enough to offend Christian passersby. Now, however, large numbers and powerful forces were involved, and the old one-sided and clear-cut rules were impossible. Public space became an area of contention and the city soundscape a zone of battle. Public processions marked territory, and bearing a Roman Catholic relic through a Protestant neighbourhood was an act of intentional aggression. In such a tense context even the tolling of church bells, familiar time markers useful to everyone, could now become an offensive claim to a specifically Catholic urban soundscape. Even in Augsburg, the "bi-confessional" city famous for the peace treaty of 1555, the tensions of religious diversity continued to be played out on the street. As Alexander Fisher demonstrates, by the early seventeenth century, the traditional format of religious processional was combined with the aggressive forms associated with military parade in an effort to control the city's soundscape.

While internal boundary markers were being challenged in German cities, they seemed to be unacceptably eroding in Amsterdam, at least in the view of many outsiders. The reactions of Christian tourists to the prominent synagogues erected there in the 1670s are understood by Saskia Coenen Snyder as largely reflections of the assumptions and conventions about Jews that these outsiders had brought with them from their home cities. Coenen Snyder's chapter is a contribution to the increasingly important field of tourism studies, an approach that emphasizes the nature of the interaction between observer and observed, between the fixity of a physical given and the volatility of spatial experience, between what is there and what we bring to it. In the specific case of Amsterdam, Coenen Snyder finds a marked difference between the tolerance implicit in the reactions of Dutch (and some British) observers and the hostility expressed by most travellers from France and, especially, Germany. She attributes the difference in response to the greater appreciation in Holland and England of the utilitarian benefits to be derived from a Jewish presence. In doing so, Coenen Snyder has moved the question back one step: what must now be explained is not the reaction to the architecture but the initial tolerance from which it derived. Thus, the issue of borders with which we began leads us ineluctably back to the apparently opposite question of tolerance and openness. But tolerance is not a simple or univalent concept, as we can demonstrate when we examine another aspect of Amsterdam's pattern of sacred architecture: while Jews already had an open synagogue by the second decade of the seventeenth century, Catholics were required to pray in *schuilkerken* – ostensibly hidden chapels maintained behind the façades of private homes. Though these chapels were not secret in any true sense, they did allow for a distinction between public and private worship and, thus, a division between public and private space that served as a major mechanism for tolerance of religious dissent in many areas of Europe into the nineteenth century. This distinction points the way to emerging concepts of civic discourse that define the modern pubic arena.[6]

Deviance is of course not limited to religion, nor is diversity merely the passive object of urban control systems. Even a group perceived by authorities as most dangerous to civic peace could, concentrated in a more or less fixed neighbourhood, shape itself into a community and become an active part of the urban landscape. Even a ghetto can become a well known locale to be visited for its very differentness as much as for any licit (or illicit) service it offered. Of the groups most often understood as posing potential danger to society, sailors were certainly among the most prominent, especially when they gathered in a port where a fleet was being assembled.[7] In his chapter, one of a series of studies devoted to the theme, Isaac Land looks at "sailortown" – particularly London's

Wapping neighbourhood – as a separate cultural space within the city. Here sailors are a spectacle for border-crossing tourists, but they, and the myriads of others who served their needs, are also creating and playing out quite clear identity roles for themselves. In his work, Land adds another theoretical rubric to our urban studies arsenal – that of "subculture studies." Land sees Jack Tar and his comrades as a subculture rather than as a counterculture, appropriating elements of the dominant culture but intentionally making these opaque as a method of regaining "subjecthood" vis-à-vis the dominant society. In this, Land is specifically distinguishing his approach from the mainstream of Atlantic historians who have declared the boat and the sailor as transnational elements creating a common set of values. Rather than emphasizing the sailors' cosmopolitanness, Land explores the manner in which sailors are interacting with the specific urban environment in which they are rooted. That environment, in turn, co-opts the spectacle of the local sailortown for its theatrical or political needs. Thus, the circle was closed, and boundaries of space and behavioural norms became themselves part of the urban essence.

It is fitting that we close our discussion with the literary invention of neighbourhood and city. As Arnold Weinstein has noted, literature can provide us with a unique map to the city and its soul,[8] and the artist's sharp eye can pick out landmarks and divisions that might not be noted by less artistic observers. The importance of specific urban environments for given writers is, of course, well known: we need only mention St Petersburg for Dostoevsky or Dublin for Joyce to make the point clear. And criticism of urban social evils has been a prominent literary theme from Charles Dickens to Upton Sinclair. However, in his chapter on treatments of London in Blake and Wordsworth, Jon Saklofske focuses our attention not on any specific cityscape but, rather, on the artists' understanding of the city per se, of the artists' simultaneous observation of, and distance from, the urban panorama. Indeed, Saklofske wishes to move beyond any straightforward link between poet and perceived reality, exploring not so much the borders within a specific time and place as the creative lines separating and joining "mind-forg'd" cities – real, mythic, and imaginative. Just as the author seeks to go beyond Blake as an "urban poet" objecting to social evils, so he also insists on widening our understanding of Wordsworth as more than an anti-urban Romantic. In both writers, he argues, the city is a place of potentiality and vitality, beautiful not only in the calm of earliest morning ("Dear God! The very houses seem asleep; And all that mighty heart is lying still")[9] but also when it lives and bustles.

Though Saklofske doesn't say this, it seems that, in Wordsworth, we already see the artist on the way to becoming the *flâneur.* He observes the overwhelming divisions and multiplicities of modern urban life and, by giving them structure and meaning, unites them. City dwellers are caught up in the confusing trivialization of reality, in the "perpetual whirl / Of trivial objects, melted and reduced / To one identity, by differences / That have no law, no meaning, and no end." But the poet observer can lend significance to urban experience because he has "among least things / An undersense of greatest; sees the parts / As parts, but with a feeling of the whole."[10] In a sense, that is the purpose of this entire volume, and of urban studies as an endeavour – to cross the boundaries and gain a feeling of the whole.

NOTES

1 For example, when Spiro Kostof set about answering the question "What is a City?" he necessarily included "a specialized differentiation of work," unequal distribution of wealth, social hierarchy, and differentiated ethnicity in his definition. See Kostef, *The City Shaped,* 37–41.

2 For a model reconstruction of the role of various urban groups in a confrontation, see Weinberg, "The Pogrom of 1905 in Odessa."

3 One need only think of the struggles over the constitutional implications (as well as the theatricality) of the royal or lordly "joyeuse entrée" into the city. See, for example, Bryant, *King and City in the Parisian Royal Entry Ceremony*; and Arnade, *Realms of Ritual.*

4 For a useful discussion of the literature and a possible model of relevant factors for the specific case of York, England, see Galley, "A Model of Early Modern Urban Demography."

5 Illuminating comparisons can be drawn with the situation in London, where the population pressure was even greater and where records allow us a quite detailed picture of the urban institutional response. See Kevin P. Siena's *Venereal Disease Hospitals and the Urban Poor.*

6 See Kaplan, "Fictions of Privacy."

7 See, for example, the concerns of the Bishop of St Malo in 1675, quoted in Cowan *Urban Europe*, 179, who, in turn, is quoting from Y. Garlan and C. Nières, *Les révoltes bretonnes de 1675* (Paris: Éditions sociales, 1975), 43.

8 Weinstein, *Soul and the City*. I might note here that I have had excellent results assigning this stimulating series of recorded lectures produced by the Teaching Company as background for first-year students in university courses on urban history.

9 Wordsworth, "Composed Upon Westminster Bridge," 1802.

10 Ibid., *The Prelude* (1850), bk. 7, lines 722–36.

10

Alls wie mann inn krieg pflegt zue thuen: Music and Catholic Processions in Counter-Reformation Augsburg

ALEXANDER J. FISHER[1]

In many ways, the southern German city of Augsburg was a microcosm of the religious divide that destabilized the early modern Holy Roman Empire as a whole. The largest of the so-called "biconfessional" cities, Augsburg's 1555 Constitution guaranteed the religious rights of both its Protestant majority and its Roman Catholic minority, its imperial status exempting it from the rule of *cuius regio, eius religio* that was to prevail in the rest of the empire. Étienne François has described an "invisible boundary" in the city between the two faiths, and, indeed, Augsburg's economic well-being and social peace depended to some extent on this boundary remaining intangible.[2] The years leading up to the outbreak of the Thirty Years War, however, were a period during which confessional distinctions were hardening. Perhaps no other phenomenon expressed these differences more publicly and more dramatically than the Catholic processions that began to extend into Protestant neighbourhoods around 1600, particularly on Good Friday and on the feast of Corpus Christi. Numerous contemporary sources suggest that Catholics as well as Protestants saw these events in a political light.[3] One Catholic tract from Ingolstadt, for example, describes a Good Friday procession from 1605 and its alleged effect on one poor Lutheran bystander:

> A procession went out with such religious pomp that a certain tailor, from the Lutheran flock, was a spectator. He saw in long order a great crowd carrying statues of Christ depicting his

> diverse torments, followed by a troop of horses most splendidly decorated and laden with [an image] of the crucified Christ, boys under the embellished standards of the Angels singing songs, [a representation] of the earth shaking made from beams, [he heard] the striking of scourges, [he saw] the heavens burning with fire, and all of the Catholics imflamed with piety; he was wracked, seething, envious, and indignant on account of these wondrous ways, and everything was burdensome and sorrowful to him. What more is there to say? He went immediately home, and shut his wretched soul away from this snare. It is uncertain whether he did so out of his own desperation or out of envy of us. Afterwards the Catholics joked cheerfully about why Lutherans would not want to be willing spectators. For while the Catholics would represent the sufferings of Christ, the [Lutherans] would represent Judas.[4]

Another document, a request for papal indulgences by a local confraternity, illustrates the effect that Catholic partisans hoped to have on their Protestant observers:

> Here in Augsburg, and in the countryside, this praiseworthy brotherhood has carried out many devotions and divine services (and still does); thus pious, Catholic, and ardent Christians have held public processions with banners into and out of all of the [city] gates, and organized several choirs in great numbers which sang German and Latin Litanies of All Saints, and many Protestants walking by saw this and stood there with terrified hearts, and many of them showed reverence to the clergy.[5]

Much has been written about the visual stimulus of early modern Catholic culture, the impulse to make Catholic truths immediately tangible through image, gesture, and theatre.[6] Catholic processions, however, were multimedia spectacles, and the aural dimension, including songs, litanies, and instrumental music, arguably had at least as much impact in this urban context as this music could be heard even in those areas far removed from the sight of the procession itself. It is conceded that religious devotion, instead of politics, would have motivated many of the marchers, and one must also bear in mind that a significant proportion of the participants – including many of the professional musicians engaged for the event

– were bound to take part out of obligation to their respective institutions. From the perspective of the organizers and many Protestant bystanders, however, these processions aggressively appropriated space, both public and private: not only the physical space occupied by the marchers themselves as they filed through public squares and by Protestant households but also the much larger space defined by the procession's sonic imprint.[7] By the early seventeenth century, this imprint could conceivably encompass the entire city as the addition of trumpets and drums, not to mention the roar of cannon and musket fire on particularly festal occasions, transformed Catholic processions into explicit symbols of military triumph over the doubts of unbelievers. The inescapable sound of military fanfares, gunfire, and the strains of Catholic litanies undermined, if only temporarily, the delicate confessional equilibrium.[8]

TRADITIONS OF LITURGICAL AND OCCASIONAL PROCESSIONS

While the elaborate Good Friday and Corpus Christi processions of the early seventeenth century could not have had such a profile without the agitation of zealous Jesuits, patricians, and clerics, these phenomena had long-standing roots in sanctioned ritual practices. Surviving liturgical books from the mid-sixteenth century record regular Sunday processions past the tombs of the departed inside the cathedral's cloister, Vespers processions on major feasts, and processions during Rogation Days, specifying various litanies, antiphons, and responsories to be chanted by the clergy. These prescriptions, however, reflect a usage that is distinct from the later, more theatrical variety: there is no suggestion of the laity's inclusion, music is restricted to Latin chant, and the processions remain entirely within church grounds, with rare exceptions.

To these liturgical processions we can add a second category that appears more and more frequently in the later sixteenth century: occasional processions as supplications for weather, deliverance from plague or the Turks, or for celebrations and commemorations for prominent political figures or churchmen. As Philip Soergel has written, these processions fulfilled a spiritual function in that they embodied the community's appeal to God, Christ, the Virgin Mary, and the saints to come to its aid in times of great need. In this sense they played a role in a spiritual economy not unlike that played by pilgrimage shrines, in which devotion could be exchanged for intercession.[9] On the other hand, the expressive boundaries between supplication and politics are not always clear. That a procession commemorating the election of a new bishop had a political dimension is obvious, but even weather processions reinscribed the distinctively Catholic doctrine of sanctoral intercession.

Before the late 1590s, there seems to be no evidence that liturgical or occasional processions in Augsburg ventured far beyond their home churches, and the lack of documentation for lay participation suggests that the overall numbers of marchers remained low compared to later spectacles. Musically, the modesty of these processions was matched by the rather strict prescriptions for Latin plainchant and the seemingly limited scope for vernacular songs or instrumental music. The distinction in musical embellishment between prescribed liturgical processions and those on the greater feasts like Corpus Christi may be seen already in Bishop Marquard von Berg's 1580 Ritual for the Augsburg diocesan liturgy: while the Corpus Christi procession, for example, could enjoy the participation of "trumpets, pipes, organs, and other musical instruments, employed for the glorification of Christ and the devotion of the faithful" to augment the Latin chant, the prescribed processions during Rogation Days allowed for no instruments, only chant and "approved German songs" with the admonition that "the voices of those singing in German should be pious, sweet, and consonant."[10] Even on the feast of Corpus Christi, most Protestant residents of Augsburg could expect to be spared from the sights and sounds of these events.

Indeed, Catholics had reasons to fear the consequences of marching into Protestant neighbourhoods. Writing in 1640, the Catholic chronicler Reginbald Möhner recalled that, in 1595, public processions began to be organized in Augsburg, processions "which previously were not held except within the churches and their environs due to fear of the Lutheran masses."[11] The risks would be made clear in the nearby imperial city of Donauwörth, where Protestant mobs physically attacked Catholic marchers on Corpus Christi in 1606, a conflict later dubbed the *Fahnenschlacht* and one that triggered a forcible takeover and re-Catholicization of the city by the Bavarian army the following year.[12] Nevertheless, the turn of the new century saw the rise of a more daring, and indeed propagandistic, attitude on the part of Catholic organizers in Augsburg.

THE GOOD FRIDAY PROCESSION

Between 6 and 7 o'clock on Good Friday evening in 1604, Augsburg's Catholic community began a procession that far outstripped previous efforts in audacity, if not in scope. Some 150 participants, led by the newly founded Corpus Christi brotherhood, departed from the church of Heilig Kreuz, in the northwest corner of the city, and wound their way towards the basilica of SS. Ulrich and Afra in the southern quarter, making stations at the cathedral and the Jesuit church of St Salvator. Surviving accounts describe images of and actors representing the events of Christ's Passion from the Mount of Olives to the tomb. Accompanying this were several groups of singers, including "a chorus of four boys singing a tearful dirge to Christ," a "mournful symphony," a "doleful funeral song sung by a choir of angels," and another group of musicians at the very end of the procession.[13] Multiple institutions, then, including the confraternity, the cathedral choirboys, and instrumentalists either from the cathedral or from the company of city pipers, would have been involved in creating this spectacle of sight and sound.

A tract printed at the nearby Jesuit university of Ingolstadt later that year summarized the goal of this procession:

> The praiseworthy zeal for a Christian, godly, and spiritual life [was seen] particularly in the edifying example of the devout, magnificent, well-considered and orderly procession through the whole city of Augsburg last Good Friday, in which various images of the bitter sufferings of Jesus Christ, our sole redeemer and savior, [were carried,] along with other severe acts of penitence [i.e., flagellation] done to yourselves, through which not only the hearts of Catholics, but also those of Christians deceived in religion, were moved and softened, so that [their hearts] must have burst at the same time from inner sighs and hot tears.[14]

The tract concludes with an admonishment that the brotherhood not be dissuaded from their tasks by Protestant mockery. But were Protestants watching and listening to the procession? They were indeed, if we can believe the pastor of the Protestant church of St Anna, Melchior Volcius, who published two sermons in 1607 specifically attacking the Good Friday procession in his city. Having expressed his distaste for the grotesque images and for the gruesome bloodletting of the flagellants, he decried the holding of the procession in public view:

> [They] began not only to flagellate themselves privately and in secret, but also to hold public processions, just like those old heretical flagellants condemned by the Pope; [they held them] particularly in those places where proper, true Lutheran Christians lived, not keeping them in those places and streets where they had always held them; rather [they] crawled out of the alleys and came into the public, most prominent streets, where others joined the spectacle with their naked, cut, lashed, and bloody backs and haunches, not without particular horror and revulsion of honest, knowing persons; and they whipped themselves in great numbers longer and harder, all for the purpose of gaining followers and making a special demonstration of their zeal for their religion, and for deceitfully catching and taking unto themselves pious, simple, and innocent hearts under the pretense of great holiness.[15]

Surely many Protestants observed these spectacles since Volcius felt the need to admonish his flock to avoid them:

> And what do [these Catholics] do? They forbid their people to visit our church, hear our sermons, and attend our services, in which they would hear nothing but God's pure, unsullied word, along with pure Psalms and sacred songs; they would see nothing but the holy Sacrament as it was given to us by Christ himself. But you run to this blasphemous, abominable event in night and fog, where you see nothing but sheer atrociousness and idolatry; you hear nothing by which you can better yourself.[16]

Furthermore, he writes: "When these flagellants' processions are held, for our part many Lutherans go there in great numbers, and fill all of the alleys and streets so full that it seems as if there are often more of our people there than those marching in the procession."[17]

Volcius's dismay at the presence of his flock at these events made him an easy target for the mockery of the Ingolstadt Jesuit polemicist Conrad Vetter, who responded in the following year with his own "Flagellant's Zeal" (*Flagellifer*). In it he joked that Volcius's warning to his flock was so effective that, on the previous Good Friday, "not a single Lutheran (excepting women and men, young and old) would allow himself to be seen on the streets or in the windows" during the procession.[18] Furthermore, Vetter claimed that Volcius himself would be unable to resist its power. Referring to a different procession on Ascension Day, Vetter wrote:

> This procession, I say, should not displease our Herr Volcius at all, because it is held in the full light of day. I also have no doubt that his own heart would leap in his breast if he heard the singing of so many choirs of musicians, and the magnificent ringing of the great bell of St. Ulrich in his ears, and saw the whole procession pass by St. Ulrich's church before his own eyes.[19]

Volcius's reference to "pure Psalms and sacred songs" and the "many choirs of musicians" (*so vil choros musicorum*) praised by Vetter point to a fundamental way in which music helped to constitute religious and cultural differences between the Protestant and Catholic communities in this confessionally divided city: while Volcius alludes to the decades-old Protestant tradition of vernacular Psalms and chorales, Vetter's text suggests the role of music as part of a sensually overwhelming dramatic spectacle. Catholics increasingly turned to explicit, public demonstrations of their faith, which were designed not only to promote unity within their own ranks but also to impress the city's Protestant majority. Although Volcius and Vetter do not describe the musical element of these processions in great detail, their tracts, in general terms, suggest that music was a vital part of a richly layered spectacle involving different media.

THE CORPUS CHRISTI PROCESSION

The yearly procession on the feast of Corpus Christi was the most elaborate Catholic public spectacle in early seventeenth-century Augsburg. It was not only the largest and most varied procession, involving the contributions of hundreds of clergy and laypersons with images, banners, theatrical displays, self-flagellation, and musical performances, but also the most potent symbolic expression of the church militant. Bishop Heinrich V von Knöringen made this explicit in the section of his 1612 diocesan Ritual devoted to the celebration of Corpus Christi:

> Among all of the celebrations of the Catholic church there is not one which is more exclusive to Catholics, and offends the eyes of the heretics more acutely, than [that of] the most holy body of CHRIST alone. Thus it is fitting that this [feast] be celebrated most solemnly both in the Divine Office as well as in processions, according to the abilities of the place. Therefore, let the priest take care that all things are well prepared, and that all persons are brought together in order, who proclaim and confirm their true Catholic faith in an outward manner.[20]

Sacramental devotion, of course, had enjoyed a centuries-old history and indeed formed a dominant thread in medieval pilgrimage traditions in Bavaria.[21] After a hiatus in the wake of the Reformation, the cult of the "Real Presence" in the sacrament experienced an intense revival at the hands of Counter-Reformation ideologues like Heinrich von Knöringen, who conceived it as a militant symbol of Catholic truth in the face of heretical opposition. Nowhere was this more true than in nearby Munich, where the ducal establishment actively promoted the yearly Corpus Christi procession, an event that, by the late sixteenth century, reportedly involved the annual participation of several *thousand* individuals, indeed, a substantial percentage of the entire city's population.[22] Organizers in that staunchly Catholic city, however, could hardly count on the numbers of Protestant observers that would have watched and heard the same procession in Augsburg.

Not surprisingly, the Corpus Christi confraternity also took a leading role in the organization of the procession on that feast. Founded in 1604, the group devoted itself to the veneration of the so-called *Wunderbares Gut*, an allegedly miraculous host housed at the local church of Heilig Kreuz that represented the centre of sacramental devotion in the city. According to the legend, in the year 1194 a local woman visited the church of Heilig Kreuz, where, instead of swallowing the host, she took it home secretly and encapsulated it in wax. Having revered the host for five years in her home, she was plagued by guilt and returned it to the head of the church's chapter, who noticed that it had physically changed to resemble flesh and blood. After consulting with the bishop, the host was exposed for veneration on the cathedral's altar, where it grew dramatically in size, bursting out of its wax capsule. The bishop had the miraculous host and its wax container placed in a crystal monstrance and delivered in a festal procession to Heilig Kreuz, where it was to remain.[23] Initially founded by Marcus Fugger and other noble persons, the brotherhood honouring this host quickly expanded its ranks into the lower rungs of society; among its members was Gregor Aichinger, Augsburg's most prominent Catholic composer and an ordained priest, who would dedicate a printed collection of Eucharistic music to the confraternity in 1606.[24]

Not coincidentally, it was around the same time as the founding of Aichinger's brotherhood that the Corpus Christi procession expanded in size and range. Documents from 1599 and 1603 indicate that the procession had already been extended to include the churches of Heilig Kreuz and St Salvator in the northern quarter of the city, but, in 1604, the city's Catholics finally resolved to march to the basilica of SS. Ulrich and Afra in the south. The moment of the decision was recorded by the cathedral chapter's notary:

> As my gracious lord, the cathedral dean, has reported, as well as Herr Cleophas Distelmayr [the cathedral preacher], that certain zealous Catholics, and particularly Herr *Stadtpfleger* Welser, have wished to further promote the Corpus Christi procession, and indeed to extend it to St. Ulrich, to sing the four Gospels, and to have the canons carry torches; also, as my gracious lord, the cathedral dean, has reported that Herr Marcus Fugger wishes that he and his company, the Corpus Christi Confraternity, would like to carry the canopy [over the Eucharist], and that his Grace [Bishop Heinrich V] has told him that he would approve, and that Herr Fugger said that he would appear in stately dress. So it is resolved, for sake of Catholic zeal, that this procession, since it should make a circuit and not travel on the same street twice, should proceed over the Perlach, and through the Steingasse toward the Heilig Kreuz gate; then it should proceed down the Kreuzgasse to the gate of Our Lady, and then return back into the cathedral. The four Gospels are to sung at four different places, where they may be the most appropriate.[25]

The most prominent roles were taken by the Corpus Christi Confraternity and patricians of the Fugger and Welser families; indeed, the advocacy of Marcus Welser, one of the two *Stadtpfleger* in the highest reaches of the city government, represents a notable departure from the confessionally neutral politics typical of Augsburg's patrician council. The entry confirms that the procession was no longer restricted solely to the ecclesiastical quarter of the city but that it marched into largely Protestant neighbourhoods as well. According to liturgical tradition, the procession was to make four stations along the route where the four Gospels would be chanted in front of altars erected for the occasion; vocal and instrumental music would typically welcome the procession as it arrived at each altar. It is unclear what the notary intended as the "most appropriate" places for the singing of the Gospels, but the extension of the procession over the major north-south axis of the city may have been sufficiently provocative in itself.

Although the Augsburg Corpus Christi procession adhered to this framework, contemporary documents show that the musical embellishment at times went far beyond the bishop's prescriptions. A chronicle of the Augsburg Jesuits describes a particularly elaborate four-hour procession in 1606 that involved over 2,700 participants, including numerous musicians.[26] The procession made its way from the cathedral southward and made its first station before the Ilsung residence near city hall. Either before or after the Gospel was sung,

> A chorus of angels from our [Jesuit] schools who were present [entreated] Christ, singing a song most sweetly and with gestures. In the same way, in the vicinity of the city hall and towers, the city trumpeters, at the command of the magistrates, received the coming [body of] Christ with the sweet harmony of instruments, and followed it as it departed. In the meantime, the festal, ringing harmony of military drums and trumpets along the route and at the same altars made the entire city joyful, as did the choirs of musicians, of which there were many.[27]

From the first altar the procession proceeded south through the wine market and made its second station before the business quarters of the Fugger family; subsequently, upon passing the Göggingen gate on the western wall, a group of armed soldiers from the city militia "magnified the triumph with the beating of four drums."[28] From there the procession went past the Protestant church and school of St Anna – surely a provocative act – to the courtyard of the patrician Bernhard Rehlinger, where the third altar and a "most sweet symphony of the musicians" awaited the arrival of the host.[29] The final station was held at the Jesuit church of St Salvator before the procession returned to the cathedral.

The chronicler goes on to describe the constitution and the order of the procession in greater detail, and from his remarks we can get a fuller picture of the musical complement. Amidst the Marian Congregation, for example, was a choir of twenty-seven Jesuit students. The clerical confraternity of St Sebastian was followed by "seven trumpets, all dressed in silk, and a military drum carried by two persons and crowned with the insignia of the Corpus Christi sodality; alternating with these was the chapel master of the musicians from the cathedral, of which there were thirty-three, all clothed in white."[30] A document from the Corpus Christi brotherhood itself, by contrast, indicates that "*sixteen* trumpeters and two military drummers were engaged to walk in front of the musicians of the cathedral, and who performed their service before and after the sung Gospels and benedictions, as well as at other places, and gave the procession a fine character [emphasis mine]."[31] Also participating was the cathedral choirmaster with thirty-three musicians, all clothed in white, followed by twenty choirboys "dressed as angels," of which eight sang before the four altars.[32] The militaristic aspect of the musical accompaniment would not have been lost on the onlookers or the participants. One Protestant chronicler, Georg Kölderer, lamented the presence of many Protestant bystanders, who heard trumpets and drums "as used in warfare" (*alls wie mann inn krieg pflegt zue thuen*).[33] The participation of trumpets and drums, documented in the Corpus Christi procession at least into the 1620s, underscored the symbolism of feast as an occasion to celebrate the triumph of the Roman Catholic Church over its antagonists. The combination of Eucharistic and military imagery, however, would reach its peak in the following decade, when the miraculous host of Heilig Kreuz was triumphantly returned from its wartime hiding place in 1635.

THE TRIUMPHANT RETURN OF THE *WUNDERBARES GUT*

This remarkable event capped several disastrous years of war, plague, and famine. In the wake of his military successes in the opening phases of the Thirty Years War, Emperor Ferdinand II issued the Edict of Restitution in 1629; Augsburg, as all Imperial cities, saw the installation of an entirely Catholic city government that radically curtailed the rights of local Protestants. This state of affairs persisted until April 1632, when the Swedish army of Gustavus Adolphus took the city without resistance. Just over two years later, his army was routed at Nördlingen (Gustavus Adolphus himself had been killed previously at the battle of Lützen in November 1632), and by October 1634 Catholic troops had surrounded Augsburg. The Swedish garrison refused to surrender, and a disastrous siege ensued through the winter of 1634–35, during which thousands died of hunger and disease. The remaining Swedish soldiers having fled, the Catholic clergy returned on 28 March 1635. That spring the traditional processions on Good Friday and Corpus Christi would be restored, but the general economic ruin prevented any repeat of the spectacles of previous decades.

Those processions, however, would pale in comparison to that organized upon the return of the *Wunderbares Gut* to Augsburg in May 1635, when the miraculous host arrived back from its wartime home at Chiemsee and was carried in a triumphant procession to its original abode at Heilig Kreuz. Several accounts of this procession survive, but surely the most vivid is found in a letter to Bishop Heinrich V from his vicar general, Caspar Zeiller, written the day after the event unfolded:

> The suffragan bishop in pontifical dress arrived, took the most worthy Sacrament, and placed it, with the usual ceremonies, upon an altar erected in a field for that purpose, while several pieces were played by the trumpeters, military drummers, and musicians. Then a short exhortation was given by the preacher from Heilig Kreuz ... accompanied by a threefold [fanfare] with military drums and trumpets in honor and thanksgiving. Finally, the suffragan bishop gave the benediction, and all of the people present shouted "JESUS, JESUS, JESUS" three times, not without some tears. Then the musketeers ... fired all of their weapons, as did those who were standing atop the fortifications. At this, the procession made its way in good order toward the city.

The marchers included the (still modestly sized) clergy, foot soldiers and cavalry, city and imperial officials, and lay pilgrims, some of whom had come from Munich for the occasion. As the procession reached the city, an overwhelming visual and aural spectacle unfolded:

> As [the procession] approached the Red Gate, the muskets were fired again, and at Ulrich and Afra the holy Cross [of St Ulrich] was left, and the people rested for some time during the music. From there [the procession] went through the Weinmarkt and by the Perlach. In the finest squares [of the city] the regiments lined themselves up in good order, and where the Holy Sacrament was carried, all of the soldiers fell to their knees, placing their axes, pikes, muskets, and guns underneath them ... Under the great door of the city hall an altar had been erected, decorated like that in the cathedral, and the people sang for some time. Then the procession made its way to Heilig Kreuz with a magnificent *Te Deum laudamus* and Vespers; during the *Te Deum laudamus* a salute was again fired by all of the musketeers and guns around the city. On the streets, where the Catholics were standing or walking, there was a general weeping for joy, that finally, after having endured so much misery and sadness, that the city could be blessed with this great treasure and Catholic ceremonies.[34]

Although one can expect that Zeiller's account may have been somewhat embellished to please his superior, the description closely resembles a series of engravings of the event executed by Wolfgang Kilian and reproduced as figure 10.1 and figure 10.2. Zeiller's letter and the engravings suggest that the procession, and its associated music, had an undeniably militaristic quality. Figure 10.1 shows that trumpeters, military drummers, and other musicians performed as the clergy and laity venerated the sacrament upon a makeshift altar outside of the city walls; the sacrament was flanked at the left by a pair of kettledrums and at least seven trumpeters, and at the right by a choir of at least fourteen singers, led by a conductor with a baton and accompanied by one musician on what appears to be a slide trumpet or trombone. The noise of muskets and cannon fire from the city fortifications was the signal for the procession to proceed into the city via the so-called "Red Gate" on the southern wall. Figure 10.2 shows the long line of marches heading into the city; the trumpeters, drummer, and choir are located just behind the

Figure 10.1
Engraving by Wolfgang Kilian of ceremonies preceeding the return of the *Wunderbares Gut* to Augsburg. Staats- und Stadtbibliothek Augsburg, Graphiken 28/44.

Figure 10.2
Engraving by Wolfgang Kilian of the procession into the city of Augsburg, 10 May 1635. Staats- und Stadtbibliothek Augsburg, Graphiken 28/45.

confraternities with their banners, and immediately preceding the higher clergy accompanying the sacrament under a canopy. Zeiller tells us that, before proceeding northward towards the Rathaus, the participants rested and listened to some music at the basilica of Ulrich and Afra; we also hear of general singing as the sacrament was venerated in front of the Rathaus, the seat of secular power. Another, shorter account of the proceedings claims that the music heard here included a sung collect for the emperor and other polyphonic motets.[35]

We are not precisely informed of the music heard while under way, but we can speculate that it may have included military fanfares, simpler part music by the choir, and/or sung litanies, traditionally a characteristic feature of Catholic processions. Nor are we told of what Augsburg's remaining Protestant population might have thought of these ceremonies, but the route of the procession and its accompanying music make clear that few residents would have been able to escape its sound, even if some could escape its sight.

CONCLUSION: MUSIC AND PROCESSIONS IN A BICONFESSIONAL CITY

For the Protestant citizenry of Augsburg that had managed to survive the years of political turmoil, pestilence, and the terrible siege of the winter of 1634, the impression of the procession accompanying the *Wunderbares Gut* back to Heilig Kreuz was inescapable, not in the first place because of its visual splendour, but principally because of its aural dimension. The marchers physically appropriated space by formally reoccupying churches formerly in Protestant hands, by travelling down prime thoroughfares, and by making stations in the city's principal squares. Yet, the procession was accompanied by a sonic envelope that would have been audible before the Catholics even reached the city gates; by the time the cohort entered the city, the din of gunfire, trumpets, and military drums would have encompassed the entire community. For those closer to the procession some of the music would have been explicitly marked as Catholic – notably the repetitive invocations and responses of litanies in Latin or German – but even genres of a more neutral quality like instrumental music and simple songs would have taken on a quite different cast in the context of confessional demonstration and provocation. Furthermore, the provision of a militaristic clamour on special occasions would inevitably have coloured impressions of the more modest and frequent Catholic processions (both liturgical and paraliturgical) whose ambitions were not necessarily, in the first place, political.

The study of Catholic processions and their music in biconfessional cities provides some balance to accounts of Counter-Reformation culture that emphasize the element of visual spectacle at the expense of the aural. In constricted urban spaces the music performed by instrumentalists, trained choirs, and the laity arguably were heard by many more people than observed the processions directly; the addition of gunfire on extraordinary occasions had the effect of extending a curtain of sound over the entire community. Indeed, contemporary accounts demonstrate that organizers felt the aural component to be an indispensable contribution to these events' potential for propaganda. Much comparative work remains to be done on the musical profile of Catholic processions not only in biconfessional cities but also in more confessionally homogenous areas. This work, in turn, should feed into a broader consideration of urban soundscapes and the ways in which sound – musical and otherwise – shaped the political and religious identities of early modern subjects.

NOTES

1 The present chapter expands some ideas presented in my book *Music and Religious Identity*, esp. chaps. 5 and 9. I am grateful for the comments of Judith Owens, Greg Smith, and Glenn Clark, the organizers of the conference of which this chapter was a part.

2 François, *Die unsichtbare Grenze*.

3 See also Wolfart (this volume) on confessional historiography in Germany in this period and Blackstone (this volume) on the civic and religious functions of pageants and processions in sixteenth-century Norwich. Eds.

4 Kaspar Lechner, *Sodalis Parthenius. Siue libri tres qvibvs mores sodalivm exemplis informantur. Operâ maiorvm sodalivm academicorvm B. Mariæ Virginis Annunciatæ in lucem dati* (Ingolstadt: Gregor Hänlin, 1621), 108–11.

5 "Concept der Bruderschafftt zum Heÿ: Berg Andex Suplication an die Bäbst: hey: zu Rom vmb zuerlanngen ettliche Indulgentias Anno Christi 1586." Stadtarchiv Augsburg, Katholisches Wesensarchiv E458.

6 Among recent literature on this topic, see Smith, *Sensuous Worship*; Hecht, *Katholische Bildertheologie im Zeitalter von Gegenreformation und Barock*; Appuhn-Radtke, *Visuelle Medien im Dienst der Gesellschaft Jesu*; and Ostrow, *Art and Spirituality in Counter-Reformation Rome*.

7 Although space does not permit an extended historiographical detour, the present chapter is a small contribution to a growing literature on early modern space and the role of sound in shaping the conceptualization of space – the creation of a "soundscape," so to speak. See, for example, Schafer, *The Tuning of the World*; Feld, *Sound and Sentiment*; Smith, *The Acoustic World of Early Modern England*; and Coster and Spicer, *Sacred Space in Early Modern Europe*, esp. J. Craig, "Psalms, Groans and Dog-Whippers: The Soundscape of Sacred Space in the English Parish Church, 1547–1642."

8 See also Land (this volume) and Warne (this volume) on other kinds of appropriations of city streets and spaces; and Hammond (this volume) on other ways in which music defines civic identity. Eds.

9 Soergel, *Wondrous in His Saints*, 20–21.

10 With respect to Corpus Christi, "Chorus in Processione decantat Responsorium, *Homo quidam fecit cœnam magnam*. & Hymnos. *Pange lingua gloriosi. Sacris solemnijs*. Et id genus plura cantica. Nonnunquam tubæ, fistulæ, organa & alia instrumenta musica eidem Processioni, ad Christi gloriam, & pro deuotione fidelium adhibentur, sicut & Dauid adhibuit, ob Arcam Domini in Processione delatam." By contrast, during Rogation Days "Cantionum veterum vsus, cum eas catholicas & probatas esse constat, populo permittatur. Sint autem Germanicè canentium voces piæ, suaues & consonæ." From *Ritus ecclesiastici Augustensis episcopatus* (Dillingen: Johann Mayer, 1580), 604–13 and 621–4.

11 "Anno 1595 publicè Proceßiones in Vrbe ecclesiastico ritu haberi cæptæ sunt, et à multis annis ob timore Luteranæ plebis non nisi in templis eoru[n]demque; ambitu haberentur. Prima autem publicæ supplicatio totius Cleri instituta i Dominica III post Paschæ ex cathedrali templo ad S. Vdalricum, ubi solennißimè deca[n]tato hymno Te Deu[m] laudamus, et officio decantato per Suffraganeu[m], campanæ totius vrbis ecclesiaru[m] insonuerunt, et maiora tormenta in propugnaculis explosa sunt, in gratiaru[m] actionem, ob receptu[m] Jaurinum." Reginbald Möhner, "Annales Augustani Reginbaldi Moehneri," Archiv des Bistums Augsburg, Hs 52, 2:1437–38. The Christian conquest of Györ in Hungary (Ger.: Raab; Lat.: Iaurinus) actually took place in 1598; Möhner seems to have misremembered the date.

12 The only large-scale study of this event remains Stieve, *Der Kampf um Donauwörth im Zusammenhänge der Reichsgeschichte*; see also Lossen, *Die Reichsstadt Donauwörth und Herzog Maximilian*.

13 From "De initijs ac progressu omnium Fraternitatum, quæ in alma hac vrbe Augustana fuerunt diversis temporibus erectæ à Christi fidelibus, narratio MDCXVII," Staats- und Stadtbibliothek Augsburg, 2° Aug. 346, 22r–22v.

14 *Gratulation An die andächtige deß Heiligen Fronleichnams JEsu CHristi, vnd andere Brüderschafften zu Augspurg* (Ingolstadt: in der Ederischen Truckerey, durch Andream Angermayr, 1604), 3–4.

15 Volcius, *Zwo Christliche Predigten,* 23–4.

16 Ibid., 52.

17 Ibid., 51.

18 Vetter [a.k.a. Andreae], *M. Conradi Andreæ &c. Volcius Flagellifer*, 28–9.

19 Ibid., 12.

20 "INTER omnes Catholicæ Ecclesiæ festiuitates non est, que Catholicorum magis propria sit, Hæreticorumque ocluos offendat acriùs, quàm sola sacratissimi Corporis CHRISTI. Vndè decet eam pro cuiusq; loci facultatibus solemnissimè tàm in diuinis Officijs, quàm Processionibus celebrari. Det igitur operam Parochus, vt omnia tempestiuè parentur, omnesque hominum ordines congregetur, qui veram & Catholicam fidem suam externo etiam ritu declarent & comprobent." *Liber Ritualis, Episcopatus Augustensis* (Dillingen: Johann Mayer, 1612), 3:177–8.

21 A keen interest in Eucharistic pilgrimage, in part to "bleeding host" shrines whose legends revolved around tales of Jewish host desecration (Deggendorf, Schöne Maria at Regensburg), can be traced to the thirteenth century, especially in the Danube valley. See Soergel, *Wondrous in His Saints*, 23–4.

22 For example, Mitterwieser, in his *Geschichte der Fronleichnamsprozession in Bayern*, 35, cites contemporary documentation for over three thousand participants in the 1582 Corpus Christi procession.

23 The early modern literature on this miracle is extensive; some representative works are Bremens, *Historia Sacramenti Miraculosi*; Scioppius, *Emmanuel Thaumaturgus Augustae Vindel*; and Lader, *Historia dess Sacraments.*

24 Aichinger, *Solennia Augustissimi Corporis Christi.* For commentary on this collection, see Fisher, *Music and Religious Identity*, 144–9.

25 Domrezessionalien, 11 June 1604. Bayerisches Staatsarchiv Augsburg, Hochstift Augsburg/Neuburger Abgabe, 5527.

26 "Historia collegii Augustani", Bibliothèque cantonale, Freiburg/Switzerland, L951, 1:443–50.

27 Ibid., 433–44. There is a pagination error at this point in the Jesuit chronicle.

28 " ... ad portam ciuitatis Gögginganam, ubi cohors ex pr[æ]sidio militum in ordines digesta, armis tormentisq; instructa, quaternis tympanis concrepantibus triumphum auxit." Ibid., 1:444.

29 "Descensum indè uia regia per S. Annæ uicum usq; ad Bernardi Rehlingeri uestibulum, in quo extructa ara, nobiliq; pictura uisenda, cum suauissima Musicorum Symphonia Christus expectabatur." Ibid.

30 Ibid., 446.

31 "Kurtze beschreibung, wie die andächtige bruederschafft des allerheiligsten Fronleichnambs *Jesu Christi* ... wider vfgericht, und was weither darinn geordnet, vnd fürgenom[m]en worden," 7v. Archiv des Bistums Augsburg, BO 2480, no. 2.

32 "uiceni pueri cælitum habitu, ex quib[us] octo ad altaria, ut dixi, cantauere;" "Historia collegii Augustani," 1:446.

33 From Staats- und Stadtbibliothek Augsburg, 2° Cod. S. 44, fol. 51, qtd. in Roeck, *Eine Stadt im Krieg und Frieden*, 184–5.

34 Letter from Caspar Zeiller to Bishop Heinrich V, 11 May 1635, Archiv des Bistums Augsburg, BO 2308. About a week previously Zeiller helped plan the procession together with the cathedral chapter. See Domrezessionalien, Bayerisches Staatsarchiv Augsburg, Hochstift Augsburg/Neuburger Abgabe, 5551, 5 May 1635.

35 "... von darauf d[en] berlach (alla vnd[er] dem Stathaus ein Altar auf gemacht word[en], vnnden 1 Collect für den Kaiser gesung[en] vnnd andre *muteten*), vnnd forth ins thumb zue vnser l: frauen." From "Diarium Augustanum" (c. 1652) by Johann Georg Mayr, priest from Oberhausen, 10 May 1635. Bayerische Staatsbibliothek, Cgm 3313. While the collect would likely have been sung in plainchant, the term *muteten* would indicate a composed musical work on a Latin, religious text for roughly four to six voices.

11

"Madness in a Magnificent Building": Gentile Responses to Jewish Synagogues in Amsterdam, 1670–1730

SASKIA COENEN SNYDER

Over the course of the seventeenth century, travelling abroad became a fashionable social practice among well-to-do Europeans. The foreign journey was no longer limited to the realms of health or business but, rather, developed into a leisure activity vigorously pursued by men as well as by women, who proudly recounted their experiences in travelogues and diaries. Indeed, observing the novelties of foreign places and cultures was considered an edifying experience in the higher echelons of European society and became an indispensable part of a young man's education. An attractive site on the tourist map of Europe was Amsterdam, a city widely referred to at this time as the "trading Mecca" of the world. The capital of the Dutch Republic, which during the Golden Age experienced an unprecedented growth in economic activity and colonial trade, drew a growing number of curious travellers who could not but admire and envy its commercial power, prosperity, and cosmopolitanism.[1]

A major attraction in this port city was the so-called *Joodse buurt* (Jewish neighbourhood), which over the course of the seventeenth century, had become an integral part of Amsterdam's urban landscape. Visitors could easily identify this district as the centre of Jewish settlement within the city as two monumental structures clearly demarcated it as a Jewish space: the Spanish-Portuguese synagogue and the smaller, but nonetheless prominent, German-Jewish synagogue. These religious structures became, together with the stately City Hall and the "Beurs" (the Amsterdam Exchange), the city's landmarks, widely analyzed and described in what one might call an early form of tourist literature. Such texts are of particular value as they offer a window into the perceptions of contemporary observers not merely with regard to the presence of Jewish religious structures in the city but also with regard to the place and participation – that is, the level of toleration – of Jews in the Dutch Republic at large. That a variety of foreign and Gentile visitors, for instance, refer to Amsterdam as the "New Jerusalem" of Europe suggests that the contours of Jewish life in the republic followed certain conditions unique to the Dutch landscape – conditions that caused travellers to experience a mélange of emotions when observing the Jewish neighbourhood. They were baffled, surprised, confused, or outright annoyed by what they witnessed inside and outside the boundaries of the local Jewish quarter. Their views about the presence of "Others" were challenged as observers were asked to acknowledge a link between Jews, on the one hand, and beautifully built monumental architecture, on the other – a relationship previously considered implausible. Christians, in particular, had difficulty connecting the values associated with this type of architecture, such as aesthetic sophistication and religious respectability, with Jews. Christian discourse, after all, had consistently depicted the Jews as the epitome of cultural primitiveness and incivility, as being incapable of producing refined works of art. Consequently, many Christians visiting the Amsterdam synagogues lauded the buildings for their elegance, but they denounced the people who actually built and used them because they could not harmonize what, in their minds, constituted unequivocal opposites. Early modern travel descriptions, then, offer a glimpse into the perceptions of contemporary observers and reveal how well-to-do Gentiles responded both to the public presence of Jewish architecture in the city and to the participation of Jews in the republic at large.[2]

The Spanish-Portuguese and German-Jewish synagogues, known in local parlance as the Esnoga and the Great Synagogue, respectively, served as a metonymy for the Jewish neighbourhood. Built right across from each other on a prominent location in the early 1670s, they visually identified the site as the city's Jewish quarter and bestowed, as one scholar phrased it, a particularly "Jewish character" onto this urban space.[3] The public presence of these structures, enhanced by their sheer size and monumental architectural form, made the clear statement that it was here that the local Jewish population lived, worked, and openly worshiped its faith.

Figure 11.1
The Spanish Portuguese Synagogue (1675), Collection Jewish Historical Museum, Amsterdam.

The establishment of this neighbourhood thus created a religiously and ethnically defined locality that gave physical shape to the voluntary process of organization and self-segregation from the larger Dutch population. However, the way in which the Jewish quarter openly announced its presence, attracting a growing number of tourists, scholars, artists, and Sunday afternoon strollers into its midst, also suggests the formation of this district as a public space to walk through rather than around – one that blended with, rather than segmented, the city's architectural landscape. In other words, the inviting grandeur of the synagogues rendered the Jewish district an accessible urban neighbourhood that signified the entry of Jews into Dutch public life.

Gentile visitors were witnesses to the establishment of this Jewish space. Tempted by curiosity and invited by the magnetism of the Esnoga, tourists began to attend services, chatted with local Jews, and related their experiences and interpretations in letters and diaries. Locals, too, strolled into the streets where Jews lived to observe a world that was largely unknown to them. Their curiosity grew partially out of the challenge that Amsterdam Jewry posed – particularly Sephardim – to the familiar stereotype. Gentile perceptions of Jews had for the most part been constructed by folklore, Christian sermons, hearsay, and – in educated circles – by books, the majority of which were hostile in tone. Jews were considered a contemptible breed stubbornly resisting the acknowledgment of Christianity as the true religion, whose lack of education found expression in their bad manners and shabby appearance, and whose speech was inarticulate. This image, however, was challenged by Amsterdam's Portuguese Jews, whose behaviour and customs appeared refined and cultured. Instead of pushing a peddler's cart, they engaged in international commerce and maintained important economic relationships with Gentile elites. They displayed an impressive level of what in Germany would come to be known as *Bildung*, a cultural sophistication that was generally reserved for the Christian gentility. These Portuguese Jewish merchants built large residences, schools, and houses of worship, structures that were no longer modest and obscured from public view but that, rather, were meant to be seen and admired. The new "aura of mystery," as historian Yosef Kaplan phrased it, surrounding Amsterdam's Sephardim aroused great interest and invited local and foreign visitors into the Jewish neighbourhood to observe at close hand their daily behaviour.[4]

It is the dynamic exchange between these observers and Jewish religious buildings, described in late seventeenth-century and early eighteenth-century tourist literature, that is under scrutiny here. The interaction of human actors with the architecture, or, as critical theorist Lindsay Jones calls it, the "human experience of architecture,"[5] produced interpretations that are useful in determining the responses of Gentiles to a growing Jewish presence in the city. After all, the aesthetic product that is a synagogue, however grand it might be, generates no valuable information as buildings in and of themselves have no meaning. Only through the interaction between the built form and human actors are perceptions and interpretations generated and can we begin to understand what the emergence of these synagogues meant in Amsterdam at this particular time. An important question to ask, then, is how contemporary observers *created* meanings as a result of negotiations between the physical object (the synagogue) and the human subject. From this perspective, meaning is not owned by the buildings themselves but is a product of the beholder's engagement with it. It is, in Jones's words, an effect that is experienced, not a message that must be found.[6] As visitors to the Jewish neighbourhood observed, paused, and reflected, they engaged in a conversation with the built form, giving voice not merely to their own tastes and viewpoints but also to a larger cultural response that illuminates the receptivity to public expressions of Jewish presence.

This is not to say that late seventeenth-century Amsterdam synagogues had only one inherently stable meaning. Indeed, multivocality rather than univocality, and fluidity rather than permanency, characterize the human response to architectural edifices and generate interpretations that are highly dependent on context. This means that gaining insight into how Jewish religious structures were seen and understood is contingent upon locating them in space and time, particularly with respect to socio-cultural conditions, attitudes, aesthetic traditions, and rituals. This is a complicated process, for not only did each of our travellers have a different set of assumptions and expectations guiding his or her interpretation but they were also influenced by age, social position, occupational and educational background, gender, and nationality. All of these factors, Jones teaches us, "intrude upon the preparedness that people bring to their respective experience of one and the same architectural configuration" and influence the ways in which architecture is experienced. Synagogues are therefore, to borrow Umberto Eco's term, "open works" insofar as they are "susceptible to accommodating several meanings, each validly posited by a different beholder."[7]

However, despite the fact that Gentile responses to synagogues were subject to a widely diverse spectrum of interpretations that can be deconstructed and unpacked, surprisingly similar response patterns emerged. This can be explained to a large extent by the shared social background from which many of our visitors came. Most were upper-class males from western and central Europe who often made extensive journeys that lasted for weeks, if not months. Virtually all travellers were well educated and practising Christians and often held firm convictions concerning religious observance, cultural manners, and socio-economic customs. It should therefore come as no surprise that these travellers also expressed strong opinions when observing synagogues, many of which reflected, as we shall see, the cultural codes dominant in the social circles from which they came. In fact, their descriptions often expose more about the travellers themselves than about the object under scrutiny.

A number of refractions thus take place when examining the Gentile population's reception of conspicuous Jewish structures and their public display of architectural splendour and prosperity. The lens through which our culturally biased visitors observed synagogues and the twenty-first century lens through which *we* interpret *their* experiences prevent an easy or final interpretation of the literature. However, despite the improbability of a once-and-for-all analysis, a careful synthesis of built form, human actors, and historical context does allow a number of suggestions to be made. Written responses by foreign visitors, for instance, generally included very positive descriptions of the buildings themselves, but they expressed long-held stereotypes about the Jews. They appreciated the architectural achievements but resented what these buildings represented, that is, two prosperous and growing Jewish communities taking full advantage of Holland's relatively liberal religious climate.[8] Dutch comments on the other hand – as well as an occasional British response – seemed to be more accepting of, or at least less negatively predisposed towards, Jews in their midst as they realized that the unprecedented prosperity and blossoming of the city and the republic was, to a large extent, contingent upon the presence of "Others." They were more willing to welcome a foreign element into the realm of the familiar, a sentiment based more on economic concerns than on heart-felt sympathies towards the Jews. Whereas the entry of Jews into Dutch public spheres, among other ways by making their religious buildings prominent contributions to the city's urban panorama, occasioned surprise and sometimes scorn from foreign travellers, native observers viewed this process as much less of a threat.

In this climate of cosmopolitanism and relative tolerance, Amsterdam synagogues transformed from converted warehouses inconspicuous to the public eye into monumental structures that rendered Jewish worship not an activity largely directed at the inside but, rather, one that incorporated public representation into its celebration of Judaism.[9] These highly visible synagogues became public markers of the prosperity, sense of comfort, and prestige the city's Jewish communities enjoyed during these years and illustrate how much they had become an integral part of the socio-religious panorama of the city. Their emergence is particularly striking when one considers the caution with which other religious minorities kept out of the public realm, particularly Dutch Catholics, who worshiped in so-called *schuilkerken*, or concealed chapels.[10] While Catholics, due to strong anti-Spanish and anti-Catholic sentiments, gathered in private homes, the Jews erected two monumental structures that were to form the heart of the most imposing synagogue complex in the world and that, together with the communities' slaughterhouses, residences for the rabbis, gambling and coffee houses, Jewish schools, and printing facilities, "gave the neighborhood the quality of a Jewish center not seen anywhere else in Europe at this time."[11]

The construction of highly visible Jewish prayer houses on prominent sites extended an invitation to outsiders to come and observe the fruits of religious freedom. And Gentiles, in increasing numbers, did. Sightseeing in the Jewish neighbourhood became part of the tourist agenda while visiting Amsterdam. Jewish communal leaders favoured this growing interest in the synagogue. They encouraged Gentiles to enter its domain by attempting to foster an elegant and respectful image of the congregation. Yosef Kaplan even found a number of special regulations introduced as early as the late 1640s that were intended to create a sense of earnestness and decorum that would please Christian guests:

> In contrast to the policy of segregation that characterized many Jewish communities in Europe, the Portuguese community of Amsterdam showed great openness toward Christian visitors and even stated in a special regulation adopted in September 1649 that "the gentlemen who sit behind the *tebah* [reader's platform] will be permitted to offer a seat to any man [who might visit the synagogue] without disturbing the congregation of worshippers." Since this regulation had previously mentioned that "no man shall rise from his seat in order to greet *goyim* [sic] without permission of their lordship of the Mahamad," we may conclude that its intention was to permit non-Jewish visitors to sit in the synagogue, on condition that this was arranged in an orderly manner, by having the worshippers behind the *tebah* function as ushers when necessary, as in a theatre![12]

By making visitors feel welcome, Jews could personally demonstrate their cultured behaviour and good taste, thereby inviting curious Christians to rethink the validity of traditional stereotypes. Replacing "improper" codes of conduct with ones Gentiles could recognize and appreciate thus diminished the possibility of rejection. Taking pinches on the Sabbath thus became inappropriate as such behaviour aroused "great reproach not only among the members of our nation but also among the *goyim* who are present in the place, who whisper about these things and others which constitute a desecration of [the name of] heaven." At the end of the seventeenth century the act of leaving one's seat during the service, too, was considered improper as it "arouses great reproach among the strangers."[13] These communal regulations suggest not only that Christians visited these Jewish religious spaces but also that Sephardim took great pains to convince them of their moral behaviour and "worthiness" by presenting an orderly and dignified Jewish service.

The observations that travellers made of Jewish religious edifices were influenced, as mentioned earlier, by the context in which their interaction with the buildings took place, that is, within a relatively liberal religious and multi-ethnic Dutch milieu that permitted Jews a greater number of privileges than the majority of foreign visitors were used to. Their bafflement emerged largely from their unfamiliarity with the status of Jews in Amsterdam as a generally tolerated religious and ethnic minority. This element of surprise is, according to Jones, a fundamental component in the experience of architecture as its interpretation and meaning emerge out of the "tension between on the one hand a building's conformity to a collectively shared schema, and on the other hand its undermining of habits of perception."[14] Hans-Georg Gadamer, who is best known for his theoretical explorations in *Wahrheit und Methode* (1960), made a similar point when he spoke of a "double mediation," referring to the juxtaposition of paired components required for architecture to become productive – namely, those of conventionality on the one hand and innovation on the other, familiarity and deviation, predictability and surprise.[15] The conventionality of the Esnoga and the Great Synagogue is located in their very form: they were built in a Protestant Baroque style and fit into a familiar European cultural tradition, one with which virtually every tourist could identify. However, the association of these structures' monumentality and public presence with *Jews* challenged many of the observers' expectations. In the eyes of foreign travellers, these components did not or should not match, thereby generating a great sense of perplexity. For these beholders, Dutch synagogue architecture served as a disrupting force as it undermined their understanding of the Jews' place in society, exposing instead an alternative status quo with which they were utterly unfamiliar. Most foreign tourists translated their surprise into resistance, which found its expression in the confirmation of long-held stereotypes. For others – predominantly Dutch observers – monumental synagogues were increasingly accepted as familiar urban structures, the presence of which served to expand, rather than test, the limits of toleration.

The more willing travellers were to engage in a dialogue with the built form and to question the juxtaposition between individual expectation and actuality, the more revealing are their responses. Three different types of reactions to Amsterdam's Jewish synagogues emerge in reading contemporary travel literature, the first of which reveals the lack of any kind of willingness to deal with the Jewish presence in the city. Whereas Jewish synagogues had become sites on the tourist map of Europe by the end of the seventeenth century, a number of travelogues either do not mention them at all or give what seems to be a brief obligatory description. Maximilien Misson reports in his 1699 *New Voyage to Italy: With Curious Observations on several other Countries* that "Amsterdam is without doubt one of the most beautiful, admirable, and important Cities in the World ... the great Magazine of Europe," but he leaves out any mention of the city's Jews. Misson, who finds all Dutch cities "of a sparkling Beauty" and concludes that "every Man in Holland is a kind of Amphibious Creature, equally accustom'd both to Sea and Land," refers to Dutch Jews once in a description of Frankfurt. In this German city "there are a great number of Jews, but they are as beggarly as those of Amsterdam are rich."[16] William Bromley, too, glances over the new synagogues in his elaborate travelogue *Several Years Travels through Portugal, Spain, Italy, Germany, Prussia, Sweden, Denmark, and the United Provinces, Performed by a Gentleman.* Whereas this travel-curious gentleman describes Amsterdam's City Hall as "the first to be taken notice of, as being the most magnificent Structure of its kind in Europe" and refers to "other publick buildings,"[17] the *Joodse buurt* was clearly not on his busy agenda.

Of course, the absence of synagogue references in some of the travel literature does not necessarily mean that the authors refused to go and see Jewish prayer houses or that they harboured anti-

Jewish sentiments; perhaps synagogues were not a priority on a long list of sites to see in a relatively short period of time. Moreover, brief descriptions of Jewish religious structures were often accompanied by equally brief paragraphs on Lutheran, Catholic, Armenian, or Quaker houses of worship, suggesting that the purpose of writing their particular travelogue was not to analyze these urban sites but, rather, merely to report them in order to convey to the reader the impressive array of sites the author had observed within the city centre. However, the fact that other travellers around this time talk about the "famous synagogues" in Amsterdam does suggest the latter were most likely highly popular tourist sites and that a conscious decision was made not to go and see or write about them (or to mention them only in passing).

A second group of responses includes an elaborate and overall positive description of the synagogues but is followed by a rather quick and firm rejection of the larger implications of these buildings. These visitors, most of whom came from France and Germany, wandered into the Jewish neighbourhood, observed the exterior as well as the interior of its religious structures, and occasionally attended services. Many of them were in awe of the buildings' elegant grandeur but were not willing to accept their message: that non-Christians could enjoy some of the same privileges – freedom of conscience, ownership of land, a sense of security – as Christians. In fact, many saw the Esnoga and the Great Synagogue as confirmations of their own preconceived notions of Jews, whether with respect to Jewish malevolence or Jewish domination. These foreign visitors were thus drawn to Amsterdam's synagogues but refused to interpret them as representations of progress towards a greater tolerance and instead translated them as "proof" for traditional Jewish stereotypes.

This is particularly evident in a recurring story in late seventeenth-century travel literature that explained the construction of the Esnoga as an act of conspiracy against the Dutch authorities: rich and powerful Jews were secretly building a large fortress, disguised as a synagogue, in order to take over power in the city. It recounted how local officials expressed growing concerns during the construction process as the building increasingly resembled an intimidating fortress rather than a house of worship. The outwardly slanting buttresses, similar to the design of Solomon's Temple, intensified this speculation. As a result of this "threat," the story went, the local authorities put a stop to the project by demanding the Jewish community build a roof on the unfinished structure. The anonymous French traveller B.F., whose elaborate travel account *Voyages historiques de l'Europe* was published in Paris in the late 1690s and was translated into English and German in the following decade, told his readers:

> When you have visited the Arsenals, if you have not a mind to keep along by the Port, you must cross the Jews' Quarter, which would be one of the most Beautiful in the City, were those Disciples of Moses as neat as the Hollanders. There are two Synagogues, one for the Greek and German Jews, another for the Portuguese. This is much the fairer, being built in a great Square, cover'd with a Duomo, and resembles rather a Citadel than a Jewish Temple; So that when the Jews built it so high, and so thick, the Magistracy began to grow jealous, afraid, left under the pretense of a Temple they were building a Fortress, that might one day trouble the repose of the City; and out of this fear it was, that the Jews were commanded to go no further; so that they were forc'd to cover it, before the Structure was brought to its intended Perfection; and this is the only reason of the Defects which the Architects observe in the Building.[18]

To this observer, the roof was the element of disorientation in his experience and interpretation of this architectural edifice. He considered it a "beautiful" structure, but he could not resist linking it and its construction with the persistent stereotype of Jews as malevolent and untrustworthy. Despite its beauty, the Esnoga still remained a suspicious artefact and a potential threat to Christian society.

Johann Jacob Schudt (1664–1722), a high school principal in Frankfurt, repeated the fortress story in his well known publication *Jüdische Merkwürdigkeiten* (1714), in which he presented a list of "peculiarities" concerning the "allzugroße Freitheit der Juden in Holland" (the excessive freedom of the Jews in Holland). His main concern, however, was not the Jewish attempt at building a fortress, which, in his mind, was not an unexpected move on the part of those power-hungry Jews. Schudt was much more upset by the scandalous fact that Christians had assisted in financing the construction of both synagogues. He could not understand "that these Jews are allowed to build such a magnificent synagogue, one that is praised as a house of God, the construction of which even receives financial support."[19] Did Dutch Christians not understand that the splendid façades of these synagogues and other "exquisitely built Jewish palaces" were hiding nothing but viciousness, that once inside of these buildings all one finds is "Jews smelling like garlic [and] old Jewish women with big Jew-noses and glasses reading books"? Did the local officials not see that, by granting a loan, they were contributing to their own ruin? Presenting himself as a defender of Christianity, Schudt could only explain this financial gesture by the Dutch authorities as a purely economic act performed by "Dutch men of the highest standing in the city of Amsterdam. [They] granted Jews the liberty to build a synagogue and loaned them the money to complete a wonderful and exquisite building, which certainly did not come without significant advantages to the moneylenders. Holland has reached the point of favoring small profits made in the name of God over conscience and Christian well-being."[20] According to Schudt, money had clearly taken priority over religion in this mercantilist society, an observation – as we see below – that was not at all an overstatement.

Equally disturbing to Schudt was the treatment of the Spanish-Portuguese synagogue in Dutch art and literature, in the painting and poetry of, among others, Romeyn de Hooghe, Pieter Persoij, Balthazar Bernaerts, and Emanuel de Witte. De Hooghe, in particular, received much criticism. A well known Dutch artist at the time and a member of Stadholder William III's circle, de Hooghe had lauded the new synagogue in a unique series of prints that appeared, together with the inaugural sermons, in a commemorative book entitled *Sermoes que pregarão os doctos ingenios do K. K. de Taalmud Torah des ta cidade de Amsterdam* (1714). His engravings portrayed elegantly dressed Jews as well as representatives of the Dutch government gathered inside of the new building. One particular scene, framed by medallions bearing the names of the *parnasim*, was complemented by small-scale representations of the exterior and the building plan placed at the top margin of the engraving. To complete the picture, allegorical figures representing the Republic of the United Provinces, Liberty of Conscience, and Judea and the High Priest holding the Scroll of the Law were added in the corners, reinforcing with the Latin phrase *Libertas conscientiae incrementum reipublicae* (Freedom of worship is the mainspring of the republic) the notion of religious freedom as vital to its growth and prosperity. De Hooghe complemented his engraving with a poem that extolled the new synagogue:

> This is the school of Law, the Jews' house of prayer;
> A builder's masterpiece,[21] the glory of the Amstel and the Y;
> This church dedicated to God, Fears no coercion, nor pain nor death;
> This honorable tribe of Judae, let your shoots blossom;
> The growth of burghers will only increase the power of this land.[22]

Schudt could only be amazed "that this house of vice, the Portuguese Jewish synagogue, is honored so highly, that its interior, decorated with wonderful pillars, costly lanterns and lamps in large and very small sizes, is publicized so widely ... that not just Jews but also a Christian, Romanus de Hooghe, has inflicted ridicule on to Christianity by adding his name to Dutch, Latin and French verses, as the educated reader can, with astonishment, gather from the present edition."[23] Shocked by the warm approval expressed in the writings of both Jews and Christians, Schudt could only sigh and exclaim "O! In was für Zeiten sind wir gerathen!" (O! In what times do we find ourselves!).

Schudt finds de Hooghe's poetry so disturbing not merely because it celebrates the Esnoga and Dutch Jewry at large but also because it undermines the idea that the Dutch authorities objected to the construction of a Jewish synagogue on a very public site. De Hooghe's references to the Esnoga as "Bouman's masterpiece" and "the glory of the Amstel" challenged Christian suspicions about the building. When Stadtholder Prince William III of Orange thus offered to replace the wooden columns in the Esnoga with stone ones after his visit in 1690, the only interpretation available to Schudt involved some ulterior motive – namely, economic interests.[24]

It was not uncommon for this type of criticism to go hand in hand with negative views of Dutch society at large. Travel accounts by Schudt and others expressed hostile views of Amsterdam's Jews and their new synagogues within the context of what was perceived as an increasingly secular society tolerating this "allzugroße Judenfreiheit." British traveller Owen Felltham, for instance, did not specifically mention Amsterdam's Jews or their houses of prayer in his 1672 *Batavia, or the Hollander*, but he created the connection between Jewish stereotypes, on the one hand, and the decline of Dutch society due to a preoccupation with money and trade, on the other. To Felltham the Dutch are "the Jews of the New Testament that have exchanged nothing but the Law for the Gospel; and this they rather prosess [sic] than practice."[25] Annoyed with Dutch prosperity and importance in international trade, and resentful towards the Dutch as a result of ongoing Anglo-Dutch conflicts, Felltham presented a scathing and vicious account of Holland, a country inhabited by "savages," "water devils," and "cowards [who] live lower than the fishes." Despite this barbarity and uncivilized behaviour, however, Dutch houses and public buildings, "especially in their Cities, are the best eye-beauties of their Countrey. For Cost and Sight they far exceed ours."[26] Felltham seemed to follow the pattern of praising the aesthetic quality of the built environment while disapproving of those who actually inhabited it. The well known stereotype of the Jew – his supposed wealth at the expense of others, the thin veneer barely covering his boorish and savage nature – served in this case as a model to describe the Dutch population at large.

Felltham and Schudt are admittedly rather extreme examples of this second type of response, namely, that of visitors whose observations and descriptions of the religious buildings themselves were favourable but who ultimately arrived at a negative judgment regarding their representation. They were drawn to these monumental synagogues, yet they had difficulty accepting the prevailing tolerance of Jews in Dutch society. Whereas this tone is equally detectable in other travel accounts, the majority was considerably less aggressive. One might even call this "category" of responses to Jews and their synagogues rather mild in nature, perhaps even innocent, as they emerged not from an anti-Semitic disposition but, rather, from Christian travellers' unfamiliarity and misunderstanding of Jewish culture. The British traveller Thomas Penson, for instance, was not shy of repeating negative Jewish stereotypes in an account dated from 30 July until 6 October 1687: "Nor did I only visit the Christian churches, but also the Jews, whose temple or synagogue is a magnificent building, to which I repaired more than once, being informed of some of their great days on which they performed some extraordinary ceremonies, which seemed to me more like madness than order."[27] Penson recognized the architectural value of the building, but, as he was utterly unfamiliar with Jewish religious customs, he described the events taking place inside it as uncivilized chaos. Gregorio Leti, who visited Holland in the 1680s, was equally complimentary of the Jews' outward appearance and manners, but he could not hide his displeasure with what, to him, appeared to be a noisy, disorganized bunch.[28] The British physician John Northleigh, too, reported that he saw "near Two thousand Souls ... in their great Church, all habited in White Silk Hoods over their Shoulders, Men and Boys [who would at times] be laughing, talking, and idly wandering, as if about profane Affairs, though in a Presence so sacred."[29] And "when they were dismissed," wrote Phillip Skippon in amazement, "many of them went down singing till they came to the street!"[30] For Mrs Calderwood, an upper-class woman of Polton, this "disorder" and "carelessness" in religious services rendered the Jews "the drollest set [she] ever saw." She reported:

> I went into their synegogue [sic] one morning, and they were at service, but what kind I could not find out, but I suppose it was a fast-day, for there were two men standing on the altar, I suppose, for it was raised higher than the rest, in the midst of the room; there was a lamp burning, though the sun was shining. They were both reading aloud, with harn clouts [literally, brain cloths, a cloth around the head] on their heads, and several of the congregation had harn clouts likeways. Some were sitting with books in their hands, some standing, reading or looking on a book, some walking about, snuffing and cracking [conversing, gossiping] as loud as if they had been in the street; in short you never saw such a congregation; some were coming in, some going out, and those who went out had their harn clouts in their pockets.[31]

This snuffing and cracking during the service must have made some impression on Mrs Calderwood as she refrained from mentioning that which nearly all visitors noticed at first sight – that is, the grandeur of the actual building. This was the first thing that struck William Carr, who reported in his *Travellours Guide and Historians Faithful Companion*, published in London in 1690, that "the *Jewes*, who are verie considerable in the trade of this citie have two synagogues, one whereof is the Largest in Christendom, and as some say in the world, sure I am, it far exceeds, those in *Rome*, *Venice*, and all other places where I have bin."[32] However, within the synagogue's court yard, he added with a disapproving voice, "they have several Roomes or schools, where their children are taught Hebrew, and verie carefully, to the shame of Christians negligence, brought up and instruckted in the Jewish principles." While acknowledging the Esnoga exceeded any other synagogue he had ever encountered, Carr could not hide his hope that the Jews would eventually convert to the Christian faith.

Despite their admiration of the synagogue's architecture and their descriptions of Amsterdam as "one of the beautifullest cities in the world," these visitors thus echoed long-standing prejudices regarding Jews. Penson emphasized that he "must not omit (by way of caution) to speak of the Jews who are nicknamed Smouces. They are the money-changers ... [who] will cheat a man to his face."[33] Mrs Calderwood informed her readers they were called, "by way of reproach, *smouce*, but that is only a name for a certain sort of them; I asked a man if he was a smouce, and he said, 'Ya, Mefrowe' [yes, ma'am]."[34] The "certain sort" of Jews in her presumably light-hearted remark were clearly the Ashkenazi peddler or moneylender, whose appearance, occupation, and manners could not but earn him this derogatory name. Carr, too, warned his readers to be careful of the shady way Jews did business, which was "a great mystery of Iniquity [that] inricheth one man and ruins a hundred." He elaborated extensively on the process of buying and selling of "Actions of the Company" at the Dam Square, the Exchange, and "in the Coledges or Clubs of the Jews," the price of which was apparently influenced by "Crafty Jews and others [who] Connived to Coine bad newes to make the Action fall, and good newes to raise them, the which craft [sic] of doing at Amsterdam is not taken notice of, which is much to be wondered at, in such a wise Government as Amsterdam is, for it is a certain trueth they many times spread scandalous reports touching the affaires of State, which passe amongst the Ignorant for truth."[35] Jews might have had a splendid and state-of-the-art synagogue, but they were still not to be trusted.

The third and last group of responses reveals a genuine interest in synagogues. These travelogues disclose at least a partial acceptance of Jewish religious structures as an integral part of the cityscape as well as of Dutch society at large. This group, many of whom were native Dutch visitors and an occasional British tourist, was more appreciative of conspicuous synagogues as it tended to see Jews – especially Sephardim – as beneficiaries to the overall well-being of the Dutch Republic. That their tone and receptivity differ substantially from those of previously discussed observers can, to a large extent, be explained by the political and cultural codes prevalent in the societies from which they came. As Amos Rapoport suggested almost thirty years ago, "people's responses [to built and natural environments] depend upon the meaning which they attach to stimuli, which is associational and, in turn, depends on past experience, and culture influencing standards and environmental evaluation."[36] Our travellers' dialogue with the Esnoga and the Great Shul, in other words, was coloured by the place and participation – or lack thereof – of Jews within their own socio-cultural, economic, or religious spheres as well as by popular perceptions of Jews within their immediate surroundings. Both the Dutch Republic and Britain at this time were religiously diverse societies. Jews were only one of a multitude of religious minorities, and most people did not perceive them as a threat to the existing order. In fact, the Dutch authorities, who increasingly valued commercial interests over Church dogma, fully realized that allowing a Jewish community into their midst led to an accumulation of resources and knowledge highly lucrative to a republic deeply involved in international trade, particularly if that community was completely self-organized and self-sufficient. The commercialization of the traditional ruling classes in combination with religious diversity created a milieu in late seventeenth-century Holland that not only permitted Jews to gradually enter Dutch public space, albeit within certain boundaries, but also led to a less hostile reception on the part of Gentiles. Coming from a culture in which the Jewish "Other" did not pose a threat and that lacked a tradition of vicious discrimination against Jews – largely due to the long absence of an organized Jewish community in this part of Europe – most Dutch and British visitors were more willing to engage in a meaningful conversation with Jewish religious buildings. Consequently, majestic synagogues built "on a publick road" did not generate the same feelings of shock and surprise as it did among German or French visitors; rather, the very presence of these urban structures advanced confessional toleration as they expanded the limits of what was considered acceptable within the public realm.

An obvious exception to the German response pattern is a letter written by a German baron called Karl Ludwig, Freiherr von

Pöllnitz, on 2 February 1733, which reveals a rare moment of self-examination and self-criticism after he had observed Jews in Amsterdam's Jewish neighbourhood. When describing the Sephardim, Pöllnitz warned the recipient of his letter not to take the Esnoga's popular architectural style as a sign of Jewish authority over Dutch urban aesthetics. Instead of falling victim to "presumptions" that associated anything Jewish with vice and transgression, a very un-Christian tendency in his opinion, this foreign traveller presented an alternative interpretation:

> You will no doubt think it a Phæneomenon to find that a Hebrew, whom in Germany we treat with a Sort of Disdain, *which perhaps is neither very Generous, nor very Christian*, should concern himself in the Spectacles, and presume to force an entire Town to conform to his Taste; but you are to know, Sir, that the Jews are treated in this Government, upon quite another Footing than they are elsewhere; and really, as for the Portuguese Jews, *they deserve it*; for a *Texeyra*, a *Schwartzo*, a *Dulis*, have done such generous Actions as are worthy of the most virtuous Christians. They live like Noblemen, and indeed, such you would take them to be. They are admitted into all Assemblies, and even their Wives appear there: They treat and receive all Persons of Distinction at their Houses: They relieve our Poor, contribute to our Churches, and *differ in nothing from us but in frequenting the Synagogue*.[37]

Freiherr von Pöllnitz's early eighteenth-century comments were not unlike the arguments brought to the fore by liberal-minded and Reformed German Jews a century later, which stated that the only distinction between Jews and Gentiles was their religious faith and that they were "worthy" of better treatment – that is, Emancipation. This traveller's observations of Amsterdam's Sephardim in the context of Dutch religious progressivism, in combination with his own cultural background, produced an interpretation that not only denounced the negative stereotyping of Jews but also hinted at an alternative outlook – one that viewed Jews as part of, rather than a threat to, Western culture and society. "As for the Portuguese Jews, they deserve it," contended Pöllnitz, as in his eyes these "gentlemen" seemed to have adopted the dominant social and cultural values of Dutch society. Although he refrained from elaborating on the city's Ashkenazim, we can only guess that he might not have considered them "qualified" for this kind of honour.

The outlook that prevailed in Holland, which gave rise to what Pöllnitz called the "phenomenon" of Jewish "Spectacles," was deeply embedded in the economic make-up of the Dutch Republic. In fact, the general lack of suspicion or bias towards Jews and their synagogues in late seventeenth-century and early eighteenth- century Dutch travel literature can be partially ascribed to the role Jews played in Amsterdam's economy, and it reflects the mercantilist lens through which many natives observed their surroundings. It was well known that the presence of Jews attracted trade and investors to the city and that a considerable contribution was made on their part in financing the three Anglo-Dutch wars between 1652 and 1678. Cornelis de Witt explains in a letter dated in 1688 and addressed to a British friend that many Jews and other "Refugees consist of Merchants, Artifficers [sic], or Laborious Tradesmen, that like Bees, wherever they come, bring in Honey to the common Hive."[38] Their extensive network of commercial and financial relations, an enterprise that proved particularly beneficial to the Dutch war effort, contributed to the overall well-being of both the Jewish community and the republic at large. Jews were thus closely connected to economic success and power, and Dutch contemporaries were only too proud to attribute the republic's prominence on the world map to Holland's cosmopolitan and religiously diverse character. Moreover, the prevailing ethos of commercial gain prevented a stigma from being attached to the financial and commercial activities in which the majority of Jews were involved. In other parts of Europe, particularly central Europe, it was not uncommon for these kinds of activities to be perceived as suspicious and lacking in nobility, and the fact that a disproportionately high percentage of Jews found their profession in commerce and trade aggravated an already strained Christian-Jewish relationship. In the Dutch Republic, however, these occupational spheres were highly respected and Jewish pre-eminence in this line of work much welcomed. Commercial power, mercantilist ideology, and the principle of "freedom of conscience" thus constituted vital components in Holland's success formula. Casper Commelin, whose *Beschryvinge van Amsterdam* (Descriptions of Amsterdam) appeared in 1694, informs his audience of the important connection between religious diversity and the capital's power:

> [T]his unconstrained Liberty from a dismal and ungodly coercion of conscience is the primary reason for the blossoming state of this city, since it invites all kinds of people from all corners of the World, especially those who cannot practice nor experience their Religion publicly, to come and live in this City … Lutheran, "Remonstranten" or Arminians, Mennonites or "Doopsgezinden" also have their Churches; there is an English Brownist Church located in the Barnesteeg … as well as Jewish synagogues where Jews openly practice their Religion. This almost appears to be the only reason for the rise and preservation of this City, which will, without doubt, continue to prosper as long as everyone is permitted the liberty to practice their Religion and the liberty of Conscience.

To strengthen his claim, Commelin includes a poem by the well known contemporary poet and playwright Joost van den Vondel entitled "To Religious Liberty," which directly links Amsterdam's prosperity to the freedom of conscience:

> Alongside the Amstel, and alongside the Y is wonderfully exposed, she who, like an Empress, wears the crown of Europe;
> Amsterdam, raising her head toward the Heavens, and pounding poles into its marshes, as if in Pluto's chest;
> Which waters do not see the shadows of her sails? At what markets does she not sell her goods?
> Which peoples does she not see in the light of the moon? She who lays down the laws to the grey Ocean,
> She extends her wings further by an accumulation of souls, And carries her overstocked keels into the World;
> This prosperity will be hers, as long as the distinguished [city] Council denies religious coercion her evil will.[39]

Although Dutch tolerance of religious minorities resulted more from practical commercial interests than from a principled belief in the moral superiority of religious diversity,[40] it nevertheless allowed the Amsterdam Jewish communities to thrive and to become a visible and common component of the city's urban landscape. And it is this visibility that, in the words of the British ambassador Sir William Temple, "contribute[d] much to make *conversation*, and [that made] all the offices of common life so easie, among so different opinions, of which so many several persons are often in every man's eye; [N]o man checks or takes offence at faces or customs, or ceremonies he sees every day, As at those he hears of in places far distant, and perhaps by partial relations."[41] Although Temple's descriptions admittedly have an idealized tone to them, at the very least they suggest that anti-Jewish sentiments did not constitute an intrinsic and overt element in the structure of Dutch society.

The realization that the Jewish community was not merely a religious body but also a highly lucrative economic entity that greatly benefited the city's financial interests rendered potential Christian objections to granting Jews certain privileges less and less urgent.[42] This civic toleration went hand in hand with the gradual reduction of the Church's influence in the economic and political spheres in the late seventeenth century. A mercantilist ethos that welcomed religious diversity, and that considered the meddling of the Dutch Reformed Church in political and commercial activities increasingly inappropriate, challenged both the authority of the Church and the belief in its omnipotent power in every facet of society. This process, maintains historian Daniel Swetschinski, led to "the delimitation of a sphere of public life in which religious opinions [were] not of primary concern"[43] and in which the public presence of Jews was not perceived as a threat to Dutch religious identity. In other words, an early form of realpolitik on the part of the local magistrates, in which a pragmatic mindset prevailed over religious ideology, permitted the Jews to build stately synagogues on prominent locations as the former were willing to subordinate purely religious considerations to the attractions this commercially valuable group had to offer. The risk of having Sephardic merchants – as well as the less wealthy but still tax-paying Ashkenazim – leave for such places as London or Hamburg, the result of which would mean a significant loss of enterprise and revenue, was simply too great. Jews, as well as other religious minorities in Holland, thus profited from the mounting tension between jurisdiction and local legislation.[44]

The relatively liberal conditions in which Jews lived also derived from the ruling classes' awareness that powerful minorities pose less of a danger to the existing social order when tolerated publicly than when they are condemned to practise in secret. Cornelis de Witt gave voice to this view in his 1688 *Letter from Holland*, in which he writes that "granting Liberty of Conscience secures the

Government and renders it easy; takes away all Colour for Faction or Rebellion: Nothing binds more firmly than Interest, and no Interest is more strongly obliging, or more beloved, than this Freedom; and therefore ties all the Inhabitants where they have it, into a strict Fidelity to that Power which grants it."[45] Peace and stability, or, as historian Joris van Eijnatten phrased it, a "calculated peace,"[46]outweighed the potential annoyance of Christians at the growing presence and participation of Jews in the public sphere. In fact, tolerating a minority sect often proved far easier than putting up with a rival denomination, which partially explains why Jews received considerably less attention than did local Catholic dissenters whose religious identity was much closer to the norm.[47] The Remonstrant Johan Uytenbogaert was not far off when he remarked: "You [Hollanders] are a strange kind of people; you bear harder upon those that differ but little from you, than upon those who differ much."[48]From this perspective, concealed Catholic chapels were much more dangerous to the establishment than was a monumental and conspicuous Jewish synagogue.

It is from this milieu that most of our Dutch travellers to the Jewish neighbourhood came, and it is these notions of civic toleration and religious pluralism, as well as the passion for commerce, that reverberate in their observations of synagogues. Whereas foreign travellers were often surprised or annoyed with what they perceived as Dutch laxity towards the growth and prosperity of Amsterdam's Jews – "as long as you are a good and faithful burgher, nobody cares what you believe!" reported the astonished author of *Curieuse und Historische Reisen* in the late 1600s[49] – contemporary Dutch writings overall lack these strong sentiments. In fact, the Dutch contemporary poet Roeland van Leuve, whose book on Amsterdam is written entirely in rhyme, labelled anyone who uses such derogatory terms as "smous" for a Jewish burgher "slegt volk," or "bad people," and counted Jews among "Amsterdam's virtuous Fathers."[50] Travel accounts by, among others, Casper Commelin, Olfert Dappert, Jacob de Riemer, and a variety of anonymous authors, as well as contemporary writings and paintings by Romeyn de Hooghe, Joost van den Vondel, Pieter Persoij, Balthazar Bernaerts, Emanuel de Witte, and Bernard Picart, vary from rather neutral to highly positive receptions with regard to the emergence of Jewish religious structures. Their engagement with the built form within the context of a relatively liberal religious, political, and economic climate produced an interpretation that rendered the Esnoga and the Great Shul respectable products of the Golden Age. That their positive descriptions and depictions also indirectly confirmed the virtuousness of the Dutch themselves – and thus of the individual author or painter – was, certainly, a nice encore.

This is, of course, not to say that there were no oppositional voices in Holland at this time or that Jews were fully accepted burghers untouched by prejudice or intolerance. A number of Calvinist preachers and theologians, in particular, expressed anger and anxiety about "deceitful" Jews, whose increasingly public form of Jewish worship was a blasphemous and scandalous development. Van Eijnatten also informs us that the majority of seventeenth-century and eighteenth-century Dutch intellectuals still favoured some form of religious uniformity over principled diversity and that much of the toleration debate centred on the importance of religious unity rather than on the virtues of religious plurality. However, whereas these voices were heard, they failed to have an impact on the position of Dutch Jews, who progressively gained access to public domains, nor did they give rise to a literary tradition of demonization.[51] The main target remained not the Jewish minority but the Catholic minority. Similarly, we do not know whether the generally positive attitude of well-to-do Dutch travellers or educated artists represents the mainstream burgher in Holland. Late seventeenth-century travel accounts – offering elite rather than popular "readings" of the city – do not tell us whether the average Christian shopkeeper harboured virulent anti-Jewish sentiments or whether his wife believed local Jews were conspiring against the Christian authorities by building a fortress in the Jewish neighbourhood so they could finally achieve the power they had always craved. However, what we do know is that, in the late seventeenth and early eighteenth centuries, a certain segment of Dutch society produced a body of art and literature that seems to be less negatively predisposed towards the emergence of the Esnoga and the Great Synagogue. Many of these interpretations have an almost self-congratulatory tone to them, reminding readers that these exquisite buildings were part of Amsterdam's urban panorama only because of the virtue and generosity of the larger Dutch society. It was thus not unusual for Jewish synagogues to be used as evidence of Dutch exceptionalism regarding its religious climate and commercial power, even though, in the early eighteenth century, the latter already showed serious signs of decline. The atypical status of Sephardim and Ashkenazim in Holland during this time, one might conclude, thus generated an equally unconventional response on the part of affluent Dutch observers to the emergence of prominent Jewish synagogues.

NOTES

1 See also Perkins (this volume) on tourists in Edinburgh. Eds.
2 See also Friedrichs (this volume), who alludes to the importance of intercontinental exchanges in shaping religious and social perceptions. Eds.
3 Michman, Beem, and Michman, *Pinkas*, 53.
4 Kaplan, "Gente Política," 21–2.
5 Jones, *Hermeneutics of Sacred Architecture*, 29.
6 Ibid., 189. [See also Blackstone (this volume) on how the buildings in Norwich registered the presence of community figures; and Hoople (this volume) on Henry James's responses to Florentine architecture. Eds.]
7 Eco quoted in Maquet, *The Aesthetic Experience*, 159.
8 It is important to make a distinction between what the Esnoga and the Great Shul represented to gentiles – namely, wealth and power – and the actual conditions in which Amsterdam Jews lived. The privileges that the Jewish communities enjoyed were both limited and very much dependent on the goodwill of the local authorities and could be reversed at any time. Moreover, despite highly successful segments of the community, a substantial number of local Jews – mostly Ashkenazim – lived in poverty.
9 The synagogues of Amsterdam may, in this respect, be seen as precursors to the impressive building programs initiated in Europe in the second half of the nineteenth century. Whereas synagogues were generally small and inconspicuous in the premodern period, the Esnoga and the Great Shul were the first to break with this pattern. This is one of the main reasons why they attracted so much attention by Jews and gentiles alike.
10 See, for instance, Israel's discussion of toleration in *The Dutch Republic*, 637–76 and 1019–30.
11 Michman, *Pinkas*, 53.
12 Kaplan, "Gente Política," 27.
13 *Livro de Ascamoth B,* Amsterdam Community Archives, PA 334, no. 20, fol. 248, cited in Kaplan, "Gente Política," 28.
14 Jones, *Hermeneutics of Sacred Architecture*, 67.
15 Ibid., 71.

16 Misson, *A New Voyage to Italy*, 22, 54.
17 Bromley, *Several Years Travels*, 275.
18 B.F.'s *Voyages Historiques de l'Europe* was translated into German by August Bohse (1661–1730) under the title of *Curieuse Reisen durch Europa* and into English under the title of *A New Description of Holland and the Rest of the United Provinces In General: Containing Their Government, Laws, Religion, Policy, and Strength; Their Customs, Manners, and Riches; Their Trade to the Indies, etc.*. This quotation is from the English translation, which was published in London in 1701. That this travel account appeared in three languages suggests the high demand for popular travel literature at the end of the seventeenth century.
19 Schudt, *Jüdische Merkwürdigkeiten*, 278.
20 Ibid., 281.
21 This line of de Hooghe's poem is a pun on the name of the Esnoga's architect, Elias Bouman. The Dutch word for builder is "bouwman," which has the exact same pronunciation. The "Amstel" and the "Y" in the next phrase refer to two rivers that run through Amsterdam.
22 See de Castro, *De Synagoge der Portugees-Israëlitische Gemeente te Amsterdam*, 34–5.
23 Schudt, *Jüdische Merkwürdigkeiten*, 281.
24 Apparently, his highness expressed his surprise over the wooden columns, which had been the result of failed orders for stone materials from Germany and Italy. William intervened, which resulted in the wooden columns' being replaced by stone.
25 Felltham, *Batavia, or the Hollander Displayed*. This source lacks page numbers.
26 Ibid.
27 Thomas Penson, *Penson's Short Progress into Holland, Flanders, and France, with Remarques* (1687), cited in van Strien, *Touring the Low Countries*, 41.
28 Gregorio Leti, *Teatro Belgico, o vero ritratti historici, chronologici, politici, e geografici, della sette Provincie Unite*, vol. 2 (Amsterdam, 1690), cited in Brasz and Kaplan, *Dutch Jews*, 26.
29 John Northleigh, *Topographical Descriptions*, in Swetschinski *Reluctant Cosmopolitans*, 210.
30 Phillip Skippon, *Account of a Journey*, in Swetschinski, *Reluctant Cosmopolitans*, 209.
31 Fergusson, *Letters and Journals of Mrs. Calderwood of Polton*, 104–6.
32 Carr, *Travellours Guide*, 23.
33 Penson, *Short Progress*, 46.

34 Fergusson, *Letters and Journals of Mrs. Calderwood*, 104–6.
35 Carr, *Travellours Guide*, 54–5.
36 Rapoport, *Human Aspects of Urban Form*, 320.
37 von Pöllnitz, *Memoirs of Baron Charles Lewis von Pöllnitz*, Letter 52, 2 February 1733, 410.
38 de Witt, *Letter from Holland*, 2.
39 Commelin, *Beschryvinge van Amsterdam*.
40 De Witt fully realized that the scales increasingly favoured economic concerns over religious dogma. He reported: "thô I know Peoples Passions have a strange Byas on their Judgments, yet a Wise Man may be tempted to suspect something more in this case [concerning Liberty of Conscience], and that the Humour is fomented and encouraged by the secret Influences of some powerful interest: for 't is That commonly moves the Wheels, though Religion may be made the pretence." De Witt, *Letter from Holland*, 1.
41 Temple, *Observations Upon the United Provinces of the Netherlands*, 207.
42 Vlessing, "The Excommunication of Baruch Spinoza," 143.
43 Swetschinski, *Reluctant Cosmopolitans*, 39.
44 Michman elaborates on this dualism in *Pinkas*, 15. Whereas the Dutch Calvinist Church enjoyed a special status, Michman contends it no longer had a decisive voice in local politics – as opposed to the case in Britain. This does not necessarily mean that religious ideology weakened; rather, it merely suggests that, in the political and economic realm, the civil authorities had become more influential.
45 De Witt, *Letters from Holland*, 1.
46 van Eijnatten, *Liberty and Concord in the United Provinces*, 18.
47 Bodian makes a similar point in *Hebrews of the Portuguese Nation*, 55.
48 See Swetschinski, *Reluctant Cosmopolitans*, 26.
49 Anonymous, *Curieuse und Historische Reisen durch Europa*, 754.
50 Roeland van Leuve writes: "who does not honor the virtue of Amsterdam's Fathers? / Each of whom approaches God his own way, whether Roman or non-Roman, whether Christian or Jew. / The latter own a large and beautiful synagogue, built by prosperous Portuguese who disobey the Law of Moses / And another synagogue, smaller but equally beautiful, was built by what bad people would consider Smousjes." See van Leuve, *Werelds Koopslot*, 84.
51 That the Jews received a relatively mild response from Calvinist circles might also have been related to the latter's interests in the study of Hebrew. Yosef Kaplan states at one point that Jews were not the "aver-

age" religious minority as many theologians became increasingly interested in exploring the links between the roots of Christendom and Hebrew texts. The religious discussions between Christian scholars and Jewish intellectuals in the course of the seventeenth century, maintains Kaplan, not merely strengthened an often recently acquired Jewish religious identity but also created – albeit modest – bridges between two different religious and intellectual traditions. Christians, however, engaged in these discussions primarily with the intent to convert Jews to Christendom. See Kaplan, "De Joden in de Republiek tot omstreeks 1750," 166–8.

12

Between History and Hope: The Urban Centre of William Blake and William Wordsworth

JON SAKLOFSKE

Thy scenes,
Thy tainted scenes, proud city, now detain
My restless feet. 'Twill soothe a vacant hour
To trace what dim inexplicable links
Of hidden nature have inclined my soul
To love what heretofore it most abhorred.

From "London" by Charles Lloyd and Charles Lamb

Jean Paul Sartre suggests that a city, for Europeans, "is, above all, a past," whereas for Americans "it is mainly a future; what they like in the city is everything that it has not yet become and everything it will be."[1] Cultural and geographical generalization aside, this statement identifies a useful perceptual difference in the apprehension of the urban landscape: the city can be a metaphor for history or futurity, an established traditional structure or a fluid space of evolutionary possibility and hopeful excess.[2] Situated between Europe and America, William Blake and William Wordsworth variously engage with each of these perspectives in relation to late eighteenth-century London. A close comparison between their poetic responses to the city challenges a number of assumptions regarding Romantic attitudes towards the cityscape, illuminates some symbolic associations between England and its largest urban sprawl, and demonstrates the effects of a "mutual imposition" or interactivity between city and author.

Romantic literature is often stereotyped as being generally hostile towards urban settings, and some of William Blake's *Songs of Experience*, including "London," "The Chimney Sweeper," and "Holy Thursday" appear to fortify such antagonism. These poems reveal the decay of England's social, political, and religious traditions through definitive and richly symbolic images gathered from the streets of the empire's capital. These urban images are refracted through the songs of an imaginative (and often economically, socially, and politically frustrated) city dweller who, perhaps, is too close to his subject (or too much of a subject of urban life) to objectively present it as anything other than a threat to individual energies. As well, in a cancelled plate from Blake's forward-looking work entitled *America: a Prophecy*, Blake criticizes "Infinite Londons [sic] awful spires [for casting] a dreadful cold / Even on rational things beneath."[3] Blake's association of the cityscape with the "dark Satanic Mills" of industry in his poem *Milton a Poem in 2 Books* and the "mind-forg'd manacles" of the city crowd in "London" anticipates Friedrich Engels' and D.H. Lawrence's later condemnations of urbanized industry and its effects on humanity.[4]

Curiously, though, the narrator of Blake's "London" reveals a "wandering" capability and agency amidst London's "charter'd" streets. While all faces in the crowd are marked with weakness and woe, it is the narrator's unconventional perceptual ability that notices or remarks upon this reality. Indeed, in the midst of the crowd, Blake's narrator is uniquely removed from it, revealing it but not sharing its scars, its chartered echo of the streets that contain and channel it. However, repetitions of the word "mark" as both action and effect – "I mark in every face I meet / marks of weakness, marks of woe" – implies a creative complicity that places this speaker on par with the affective properties of the cityscape. In other words, the marking activity of the speaker is a power he shares with the city: the responsive but still limited speaker only notices and condemns London's repressive institutions, and his lack of imaginative vision ironically reveals that he is part of the problem that he identifies, condemns, and from which he cannot emerge. This poem offers little choice for London's citizens: be silently marked and victimized by institutional collectives or individually emulate the ignorant monstrosity that produces such victimization.

"London", however, is a song of "Experience" – a perspective that is revealed to be just as limited as its innocent counterpart when one takes a more comprehensive look at Blake's collected *Songs of Innocence and of Experience*. Blake, an author who is able to simultaneously consider the unresolved interplay of the contraries of Innocence and Experience, creates a speaker who is thus limited in his capabilities to define, to comment upon, and to fully comprehend London's character. While this poem has often been noted for its scathing indictment of urban ills, too easily aligning with the problematic speaker who is too preoccupied with adding his own cries of weakness and woe to the chorus that he maps out will reveal a reader's own ignorance and, possibly, complicity in a misrepresentation of Blake's city. Indeed, it is not "London" itself that is harmful; London, as presented here, is a concentrated arena of individual and institutional arrogance and ignorance that the partial perceptions of Blake's cynical narrator highlight and participate in, yet condemn.

It is no wonder, then, that Blake's later works associate London with symbols that often contradict the perceptions of the aforementioned speaker. Even the earlier mentioned quote from the deleted plate of *America: A Prophecy*, in which Blake seemingly criticizes "Infinite Londons [sic] awful spires [for casting] a dreadful cold / Even on rational things beneath," is problematized when one becomes aware of the value that Blake elsewhere places on imaginative infinity, the characteristic reversals in which he often aligns himself with conventionally negative images such as hell and devils, and his distrust of rationality and analytics.[5] Without becoming ensnared in the debate surrounding Blake's ambivalent "meanings" here, suffice it to say that, while Blake's reference to London in *America* apparently supports the stereotype of Romantic condemnation of urbanity, subtly condemning the religious and political architectures that unnaturally eclipse the heat and light of life and sunshine, it also potentially recognizes the seeds and fires of America's antithetical and prosperous futurity in London's spires and shadows. While this excerpt does sustain the critique that "London" offers against a nation and its institutions through the critical presentation of a representative cityscape, it additionally and subtly acknowledges a combative vitality, procured by the intersection of cumulative European historicity and the futurist hope generated by the prodigal revolution of England's imperial offspring, in a complex image of London that Blake increasingly contemplates beyond the limited perspectives of *Songs of Experience*.

Kenneth Johnston, following Frank Kermode and Northrop Frye, affirms Blake as "English Romanticism's most urban poet and the modern city's first myth-maker" and suggests that Blake's urban imagery evolved over time to encapsulate both the heavenly and fallen cities of biblical myth.[6] His argument envisions Blake as a poet concerned with urban reality who appeals to complex mythic imaginings to suggest that England will be renewed in and through a literal process of unified urban renewal. This perspective, although tidy, is partly misled by a historicist predisposition, subjecting myth to history in an attempt to demonstrate Blake's "application to everyday life."[7] The limitations of Johnston's appeal to this binary between history and myth can be overcome by focusing on the temporal parameters that Sartre's earlier quote brings to bear on this chapter's particular focus.

Rather than seeing Blake's writings as marking a progressive path towards the actual resolution of the urban ills featured in the "London" of *Experience*, the London of Blake's last major prophetic work, *Jerusalem: The Emanation of the Giant Albion*, overwhelms his earlier speaker's perceptual participation in human limitation and further emphasizes that such partiality is antithetical to, and perhaps even unnatural in relation to, the manifest and potential human capability signified by his city. Blake's London comes to signify an imaginative presentness, a density that actualizes mythical and historical pasts and anticipates apocalyptic and paradisiacal futures. This shifting symbolic potential of London within *Jerusalem* incorporates but also overwhelms the applicability of his considerations to actual urban reformation. Blake was not an urban reformer; he was a difficult poet who promoted imaginative freedom and perceptual awakening – and the city of London becomes an appropriate nodal point of symbolic association, functioning as both cause and effect in relation to Blake's creative ends.

In *Jerusalem*, Blake considers London in relation to the mythically infused cities of Babylon and Jerusalem as well as to the purely imagined city of Golgonooza. Jerusalem and Babylon are defined by Blake as a straightforward opposition between a heavenly centre of human imagination, liberty, and divine form and a hellish centre of misery, destruction, and torment, respectively.[8] Unlike the Babylonian London presented in Blake's *Songs of Experience*, though, *Jerusalem*'s London houses both extremes. While temporal shifts, inconsistencies, and a frustrating host of symbolic associations often interrupt narrative expectations throughout Blake's *Jerusalem*, the "City & ... temple" of Jerusalem is initially built within London.[9] Situating a symbolic Jerusalem within the actual city of London is both a narrative reversal and a fortification of the interactivity signified by London's current containment in Blake's *Jerusalem*. However, the fertile unification of London and Jerusalem is revealed as a distant past (and as a persistently hopeful future), for London has declined and has become a mere stone of Jerusalem's ruin that now hosts Babylon or can now be associated with the abovementioned Babylonian qualities.[10] London and Jerusalem are still linked in that they share the same condition of ruin, and Blake reverses the subjection of London to Jerusalem by personifying Jerusalem as being "in ruins wandering about from house to house" within London.[11] "Jerusalem" names a city, a temple, and a human figure in Blake's work, and its association with London suggests that London can be perceived with the same density of association. Indeed, just as Jerusalem is represented as more than a mere place or setting, London is also personified "as blind and age-bent begging thro the Streets / of Babylon."[12] Blake creates a shifting interdependent and interpenetrating relationship here: Jerusalem, once located within London, now wanders within the ruin of Babylonian London; but London is a mere fragment of Jerusalem's ruin that wanders within Babylon. What emerges from this layering is a richness of association that includes but also exceeds the isolated London of *Experience*.

In chapter 1 of *Jerusalem*, London is presented both as being in ruins "rent away and dissipated, in Chasms & Abysses of sorrow, enlarg'd without dimension, terrible" and yet as also containing every nation and being contained in every nation, "mutual in love & harmony."[13] This concentration of cynicism and idealism demonstrates the potential that resides in the contradictory excesses of London's presentness, in which aging traditions collide with hopeful ambitions on many scales on a modern empire's urban stage. If, as Shakespeare's Jaques suggests in *As You Like It*, "All the world's a stage," by Blake's time, London's urban density and scope had become the symbolic centre and ironic reality of a powerful nation's ideals. Indeed, "London cover[s] the whole Earth" at the beginning of *Jerusalem*'s chapter 4.14

Just prior to this, in chapter 3, Blake equates London with another city – Golgonooza. Both are "created continually East &

West & North & South" and also provide the origin of "all the nations of the world."[15] London's exponential growth and status as a symbol of the British Empire during Blake's time justifies such characterizations. Golgonooza, though, is a city of imagination and process, and it is unlike the archetypes of Jerusalem and Babylon, which, despite their opposition to one another, are static products of history and myth that can be seen as either precedents or prophetic destinations. In chapter 1, Golgonooza, like Jerusalem, is being created in the midst of London by a character, ironically, or perhaps fittingly, named Los.[16] In Blake's *Milton*, published in 1804, the same year as *Jerusalem*, Golgonooza is associated with a Miltonic Satan and related to a "spiritual, four-fold London eternal / in immense labours and sorrows, ever building, ever falling."[17] In chapter 3 of *Jerusalem*, this relationship between Golgonooza and London is extended to an equation, and both are said to be in a state of continual construction and decay because of love and jealousy.[18] Golgonooza, London's equal prior to Jerusalem's return, is thus presented as a creative and imaginative eternal process that at once fulfills time yet lies outside of time: a "continuing city" as Morton Paley suggests.[19] It is a cyclical ideal in the process of endless realization and revision. However, Golgonooza, a hopeful creation without the necessary roots of conventional symbolic history, also has its limitations. "Named art and manufacture" (it is unclear whether Blake is referring to artistic expression or artifice) it is "Outside of the gates of the human heart" and is built in "fears," "rage & fury," and, thus, "the separate Nations wait for the return of Jerusalem."[20] While Golgonooza is not an ideal, finalized city, then, it exemplifies imagination, regeneration, and process, adding hope to the images of London's present decay.[21] By itself, though, Los's particular project appears similar to the self-centred and ignorant "marking" actions of the speaker in Blake's *Songs of Experience* in that the individualized construction of Golgonooza, the material realization of Los's vision, is a loss of vision that ultimately prevents the ideal reconstruction of a dematerialized and universal Jerusalem. However, despite a name that suggests deprivation and an activity that will never be completed, Los's imaginative efforts in the building of Golgonooza extend beyond the "mind-forg'd manacles" of cynical *Experience*. London, within the literary realization of *Jerusalem*, is the foundation for this creative and constructive act, and it is an essential vehicle of union that contains and amplifies, but also surpasses, the individualism of Los and becomes an intersection of history, hope, and process. In *Milton*, Blake defiantly asserts: "I will not cease from Mental Fight / Nor shall my Sword sleep in my hand: Till we have built Jerusalem, / In England's green & pleasant Land."[22] Although in figurative ruins, London is the material centre and symbol of Blake's own constructive idealism in *Jerusalem*. As both setting and symbol, London is neither exclusively celebrated nor condemned here, but it is much more than Blake's experienced narrator from his earlier work could perceive.

Real, mythic, and imaginative cities are thus embedded within each other and equated with each other in the midst of a narrative that alternatively and inconsistently associates London with images of heavenly potential, hellish ruin, and endless inconsequence. Blake further illuminates London's complexity and necessity by presenting it, like his Jerusalem, as both a literal cityscape and as a personification. It is described as "a Human awful wonder of God" and as an "immortal Guardian," again demonstrating its containment of contrariety.[23] One of the most powerful passages in *Jerusalem* occurs when Blake gives London a voice that commits itself to Albion (England) and equates the human body with the cityscape:

> Return, Albion, return! I give myself for thee:
> My Streets are my, Ideas of Imagination.
> Awake, Albion, awake! And let us awake up together.
> My Houses are Thoughts: My inhabitants, Affections,
> The children of my thoughts, walking within my blood vessels,
> Shut from my nervous form …
> … while my vegetating blood in veiny pipes
> Rolls dreadful thro' the Furnaces of Los and the Mills of Satan.
> For Albions sake, and for Jerusalem, thy Emanation
> I give myself [24]

The human city of London transcends, yet is essentially composed of, the individuality of its inhabitants, who are equated with insubstantial but necessary emotions that circulate throughout its machinery. London, a human creation, echoes the contradictory meeting of mind and matter, of spirit and nature, in its human makers, and it also strives for spiritual transcendence and resurrection through diversity and complexity. As a personified character, London commits its ruinous reality to an ideal, an ideal that is fed by figurative language that dematerializes London and associates it with human imagination, thoughts, and affections. The promise of *Jerusalem* is that, if London can keep Babylonian urges at bay with Golgonoozan imagination, hope and renewal, the worldly city and symbol of the British Empire, will survive ruin and corruption, will be redeemed and resurrected as something ideal, just as fallen human beings who do not give in to sin are promised resurrection in the Book of Revelations. Blake's *Jerusalem* is a retelling of biblical myth for the British citizen, extending moral consideration beyond the human condition to include human creations such as art, city, and empire. *Jerusalem* is an imaginative attempt to shift away from the microcosmic limitations of the narrator of *Experience*'s present-day "London," perceiving the city from a macrocosmic perspective and associating it with future redemption. As Johnston has suggested, Blake is certainly trying to perform a mythic conversion of London here, to revise and renew a familiar landscape through symbolic and imaginative creativity. He is also implicitly encouraging the same type of perceptual rebirth on the part of the city's inhabitants, defining them as emotive agents who are able to open the doors of perception and circulate through the dynamic process that is London, recognizing its mythic potential and preserving creative hope while respecting the realities and the history of its charter'd streets. Stereotypical views of Romantic hostility towards the cityscape are thus undermined by *Jerusalem*'s perceptual shift and can be seen to echo the limitations of their key examples, just as the limited perception of "London's" narrator determines the condition of his urban reality.

This challenge to the Romantic stereotype highlights the persistent critical difficulty and impropriety of attempting to associate writers of the same period with the same generalized opinions and perspectives. Indeed, the well documented differences between William Blake and William Wordsworth's ideas and writings effectively exemplify the period's variety. Wordsworth, generalized as a poet devoted to the inspirational power of the natural world, is often cited as the representative voice of Romantic anti-urbanism. Many examples fortify this opinion. In "Book First: Home at Grasmere" (1800–06), which was intended as a beginning for his unfinished work, *The Recluse*, Wordsworth associates undesirable solitude with the city dweller and offers the counter-argument that the forest Hermit benefits from a much more communal and spiritual surrounding:

... he truly is alone,
He of the Multitude whose eyes are doomed
To hold a vacant commerce day by day
With objects wanting life – repelling love;
He by the vast metropolis immured,
Where pity shrinks from unremitting calls,
Where numbers overwhelm humanity,
And neighbourhood serves rather to divide
Than to unite – what sighs more deep than his,
Whose nobler will hath long been sacrificed;
Who must inhabit under a black sky
A city, where, if indifference to disgust
Yield not to scorn or sorrow, living men
Are oftentimes to their fellow-men no more
Than to the forest Hermit are the leaves
That hang aloft in myriads; nay, far less
For they protect his walk from sun and shower,
Swell his devotion with their voice in storms,
And whisper while the stars twinkle among them
His lullaby. From crowded streets remote,
Far from the living and dead wilderness
Of the thronged world, Society is here
A true community – a genuine frame
Of many into one incorporated.[25]

While Wordsworth offers scathing commentary on the urban condition, note that his criticisms are explicitly levelled at "living men" and "society." Indeed, it is better to live as a solitary human being in the frame of natural surroundings than to give up your "nobler will" in the crowded streets of a city where "numbers [of people] overwhelm humanity." Cities themselves are not the problem, then; rather, the inhuman behaviour of proximate humanity is the cause of the poem's justification for an escape to and seclusion within nature. It might be suggested, however, that the city as described in the above excerpt is an essential ingredient in the reinforcement of the behavioural indifference, scorn, and sorrow that Wordsworth condemns: it is a materialization of human nature, industrially blackening the sky with pollution that overhangs undersized streets that become overpopulated with a doomed multitude drawn to the vacant commerce that it symbolizes. In this way, Wordsworth's cityscape is as dangerous as Blake's "Mills of Satan" or "Furnaces of Los." However, just as Blake's imagery reveals a much more complex picture of the city overall, some of Wordsworth's images problematize an inclusion of the city in the above condemnation. In the same way that he compares people to leaves for the eventual purpose of contrasting their function to further his indictment of urban indifference, Wordsworth initially likens the city to a "living and dead wilderness," then subsequently favours the "genuine community" of an actual forest in nature.[26] Unlike Blake, then, Wordsworth favours tangible reality over imaginative association. Yet, Wordsworth's metaphoric association between city and wilderness is not completely negated by the implied contrast. Indeed, while nature shelters, comforts, and soothes the Hermit and is associated with stasis and dependability, the city is both living and dead – an intersection of motion and stasis, vitality and impotence. Wordsworth, like Blake, associates the city with possibility rather than with predictability; the difference lies in the value that each poet associates with this quality. Wordsworth's preference for stability and sanctuary over a diverse and unpredictable wilderness is a choice that aligns his speaker with the ignorance of Blake's speaker in *Experience*. Indeed, the comparison of the city to a natural wilderness and the subsequent condemnation of that wilderness explicitly challenge the exclusive partiality of the natural ideal that Wordsworth goes on to define and promote. His imaginative idealization of a nature that possesses limited capabilities, asserted against the realistic potential for variety ascribed to the city, ironically reverses the explicit argument that favours "a genuine frame / Of many into one incorporate." While Wordsworth's wording may formally interrupt his intended message, his hostility to the urban cause of human isolation and dejection is not completely eradicated. Yet, what exactly the city represents for Wordsworth remains unclear.

A frequently studied sonnet, entitled "Composed upon Westminster Bridge, Sept. 3,1802" furthers this exploration of Wordsworth's engagement with London:

Earth has not anything to show more fair:
Dull would he be of soul who could pass by
A sight so touching in its majesty:
This City now doth, like a garment, wear

The beauty of the morning; silent, bare,
Ships, towers, domes, theatres, and temples lie
Open unto the fields, and to the sky;
All bright and glittering in the smokeless air.
Never did sun more beautifully steep
In his first splendour, valley, rock or hill;
Ne'er saw I, never felt, a calm so deep!
The river glideth at his own sweet will:
Dear God! the very houses seem asleep;
And all that mighty heart is lying still![27]

The tone of the poem is celebratory, asserting London in the present moment as a majestic sight in a manner that seemingly contradicts the condemnations of "Home at Grasmere."[28] One could argue, though, that the city is only worth Wordsworth's praise here because it receives its attributes from the "beauty of the morning" and remains safely framed by natural images of fields and sky.[29] It is also a city out of time, frozen by words in an artificially imposed stasis that anticipates the problematic idealism of Keats's "Ode on a Grecian Urn." Wordsworth defines it here as an empty sanctuary that is quite unlike the overcrowded wilderness mentioned in *The Recluse*. It is asleep, still, calm, smokeless, silent, open – bearing a tranquillity and idealism that Wordsworth more often associates with natural surroundings. Perhaps, then, this is a natural extension of the metaphoric association between the city and nature in *The Recluse* – demonstrating that the city, in all of its variety, can also become the ideal that Wordsworth has insufficiently asserted against urbanity. This frozen ideal is temporary, though, and anticipates future movement because it is dawn and the city is about to awaken, continuing a cyclical process of waking and sleeping that reminds us of Blake's ever-building, ever-falling Golgonooza. Curiously, whereas Blake's ideal London is one that awakes and transcends Golgonooza's oscillatory revolutions but retains its imaginative dynamism in contrast to the static opposition between the traditional myths of Babylon and Jerusalem, Wordsworth's ideally still and sleeping London, while associated with nature, seems unnatural in that its celebrated stasis and slumber are always temporary and embedded in the cyclical processes of the natural world. Wordsworth's idealizations of the London cityscape in this poem and the natural landscape in *The Recluse* are exclusive and partial, and yet they are essentially the same, problematizing any attempt to stereotype Wordsworth's supposed preference for nature over the city.

Indeed, in "Composed upon Westminster Bridge," while the city does wear the beauty of the morning like a garment (implying that such beauty is not an inherent quality of the city but is a value added by its engagement with nature), "Never did sun more beautifully steep / In his first splendour, valley, rock or hill," suggesting that the city's qualities and features have an innate beauty that natural elements do not possess. The first line of the sonnet confirms this: "Earth has not anything to show more fair" than a cityscape clothed in the stillness of the morning. This human achievement, framed by nature, exceeds anything exclusively "natural." Although Wordsworth praises this human accomplishment, he also prefers an ideal urban scene devoid of human presence, where numbers and noise do not overwhelm his own solitary voice. There are no faces of weakness and woe to mark or to echo, no evidence of indifference, scorn, or sorrow. Although Wordsworth personifies London here (it sleeps, has a "mighty heart," and wears the beauty of the morning like a garment), the city, framed within this natural setting, exceeds anything exclusively human. It is an ideal space because it has been created by humans and represents humanity but, for this moment at least, is devoid of human presence. Johnston claims that Wordsworth anthropomorphizes the city in an attempt to reconcile himself to it.[30] Gassenmeier and Gurr too hastily interpret Wordsworth's personification of the city as a sleeping female figure whose "domes, theatres and temples" lie exposed[31] and whom Wordsworth can only bear or voyeuristically peruse as long as she is sleeping. While this interpretation reveals more about the critics' preoccupations than the work, it is useful to note that Wordsworth also repeatedly anthropomorphizes *nature* as a female figure throughout his works, potentially establishing yet another intersection between his visions of the city and of nature (if we accept Gassenmeier and Gurr's interpretation). Curiously, Blake's ideal figure of liberty and imaginative inspiration is Jerusalem, an intersection of past, present, and future that is simultaneously depicted as a female figure and a cityscape, whereas Wordsworth's ideal figure of liberty and imaginative inspiration is either a partial and timeless vision of nature anthropomorphized as a nurturing female figure or an artificially frozen portrait of London anthropomorphized as a sexual yet passive female figure exposed in the dawn's early light and viewed from a distance. While this comparative connection between femininity and liberty is worthy of another chapter, the equalities between these poets' visions of London establishes a thematic and potentially revolutionary fraternity between the two.

However, we must be careful not to generalize too extensively between these two writers: Blake gives his London a creative voice that calls for its own awakening, while Wordsworth's city, beautiful without human activity, is presented as a sleeping figure. More important, though, both Blake and Wordsworth are doing more than just describing and assessing cities in general: they are commenting specifically on London. As the economic and political centre of the British Empire, London potentially symbolizes that empire, and literary portraits of the city can be seen as indications of the nation's highs or lows. Blake's criticism of the minute particulars of the city in his poem "London" connotes a broader criticism of Britain's religious, political, and social shortcomings. This lack of patriotic commitment is safely asserted by a persona who is not subject to the same fears of being accused of sedition as was its author. However, the complexity of *Jerusalem* introduces the possibility of future hope and redemption for London and the empire that it represents by associating the actual city of Blake's present with mythical cities of history and imagination. For Wordsworth, London in *The Recluse* symbolizes a flawed society that encourages isolation. Yet, the rural isolation from a flawed human society prescribed by the poem is, itself, a flawed solution, a better-than-nothing retreat rather than a constructive engagement with the problems that London represents. Like the narrator of Blake's "London," Wordsworth's speaker reproduces the very problems that he identifies. "Composed upon Westminster Bridge" conversely praises London, the mighty and majestic centre of the British Empire from within, but can only do so before the dawn of its human activity. This reclusive tourist, appropriately utilizing the Italian sonnet form, thus marvels at the abstract scope of London's "slumbering" architectural monolith as one might be safely awed by the empty ruin of the ancient (and thus dead) Roman forum and its hints of past glory. While Wordsworth's speaker describes the beauty and power of London, its life is limited by forced idealization, by the selective and partial nature of the portrait that ambiguously presents it as a glorious corpse or as an awakening God. In this way, Wordsworth uses images of a still, sleeping, but not completely lifeless present to celebrate the cumulative, ideal result of British achievement, and, for the moment at least, London is able to transcend its human particulars. The ideal London for Wordsworth is thus slumbering form without function or human activity, whereas Blake's ideal depends on the flexibility of London's functional potential and the human agency that it exemplifies and inspires.

Perhaps this difference can be further accounted for by appealing to the actual relationship that each poet has with London. Blake is primarily a city dweller, one who is daily immersed in the vitality, inspiration, and antagonism of a human arena that unfailingly responds to social and individual overtures. In contrast, Wordsworth's rural perspective situates him as a solitary visitor to, rather than as a resident of, London, which may explain why "Composed upon Westminster Bridge" reads like a distant and abstract postcard. Indeed, Wordsworth describes himself as a "transient visitant" who initially idealizes, subsequently encounters, then poetically interprets the shocks of mighty London's "endless streets" in Book Seventh of his autobiographical poem *The Prelude*.[32] Significantly, the formation of *The Prelude*, like Blake's city of Golgonooza, can be described as a continual process of expression and revision that was only fixed when the poet's "mighty heart [lay] still," like the sleeping London of "Westminster Bridge." *The Prelude* is a work of recollection, in contrast to the prophetic directions of Blake's *Jerusalem*, but it is still subject to a similar conflation of temporal perspectives and idealization. It combines memory, interpretation, and speculation and shifts the relationship between its past, present, and future conceptions with each revision. While Wordsworth increasingly emphasizes a desire to maintain a conceptual distance between himself and London by refusing to call it "home" and by presenting himself in the 1850 version as an antithetical "idler" in the midst of a "concourse of mankind" where "life and labour seem but one," he also identifies the pleasures and incessant whirl of London and reflects these through his own uncertainty, indeterminacy, and "unchecked fancy."[33] This tension between intended independence from and unavoidable interdependence with London's energies persists throughout Book Seventh.

Early on in this portion of *The Prelude*, Wordsworth discusses the distance between his ideals and imaginings of the city and his actual experience of it in 1791, and he emphasizes his overall disappointment with it. Yet, in a passage that underwent significant changes between 1805 and 1850, Wordsworth initially identifies the city as a vital experience, as a "vivid pleasure of [his] youth" and as a valued memory, a "frequent daydream for [his] riper mind."[34] In 1850, Wordsworth replaces these identifications with a description of the city as a "monstrous ant-hill on the plain / of a too-busy world."[35] Further, in 1805, echoing Blake's "London" narrator, Wordsworth writes of his immersion in the "endless stream of men and moving things."[36] While he describes London's "quick dance" and "Babel din" from within, reflecting the speed, motion, and variety of shops, houses, and people in an appropriate poetic excess, the energy of this poetic expression distinguishes him from the "weary throng" that he sees "here, there and everywhere" in the city. While the citizens described by Blake are miserable reflections of their hellish urban surroundings and of the narrator's own cry of woe, Wordsworth's "weary throng" seems out of place in the midst of the energy and vitality of London's images and the poet's own responsive energy. Indeed, the mature Wordsworth describes his youthful mind as "sportive and alert / And watchful, as a kitten when at play" in the midst of the city's spectacles, realizing that "Life then was new, / The senses easily pleased."[37] It becomes clear, though, that Wordsworth perceives human exhaustion and disillusion as effects of the city's excesses and makes a poetic and narrative effort to protect himself from these seductions by turning into a "sequestered nook" (still within the city) to escape from the human roar of London "as from an enemy."[38] Here, too, the enemy is not the city in general but, rather, the roar of human activity that it catalyzes, contains, and blurs. Wordsworth, whether amidst the crowd or passing through the "sequestered nook," observes this roar from within but does not fully give himself over to its triviality or anonymity. By the 1850 version of *The Prelude*, Wordsworth not only increases this distance between his own agency and the subjectivity of the weary crowd but also retreats from his earlier immersions in the urban landscape, perhaps to ensure that he does not lose his voice and energy to the demands of city life. He authoritatively diminishes the excessive catalogue of images from his earlier version and, like a god, commands the city to "Before [him] flow."[39] This revision does not supplant the recollection of the youthful experience, but it does modify the subsequent perception of such experience.

Yet, Book Seventh is affected by constant indecisiveness, as Wordsworth condemns the human roar, then celebrates its variety, "well pleased to note / Among the crowd all specimens of man."[40] He symbolizes the artifice and contrived spectacle of the city through his particular attention to London's panoramas, exhibitions, theatres, and carnivals, but he also uses memorable images from this time in London to demonstrate how "casual incidents of real life / … / Outweighed … the set events / And measured passions of the stage."[41] In one episode, Wordsworth sees a beautiful child and observes how out of place it seems in the folly, vice, misery, strife, and artifice of its urban surroundings, concluding that it would be better to die young in natural surroundings than to survive and grow in London.[42] Following this, however, Wordsworth contemplates that "foolishness and madness in parade, / Though most at home in this their dear domain, / Are scattered everywhere," and are not exclusive to the city streets.[43] This furthers the earlier suggestion that *human* foolishness and madness in general are the targets of Wordsworth's condemnations. Aside from this human blemish, the sublimity and accomplishment that London's spaces signify are cause for celebration and awe, as in "Composed upon Westminster Bridge." Indeed, Wordsworth's later revisions of Book Seventh suggest that examples of "courage, or integrity, or truth" found in the cityscape "appeared more touching" as they are set off in stark contrast to "that huge fermenting mass of human- kind" that inhabits London.[44]

For Wordsworth, then, there is a silver lining of inspiration within the dark crowds of the city. Indeed, the variety and mystery of the busy cityscape overwhelm him to the point of visionary transcendence, taking him "beyond the reach of common indication," beyond his own individual hopes and fears.[45] In this near-Blakean state in the midst of the crowd, he sees a figurative reflection of himself, a stationary blind beggar "Wearing a written paper, to explain / His story, whence he came, and who he was."[46] This figure silently admonishes the poet not only for his similarities but also for his differences. Wordsworth and his *Prelude* are as potentially limited as the beggar, sharing the man's blindness and affected by the same communicative limitations in a crowd that is moving too quickly to pay attention to written signs. Indeed, for Wordsworth, who is immersed in the motions of the urban crowd, the image of the beggar is much more important than what is written on his "label." More important, though, the beggar is also a crucial point of stillness and sensory exemption in the midst of London's perpetual whirl, possibly admonishing Wordsworth for being seduced by the spectacle of this anonymous tide, for forgetting his role as an "idler." Encountered in 1791 and reflected upon in the initial writing of Book Seventh in 1804, the figure causes the poet to reflect on the beauty, peace, and solemnity of the stillness that he recognizes in 1802 in "Composed upon Westminster Bridge." During a later effort to parallel the city to Bartholomew's Fair, Wordsworth attempts to both emulate and exceed this beggar, suggesting that a steady, self-aware, and confident gaze, likely inspired by the presence and possibility of stillness within the city's dynamism, will allow the poet to unravel some of London's mysteries and to survive amidst its carnivalesque "Parliament of monsters":

> Oh, blank confusion! True epitome
> Of what the mighty city is herself
> To thousands upon thousands of her sons,
> Living amid the same perpetual whirl
> Of trivial objects, melted and reduced
> To one identity, by differences
> That have no law, no meaning, and no end –
> Oppression, under which even highest minds
> Must labour, whence the strongest are not free.
> But though the picture weary out the eye,
> By nature an unmanageable sight,
> It is not wholly so to him who looks
> In steadiness, who hath among least things
> An under-sense of greatest; sees the parts
> As parts, but with a feeling of the whole.[47]

Stillness, then, relates to a sense of wholeness and timelessness, a perceptive awareness that encapsulates past and future – similar to the ideal offered by Blake's "Auguries of Innocence" of being able to perceive "a World in a Grain of Sand / … / And Eternity in an hour."[48] For Wordsworth, this awareness significantly depends on the preservation of his individual poetic self-consciousness against the meaningless singularity and oppressive emptiness of a collective identity. Yet, the blind beggar's distinction and destitution assert and question the ideals of such individualism, and Wordsworth's continual revisions of and alterations to *The Prelude* lend to it a sense of unfinished dynamism rather than definitive steadiness. Indeed, the motion and change of the crowd are necessary conditions for the initial inspiration and constantly changing reflections of Book Seventh, providing an essential foil of awareness that focuses Wordsworth's attention on the stillness of the beggar and prompts him to define the timeless level of steady understanding promoted by the above passage.

Exclusively favouring stillness and stability in a dynamic work about a vibrant subject seems as flawed as the image of the city presented in "Composed upon Westminster Bridge." However, the last lines of Book Seventh qualify Wordsworth's apparent self-contradiction:

> The Spirit of Nature was upon me there;
> The soul of Beauty and enduring Life
> Vouchsafed her inspiration, and diffused,
> Through meagre lines and colours, and the press
> Of self-destroying, transitory things,
> Composure, and ennobling Harmony.[49]

Wordsworth appeals to an abstract "Spirit of Nature" as the preserver of composure and harmony in the midst of transitory things, comparing it to eternal ideals of Beauty and Life (as opposed to their actual mortal counterparts, which are subject to change and corruption). Yet, it is unclear whether he means to suggest that this timeless ideal of nature and its inspirational potential persists despite the temporal reality of the city's perpetual motion or is generated and emulated by the city's vastness and vitality. Walter Reed's commentary on Romantic writing in general seems to favour the latter possibility and supports the current challenge to the anti-urbanism stereotypically attributed to Wordsworth. He suggests that "Romanticism never wants simply to return to a state of nature, but to recapture something of the vital power of that state."[50] For Wordsworth, it seems that London is able to do just that. In the 1850 version of Book Seventh, Wordsworth precedes his conclusion with an appeal to natural images of "everlasting streams," "desert sands," oceans and clouds, noting that both "forms perennial" and "the changing language of their countenances / Quickens the slumbering mind and aids the thoughts, /

However multitudinous, to move / with order and relation."[51] The mixture of permanence and change, of timelessness and temporality so evident in these natural images, is also experienced by Wordsworth in "London's vast domain"[52] and allows him to resolve the earlier exclusions and problems of "Composed upon Westminster Bridge." The final lines of Book Seventh evolve the figurative connection between nature and urbanity that Wordsworth establishes in *The Recluse* and "Composed upon Westminster Bridge," allowing him to expand beyond the limitations of his earlier idealization of nature to include the possibility of motion and stasis and to reassert London's replication of nature's "vital power" through its containment of vitality and stability.

This optimistic acceptance and celebration of the motion of modern life, reminiscent of Blake's hopeful prophecies, is confirmed in a lesser-known sonnet by Wordsworth, entitled "Steamboats, Viaducts and Railways":

> Motions and Means, on land and sea at war
> With old poetic feeling, not for this,
> Shall ye, by Poets even, be judged amiss!
> Nor shall your presence, howsoe'er it mar
> The loveliness of Nature, prove a bar
> To the Mind's gaining that prophetic sense
> Of future change, that point of vision, whence
> May be discovered what in soul ye are.
> In spite of all that beauty may disown
> In your harsh features, Nature doth embrace
> Her lawful offspring in Man's art; and Time,
> Pleased with your triumphs o'er his brother Space,
> Accepts from your bold hands the proffered crown
> Of hope, and smiles on you with cheer sublime.[53]

Composed in 1833 and published in 1835, two years before Queen Victoria's reign begins, this verse embodies much of the enthusiasm and confidence associated with the early years of her reign. Curiously, its promotion of movement, change, and mechanical innovation counters Gassenmeier and Gurr's suggestion that Wordsworth became more quietist and conservative in his later writing. His hearty embrace of an admittedly ugly variety of technological and industrial progress further justifies his acceptance of London's carnivalesque variety and activity in *The Prelude*. Just as Wordsworth locates a national strength and established stasis in the London of "Composed upon Westminster Bridge" and adds to this a dynamic vitality associated with nature's powers in *The Prelude*, so the potential motion and expansion signified by England's transportation innovations are welcomed as "lawful offspring" that are approved and embraced by nature, even if they mar nature in the process. The "motions and means" of which Wordsworth voices his approval symbolize the imperialistic expansion of the British Empire and are described as boldly triumphant in their war with tradition and "Space." Reversing "Composed upon Westminster Bridge's" celebration of a slumbering monument to tradition and past accomplishment, this expansion of the city's commerce and vital energy into a powerful imperial network promotes a visionary awakening of the mind, procuring an openness to future change that crowns time with hope. Wordsworth's acceptance of the potential of powerful activity over considerations of beauty and loveliness is the endpoint of a process that begins with an appreciation of a morning vision of London and presents an overall challenge to the stereotype that Wordsworth is *consistently* antagonistic to the city. Like steamboats, viaducts, and railways, the city is increasingly recognized by Wordsworth as another example of "Man's art," which qualifies as nature's "lawful offspring" because it still embodies and reflects "Nature's spirit," despite its "harsh features" and affront to "old poetic feeling." This perspective is already anticipated in Book Thirteenth of *The Prelude*, which concludes that "the forms / Of Nature have a passion in themselves, / That intermingles with those works of man / To which she summons him; although the works / Be mean, have nothing lofty of their own."[54] If Wordsworth can separately celebrate the dynamic, hopeful nature of human (and, more specifically, British) innovation and the symbolic power of a frozen cityscape at dawn, then his acceptance of London as an amalgamation of both contraries at the end of Book Seventh of *The Prelude* signifies an expansion of his own perception of the city to "that point of vision" that Blake realizes in *Jerusalem*.

Indeed, between 1809 and 1812, Wordsworth writes a section in his work *The Excursion*, entitled "Cloudscape New Jerusalem," which describes a vision of a city in the clouds that elevates his developing associations between natural vitality, spirituality, and the city to new heights. This lofty revelation, a "gorgeous spectacle

… bright and fair," is described as "Glory beyond all glory ever seen / By waking sense or by the dreaming soul."[55] It is a storm cloud formation that, in its collision with surrounding "mountain steeps and summits," takes the shape of "a mighty city," which Wordsworth describes as "a wilderness of building."[56] This familiar association again links natural wilderness with the cityscape; however, rather than London's wearing the beauty of the morning, nature's most glorious form is an overwhelming version of urbanity. The components of this "New Jerusalem" are "confused, commingled, mutually inflamed, / Molten together" in "forms uncouth of mightiest power, / For admiration and mysterious awe."[57] Like the variety ascribed to London in *The Prelude*, this shifting "pomp of structure" also features fixed positions and "fixed resemblances" yet transcends its earthly, British counterpart in that it is imagined to be the "the revealed abode / Of spirits in beatitude" rather than housing a parliament of human monsters.[58] This depoliticized vision of a synthesis between nature and urban formation inspires the poet, who exclaims: "I have been dead … / … And now I live. Oh, wherefore do I live?"[59] However, the resurrection of his awareness reminds Wordsworth that this universal city is open to spirits but closed to his living being. This confirms the position established by Wordsworth in poems previously considered: that, while a human presence lends a necessary vitality to London and brings it closer to a comprehensive ideal, materiality and human mortality also subject London and the empire that it represents to a dynamic temporality, just as Blake's Golgonooza embodies present energy and hopeful ambition for future success, yet is ultimately associated with Los and natural cycles of growth and decay. The ultimate setting for spiritual and natural ideals that transcend imperial concerns is a visionary, heavenly city, a New Jerusalem whose possibility is recognized by the poet as he gazes upon natural elements. Wordsworth's glimpse of a temporary manifestation of this ideal spirit of human construction transcends natural cycles and his limited sight, however, by inspiring a vision in which fixity and change are timelessly synthesized and ideal human spirits are housed in an ideal state of happiness. Although this reminds the poet of his fallen state and the limitations of his subjection to time, he is offered a transcendent, urban vision of hope and future promise, much in the same way that Blake's visions of *Jerusalem* offer hope for the "London" of *Experience*. Although both poets eventually move beyond a direct consideration of London, the city continues to be a point of inspiration for their optimistic visions, despite all of its recognized shortcomings.

This comparative study provides a number of challenges to the stereotype that holds that Romantic writers were generally hostile to the city. When considering the relationship of this period's writers to the city, perhaps it is less useful to evaluate them based on a condemnation/celebration binary than it is to explore the functional capabilities each attributes to the cityscape. Certainly, in these two poets, who are often seen as so different from one another, there is a similar tendency towards idealizing the symbolic potential of the urban landscape that represents the British Empire. Wordsworth, London's tourist, idealizes the present moment of the city by initially excluding its people and viewing it as an aggregate of past achievement, then by embracing its perpetual motion and variety as indicators of present strength and future hope. As well, for Wordsworth, natural vitality informs the human imagination, which is realized and embodied by the city, and it is up to individual observers to expand their perceptions so that nature's presence can be recognized in the creative offspring of this imagination. Blake, London's resident, realizes the ideal of England's urban cornerstone by imaginatively redeeming its people and by linking it with past myth, present possibility, and future hope. The ideal city for Blake is the symbol of the triumph of the human imagination over natural cycles of growth and decay. Blake's *Jerusalem* idealistically focuses on a future in which time and change are defeated, whereas Wordsworth celebrates a present defeat of spatial limitations and deems time triumphant but also looks forward to an urbanized vision of spiritual eternity. In their progressive contemplations of London, both Wordsworth and Blake find, "through meagre lines and colours, and the press / Of self-destroying, transitory things, / Composure and ennobling Harmony."[60]

What fundamentally links these overlapping, but ultimately contrary, approaches is a common act of interpretative agency in the service of idealism, an imposition of imaginative human perception on actual human construction. This narcissistic activity, which is the foundation of literary creation and criticism, exemplifies many literary encounters with and translations of urban locations throughout history. The contrasts and connections between the Londons of Blake and Wordsworth, though, raise a specific theoretical question regarding literary representations (or transformations) of the historic city: If the imagined cityscape is simultaneously a future, a present, and a past, where is the historic city located within such fiction? Does it ultimately lay outside of words, outside of what Ihab Hassan terms the "inscape of mind?"[61]

NOTES

1 Sartre, "American Cities," 201.

2 See also Hoople (this volume) on Henry James's distinctions between Europe and America, especially the continuity of past and present apparent in European architecture; and Perkins (this volume) on eighteenth-century Edinburgh as an amalgam of past and future. Eds.

3 Blake, *America*, 59, *Complete Poetry*, ed. D. Erdman. All subsequent references to Blake's works are from this edition.

4 Blake, *Milton*, 95; "London," 26–7; See Friedrich Engels' *Condition of the Working Classes in England* (1844); and poems such as "The Ignoble Procession," "Dark Satanic Mills," "We Die Together," and "City-Life" from D.H. Lawrence's *Pansies* and *More Pansies* collections, reprinted in Lawrence, *Complete Poems*. [See also Bailey (this volume), who traces more optimistic responses to upheaval on the part of journalists in mid-nineteenth-century Paris. Eds.]

5 Blake, *America*, 59. Such reversals are stated and amply illustrated in the complexities of Blake's *The Marriage of Heaven and Hell*.

6 Johnston, "Blake's Cities," 413.

7 Ibid., 440.

8 Blake, *Jerusalem*, 169.

9 Ibid., 243.

10 Ibid., 191, 243.

11 Ibid., 229.

12 Ibid., 243.

13 Ibid. 147, 170.

14 Shakespeare, *As You Like It*, 2.7.147; Blake, *Jerusalem*, 234.

15 Ibid., 227.

16 Ibid., 153.

17 Ibid., 114, and 99.

18 Ibid. 203, 227.

19 Paley, *Continuing City*, 137.

20 Blake, *Jerusalem*, 120, 203, 227

21 Paley, *Continuing City,* 141.
22 Blake, *Milton,* 95–6.
23 Blake, *Jerusalem*, 180.
24 Ibid., 180.
25 Wordsworth, "The Recluse, Part First, Book First," 592–616.
26 Wordsworth does something similar in Book Thirteenth of *The Prelude*, where he describes the city as a "heart-depressing wilderness" then goes on to celebrate the "human kindnesses and simple joys" that enrich rural paths and lonely roads (1850, 114–19). This metaphor of city-as-wilderness problematizes Wordsworth's exclusive preference for nature's wilderness in both *The Prelude* and *The Recluse*'s "Home at Grasmere."
27 Wordsworth, "Composed Upon Westminster Bridge," 296.
28 Wordsworth returns to a very similar situation and theme in an unpublished poem composed in 1808 entitled "St Paul's." In this verse, Wordsworth is beginning his journey home to Grasmere through an early winter morning in London after a visit with Coleridge. The "noiseless and unpeopled" city offers a "visionary scene" that provides an "anchor of stability" for his uneasy melancholy (20, 11). Unlike in "Composed upon Westminster Bridge," Wordsworth finds an architectural focal point in the "pure, silent, solemn, beautiful … / … majestic temple of St. Paul" (25–26), which is isolated by a "sacred veil of falling snow." As a result, the poet gains spiritual inspiration from the form and function of this cathedral. Like "Composed upon Westminster Bridge," however, this portrait of London is devoid of the "moving form[s]" of people and is harmoniously integrated with its own natural garment of "fresh and spotless" snow.
29 See also Land (this volume), who draws different implications from this poem. Eds.
30 Johnston, "Blake's Cities," 441.
31 Gassenmeier and Gurr, "Experience of the City," 319.
32 Wordsworth, *Prelude* (1850), 68.
33 Ibid., 58–9, 69–72, 75.
34 Ibid., 151–4.
35 Ibid., 149–50.
36 Ibid., 158.
37 Ibid., 471–2, 440–1.
38 Ibid., 169.
39 Ibid., 150.
40 Ibid., 220–1.
41 Ibid., 402–5.

42 Ibid., 331–81.
43 Ibid., 589–91.
44 Ibid., 600, 602, 621.
45 Ibid., 593–8 and 636.
46 Ibid., 641–2. [See also Warne's discussion (this volume) of Wordsworth's blind beggar. Eds.]
47 Ibid., 722–36.
48 Blake, "Auguries of Innocence," 490.
49 Wordsworth, *Prelude* (1850), 766–71.
50 Reed, *Meditations on the Hero*, 13–14.
51 Wordsworth, *Prelude* (1850), 745–61.
52 Ibid., 765.
53 Wordsworth, "Steamboats, Viaducts and Railways," in George, *Complete Poetical Works*, 721.
54 Ibid., 290–4.
55 Wordsworth, "Cloudscape New Jerusalem," 866, 862–3, cited in Wu, *Romanticism*, 410–11.
56 Ibid., 884, 870–1.
57 Ibid., 890–1, 903–4.
58 Ibid., 899, 908–9.
59 Ibid., 910–11.
60 Wordsworth, *Prelude* (1805), 769–71.
61 Hassan, "Cities of Mind, Urban Words," 94.

13

The Humours of Sailortown: Atlantic History Meets Subculture Theory

ISAAC LAND

The character of a British Seaman exhibits so many striking singularities, that blend themselves so much with all his habits, that a thorough acquaintance with them becomes necessary to both officer and physician, in their respective stations. These peculiarities are the offspring of a sea-life, from the little communication it affords with the common manners of society.[1]

Thomas Trotter

William Wordsworth's sonnet, "Composed upon Westminster Bridge," captures London's skyline at daybreak with an instructive list: "Ships, towers, domes, theatres, and temples lie / Open unto the fields, and to the sky; / All bright and glittering in the smokeless air."[2] The poet may have placed ships first for reasons of scansion, but the prominence of ships *in* urban space, to the extent that they could be seen as an integral part of the city's own architecture, implies something about the city's human architecture as well. In many parts of Europe, urban space was predominantly coastal and harbour-oriented until the advent of railroads.[3] Railroads actually accelerated the growth of certain port cities, as did the decline of malaria, which, in the nineteenth century, permitted still greater concentrations of population along the coastline.[4] Yet urban history – for all its sophisticated debates about the meaning of theatres, towers, and temples – has offered surprisingly few insights into the forest of masts in the harbour.

London's Wapping neighbourhood, which became known across the Atlantic as the definitive sailortown in the eighteenth and early nineteenth centuries, was seen by the affluent as a place to titillate the ear with impenetrable jargon, marvel at the outlandish behaviour of "Jack in Port," and perhaps share in his liberating transgressions. "Explore Wapping," Dr Johnson urged his young protegé Boswell.[5] While writers describing parts of London such as St Giles, Marylebone, or Whitechapel emphasized their extreme poverty, Wapping – in contrast – was represented in art and literature as a riotous, comical party. It is time to acknowledge neighbourhoods like Wapping *as* neighbourhoods, as sailortown communities rather than as licentious playgrounds or as a mere enclave of oceanic space carved out of the city.[6] Sailortown was a dangerous place where the weak or unwary might quickly lose all they had, but we know that this was characteristic of urban life more generally. We should acknowledge the predatory behaviour, but place it alongside the networks of pleasure, mutual aid, friendship, and even civic cooperation that shaped the sailortown experience.[7] I argue in this chapter that we must also consider the behaviour of sailors in port as a form of resistance, a subcultural dialogue with the city and its authorities.

SAILORTOWN AS SPECTACLE

Thomas Rowlandson's *Portsmouth Point* (1811) is one of the most famous representations of sailortown in art. Portsmouth was Britain's main naval base on the English Channel. In time of war, to keep its French counterpart bottled up, the Royal Navy maintained a vast fleet in Channel waters. In *Portsmouth Point*, that fleet is plainly visible in the distance, but Rowlandson's focus is on the urban consequences of the navy's presence. An unpaved street, predictably lined with drinking establishments and pawn shops, takes an abrupt dive down a sandy slope, terminating obscurely at the water's edge. The tilted and premature horizon formed by the sandy slope cuts across the middle of the picture. By positioning the looming fleet above the false horizon where urban space loses its remaining coherence, the artist suggests that Portsmouth is where the city meets the navy, and the city loses. The movement of a swarm of vague human figures on and over that horizon line, disappearing into the invisible beach, is only accentuated by the way that sailors and their female companions lean, stagger, grope, and roll their way

Figure 13.1
Thomas Rowlandson, *Portsmouth Point*, 1811. Courtesy of the Lewis Walpole Library, Yale University.

across the picture. Although *Portsmouth Point* is a built-up and densely populated cityscape filled with cheerful activity, it is hard to avoid the sense that the people, like the street, are in the process of falling, of losing their balance, of descending from the dignity of urban life (figure 13.1).

It is true that Rowlandson was a well-known social satirist with a terrific eye for human foibles and absurdities, so contemporaries may have discounted a certain amount of grotesque caricature.[8] However, a comparison of Rowlandson's sailortown with his pictures of high society at Bath, or even at the less elevated venue of Vauxhall Gardens, underscores the madcap disarray of *Portsmouth Point*. As a London artist who made his living principally as a chronicler of urban life, Rowlandson would probably have been aware of some earlier precedents for *Portsmouth Point*, such as Arnold Vanhaecken's *The View and Humours of Billingsgate* (1736). Vanhaecken's image of the fish market and the wharves also featured dogs, unseemly behaviour, and crooked, indecorous

Figure 13.2
Arnold Vanhaecken, *The View and Humours of Billingsgate*, 1736.

postures. The "humours" of the title referred to the classical four humours of medicine but, more pointedly, to the strange emotions and behaviour that would be produced in people whose humours were misaligned.[9] In an era characterized by new initiatives to police, clean up, and straighten up urban space, Vanhaecken and Rowlandson portrayed sailortown as skewed and screwy, unbalanced in every sense (figure 13.2).[10]

In the eighteenth century, sailors had what we would today call an image problem. Some employers considered ex-sailors and ex-convicts equally objectionable. The productions of artists and writers reinforced this stereotype. William Hogarth's "Idle Prentice" went to sea, en route to a life of crime and ultimately the gallows. Dr Johnson, notoriously, compared the ship to the prison and concluded that the ship was a worse place. Sea life was associated with some of the gravest transgressions. Lurid tales of mutiny and misadventure in foreign lands implied that the "custom of the sea" involved the systematic inversion of land-bound moral norms, through piracy, sodomy, religious apostasy, cannibalism, or combinations of these four sins.[11]

If the sea was held to be the ultimate source of these deviant behaviours, the images by Vanhaecken and Rowlandson offer a graphic reminder that the sailortown subculture itself was an urban phenomenon. Sailors expected to be looked at, they contrived to be looked at, and the special outfits – the "shore-going rigs" – that they kept for their promenades on shore contained a parodic confirmation of the spectator's presumptions about their difference. There were no standard-issue uniforms for common seamen in the Royal Navy until 1857, but sailors improvised an outfit for themselves that ensured that they would stand out on shore.[12] The basic elements of this unofficial uniform were chosen with practical needs in mind. Sailors wore comfortable trousers rather than tight-fitting breeches and, for similar reasons, preferred short jackets to long coats. The nickname "Jack Tar" came from the tar applied to these trousers to make them waterproof. But on shore, where no one could send them aloft, they chose to appear in a clean, expensive, and ornamented version of their work clothes. This outfit was never worn at sea. Decorated with silver buckles, brass buttons, "coloured tape along the seams, and ribbons in their hats," its purpose was to catch the eye of passersby.[13]

The period from roughly 1750 to 1850 is known by historians of fashion as "the Great Renunciation" in male dress – a movement towards dark or subdued colours, the removal of ornament (including wigs), and the projection of a sober and regulated demeanour.[14] In Jack Tar's clothing, we see the inversion of this (a "Great Affirmation"?): bright or light colours, ornament in the form of hats and ribbons, and an affectation of careless disorder.[15] The outfit that enticed the young Charles McPherson to join the Navy in the 1820s – white trousers, a blue jacket, a red waistcoat, and a straw hat – was essentially the same informal "uniform" that was favoured a few generations earlier, during the Seven Years War. It was variations in small, but telling, details that made the difference. Red-striped trousers were the mark of a sailor in the satirical prints from the 1770s, whereas pigtails do not appear until 1802. A nattily dressed illustration for Charles Dibdin's song "Poor Jack" in 1790 sported a yellow vest with red stripes.[16] While it is true that the purchase of "slops" sold by a particular ship's purser might create a degree of accidental homogeneity among that crew, there was nothing sloppy or accidental about the way sailors looked when they promenaded on shore.[17]

Contemporary autobiographies contain a number of loving descriptions of these extravagant displays of "rigging." Robert Hay lavished 139 words on his account of the costume, which must be quoted in full:

> [A]nd lastly the jolly tar himself was seen with his white demity trowsers fringed at the bottom, his fine scarlet waistcoat bound with black ribbon, his dark blue broadcloth jacket studded with pearl buttons, his black silk neckcloth thrown carelessly about his sunburnt neck. An elegant hat of straw, indicative of his recent return from a foreign station, cocked on one side; a head of hair reaching to his waistband; a smart switch made from the back bone of a shark under one arm, his doxy under the other, a huge chew of tobacco in his cheek, and a good throat season of double stingo recently deposited within his belt by way of fending off care. Thus fitted out, in good sailing trim, as he himself styles it, he strides along with all the importance of an Indian Nabob.[18]

Hay was not unique in his attention to the smallest detail of *how* the clothes were worn (the cock of the hat, the "careless" neckcloth): Matthew Barker wanted his readers to know that a kerchief was "loosely knotted" and remarked of one old veteran that "[h]is jacket and trowsers were patched from clew to ear-ring, but remarkably clean."[19] It was common for thieves to dress up as sailors to confuse their pursuers, and these meticulous descriptions help to explain why: an outfit like this made people see the clothes, not the man.[20]

Charles McPherson offers us this memorable glimpse of subculture on the march in the 1820s: "We sallied through the town in a body, all dressed in white trowsers, white shirts or frocks, and straw hats with black ribbons on them."[21] McPherson reminds us here that clothes do not flaunt themselves. The street theatre of group promenades invites us to reconsider the traditional interpretation of Jack Tar's characteristic stagger. This awkward manner of walking was, supposedly, the result of habits acquired on the tottering, bobbing deck of a ship. A person who had acquired "sea legs" had difficulty making the transition back to a surface that was not moving. This is a real problem, but must we assume that every aspect of the sailor's comportment was the result of a physiological constraint? If McPherson and his fellow sailors went to such trouble to coordinate their glaring white costume, could they not also choose to synchronize their steps, improvising a strut or swagger out of a stagger? Just as Jack Tar's wardrobe inverted the colour scheme of respectability, a tilted posture or an exaggerated unsteady walk may have been a form of self-parody, a way of mocking the urban connoisseurs who came to gawk at the humours of the quayside districts.[22]

Just as sailors filled the streets with bright, disorienting sartorial "noise" and crooked promenades, so they contributed a dissonant strain to the urban soundscape. Sea slang, like Jack Tar's improvised uniform, helped to define and patrol the boundaries of group membership.[23] The sailors who told Charles Pemberton, a young lad looking to join a ship's company, that their captain would "choke your luff with figgy-dowdy," were enjoying their insider status.[24] To "choke the luff" means to jam a tackle – a type of pulley – to keep it from slackening. Here, it translates to "fill your gullet" or "stuff you full" of a favourite food. Pemberton would learn it all in due course. Yet, sailors and their friends were often conducting these conversations in public places and, therefore, also performing for an audience of uninitiated ears, including sailortown tourists who would never be initiated into the secrets of sea slang. The leering Jack Tar who promised that the boy's luff would be choked with figgy-dowdy could anticipate how the anxious listener's imagination might supply dozens of meanings, including obscene or blasphemous ones, to mysterious utterances of this kind.

Consider this passage from Matthew Barker, a common seaman who published his reminiscences in 1826:

> Jack Junk was a man-of-war's man every inch of him. He was brought to bed – no, no, I mean born in an arm-chest, cradled in a frigate, rocked by the billows, and nursed by the captain of the forecastle. He soon came to be a plaything for all hands, quaffed his grog and chewed his pigtail like an angel. As soon as he could speak, the boatswain's mate tutored him in the vulgar tongue, taught him to wind his whistle, and whistle to the wind. At six years of age he had larned to read from the lids of bacca-boxes.[25]

This short text is a parable of initiation. Superficially, this text is about the way in which a sailor is an oceanic creature without knowledge of the land; yet, the operation it performs shows how this maritime identity was an invention of language. The speaker's self-correction at the beginning announces that this is a game. We are not really asked to believe in an infant who suckled on grog (though the androgynous sailor who "nursed" him is an arresting image). This tall tale is a kind of satire on the idea that the sailor *is* a being essentially separated from the shore.

Another message of Barker's parable is that attitude counts – how you tell it is what makes you a real seaman. It is a circular process. The man who talks as if he were "cradled in a frigate," and never knew any other way of speaking, *becomes* a true shipmate. To be one of us, to be a real Jack Tar, you must abandon other language, or at least make a show of doing so. By offering to translate a newcomer's past identity into the language of the sea (perhaps involving a change of name as well), sailortown demonstrated its openness but also its bounded, or boundaried, nature.

This was not always evident to outsiders. Pierce Egan's fictional Regency libertines, Tom and Jerry, visited "ALL-MAX," a public house in "the back slums" of London's East End, to learn how to really enjoy themselves:

> ALL-MAX was compared by the sailors, something after the old adage of "any port in a storm." It required no patronage; – a card of admission was not necessary; – no inquiries were made … Ceremonies were not in use, and therefore, no struggle took place at ALL-MAX for the master of them. The parties paired off according to fancy; the eye was pleased in the choice, and nothing thought of about birth and distinction … The group motley indeed; – Lascars, blacks, jack tars, coal-heavers, dustmen, women of colour, old and young, and a sprinkling of the remnants of once fine girls, &c. were all jigging together, provided the teazer of the catgut was not bilked of his duce.[26]

The shouting capitals of the pub's name underscored the sense of place, the idea that here (and only here) could we suspend the rules. As we have seen, however, the humours of sailortown were not all licentious or whimsical. Where Egan saw promiscuous mingling, a sailortown resident might well have seen a subcultural community formed by people who had gained admission and accepted a particular set of rules. It is important to emphasize that these were not necessarily Jack Tar's rules tout court; the pleasures and opportunities of this subculture were open to many people other than sailors.

SAILORTOWN AS COMMUNITY

Such uses of clothes and language have a parallel in the youth movements of the late twentieth century, which inspired a whole field of "subculture studies" devoted to explaining the extravagant displays of mods, rockers, punks, and similar groups. According to Dick Hebdige, the first requisite of subculture is *opacity*. If outsiders see, they do not understand. What distinguishes a subculture from a secret conspiracy is that its members seek to *display* the signs of their difference. Yet, these signs refuse to "normalize": they are noise, they remain opaque despite the fact that they are flaunted in public. Finally, subculture involves *appropriation*. It begins as a form of bricolage, resistance through an assembly of "'humble objects' … 'stolen' by subordinate groups and made to carry 'secret' meanings." Creating a subculture is a way to assume political agency; as Neil Nehring puts it, "to live not as an object but as a subject of history."[27] Following the methodology of the Birmingham Center for Cultural Studies, subculture theorists have placed special emphasis on the relationship between subcultures, their portrayal in the media, and the reactions of the general public. Outsiders struggle to find an appropriate reaction to the spectacular subculture, vacillating between "dread and fascination, outrage and amusement," in the end attempting to trivialize the movement or to incorporate it into the established systems of meaning by commodifying it. Subculture, then, both begins and ends in appropriation.[28]

Why use the subculture concept here? Transculture or interculture, despite their facility at describing certain Atlantic processes such as syncretism, do not lend themselves to explaining the appearance – and indeed the active cultivation – of separateness. Yet, speaking of a self-contained maritime culture would miss the point as well. Sailors were "talking back," in an intimate, if insubordinate, dialogue with a dominant political and cultural system. These gestures were more parodic than syncretic.

It is helpful to distinguish my approach here from what has been typical of the new Atlantic history. Atlantic theorists argue that people, commodities, and ideas circulated like ocean currents, touching and transforming the farthest shores. The medium for all this was the ship. Paul Gilroy's invocation of the ship in the opening pages of *The Black Atlantic* holds an implicit challenge for urban historians: "[Thinking about] the ship provides a chance to explore the articulations between the discontinuous histories of England's ports, its interfaces with the wider world." Gilroy's use of the ship is not so much an effort to centre our attention on shipboard life as to decentre us from land-bound, nationally delimited expectations. (He even suggests that we take, not merely an international, but an "outer-national" perspective.)[29] In a similar vein, Marcus Rediker and Peter Linebaugh have argued in *The Many-Headed Hydra* that sailors played a central role in the emergence of a "commonist" Atlantic culture – the Hydra of the book's title – which opposed the Hercules of capitalism. Rediker and Linebaugh offer numerous examples of sailors serving as agents of connectivity, uniting the alienated and disenfranchised elements around the Atlantic world. In this analysis, the port city serves as the quintessential site of "outer-national" encounter and mixture. If ships were the vehicle of Atlantic interculture, the cradle of Atlantic transculture, and increasingly are deployed as a metonym for the project of Atlantic history itself, what should we make of the paradox that sailors were notorious not so much for their cosmopolitanism as for their parochialism and apparent alienation from landlubbers in general?[30] Their ostentatious behviour suggests that sailors were not suffering from "little communication" with society but, rather, that they themselves had a message to send, even if that message was simply to express their own distinctive group identity.

We can do better than that, however. The sailortown subculture arose out of a specific political context. In the eighteenth century, the residents of port cities throughout the British Isles were experiencing, and resenting, new encroachments from the fiscal-military state; or, in its more concrete forms, the Customs House and the Royal Navy's Impress Service. The population of waterfront neighbourhoods mobilized itself into a covert network for hiding contraband and sheltering sailors on the run. Sailors developed opaque systems of communication to swap advice about sympathetic tavern owners, little-known detours through the countryside, and safe houses with sliding panels and hidden compartments where one could wait out the gang. Sailors did more than hide. They responded with "noise" – a combination of clothes, movements, and language that registered dissent in the face of the demands of nation-building, violent conscription, and dramatic alterations in fashionable masculinity.

Did sailors actually spend enough time in port to constitute a community or benefit from social networks? The popular fascination with deep-sea voyages makes this question appear more vexing than it should. "For years he knows not the land," Herman Melville wrote of the Nantucket whaler, but few British seamen in the eighteenth or early nineteenth centuries could have said the same.[31] The coal run from Newcastle to London, one of the chief employers of seamen, took four to six weeks round trip.[32] Traders to Germany or Norway would make four or five voyages a year.[33] A ship engaged in the Chesapeake tobacco trade would complete one voyage in about nine months, but most of this time was spent in port; it took only eight weeks to reach America and slightly more than that to return to Britain.[34] Generally, both ships and sailors spent more time in port than at sea. Waiting for suitable cargo, haggling, and loading the ship all took considerable time. In addition, the maritime labour market varied sharply depending on the season.[35] The supply of commodities such as fish, olives, and tea was at its peak only at particular times of year. A ship's timetable was further constrained by dangerous weather, such as the hurricane season in the Caribbean and the ice and storms that shut down most commerce in the Baltic and North Sea in the winter.[36] It would have been a rare sailor who was, in Thomas Trotter's words, ignorant of "the common manners of society."

Furthermore, the seafaring population was continually leavened with unexpected elements from a variety of occupational backgrounds. Impressment was a violent, clumsy instrument of conscription that shaped the cultural possibilities of sailortown more than has been acknowledged. Many individuals acquired their first deep-water experience in the Royal Navy after a press gang plucked them from trades that "used the sea" in a much more coastal and limited sense; these people included shipwrights and the operators of river boats. In Cornwall, men worked in the mines but cast nets for herring in season, making themselves liable to the attentions of some zealous young officer and to being hauled onto the deck of a warship. Such unlikely sailors had no ambition to continue in that line of work. Desertion was frequent, though of course it created fresh vacancies that were filled by further rounds of impressment. Certain trades that "used the sea" had obtained written exemptions from impressment or argued that the gangs had, traditionally, left them alone. In a "hot press," however, all exemptions and claims of privilege were ignored.[37] The culture of sailors was not, therefore, necessarily maritime culture.

Between the necessities of their work and periodic abduction by press gangs, individual sailors were – to be sure – a transient urban presence. This was less true of the women in their lives, many of whom "used the sea" in their own way, providing much of sailortown's infrastructure: maintaining lodging houses, selling sexual services, or selling marked-up provisions to anchored vessels from bum-boats. The wives and families of sailors also provided some continuity and community. Women with some claim on the wages of an absent sailor became expert in converting that claim into ready cash, sometimes with the help of other women who had acquired a reputation for skill in such matters. A significant number of sailors were themselves the sons of seafaring men, which implies that the wives of sailors may have played a major role in the reproduction of that occupational choice and probably in the reproduction of certain elements of language and identity as well. We know that the privileges and pleasures of sea slang extended beyond occupational boundaries into the taverns and dwellings of neighbourhoods frequented by sailors. Pirates may have been famous for their profanity, but it is London's Billingsgate fishwife who has earned the dubious honour of a place in the *Oxford English Dictionary* next to "scurrilous vituperation."[38]

Males in sailortown were not always transients; indeed, some capitalized on the fact of their steady presence. Sailors shared information about who could be trusted in which ports. Far from home, perhaps with no friends in town, and their pockets full of money from a completed voyage, sailors were perfectly well aware that some people were out to fleece them. They were relieved and grateful to find a safe haven. It made good business sense to cultivate a reputation as the old reliable publican or lodging-house keeper.[39] When in London, John Nicol always boarded with a man from Inverness, "as honest a man as ever lived." In Plymouth, Robert Hay would go "directly to the house of a person who used to make all my purchases ashore."[40] For sailors with the appropriate interests, the same long-term and affectionate relationships might be established with the old reliable smuggler or with the expert forger of documents (a major industry on the Channel Islands of Guernsey and Jersey). Allying with experienced lawbreakers could pay off for a sailor on the run from the press gang. In these island havens, and in smaller ports around the British Isles, a cross-section of the community would already have been deeply involved in smuggling and fending off Customs officials, so there were established hiding places and secret rooms that could easily be adapted for the purpose of hiding sailors instead of contraband.[41] The sailor who kept to himself in port – or relied only on what his shipmates could get him – might well live to regret it. On the other hand, the sailor who took advantage of the networks that were already in place could find considerable resources, and even a measure of security, in sailortown. We need to bear this in mind when we speculate about how much, or how little, the average seafaring man may have interacted with his urban surroundings.

My intention is not to exaggerate the social harmony of sailortown. The lodging house with sliding walls and hidden compartments could have been used by successive owners for a wide range of purposes, not all of them congenial to the guests. "Panel thieves," who hid behind sliding walls and plundered sleeping lodgers, were a standard urban hazard on both sides of the Atlantic well into the nineteenth century. Indeed, the same proprietor who sheltered certain sailors – perhaps men who had helped him in a smuggling operation – might be quick to rob others or inform on them to the press gang.[42] With women, this dance of companionship and betrayal was complicated further by the role of venereal disease. In the words of one ballad:

> When poor Jack awoke, and found that she was missing,
> He said damn this whore, she's made me pay for kissing,
> She's pox'd me, which is ten times worse,
> Surely I lie under a curse.[43]

The relationship between sailors and sex workers could be particularly exploitative. The expectation that someone was up to no good often prompted pre-emptive strikes. Sea songs warned of "the Plymouth girls that'll pawn and sell your clothes" or praised the sailor who robbed the prostitute: "she'll do a wiggle and you must do the same."[44] At times, life in sailortown was about who cheated first or who laughed last.

Mischief on the waterfront was often associated with men (or occasionally women) known as crimps. Crimps were publicans or lodging-house keepers who would sell the sailor's services to a merchant captain, or a press gang, in return for a commission. The Admiralty portrayed crimps as unscrupulous predators who persuaded men to desert their ships, tricked drunken sailors, and coerced indebted ones to join a new crew. At their worst, crimps were engaged in what would later be called "Shanghaing": abducting sailors for profit. From descriptions like these, we get the impression that the crimp was a villain who specialized in trickery and entrapment, and derived his principal income from the commissions he made from captains of merchant vessels.[45] However, the individuals described as "crimps" or as keeping "crimp houses" displayed a variety of roles and behaviours; if they were exploitative, their exploitation took a more complex form than the classic descriptions would suggest. The sailor's role in the crimp's transactions was not always a passive one, and well known crimps were undoubtedly sought out by sailors ready to change ships.[46] Meanwhile, the Admiralty employed de facto crimps of their own to fortify special "rendezvous houses" where men captured by the press gang would be held until they could be transferred to a tender, a floating prison ship.[47] The moral difference between a (sometimes) violent crimp and a (sometimes) violent press gang would have been difficult to explain to most sailors.

Beyond the potentially conflicting interests of sailor, crimp, and sex worker, there are other reasons to question why, or how, sailortown could have pulled together on any issue. The occupational ecology of dockside and river areas was actually quite complex. Sailortown hosted a small army of workers who mediated the relationship between ship, sailor, and shore, but unrelated trades that happened to require access to water – such as tanning and dying – also clustered along the waterfront. The cheap lodging that attracted sailors was often the garret or cellar of a house owned by an artisan who might occupy a much higher social position (e.g., an instrument maker who crafted navigational aids). Shipwrights and sailcloth makers, even though they were subject to the press gang, were not exactly interchangeable with sailors. Even among the occupations that would have routinely mixed with sailors most often, such as publicans, dock workers, and printers – there was a great market for fill-in-the-blank Last Will and Testaments – what did these people have in common, besides their customers?

We can get some insight into that question by considering the Scottish children's game, "Press gang the weaver." The *Scottish National Dictionary* records this traditional game, which it connects to the game of "Release," a variety of tag in which the players who have been touched by the catcher may be released by the touch of a free player.[48] "Press gang the weaver" sounds like a wonderfully satirical re-enactment of the dance of capture and release played out by gangs, magistrates, and mobs. Even the name of the game announces that the press gang is either unfair or incompetent since weavers clearly do not "use the sea" in any sense at all. The spectacle of kids playing press gang should remind us that the tumult of a press gang in pursuit of its prey would have been a frequent sight. As a matter of pride, sailors liked to give the gangs a run for their money. The resulting chase, through the streets and in and out of buildings, could result in property damage or worse. From the perspective of any employer or property owner, a "hot press" was a dangerous disturbance of the peace. Adult or adolescent males who lived in sailortown neighbourhoods, regardless of their occupation or relation to the sea, were at risk and had reason to resent the gang.

Sailors' greatest complaint about impressment was that the navy made no effort to compete with the high wages offered by the merchant fleet in wartime, thus adding insult to the injury of violent conscription. Women who had expected to share in those high wages – whether as spouses, as sex workers, or otherwise – had reason to resent the press gang as well. Many other sectors of sailortown felt the pain too. Press gangs found themselves in trouble when, for example, the local mayor was also a publican. As occasional fugitives and frequent smugglers, dodging the authorities was integral to the occupational culture of seafaring men, but it also became second nature to their families, friends, neighbours, and those who hoped to profit from their company.[49] Mobs pursuing press gangs often did so in the knowledge that town officials would not interfere. Even a successful gang might find that the authorities would not permit it to lodge its captives in the town jail, or that its members themselves would be imprisoned pending the release of the men they had taken. Sailortown mobilized for war – against the officers of the Crown.[50]

The interests of smugglers, publicans, crimps, and sailors often coincided, just as their identities more than occasionally overlapped. In 1794, Lieutenant William Coller, leading a press gang in Harwich, was on the verge of seizing three sailors in an alehouse called the Royal Oak when the publican, "Landlord Cole," locked the door in his face. "I remonstrated & quietly demanded admittance," Coller wrote, "which he refused me in a most insolent & daring manner, a Conduct very usual to this Man, who has long before deserved to have his License taken from him."[51] Conflicts between angry and defiant "tapsters" and officers of the press gang seem to have been fairly common, while a "notorious crimp" named Wood in the town of Deal actually assaulted a lieutenant. Many publicans along the coast were heavily involved in smuggling – an activity that did not encourage respect for the law and that also happened to be another source of prospective employment for sailors.[52]

How could the crimps and their agents advertise without betraying themselves to the authorities? Conversely, how was the sailor to guess which of these waterfront characters he could trust? Jack Tar and his collaborators cultivated verbal arts that converted occupational jargon into a secret code. Thomas Trotter observed that "[the sailor's] narrations are full of hyperboles, similies [sic] and comparisons." In particular, sailors were gifted at the art of "translating" sentences into their own occupational jargon. Trotter saw and heard a great deal, but as a naval surgeon whose identification remained with the officer class, he remained excluded in certain important ways from the opaque community formed by the common seamen. Trotter saw translation as an expression of pride: "[T]hey look upon all landmen, as beings of an inferior order. This is marked ... by applying the language of seamanship to every transaction of life, and sometimes with a pedantic ostentation."[53] The sailor's practice of using jargon in inappropriate social contexts is mistaken for a quaint habit that betrayed an unfamiliarity with the ways of the shore rather than a clever subterfuge that permitted the secure exchange of timely advice or last-minute warnings.

Trotter's sympathetic but incomplete understanding points to an important fact: translators, potentially, formed a select group even *within* the seafaring population. Press gangs were often composed, at least in part, of sailors; to confuse them, and other sailortown denizens who might be paid informers, it is likely that there were multiple schools of translation or that meanings would be reassigned periodically. The power of "translation" lay not merely in the use of sea terms but also in the knowledge of the system of rules and conventions that governed the latest set of substitutions. The method of translation, rather than the existence of translation, was the real secret. Given the many distractions and interruptions inherent in overhearing conversation through a wall or across a crowded tavern, a little occasional recoding would be enough to frustrate the eavesdropper.

To the authorities, then, sailortown presented a mask, but a showy and insubordinate one. The swaggering processions through sailortown flew the flag of defiance for an appreciative neighbourhood audience. These displays mocked the urban explorers like Dr Johnson, who went to sailortown as they would go to a theatre, but simultaneously taunted the press gang with a highly visible, and identifiable, promenade of hunted men. In the case of those tradesmen, miners, and others who had been mis-identified by the press gang and found themselves immersed in the Royal Navy despite a lack of real sea experience, engaging in playful "translation" and collective strolls while on shore must have been a particularly ironic gesture. Working under duress in unfamiliar conditions, they appropriated the vocabulary and the accoutrements of shipboard life and reinvented them as a subversive style: "You said I was a sailor."

THE APPROPRIATION OF SAILORTOWN

Roger Knight's biography of Horatio Nelson mentions in passing that the great man's letters "are sprinkled with literary and classical references, particularly from Shakespeare."[54] This side of Nelson deserves more attention. He was especially fond of the "band of brothers" line from *Henry V*. It would be easy to interpret this as a hasty and unreflective use of the Bard. Yet, Prince Hal had a lengthy history prior to his Agincourt speech, making him – diachronically, at least – one of Shakespeare's most developed characters. Stephen Greenblatt has analyzed the transition of the young prince from a habitué of taverns (and friend to Falstaff) to a ruthless king. In *2 Henry IV*, Greenblatt draws our attention to Warwick's remark: "The Prince but studies his companions / Like a strange tongue, wherein, to gain the language."[55] Warwick correctly predicts that the prince will cast off his raffish companions when the time comes. But, as the quotation suggests, the future Henry v is doing more than slumming. The Boar's-Head Tavern is more than a playground or a resort for "villanous company."[56] The prince is learning how to speak to the people that he will one day govern. Likewise, Nelson's invocation of the "band of brothers" was opportunistic at a higher level than most have recognized.[57] Agincourt marked the culmination of a long process by which Prince Hal took what he needed from his low-life friends and sublimated it into what we might today call a conservative populist rhetoric. We can discern something similar in the way that Jack Tar was plucked from sailortown and transformed into a patriotic icon.

Dr Johnson had to instruct Boswell to go play the tourist in Wapping, but by the closing decade of the eighteenth century, it had become possible to admire the humours of sailortown from the safety of a West End theatre. Charles Dibdin, a pleasure-garden entertainer who specialized in doing impressions of different social "types" to his own accompaniment on the piano, was best known for impersonating a sailor. His song "Poor Jack" (1789), which combined vigorous sea slang with a sentimental, reassuring message about fidelity to home and hearth, brought him fame and enabled him to open his own theatre in London, the Sans Souci. He also pioneered the one-man show format and toured the provinces. Dibdin's impact, however, extended far beyond the circle of those who saw him perform in person. By 1800, his sea songs "were sold in every music-shop, seen on every lady's pianoforte, and sung in every company"; Poor Jack and his many sequels were reprinted in provincial newspapers, coloured in rosy-cheeked aquatints, plastered on the sides of jugs, and rendered in porcelain effigy for display on the mantelpiece.[58] In his memoirs, Dibdin regretted that he had been robbed of most of the profits from the reproductions of the plucky, swaggering, but endearing character that he, in turn, had stolen from sailortown. Impromptu street displays, like the nascent music industry, were not protected by copyright law.

The cycle of appropriation did not end there, however. Sailors themselves formed a conspicuous and economically important constituency of the London theatre audience and were well known for shouting and even rushing the stage when maritime events were depicted.[59] The autobiographies of sailors from this period are sprinkled with couplets from Dibdin lyrics, which are often included out of context and without attribution, presuming a great familiarity. Most remarkably, the leaders of the great naval mutinies of 1797 borrowed from Dibdin's vocabulary and phrasing in their petitions for redress.[60]

George III, seeking to put the mutinies behind him, orchestrated a victory parade through the streets of London later that year. There were, in fact, several notable victories at sea to commemorate, but in the 1790s staging such a parade was a risky and nearly unprecedented undertaking. It was an imitation of French propagandistic mass rallies and, as such, would be criticized by conservatives as aping the revolutionaries. At the same time, encouraging crowds to gather could offer opportunities for disorder or even treasonous outbursts. In 1786, an attempt had been made on the king's life during a parade, and love for monarchy had not increased since then. Despite all of these hazards and misgivings, the parade went ahead on 19 December. The king and Parliament boarded coaches for conveyance to St Paul's Cathedral, where they would give thanks for the recent triumphs against the nation's enemies. The stars of the show, however, were the officers and men of the Royal Navy. Two hundred and fifty sailors marched in the parade, offering a memorable display of loyalty and discipline at the close of a year in which the Thames had been blockaded by mutineers and a few crews had even discussed defecting to the French. Seamen had, of course, been conducting their own informal parades on the streets of sailortown for years, but George III – sensing that times were changing – brought them to the symbolic centre of London and covered them with his regal mantle. A detachment of marines was also in the parade, in case the sailors proved less loyal than predicted.[61]

These changes did not mark the end of sailortown as a material space on the city map of London; indeed, with the construction of the East India and West India docks, sailortown was beginning an expansion.[62] However, the cultural space of sailortown was changing beyond recognition. The redeployment of Jack Tar to the West End stage, to the bourgeois mantelpiece, to the ceremonial parade, and to a place in memorials to the distinguished dead in St Paul's Cathedral made it considerably more difficult to construe sailortown in terms of "here" and "there."[63] The extent to which sailortown *could* be appropriated, or *could* invade other parts of the city, serves to remind us that sailortown had always been part of the urban experience. Dror Wahrman's book, *The Making of the Modern Self*, highlights the role of masquerade and performativeness in London life.[64] Sailortown, far from an oceanic aberration, was where the city was most itself.

NOTES

1 Trotter, *Medicina Nautica*, 35.
2 I am indebted to Jon Saklofske for drawing my attention to this poem.
3 Lees and Lees, *Cities*, 17, 253–5; Ellis, *Georgian Town*, app. 1; Sacks and Lynch, "Ports, 1540–1700"; Jackson, "Ports, 1700–1840."
4 Pinol, *Histoire de l'Europe Urbaine*, 2:53–4.
5 Boswell, *Boswell's Life of Johnson*, ed. Hill, 4:201. [See also Perkins (this volume) on Dr Johnson's estimation of Edinburgh. Eds.]
6 I have developed these ideas further in Land, "Tidal Waves."
7 Land, "Many-Tongued Hydra." See also Burton, "Boundaries and Identities."
8 Paulson, *Rowlandson*, 29, discusses the artist's deployment of falling or unbalanced figures in a variety of settings.
9 *Oxford English Dictionary*, s.v. "humour." The full title of Hogarth's famous 1732 series about a prostitute is *The Harlot's Progress, or Humours of Drury Lane* (Paulson, *Hogarth*, 1:247).
10 See also Johnson's (this volume) discussion of how paintings by women reflected life in fin-de-siècle Paris. Eds.
11 I have discussed these issues further in Land, "'Sinful Propensities.'"
12 Winton, *Hurrah*, 164.
13 Rodger, *Wooden World*, 15, 64–5; Lewis, *Social History of the Navy*, 75; Hope, *New History*, 248–9.
14 Kuchta, *Three-Piece Suit*, has argued for taking a somewhat longer view rather than focusing solely on the 1750–1850 transformations, but he does not disagree that elite male dress was becoming more grave and less fanciful.
15 Styles, *Dress of the People*, 198, takes note of this possibility.
16 Yellow vest with red stripes: British Museum Collection (hereafter BMC) 7817; black ribbons: Hay, *Landsman Hay*, 75. Examples of red-striped pants: BMC 5566 (1779); BMC 6267 (1783); BMC 9106 (1797); BMC 11826 (1811). Examples of pigtails: BMC 10051 (1802); BMC 10771 (ca. 1806). Other clothing references: Pemberton, *Autobiography*, 93, 151,

281; [McPherson], *Life on Board*, 1; Hay, *Landsman Hay*, 37; Kelly, *Samuel Kelly*, 129; Leech, *Thirty Years from Home*, 125–6.

17 Jarrett, *British Naval Dress*, 48, 55, 62, 69. See also Miller, *Dressed to Kill.*

18 Hay, *Landsman Hay*, 190.

19 Barker, *Greenwich Hospital*, 11, 186. Also of interest here is Parkinson, *Portsmouth Point*, 68, 103. For traditional ballad references to sailors' clothes: "The Oak and the Ash," in Stubbs, *Life of a Man*, 55; "The Bonnie Ship the Diamond," in Seeger and MacColl, *Singing Island*, 59; "The Little Cabin Boy," in Stubbs, *Life of a Man*, 48. Thanks to Anna Davin for encouraging my interest in ballads.

20 *Lloyd's Evening Post*, May 25–27, 1768; Endelman, *Jews of Georgian England*, 205; Rudé, *Wilkes and Liberty*, 99 for journeymen weavers dressing as sailors in 1763 to attack their rivals in a wage dispute.

21 [McPherson], *Life on Board*, 75.

22 See also Warne's (this volume) discussion of the appropriation of London's streets by the blind and the disabled. Eds.

23 See also Fisher (this volume) on how processions through the streets of sixteenth-century Augsburg extended the boundaries of group membership. Eds.

24 Pemberton, *Autobiography*, 94.

25 Barker, *Greenwich*, 142.

26 Egan, *Life in London*, 286.

27 Hebdige, *Subculture*, 4, 18, 100–3; Nehring, *Flowers in the Dustbin*, 297.

28 Hebdige, *Subculture*, 92–4, 97.

29 Gilroy, *Black Atlantic*, 17.

30 Ortiz, *Cuban Counterpoint*; Gilroy, *Black Atlantic*; Roach, *Cities of the Dead*; Rediker and Linebaugh, *Many-Headed Hydra*. Baucom, *Specters of the Atlantic*, identifies the city of Liverpool as central to his story, yet this book, too, is ultimately about a ship, the slaver *Zong*, and a controversy surrounding events that took place at sea.

31 Melville, *Moby-Dick*, chap. 14.

32 Horsley, *Eighteenth-Century Newcastle*, 227–8.

33 Davis, *Rise*, 205.

34 Ibid., 286–7. By the early nineteenth century, North America traders were managing two voyages a year. See Hope, *New History*, 239.

35 Davis, *Rise*, 116; Bechervaise, *Thirty-Six Years*, 43.

36 Davis, *Rise*, 216–7, 221, 231, 238, 258; Hope, *New History*, 239.

37 My discussion of impressment is based on my review of the Home Office correspondence with the Admiralty. Rogers, *Press Gang*, has supplanted Hutchinson, *Press-Gang*, as the standard one-volume reference. See also Ennis, *Enter the Press-Gang*; and Rodger, *Command of the Ocean*, despite the latter's lack of sympathy for the common seaman.

38 *Oxford English Dictionary* s.v. "billingsgate." Hunt, "Women and the Fiscal-Imperial State"; Earle, *Sailors*. For women and seafaring communities more generally, see Creighton, *Rites and Passages*; Norling, *Captain Ahab*.

39 Clark, *English Alehouse*, 205.

40 Nicol, *Life and Adventures*, 160–1; Bechervaise, *Thirty-Six Years*, 79ff; Hay, *Landsman Hay*, 189; Nagle, *Nagle Journal*, 68–9, 71, 87; for cautionary tales, see Leech, *Voice*, 229, 232–3; Cremer, *Ramblin' Jack*, 253.

41 Macarthur, *History of Port Glasgow*, 77; Hutchinson, *Press-Gang Afloat and Ashore*, 157–9.

42 Nicol, *Life*, 158–60.

43 "Portsmouth Jack," in *Portsmouth Jack's Garland*, 2–3.

44 "Rounding the Horn," in Williams and Lloyd, *Penguin Book of English Folk Songs*, 90; "Up to the Rigs of London Town," in Stubbs, *Life of a Man*, 74–5.

45 The National Archives, Home Office (hereafter HO) 28/26, Dr Thomas Trotter to Evan Nepean, 13 August 1800; *Gentleman's Magazine* 28 (1758), 195–6; Bromley, *Manning*, 137–9; "A Commander," *Hints*, 31–2. See also Bechervaise, *Farewell*, 30; Nagle, *Nagle Journal*, 262, 274; Clark, *English Alehouse*, 324.

46 "Off to sea once more," in Seeger and MacColl, *Singing Island*, 69. For a similar analysis of the crimp's role in late nineteenth-century Canada, see Fingard, *Jack in Port*, 194–241.

47 HO 28/32, John Culverhouse at Liverpool to William Marsden, 24 July 1804.

48 *Scottish National Dictionary*, s.v. "Press gang."

49 Wilson, *Island Race*, 106.

50 HO 28/7: July and August 1790, letters on 269–273ff; HO 28/8, 28 February 1791, Admiralty Office to Grenville; HO 28/19, "Extract of a Letter from Capt. R.D. Oliver of His Majesty's Sloop Hazard to Mr. Stephens dated Campbeltown, 5 Feb. 1795"; HO 28/19, "Extract of a Letter from Rear Admiral Pringle to Mr. Ibbetson, dated Greenock 22 February 1795"; HO 28/23, Capt. J. Brenton to Evan Nepean, 4 October 1797; HO 28/26, Evan Nepean to John King, 6 August 1800; HO 28/27, 23 September 1801, Evan Nepean to Sir Geo. Shee; HO 28/29, 19 June 1803, Capt.

D. Dobree to Rear Admiral Sir James Saumarez; HO 28/29, 4 May 1803, Adam Mckenzie to Evan Nepean; HO 28/31, 31 January 1804, Ph. Stephens et al. to Right Hon. Charles Yorke.

51 HO 28/16, extract of a letter from Lieut. Wm Coller, employed on the Impress Service at Harwich, to Mr. Stephens, 21 March 1794.

52 HO 28/30, 4 October 1803, Wm Marsden to J. King [in Flushing, Cornwall]; for Deal, HO 28/30, 9 November 1803, Nepean to King; HO 28/43, 2 June 1813, J. Barrow to J. Beckett, and 17 June 1813, Captain G. Watts to J.W. Croker.

53 Trotter, *Medicina Nautica*, 38.

54 Knight, *Pursuit of Victory*, 10.

55 Greenblatt, *Shakespearean Negotiations*, 48. This line from *Henry IV* also appears in the dedication (to playboy-turned-monarch George IV) of Pierce Egan's bestseller about the "rambles and sprees" of Regency rakes, *Life in London*, vi.

56 *Henry IV, Part 1*, 3.3.

57 I have developed these ideas at greater length in Land, "What Are We at War About?" See also Wilson, "Nelson and the People"; Williams, "Nelson and Women."

58 Historians of the theatre designate him "Charles Dibdin the Elder" to distinguish him from his son, also a successful entertainer. For Dibdin's life and career, see Fahrner, *Theatre Career*. For evidence of popularity, see Hogarth, *Songs of Charles Dibdin*, xxi; BMC 7817; National Maritime Museum, PAF 4028; Prentice, *Celebration*, 63; *Greenock Advertiser*, 11 June 1802.

59 Russell, *Theatres of War*, 95–121.

60 Land, *War, Nationalism, and the British Sailor*, chap. 4.

61 Knight, *Pursuit of Victory*, 260–1; Colley, "Apotheosis of George III."

62 Linebaugh, *London Hanged*, 402–41.

63 Hoock, "Nelson Entombed," 115. For an additional example involving sailor-minstrels who made their living wandering all the neighbourhoods of London and the farming communities beyond, see Land, "Bread and Arsenic."

64 Wahrman, *Making*.

Postscript

The sentence from Calvino that serves as the epigraph to this volume, "The city ... consist[s] ... of relationships between the measurements of its space and the events of its past," defines the city in ways that John Stow, the famous sixteenth-century chronicler of London, would likely have considered apt. Stow's compendious *Survey of London*, which includes densely detailed, virtually street-by-street, building-by-building, descriptions of each of the wards in London, amasses a wealth of detail not only about the built environment (the "measurements of its space") but also about the history that underlies, sometimes quite literally, the buildings and monuments that define London of the late sixteenth century. In other ways, Stow's monumental work, like the chapters in this volume, makes more concrete and specific what remains implied by Calvino's sentence. Everywhere in his survey of London's edifices, Stow suggests that the built environment does not just reflect but actually makes possible the development of civic identities and urban values, reminding his London readers, for example, that the Romans, "by adhorting the Brytaines publikely, and helping them priuately, won them to build houses for themselues, Temples for the Gods, and Courts for Iustice, to bring up the noble mens children in good letters and humanitie."[1] Although he would not have conceived the matter in such terms, Stow also implies that the building of cities can effect sea changes in subjectivities: under the ameliorating influence of the Romans, he notes, Britons who were "before (for the most part) ... naked, painting their bodies" began to "apparell themselues Romane like."[2] For Stow, the measurements of a city's spaces can never be separated from civic identities and values or from matters of governance and the city's very identity. His first mention of London's name-sake, King Lud, is linked to both the built environment and imperatives of governance, on the one hand, and edifices and city limits, on the other, as he refers to Lud's having "repaired this Cittie, but also increased the same with fair buildings, Towers, and walles, and after his owne name called it *Caire-Lud*" and to his having built "a strong gate ... in the west ... named *Ludgate*," just before turning to the issue of Lud's successors in governing.[3] Above all, Stow concedes to edifices – and to one monument in particular, one that also happens to mark limits – the power to make and to sustain the city of London. His historical and topographical survey of the wall and gates of London, which is also a story of invasions, conquests, and defensibleness, reminds us that physical boundaries produce, rather than simply delimit, civic space.

However much his vantage point, design, and motivation differ from those of our contributors, Stow's *Survey* anticipates a number of the themes and issues that link the chapters in *City Limits*, suggesting once again that, as a subject of inquiry, the historical European city invites the kinds of investigations pursued here. In the introduction, prefaces, and cross-referencing footnotes, we have identified some of the ways in which individual chapters might be grouped together to illuminate facets of European cities and urban life prior to the twentieth century. Taking our cue from Stow, we can suggest in closing other ways to group the chapters collected here.

Like Stow's London, the cities studied by our contributors reveal their histories. The relationship between past and present, as well as between past and future, occupies not only the physical space of the city but also the consciousness of citizens and visitors – as is evidenced in the otherwise very different approaches taken by Wolfart, Blackstone, Bailey, Hoople, Perkins, and Saklofske. As is the case with Stow's London, the story of a city's limits, temporal and spatial, is frequently the story of a city's place within national, even transnational, regions, which is demonstrated in a variety of ways by Hammond, Blackstone, and Coenen Snyder. Stow's emphasis on the built environment as an index to cultural and socio-political influences and agencies is shared by contributors as otherwise diverse in their interests as Blackstone, Hoople, Perkins, and Coenen Snyder. Stow's emphasis on neighbourhoods, on the boundaries within city limits, links his choreography to those of Coenen Snyder, Land, Perkins, Fisher, and Warne, while his interest in overlapping jurisdictions links his understanding of civic administration to those articulated by Friedrichs, Coenen Snyder, and Bailey. Stow's unexpressed but nevertheless implicit interest in subjectivity, in the ever-shifting boundaries between private and public, between individual citizen and corporate body, connects his endeavour to those of Bailey, Warne, and Johnson. His sense of an urban aesthetic emerges from time to time, as in his declaring that Bread Street ward has "the most beautiful frame of fayre houses and shoppes, that bee within the Walls of London"[4] or in his frequent reference to fair buildings and monuments, particularly as they evince uniformity and proportion.[5] Stow's interest in urban aesthetics is mirrored in chapters by Hammond, Bailey, Hoople, Perkins, Coenen Snyder, and Saklofske. Finally, Stow's perambulatory approach to London is recalled by the walkers and tourists who inform the cities studied by Blackstone, Perkins, Warne, Fisher, Coenen Snyder, and Land.

The chapters collected in *City Limits* thus echo themes, issues, and approaches pursued by John Stow, confirming our sense that the historical European city lends itself particularly well to multifaceted readings and generates a number of specific themes. Our contributors also differ from Stow in signal ways. Most notably, individually and collectively, our contributors posit the city as dynamic, as constitutive of civic identities in the plural, as constituted, in turn, by the identities and interests of groups, sometimes overlapping, within the city. Where Stow looks for order and stasis within the rich multiplicity of London life in his day, our contributors reveal the instabilities and reorderings that stimulate the production of urban values. Where Stow's temporal and spatial survey of London everywhere acknowledges the limits that define London, within and without, the contributors to *City Limits* show repeatedly that limits shift and dissolve in the alembic of urban life. Stow takes into account marginalized city dwellers, past and present, such as the poor and indigent and the rebellious, but with a view towards drawing them into the compass of city statutes. Those of our contributors who focus on marginalized groups – women, the poor, the impaired, the deviant – do so not only to make visible such groups but also to make visible the dynamic by which marginalized citizens both experience and challenge, to the point of redrawing, the limits that circumscribe their agency and worlds. Like the city envisioned in Calvino's sentence, Stow's London is a richly, deeply layered city, drawing energy and meaning from its histories. The historical European city that emerges from the chapters gathered here is all that and more: dynamic, creative, composed of pluralities, and *experienced* as such by its citizens.

NOTES

1 Stow, *Survey of London*, 1:4.
2 Ibid.
3 Ibid., 1.
4 Ibid., 308.
5 Ibid., 345.

Bibliography

ARCHIVAL SOURCES

[A.L.] *Journey to Edinburgh, Stirling, Loch Lomond, Glasgow, Falls of Clyde, with Mr. Heron*. Acc. 10, 285. National Library of Scotland.

Association mutuelle des femmes artistes de Paris: Statuts. Paris: Imprimerie et librairie centrales des Chemins de fer (1894). Dos 700 ART, Bibliothèque Marguerite Durand, Paris.

[Beecroft, Mrs and Miss.] *Journal of a Tour to Scotland in the Summer of 1824*. Ms. 29,500. National Library of Scotland.

Fletcher, Eliza Dawson. *A Tour through part of England and Scotland by Eliza Dawson in the Year 1786*. Acc. 12017. National Library of Scotland.

[Sherwood, Lucy Elizabeth.] *Diary*. Acc. 8679. National Library of Scotland.

Stadtarchiv Lindau, Lit.25, *Annales Lindavienses* [= "Neukomm'sche Chronik"].

Wraxall, Nathaniel. *Diary: Scotland, July – Septemr 1813*. Ms. 3108. National Library of Scotland.

PRINTED SOURCES

Abersfeld, Anne. *Théophile Gautier*. Paris: Stock, 1992.

Abrams, M.H., and Stephen Greenblatt, eds. *The Norton Anthology of English Literature*. Vol. 2A: *The Romantic Period*. 7th ed. New York: Norton, 2000.

Aczel, Amir D. *Pendulum: Léon Foucault and the Triumph of Science*. New York: First Atria, 2003.

Agee, Richard J. *The Gardano Music Printing Firms, 1569–1611*. Rochester: University of Rochester Press, 1998.

Agulhon, Maurice. *1848: Ou, l'apprentissage de la République, 1848–1852*. Paris: Éditions du Seuil, 1973.

Aichinger, Gregor. *Solennia Augustissimi Corporis Christi, in sanctissimo sacrificio missae & in euisdem festi officijs, ac publicis supplicationibus seu processionibus cantari solita*. Augsburg: Johannes Praetorius, 1606.

Alcott-Nieriker, May. *Studying Art Abroad and How to Do It Cheaply*. Boston: Roberts Brothers, 1879.

Anderson, Benedict. *Imagined Communities: Reflections on the Origin and Spread of Nationalism*, revised ed. London: Verso, 1991.

Anonymous. *Curieuse und Historische Reisen durch Europa, Darinnen aller dieses Welt-Theil bewohnenden Völker Uhrsprung, Religion, Sitten und Gebrauche nebst der Regiments-Art und ihrer Stärcke oder Krieges-Macht begriffen ...* / Trans. by August Bohse from an anonymous French work, Joh. Ludwig Gleditsch, 1699.

Applegate, Celia. *A Nation of Provincials: The German Idea of Heimat*. Berkeley: University of California Press, 1990.

Appuhn-Radtke, Sibylle. *Visuelle Medien im Dienst der Gesellschaft Jesu: Johann Christoph Storer (1620–1671) als Maler der katholischen Reform*. Regensburg: Schnell and Steiner, 2000.

Arasaratnam, Sinnappah, and Aniruddha Ray. *Masulipatnam and Cambay: A History of Two Port-Towns, 1500–1800*. New Delhi: Munshiram Manoharlal Publishers, 1994.

Archer, Ian W. *The Pursuit of Stability: Social Relations in Elizabethan London*. Cambridge: Cambridge University Press, 1991.

Arnade, Peter. *Realms of Ritual: Burgundian Ceremony and Civic Life in Late Medieval Ghent*. Ithaca: Cornell University Press, 1996.

Arnold, Denis. *Giovanni Gabrieli and the Music of the Venetian High Renaissance*. London: Oxford University Press, 1979.

Atlas, Alan W. *Renaissance Music: Music in Western Europe, 1400–1600*. New York: W.W. Norton, 1998.

Atherton, Ian, Eric Fernie, Christopher Harper-Bill, and Hassell Smith, eds. *Norwich Cathedral: Church, City and Diocese, 1096–1996*. London: Hambledon, 1996.

Backus, Irena. *Life Writing in Reformation Europe: Lives of Reformers by Friends, Disciples and Foes*. Aldershot: Ashgate, 2008.

Baer, Gabriel. "The Administrative, Economic and Social Functions of Turkish Guilds." *International Journal of Middle East Studies* 1 (1970): 28–50.

Barker, Matthew Henry. *Greenwich Hospital, A Series of Naval Sketches, Descriptive of the Life of a Man-of-War's Man. By an Old Sailor*. London: James Robins, 1826.

Barringer, Christopher. "The Changing Face of Norwich." In *Norwich since 1550*, ed. Carole Rawcliffe and Richard Wilson, 1–34. London: Hambledon, 2004.

Barrows, Susanna. *Distorting Mirrors: Visions of the Crowd in Late Nineteenth-Century France*. New Haven: Yale University Press, 1981.

Barry, Jonathan, ed. *The Tudor and Stuart Town: A Reader in English Urban History, 1530–1688*. London: Longman, 1990.

Barzun, Jacques. *Berlioz and the Romantic Century*. 2 vols. New York: Columbia University Press, 1969.

Basler, Adolphe. *Suzanne Valadon, Collection "Les Artistes Nouveaux."* Ed. George Besson. Paris: G. Crès, 1929.

Baucom, Ian. *Specters of the Atlantic: Finance Capital, Slavery, and the Philosophy of History*. Durham, NC: Duke University Press, 2005.

Bayly, C.A. *Rulers, Townsmen and Bazaars: North Indian Society in the Age of British Expansion, 1770–1870*. Cambridge: Cambridge University Press, 1983.

Beard, Charles Austin. "Written History as an Act of Faith." *American Historical Review* 39, 2 (1934): 219–31.

Bechervaise, John. *Thirty-Six Years of a Seafaring Life by an Old Quarter Master*. Portsea: Woodward, 1839.

– *A Farewell to my Old Shipmates and Messmates; With Some Examples, and a Few Hints of Advice. By the Old Quarter Master*. Portsea: Woodward, 1847.

Beik, William E. *Urban Protest in Seventeenth-Century France: The Culture of Retribution*. Cambridge: Cambridge University Press, 1997.

Beier, A.L. "Social Problems in Elizabethan London." In *The Tudor and Stuart Town: A Reader in English Urban History 1530–1688*, ed. Jonathan Barry, 121–38. London: Longman, 1990.

Belloc, Marie Adelaide. "Lady Artists in Paris." *Murray's Magazine* 8, 45 (1890): 371–85.

Benjamin, Walter. *The Arcades Project*. Trans. Howard Eiland and Kevin McLaughlin. Cambridge, MA: Harvard University Press, 1999.

Benstock, Sheri. *Women of the Left Bank: Paris, 1900–1940*. London: Virago, 1987.

Bergeron, David. *English Civic Pageantry, 1558–1642*. Columbia, SC: University of South Carolina Press, 1971.

Bergsagel, John. "Foreign Music and Musicians in Denmark During the Reign of Christian IV." In *Heinrich Schütz und die Musik in Dänemark zur Zeit Christian IV: Bericht über die wissenschaftliche Konferenz in Kopenhagen 10.–14. November 1985*, ed. Ole Kongsted and Anne Ørbæk Jensen, 19–24. Copenhagen: Engstrøm and Sødring, 1989.

Bernard, Jean-Pierre A. *Les deux Paris: Les représentations de Paris dans la seconde moitié du XIXe siècle*. Seyssel: Champ Vallon, 2001.

Bernstein, Hilary J. "The Benefit of the Ballot? Elections and Influence in Sixteenth-Century Poitiers." *French Historical Studies* 24 (2001): 621–52.

Bernstein, Jane. *Music Printing in Renaissance Venice: The Scotto Press, 1539–1572*. New York: Oxford University Press, 1998.

Berry, Mary Elizabeth. *The Culture of Civil War in Kyoto*. Berkeley: University of California Press, 1994.

Betterton, Rosemary, ed. *Looking On: Images of Femininity in the Visual Arts and Media. London: Routledge and Kegan Paul,* 1987.

Bhattacharya, Durgaprasad, ed. *Report of the Population Estimates of India*. Vol. 2: *1801–1810*. New Delhi: Office of the Registrar General, India, Ministry of Home Affairs, 1989.

Bindoff, S.T., ed. *The History of Parliament: The House of Commons, 1509–1558*. London: History of Parliament Trust, 1982.

Blackmar, Elizabeth, and Roy Rosenzweig. "Central Park." In *The Encyclopedia of New York City*, ed. Kenneth T. Jackson, 197–9. New Haven: Yale University Press, 1995.

Blair, Sara. *Writing of Race and Nation*. New York: Cambridge University Press, 1996.

Blake, Stephen P. *Shahjahanabad: The Sovereign City in Mughal India, 1639–1739*. Cambridge: Cambridge University Press, 1991.

Blake, William. *The Complete Poetry and Prose of William Blake*. Newly Revised Edition. Ed. David Erdman. New York: Doubleday, 1988.

Blickle, Peter, ed. *Fluch und Eid: Die metaphysische Begründung gesellschaftlichen Zusammenlebens und politischer Ordnung in der ständischen Gesellschaft*. Berlin: Duncker and Humblot, 1993.

– *From the Communal Reformation to the Revolution of the Common Man*. Trans. Beat Kümin. Leiden: Brill, 1998.

– *Kommunalismus: Skizzen einer gesellschaftlichen Organisationsform*. Munich: Oldenbourg, 2000.

Blomefield, Francis. *An Essay towards a Topographical History of the County of Norfolk*. Vol 3. London, 1806.

Bloom, Peter. *The Life of Berlioz*. New York: Cambridge University Press, 1998.

Bodian, Miriam. *Hebrews of the Portuguese Nation: Conversos and Community in Early Modern Amsterdam*. Bloomington: Indiana University Press, 1997.

Boettcher, Susan. "Confessionalization: Reformation, Religion, Absolutism and Modernity." *History Compass* 2 (2004): 1–10.

Borzello, Frances. *A World of Our Own: Women as Artists*. London: Thames and Hudson, 2000.

Boswell, James. *The Journal of a Tour to the Hebrides*. Harmondsworth: Penguin, 1984 [1786].

– *Boswell's Life of Johnson*. Ed. George B. Hill. 6 vols. Oxford: Oxford University Press, 1971.

Botero, Giovanni. *Le relazioni universali*. Translated by Robert Johnson as *A Historical Description of the Most Famous Kingdomes and Common-weales in the Worlde*. London: n.p., 1601.

– *Delle cause della* grandezza *delle cittá*. Translated by Sir Thomas Hawkins as *The Cause of the Greatnesse of Cities*. London: n.p., 1635.

Boudon, Jacques-Olivier. "L'essor des nationalisms français." In *Le XIXème siècle: Science, politique et tradition*, ed. Isabelle Poutrin, 343–63. Paris: Berger-Levrault, 1995.

Boulton, Jeremy. *Neighbourhood and Society: A London Suburb in the Seventeenth Century*. Cambridge: Cambridge University Press, 1987.

Bouwsma, William J. "Venice and the Political Education of Europe." In *A Usable Past: Essays in European Cultural History*, 266–291. Berkeley: University of California Press, 1990.

Brady Jr., Thomas A. "From the Sacral Community to the Common Man: Reflections on German Reformation Studies." *Central European History* 20 (1987): 229–45.

Bräuer, Helmut. "Zur frühen bürgerlichen Geschichtsschreibung in Zwickau im 16. Jahrhundert." *Zeitschrift für Geschichtswissenschaft* 20 (1972): 565–76.

Brasz, Chaya, and Yosef Kaplan, eds. *Dutch Jews as Perceived by Themselves and by Others: Proceedings of the Eighth International Symposium on the History of the Jews in the Netherlands*. Leiden: Brill, 2001.

Bremens, Gilbert. *Historia Sacramenti Miraculosi in monasterio Sanctæ Crucis Augustæ Vindelicor*. Augsburg: Christophorus Mang, 1604.

Breitwieser, Markus. *Die Stadtbibliothek Lindau im Bodensee: Eine Untersuchung zu Geschichte und Funktion*. Wiesbaden: Harrassowitz, 1996.

Bromley, J.S. *The Manning of the Royal Navy: Selected Public Documents, 1693–1873*. London: Navy Records Society, 1974.
Bromley, William. *Several Years Travels through Portugal, Spain, Italy, Germany, Prussia, Sweden, Denmark, and the United Provinces. Performed by a Gentleman*. London: Printed for A. Roper, at the Black Boy, R. Basset at the Mitre in Fleet-Street, and W. Turner at Lincolns, Inn Back Gate, 1702.
Brunton, Mary. *Discipline*. 1814. London: Pandora Press, 1986.
Bryant, David. "The cori spezzati of St Mark's: Myth and Reality." *Early Music History* 1 (1981): 165–86.
Bryant, Lawrence M. *King and City in the Parisian Royal Entry Ceremony: Politics, Ritual and Art in the Renaissance*. Geneva: Librairie Droz, 1986.
Buelens, Gert. *Henry James and the Aliens in Possession of the American Scene*. New York: Rodopi, 2002.
– "James's 'Aliens': Consuming, Performing, and Judging the American Scene." *Modern Philology* 96 (1999): 347–63.
Buitenhuis, Peter. "Aesthetics of the Skyscraper: The Views of Sullivan, James and Wright." *American Quarterly* 9 (1957): 316–24.
Burke, Peter. *The European Renaissance: Centres and Peripheries*. Oxford: Blackwell 1998.
– *The Fortunes of the Courtier: The European Reception of Castiglione's Cortegiano*. Oxford: Polity Press, 1995.
– "The Uses of Italy." In *The Renaissance in National Context*, ed. Roy Porter and Mikulás Teich, 6–20. Cambridge: Cambridge University Press 1992.
– "The Spread of Italian Humanism." In *The Impact of Humanism on Western Europe*, ed. Anthony Goodman and Angus MacKay, 1–22. London: Longman, 1989.
Burmeister, Karl Heinz. *Lindauer Studenten aus Stadt und Land: Vom Mittelalter bis zum Beginn des 19. Jahrhunderts* [= Neujahrsblatt 44 des Museumvereins Lindau]. Lindau: Museumsverein Lindau, 2004.
Burton, Valerie. "Boundaries and Identities in the Nineteenth-Century English Port: Sailortown Narratives and Urban Space." In *Identities in Space: Contested Terrains in the Western City since 1850*, ed. Simon Gunn and Robert J. Morris, 137–51. Aldershot: Ashgate, 2001.
Butler, Ruth, and Hester Parr, eds. *Mind and Body Spaces: Geographies of Illness, Impairment and Disability*. London: Routledge, 1999.
Buzard, James. "Translation and Tourism: Scott's *Waverley* and the Rendering of Culture." *Yale Journal of Criticism* 8, 2 (1995): 31–59.

Cahm, Eric. *The Dreyfus Affair in French Society and Politics*. London: Longman, 1996.

Cairns, David. *Berlioz*. London: Allen Lane, 1999.

Calvino, Italo. *Invisible Cities*. Trans. William Weaver. London: Picador, 1979.

Campbell Orr, Clarissa, ed. *Women in the Victorian Art World*. Manchester: Manchester University Press, 1995.

Carøe, K. "Stipendium Regium og dets Stipendiarier." *Personalhistoriske Tidsskrift*, 6th ser., 6 (1915): 139–53

Carr, Sir John. *Caledonian Sketches, or a Tour through Scotland in 1807*. London, 1809.

Carr, William. *The Travellours Guide and Historians Faithful Companion: Giving an Account of the Most Remarkable Things and Matters Relating to the Religion, Government, Custom, Manners, Laws, Politics, Companies, Trade, &c. in All the Principal Kingdoms, States, and Provinces, Not Only in Europe, But Other Parts of the World …* / London: For Eben Tracy, 1695.

Carter, Tim. "Artusi, Monteverdi, and the Poetics of Modern Music." In *Musical Humanism and Its Legacy: Essays in Honor of Claude V. Palisca*, ed. Nancy Kovaleff Baker and Barbara Russano Hanning, 171–94. Stuyvesant, NY: Pendragon Press, 1992.

– "The Sound of Silence: Models for an Urban Musicology." *Urban History* 29 (2002): 8–18.

Chadwick, Whitney. *Women, Art, and Society*. 2nd ed. London: Thames and Hudson, 2002.

Chard, Chloe. *Pleasure and Guilt on the Grand Tour: Travel Writing and Imaginative Geography*. Manchester: Manchester University Press, 1999.

Cherry, Deborah. *Painting Women: Victorian Women Artists*. London: Routledge, 1993.

Chevalier, Bernard. "L'état et les bonnes villes en France au temps de leur accord parfait, 1450–1550." In *La ville, la bourgeoisie et la genèse de l'état moderne (XIIe-XVIIIe siècles)*, ed. Neithard Bulst and Jean-Philippe Genet, 71–85. Paris: Éditions du Centre national de la recherche scientifique, 1988.

Chevalier, Louis. *Laboring Classes and Dangerous Classes in Paris during the First Half of the Nineteenth Century*. 1st American ed. translated by Frank Jellinek. New York: H. Fertig, 1973.

Chitty, Susan. *Gwen John, 1876–1939*. London: Hodder and Stoughton, 1981.

Chouinard, Vera and Ali Grant. "On Being Not Even Anywhere Near 'The Project.'" In *Body Space*, ed. Nancy Duncan, 170–96. London: Routledge, 1996.

Clark, Peter, ed. *The Cambridge Urban History of Britain.* 3 vols. Cambridge: Cambridge University Press, 2000.

Clark, Peter. *The English Alehouse: A Social History*. London: Longman, 1983.

Clark, Peter, and Paul Slack. *English Towns in Transition, 1500–1700.* London: Oxford University Press, 1976.

Clark, Priscilla Parkhurst. *Literary France*. Berkeley: University of California Press, 1987.

Coffin, Judith G. *The Politics of Women's Work: The Paris Garment Trades, 1750–1915*. Princeton, NJ: Princeton University Press, 1996.

Colley, Linda. "The Apotheosis of George III: Loyalty, Royalty and the British Nation, 1760–1820." *Past and Present*, 102 (1984): 94–129.

"A Commander in the Royal Navy." *Hints on the Impressment of Seamen*. London: James Ridgway, 1827.

Commelin, Casper. *Beschryvinge van Amsterdam, Zynde een Naukeurige Verhandelinge van desselfs eerste Oorspronk uyt den Huyse der Heeren van Amsterl en Amstellant, haar Vergrootingen, Rykdom, en Wyze van Regeeringe, tot den Jare 1691*. Amsterdam: Aart Dirksz, Oossaan, 1694.

The Contrast: or Scotland as it was in the year 1745, and Scotland in the year 1819. London/Edinburgh: P. Wright & Son/J. Dick and Co., 1825.

Cooke Johnson, Linda. *Shanghai: From Market Town to Treaty Port, 1074–1858*. Stanford: Stanford University Press, 1995.

Corfield, Penelope. "Urban Development in England and Wales in the Sixteenth and Seventeenth Centuries." In *The Tudor and Stuart Town: A Reader in English Urban History, 1530–1688*, ed. Jonathan Barry, 35–62. London: Longman, 1990.

Coster, Will, and Andrew Spicer, eds. *Sacred Space in Early Modern Europe*. Cambridge: Cambridge University Press, 2005.

Cowan, Alexander. *Urban Europe, 1500–1700*. London: Arnold, 1998.

Cox, J.C. "Religious Houses." In *The Victoria History of the County of Norfolk*. Vol. 2: *The Victoria History of the Counties of England*, ed. William Page, 315–466. Folkestone, Kent: Institute of Historical Research, University of London, 1975.

Cozens-Hardy, Basil, and Ernest A. Kent. *Mayors of Norwich, 1403–1835 Being Biographical Notes on the Mayors of the Old Corporation*. Norwich: Jarrold, 1938.

Craig, W.J., ed. "As You Like It." *The Complete Works of William Shakespeare*. London: Oxford University Press: 1914; Bartleby.com, 2000. Available at www.bartleby.com/70/2027 (viewed 9 February 2009).

[Creech, William]. *Letters, Addressed to Sir John Sinclair, Bart. Respecting the Mode of Living, Arts, Commerce, Literature, Manners, &c. of Edinburgh, in 1763, And Since that Period*. Edinburgh, 1793.

Creighton, Margaret. *Rites and Passages: The Experience of American Whaling, 1830–1870*. New York: Cambridge University Press, 1995.

Cremer, John. *Ramblin' Jack: The Journal of Captain John Cremer, 1700–1774*. Ed. R. Reynell Bellamy. London: Jonathan Cape, 1936.

Cuningham, William. *The Cosmographical Glasse*. 1559. Reprinted in *The English Experience: Its Record in Early Printed Books*, Published in Facsimile, 44. Amsterdam: Da Capo, 1968.

Czok, Karl. "Bürgerkämpfe und Chronistik im deutschen Spätmittelalter." *Zeitschrift für Geschichtswissenschaft* 10 (1962): 637–45.

Davidsson, Åke. *Danskt Musiktryck intill 1700-Talets Mitt: Dänischer Musikdruck bis zur Mitte des 18. Jahrhunderts*. Studia Musicologica Upsaliensia, VII. Uppsala: Almquist and Wiksells, 1962.

Davis, Natalie Z. "The Rites of Violence." In *Society and Culture in Early Modern France*, 152–87. Stanford: Stanford University Press, 1977.

Davis, Ralph. *The Rise of the English Shipping Industry in the Seventeenth and Eighteenth Centuries*. London: Macmillan, 1962.

Dawkins, Heather. *The Nude in French Art and Culture, 1870–1910*. Cambridge: Cambridge University Press, 2002.

de Castro, D.H. *De Synagoge der Portugees-Israëlitische Gemeente te Amsterdam*. Amsterdam: Ets Haim, 1950.

de Certeau, Michel. *The Practice of Everyday Life*. Trans. Steven Rendall. Berkeley: University of California Press, 1984.

de Souza, Teotonio R. *Medieval Goa: A Socio-Economic History*. New Delhi: Concept, 1979.

de Vries, Jan. *European Urbanization, 1500–1800* Cambridge, MA: Harvard University Press, 1984.

De Witt, Cornelis. *A Letter from Holland, Touching Liberty of Conscience*. London, Printed for E.R., 1688.

Defoe, Daniel. *A Tour through the Whole Island of Great Britain, 1724–6*. Harmondsworth: Penguin, 1971.

Dibdin, Charles. *Observations on a Tour, Through Almost the Whole of England, and a Considerable Part of Scotland. In a Series of Letters, Addressed to a large number of intelligent and respectable Friends*. 2 vols. London, [1801–02].

Dieter, Stefan. *Die Reichsstadt Kaufbeuren in der frühen Neuzeit: Studien zur Wirtschafts-, Sozial-, Kirchen-, und Bevölkerungsgeschighte*. Thalhofen: Bauer-Verlag, 2000.

Dowd, Margaret. "Clash of Civilizations." *New York Times*, 13 May 2004.

Driedger, Michael D. *Obedient Heretics: Mennonite Identities in Lutheran Hamburg and Altona During the Confessional Age*. Aldershot and Burlington, VT: Ashgate, 2002.

Durkheim, Emile. *Suicide: A Study in Sociology*. 1897. Trans. John A. Spaulding and George Simpson. New York: The Free Press, 1951.

Dyos, H.J. and Michael Woolf, eds. *The Victorian City: Images and Realities*. 2 vols. London: Routledge, 1973.

Dyos, H.J., and D.A. Reader. "Slums and Suburbs." In *The Victorian City: Images and Realities*, ed. H.J. Dyos and Michael Woolf, 1:359–86. London: Routledge, 1973.

Earle, Peter. *Sailors: English Merchant Seamen, 1650–1775*. London: Methuen, 1998.

Egan, Pierce. *Life in London*. London: Sherwood, Neely and Jones, 1821.

Eldem, Edhem, Daniel Goffman, and Bruce Masters. *The Ottoman City between East and West: Aleppo, Izmir and Istanbul*. Cambridge: Cambridge University Press, 1999.

Elliott, Bridget. "New and Not so 'New Women' on the London Stage: Aubrey Beardsley's Yellow Book Images of Mrs. Patrick Campbell and Réjane." *Victorian Studies* 31, 1 (1987): 33–57.

Ellis, Joyce M. *The Georgian Town, 1680–1840*. Houndmills, Basingstoke: Palgrave Macmillan, 2001.

Endelman, Todd. *The Jews of Georgian England, 1714–1830*. Philadelphia: Jewish Publication Society of America, 1979.

Engels, Friedrich. *The Condition of the Working Class in England*. 1844. Stanford: Stanford University Press, 1958.

Ennis, Daniel James. *Enter the Press-Gang: Naval Impressment in Eighteenth-Century British Literature*. Newark: University of Delaware Press, 2002.

Fabricant, Carole. "The Literature of Domestic Tourism and the Public Consumption of Private Property." In *The New Eighteenth Century*, ed. Felicity Nussbaum and Laura Brown, 254–75. New York: Metheun, 1987.

Fagus, Félicien. "Association mutuelle des femmes artistes de Paris." *La revue blanche* 24 (January 1901): 144–5.

Fahrner, Robert. *The Theatre Career of Charles Dibdin the Elder, 1745–1814*. New York: Lang, 1989.

Fehrer, Catherine. *The Julian Academy, Paris, 1868–1939*. New York: Shepherd Gallery, 1989.

Feld, Steven. *Sound and Sentiment: Birds, Weeping, Poetics and Song in Kaluli Expression*. 2nd ed. Philadelphia: University of Pennsylvania Press, 1990.

Felltham, Owen. *Batavia, or the Hollander Displayed: Being Three Weeks Observations of the Lowe Country, especially Holland, in Brief Characters & Observations of the People & Country, the Gouvernement of their State & Private Families, their Virtues and Vices: Also a Perfect Description of the People & Country of Scotland*. London: Printed by Steven Swart, 1672.

Fergusson, Alexander, ed. *Letters and Journals of Mrs. Calderwood of Polton From England, Holland, and the Low Countries in 1756*. Edinburgh: Printed for David Douglas, 1884.

Ferry, Jean-Marc. "Cultures et Civilisations: Avatars du sentiment national en Europe, à lumière du rapport à la culture et à l'histoire." *Comprendre* 1 (2000): 1–7.

– *De la civilisation. Civilité, légalité, publicité*. Paris: Éditions du Cerf, 2001.

Ferry, Susan Janice. "Bodily Knowledge: Female Bodily Culture and Subjectivity in Manchester 1870–1900." PhD diss., Johns Hopkins University, 2004.

Fingard, Judith. *Jack in Port: Sailortowns of Eastern Canada*. Toronto: University of Toronto Press, 1982.

Finnane, Antonia. *Speaking of Yangzhou: A Chinese City, 1550–1850*. Harvard East Asian Monographs 236. Cambridge, MA: Harvard University Press, 2004.

Finscher, Ludwig, ed. *Die Musik des 15. und 16. Jahrhunderts*. Vol. 2. Laaber: Laaber-Verlag, 1990.

Fisher, Alexander J. *Music and Religious Identity in Counter-Reformation Augsburg, 1580–1630*. Aldershot: Ashgate, 2004.

Flint, Kate. "Blindness and Insight: Millais' *The Blind Girl* and the limits of representation." *Journal of Victorian Culture* 1, 1 (1996): 1–15.

Fondation Pierre Gianadda. *Suzanne Valadon*. Martigny, Suisse: La Fondation, 1996.

Forth, Christopher E. *The Dreyfus Affair and the Crisis of French Manhood*. Baltimore: Johns Hopkins University Press, 2004.

Foster, Alicia. *Gwen John*. London: Tate Gallery Publishing Ltd., 1999.

François, Étienne. *Die unsichtbare Grenze: Protestanten und Katholiken in Augsburg, 1648–1806*. Sigmaringen: Jan Thorbecke Verlag, 1991.

Freedman, Jonathan. *Professions of Taste: Henry James, British Aestheticism, and the Commodity Culture*. Stanford: Stanford University Press, 1990.

Friedman, Jerome. *The Most Ancient Testimony: Sixteenth-Century Christian-Hebraica in the Age of Renaissance Nostalgia*. Athens, OH: Ohio University Press, 1983.

Friedrichs, Christopher R. "Anti-Jewish Politics in Early Modern Germany: The Uprising in Worms. 1613–17." *Central European History* 23 (1990): 91–152

– *The Early Modern City, 1450–1750*. London and New York: Longman, 1995.

– "Jews in the Imperial Cities: A Political Perspective." In *In and Out of the Ghetto: Jewish-Gentile Relations in Late Medieval and Early Modern Germany*, ed. R. Po-chia Hsia and Hartmut Lehmann, 275–88. Washington, DC, and Cambridge: Cambridge University Press, 1995.

– "Polities or Pogrom? The Fettmilch Uprising in German and Jewish History." *Central European History* 19 (1986): 186–228.

– "The Swiss and German City-States." In *The City-State in Five Cultures*, ed. Carol G. Thomas and Robert R. Griffeth, 109–42. Santa Barbara: ABC-Clio, 1981.

– *Urban Politics in Early Modern Europe*. London and New York: Routledge, 2000.

Frye, Susan. *Elizabeth I: The Competition for Representation*. New York: Oxford University Press, 1993.

Fuma, Susuma. "Late Ming Urban Reform and the Popular Uprising in Hangzhou." In *Cities of Jiangnan in Late Imperial China*, ed. Linda Cooke Johnson, 47–79, 204–14. Albany: State University of New York Press, 1993.

Galbadon Marquez, Joaquim. *Descubrimiento y conquista de Venezuela: Textos historicos contemporaneos y documentos fundamentales*. Caracas: Academia Nacional de la Historia, 1962.

Gallagher, Catherine. "The Body versus the Social Body in the Works of Thomas Malthus and Henry Mayhew." In *The Making of the Modern Body: Sexuality and Society in the Nineteenth Century*, ed. Catherine Gallagher and Thomas Laquer, 83–106. Berkeley: University of California Press, 1987.

Galley, Chris. "A Model of Early Modern Urban Demography." *Economic History Review* 48, 3 (1995): 449–69.

Galloway, David, ed. *Norwich, 1540–1642*. Toronto: University of Toronto Press, 1984.

Gamrath, Helge. *Christian IV-tidens Danmark*. Copenhagen: Gyldendal, 1988.

Garb, Tamar. *Sisters of the Brush: Women's Artistic Culture in Late Nineteenth-Century Paris*. New Haven: Yale University Press, 1994.

Garrison, Gaston. *Le suicide dans l'antiquité et dans les temps modernes*. Paris: A. Rousseau, 1885.

Gassenmeier, Michael, and Jens Martin Gurr. "The Experience of the City in British Romantic Poetry." In *Comparative History of Literatures in European Languages: Romantic Poetry*, ed. Angela Esterhammer, 305–31. Amsterdam: Benjamins, 2002.

Geertz, Clifford. *Local Knowledge: Further Essays in Interpretive Anthropology*. New York: Basic Books, 1983.

Gerber, Haim. "Guilds in Seventeenth-Century Anatolian Bursa." *African and Asian Studies* (Jerusalem) 11 (1976): 59–86.

Geismar, Maxwell. *Henry James and the Jacobites*. Boston: Houghton Mifflin, 1963.

Gillespie, Charles Coulston, ed. *Dictionary of Scientific Biography*. New York: Charles Scribner's Sons, 1975.

Gillion, Kenneth L. *Ahmedabad: A Study in Indian Urban History*. Berkeley: University of California Press, 1968.

Gilroy, Paul. *The Black Atlantic: Modernity and Double Consciousness*. London: Verso, 1993.

Ginzburg, Carlo. *Night Battles: Witchcraft and Agrarian Cults in the Sixteenth and Seventeenth Centuries*. Trans. John and Anne Tedeschi. London: Routlege and Kegan Paul, 1983.

Glahn, Henrik, ed. *20 Italienske Madrigaler fra Melchior Borchgrevinck "Giardino novo I-II" København 1605/06*. Copenhagen: Egtved, 1983.

Gleeson, Brendan. "A Geography for Disabled People?" *Transactions, Institute of British Geographers* 21, 2 (1996): 387–96.

– *Geographies of Disability*. London: Routledge, 1999.

Glendening, John. *The High Road: Romantic Tourism, Scotland, and Literature, 1720–1820*. New York: St. Martin's Press, 1997.

Göhler, Albert. *Verzeichnis der in den Frankfurter undLeipziger Messkatalogen der Jahre 1564 bis 1759 angezeigten Musikalien*. Hilversum: Frits A.M. Knuf, 1965.

Gokhale, Balkrishna Govind. *Poona in the Eighteenth Century: An Urban History*. Delhi: Oxford University Press, 1988.

– *Surat in the Seventeenth Century: A Study in Urban History of Pre-Modern India*. Scandinavian Institute of Asian Studies Monograph Series, 28. London and Malmö: Curzon Press, 1978

Golas, Peter J. "Early Ch'ing Guilds." In *The City in Late Imperial China*, ed. G. William Skinner, 555–80. Stanford: Stanford University Press, 1977.

Goldstein, Jan. *Console and Classify: The French Psychiatric Profession in the Nineteenth Century*. Cambridge: Cambridge University Press, 1987.

Govind Gokhale, Balkrishna. *Surat in the Seventeenth Century: A Study in Urban History of Pre-Modern India*. Scandinavian Institute of Asian Studies Monograph Series, 28: London and Malmö: Curzon Press, 1978.

Grafton, Anthony. *Defenders of the Text: The Traditions of Scholarship in an Age of Science, 1450–1800*. Cambridge, MA: Harvard University Press, 1991.

Grant, Mary Ann. *Sketches of Life and Manners in England, Scotland, and Ireland: Interspersed with Moral Tales and Anecdotes, In Original Letters*. London, 1810.

Great Britain. *Acts of the Privy Council of England*. Vol. 4: *1552–1554*. Ed. J.R. Dasent. London: Her Majesty's Stationery Office, 1892.

Green, Bryan S. "Learning from Henry Mayhew: The Role of the Impartial Spectator in Mayhew's *London Labour and the London Poor*." *Journal of Contemporary Ethnography* 31, 2 (2002): 99–134.

Greenblatt, Stephen. *Shakespearean Negotiations: The Circulation of Social Energy in Renaissance England*. Berkeley: University of California Press, 1988.

Greg, W.W., ed. *The Interlude of Wealth and Health*. Chiswick: Malone Society, 1907.

– *Respublica: An Interlude for Christmas 1553*. Attributed to Nicholas Udall, Early English Text Society, o.s. 226. London: Oxford University Press, 1952 for 1946.

Griffiths, Paul. *Lost Londons: Change, Crime, and Control in the Capital City, 1550–1660*. Cambridge: Cambridge University Press, 2008.

– "Inhabitants." In *Norwich since 1550*, ed. Carole Rawcliffe and Richard Wilson, 63–88. London: Hambeldon, 2004.

Grobman, Andrew. "Twice-Told Trails: Hawthorne's Boston." Paper presented at "The Scartlet Letter: 150 Years After," Hawthorne Society Conference, Boston, MA, 18 June 2000.

Groebner, Valentin. *Liquid Assets and Dangerous Gifts: Presents and Politics at the End of the Middle Ages*. Trans. Pamela Selwyn Philadelphia: University of Pennsylvania Press, 2002.

Gunn, Geoffrey O. *First Globalization: The Eurasian Exchange, 1500–1800*. Lanham, MD: Rowman and Littlefield, 2003.

Habib, Irfan. *Peasant and Artisan Resistance in Mughl India*. McGill Studies in International Development, 20. Montreal: McGill University Centre for Developing-Area Studies, 1984.

Hahn, Harlan. "Disability and the Urban Environment: A Perspective on Los Angles." *Environment and Planning* 4 (1986): 273–88.

Hale, J.R., ed. *Renaissance Venice*. Totowa, NJ: Rowan and Littlefield, 1973.

Halliday, Paul D. *Dismembering the Body Politic: Partisan Politics in England's Towns, 1650–1730*. Cambridge: Cambridge University Press, 1998.

Hammerich, Angul. *Musiken ved Christian den Fjerdes Hof: Et Bidrag til Dansk Musikhistorie*. Copenhagen: Wilhelm Hansen, 1893.

Hammond, Susan L. "Danish Diplomacy and the Dedication of *Giardino novo II* (1606) to King James I." *Danish Yearbook of Musicology* 28 (2001): 9–18.

– "Italian Music and Christian IV's Urban Agenda for Copenhagen," *Scandinavian Studies* 77, 3 (2005): 365–82.

Hanley, Susan B. "Urban Sanitation in Preindustrial Japan." *Journal of Interdisciplinary History* 18, 1 (1987): 1–26.

Hanning, Barbara R. "Guarini, Battista." *Grove Music Online*, ed. L. Macy. Available at http://www.grovemusic.com (viewed 23 January 2006).

Hansen, Mogens Herman, ed. *A Comparative Study of Six City-State Cultures*. Historisk-filosofiske Skrifter 27. Copenhagen: Det Kongelige Danske Videnskabernes Selskab, 2002.

– *A Comparative Study of Thirty City-State Cultures*. Historisk-filosofiske Skrifter 21. Copenhagen: Det Kongelige Danske Videnskabernes Selskab, 2000.

– "95 Theses about the Greek *Polis* in the Archaic and Classic Periods: A Report on the Results Obtained by the Copenhagen Polis Centre in the Period 1993–2003." *Historia* 52 (2003): 257–82.

Harris, Ann, and Linda Nochlin. *Women Artists, 1550–1950*. Los Angeles: Los Angeles County Museum of Art, 1977.

Harvey, David. *Paris, Capital of Modernity*. New York: Routledge, 2003.

Hassan, Ihab. "Cities of Mind, Urban Words: The Dematerialization of the Metropolis in Contemporary American Fiction." In *Literature and the Urban Experience*, ed. Michael C. Jaye and Anne C. Watts, 93–112. New Brunswick: Rutgers University Press, 1981.

Haviland, Beverly. *Henry James's Last Romance: Making Sense of the Past and* The American Scene. New York: Cambridge University Press, 1997.

Hay, Robert. *Landsman Hay: The Memoirs of Robert Hay, 1789–1847*. Ed. M.D. Hay. London: Rupert Hart-Davis, 1953.

Headley, John M., Hans J. Hillerbrand and Anthony J. Paplas, eds. *Confessionalization in Europe, 1555–1700: Essays in honor and memory of Bodo Nischan*. Aldershot: Ashgate, 2004.

Hebdige, Dick. *Subculture: The Meaning of Style*. London: Routledge, 1979.

Hecht, Christian. *Katholische Bildertheologie im Zeitalter von Gegenreformation und Barock: Studien zu Traktaten von Johannes Molanus, Gabriele Paleotti und anderen Autoren*. Berlin: Gebr. Mann Verlag, 1997.

Heiberg, Steffen, ed. *Christian IV and Europe: The 19th Art Exhibition of the Council of Europe, Denmark 1988*. Copenhagen: Poul Kristensen, 1988.

Helk, Vello. *Dansk-norske studierejser fra reformationen til enevælden, 1536–1660: Med en matrikel over studerende i udlandet*. Odense: Odense University Press, 1987.

Higonnet, Patrice. *Paris: Capital of the World*. Trans. Arthur Goldhammer. Cambridge, MA: Harvard University Press, 2002.

Himmelfarb, Gertrude. "The Culture of Poverty." In *The Victorian City: Images and Realities*, 2 vols., ed. H.J. Dyos and Michael Woolf, 2:707–36. London: Routledge, 1973.

– *The Idea of Poverty: England in the Early Industrial Age*. New York: Vintage, 1985.

Hogarth, George, ed. *The Songs of Charles Dibdin*. London: How and Parsons, 1842.

Hohenberg, Paul M., and Lyn Hollen Lees. *The Making of Urban Europe, 1000–1950*. Cambridge, MA: Harvard University Press, 1985.

Holland, Clive. "Lady Art Student's Life in Paris." *The Studio* 30, 129 (1903): 225–33.

Holmes, Diana, and Carrie Tarr, eds. *A Belle Époque? Women and Feminism in French Society and Culture, 1890–1914*. Oxford: Berghahn, 2006.

Holmes, Martha Stoddard. *Fictions of Affliction: Physical Disability in Victorian Culture*. Ann Arbor: University of Michigan Press, 2004.

– "Working (with) the Rhetoric of Affliction." In *Embodied Rhetorics: Disability in Language and Culture*, ed. James C. Wilson and Cynthia Lewiecki-Wilson, 27–44. Carbondale: Southern Illinois University Press, 2001.

Hoock, Holger. "Nelson Entombed: The Military and Naval Pantheon in St Paul's Cathedral." In *Admiral Lord Nelson: Context and Legacy*, ed. David Cannadine, 115–43. New York: Palgrave Macmillan, 2005.

Hoople, Robin P. "Henry James's Alphabet of Impressions: The Example of the Obelisk." Paper presented at Tracing Henry James, International Conference of the Henry James Society, Venice, Italy, 15 July 2005.

Hope, Ronald. *A New History of British Shipping*. London: John Murray, 1990.

Horsley, P.M. *Eighteenth-Century Newcastle*. Newcastle-upon-Tyne: Oriel, 1971.

Houston, R.A. *Social Change in the Age of Enlightenment: Edinburgh, 1660–1760*. Oxford: Clarendon Press, 1994.

Hughes, Merritt Y., ed. *John Milton: Complete Poems and Major Prose*. New York: Macmillan, 1957.

Hughes, Paul L., and James F. Larkin, eds. *Tudor Royal Proclamations*. 3 vols. New Haven: Yale University Press, 1969.

Humpherys, Anne. *Travels into the Poor Man's Country: The Work of Henry Mayhew*. Athens, GA: University of Georgia Press, 1977.

Hunt, Margaret. "Racism, Imperialism, and the Traveler's Gaze in Eighteenth-Century England." *Journal of British Studies* 32 (October 1993): 333–57.

– "Women and the Fiscal-Imperial State in Late Seventeenth and Early Eighteenth Centuries." In *A New Imperial History: Culture, Identity and Modernity in Britain and the Empire*, ed. Kathleen Wilson, 29–47. Cambridge: Cambridge University Press, 2004.

Hutchinson, J.R. *The Press-Gang Afloat and Ashore*. London: Eveleigh Nash, 1913.

Israel, Jonathan I. *The Dutch Republic: Its Rise, Greatness, and Fall, 1477–1806*. Oxford: Clarendon Press, 1995.

Jackson, Gordon. "Ports, 1700–1840." In *The Cambridge Urban History of Britain*, ed. Peter Clark, 2:726–31. Cambridge: Cambridge University Press, 2000.

Jacobsen, Jens Peter, ed. *Madrigaler fra Christian IV's Tid*. Dania sonans 2–3. Egtved: Musikhojskolens Verlag, 1966.

Jakobi, Franz-Joseph. "'Geschichtsbewußtsein' in mittelalterlichen Gedenk-Aufzeichnungen." *Archiv für Kulturgeschichte* 68 (1986): 1–23.

[James, Franklin.] *Franklin's Letters to his Kinsfolk, written during the Years 1818, '19 & '20, from Edinburgh, London, The Highlands of Scotland, and Ireland*. Philadelphia: J. Maxwell, 1822.

James, Henry. *The American Scene*. London: Chapman and Hall, 1907.

– *The Art of the Novel*. Ed. R.P. Blackmur. New York: Scribner's, 1934.

– *Henry James Letters*. Ed. Leon Edel. Cambridge, MA: Harvard University Press, 1974–84.

– *Italian Hours*. New York: Horizon Press, 1968.

– "The Question of Our Speech." In *Two Lectures by Henry James*. Boston: Houghton Mifflin, 1905.

James, Mervyn. "Ritual, Drama and Social Body in the Late Medieval English Town." *Past and Present* 98 (1983): 3–29.

Janssen, Carole A. "The Waites of Norwich and an Early Lord Mayor's Show." *Research Opportunities in Renaissance Drama* 22 (1979): 57–64.

Jarrett, Dudley. *British Naval Dress*. London: J.M. Dent, 1960.

Joachimsen, Paul. *Geschichtsauffassung und Geschichtsschreibung in Deutschland unter dem Einfluss des Humanismus*. Leipzig/Berlin: B.G. Teubner, 1910.

Joetze, Franz. *Die Chroniken der Stadt Lindau: Programm des Königlichen Maximilians-Gymnasium für das Schuljahr 1904/1905*. Munich: Straub, 1905.

John, Augustus. "Gwendolen John." *Burlington Magazine for Connoisseurs* 81 (October 1942): 236–40.

Johnson, Linda Cooke. *Shanghai: From Market Town to Treaty Port, 1074–1858*. Stanford: Stanford University Press, 1995.

Johnson, Samuel. *A Journey to the Western Islands of Scotland*. 1775. Harmondsworth: Penguin, 1984.

Johnston, Kenneth. "Blake's Cities: Romantic Forms of Urban Renewal." In *Blake's Visionary Forms Dramatic*, ed. David Erdman and John E. Grant, 413–42. Princeton: Princeton, 1970.

Jones, Gareth Stedman. *Outcast London*. Oxford: Clarendon Press, 1971.

Jones, Lindsay. *The Hermeneutics of Sacred Architecture: Experience, Interpretation, Comparison*. Vol. 1: *Monumental Occasions: Reflections on the Eventfulness of Religious Architecture*. Cambridge, MA: Harvard University Press, 2000.

Kalifa, Dominique. *Crime et culture au XIXe siècle*. Paris: Perrin, 2005.
– *L'encre et le sang: Récits de crimes et société à la belle époque*. Paris: Fayard, 1995.
Kaplan, Benjamin J. *Calvinists and Libertines: Confession and Community in Utrecht, 1578–1620*. Oxford: Oxford University Press, 1995.
– "Fictions of Privacy: House Chapels and the Spatial Accommodation of Religious Dissent in Early Modern Europe." *American Historical Review* 107, 4 (2002): 1031–64.
Kaplan, Yosef. "Gente Política: The Portuguese Jews of Amsterdam vis-à-vis Dutch Society." In *Dutch Jews as Perceived by Themselves and by Others: Proceedings of the Eighth International Symposium on the History of the Jews in the Netherlands*, ed. Chaya Brasz and Yosef Kaplan, 21–40. Leiden: Brill, 2001.
– "De Joden in de Republiek tot omstreeks 1750: Religieus, Cultureel en Sociaal Leven." In *Geschiedenis van de Joden in Nederland*, ed. J.C.H. Blom et al., 129–73. Amsterdam: Uitgeverij Balans, 1995.
Kelley, Donald R., ed. *Versions of History from Antiquity to Enlightenment*. New Haven: Yale University Press, 1991.
Kelly, Samuel. *Samuel Kelly: An Eighteenth-Century Seaman*. Ed. Crosbie Garstin. New York: Frederick A. Stokes, 1925.
Khoury, Dina Rizk. *State and Provincial Society in the Ottoman Empire: Mosul, 1540–1834*. Cambridge: Cambridge University Press, 1997.
Knight, Roger. *The Pursuit of Victory: The Life and Achievement of Horatio Nelson*. London: Allen Lane, 2005.
Kongsted, Ole, ed. *Motets by G. Trehou, J. Tollius and V. Bertholusius*, Music in Denmark at the Time of Christian IV 5. Copenhagen: Engstrøm and Sødring A/S, 1988.
Kornerup, Bjørn. *Biskop Hans Poulsen Resen: Studier over Kirke- og Skolehistorie i det 16. og 17. Aarhundrede, I, 1561–1615*. Copenhagen: G.E.C. Gad, 1968.
– "Reformationsjubilæet i Danmark 1617." *Kirkehistoriske Samlinger* 6th ser., no. 2 (1936–38): 33–83.
Koselleck, Reinhard. "Geschichte, Historie." In *Geschichtliche Grundbegriffe* 2:593–717. Stuttgart: Klett-Cotta Verlag, 1975.
Kostof, Spiro. *The City Shaped: Urban Patterns and Meanings through History*. Boston: Little, Brown and Co., 1991.
Kramer, Lloyd. *Nationalism: Political Cultures in Europe and America, 1775–1865*. New York: Twayne Publishers, 1998.
Kramer-Schlette, C. *Vier Augsburger Chronisten der Reformationszeit* [= Kieler Historische Studien 421]. Lübeck: Hamburg, 1970.

Kraus, Jürgen, and Stefan Fischer, eds. *Die Stadt Kaufbeuren*. Vol. 1: *Geschichte und Gegenwart*. Thalhofen: Bauer Verlag, 1999.
Kristeva, Julia. *Au risque de la pensée*. Éditions de l'Aube, 2001.
– *Etrangers à nous-mêmes*. Paris: Flammarion, 1991.
– *Sens et non-sens de la révolte*. Paris: Fayard, 2001.
Kuchta, David. *The Three-Piece Suit and Modern Masculinity: England, 1550–1850*. Berkeley: University of California Press, 2002.
Kugler, Hartmut. *Die Vortstellung der Stadt in der Literatur des deutschen Mittelalters*. Munich: Artemis, 1986.
Kusuo, Uchido. "Protest and the Tactics of Direct Remonstration: Osaka's Merchants Make Their Voices Heard." In *Osaka: The Merchants' Capital of Early Modern Japan*, ed. James L. McClain and Wakita Osamu, 80–103. Ithaca: Cornell University Press, 1999.
Lader, Octavian. *Historia dess Sacraments, so beym H. Creutz in Augspurg verehrt wirdt*. Augsburg: Andreas Aperger, 1625.
Lamb, Charles. "A Complaint of the Decay of Beggars in the Metropolis." In *Essays of Elia and Last Essays of Elia*, 134–41. London: J.M. Dent, 1972.
Lancashire, Anne. *London Civic Theatre: City Drama and Pageantry from Roman Times to 1558*. Cambridge: Cambridge University Press, 2002.
Lancashire, Ian. *Dramatic Texts and Records of Britain: A Chronological Topography to 1558*. Toronto: University of Toronto Press, 1984.
Land, Isaac. "Bread and Arsenic: Citizenship from the Bottom Up in Georgian London." *Journal of Social History* 39, 1 (2005): 89–110.
– "The Many-Tongued Hydra: Sea Talk, Maritime Culture, and Atlantic Identities, 1700–1850." *Journal of American and Comparative Cultures* 25, 3–4 (2002): 412–17.
– "'Sinful Propensities': Piracy, Sodomy, and Empire in the Rhetoric of Naval Reform." In *Discipline and the Other Body: Humanitarianism, Violence, and the Colonial Exception*, ed. Anupama Rao and Steven Pierce, 90–114. Durham: Duke University Press, 2006.
– "Tidal Waves: The New Coastal History." *Journal of Social History* 40, 3 (2007): 731–43.
– "What Are We at War About?" *London Review of Books*, 1 December 2005.
– *War, Nationalism, and the British Sailor, 1750–1850*. New York: Palgrave Macmillan, 2009.
Langdale, Cecily. *Gwen John: With a Catalogue Raisonné of the Paintings and a Selection of the Drawings*. New Haven: Yale University Press, 1987.

– and David Fraser Jenkins. *Gwen John: An Interior Life*. London: Phaidon Press, Barbican Art Gallery, 1985.

Laslett, Peter. *The World We Have Lost*. 2nd ed. London: Methuen and Co., 1971.

Lathers, Marie. *Bodies of Art: French Literary Realism and the Artist's Model*. Lincoln: University of Nebraska Press, 2001.

Lawrence, D.H. *Complete Poems*. New York: Penguin, 1993.

Laursen, L. *Kancelliets Brevbøger vedrørende Danmarks indre Forhold i uddrag, 1596–1602*. Copenhagen: C.A. Reitzel, 1913.

Leech, Samuel. *Thirty Years from Home, or, A Voice from the Main Deck*. Boston, MA: Tappan, Whittemore and Mason, 1843.

Lees, Andrew, and Lynn Hollen Lees. *Cities and the Making of Modern Europe, 1750–1914*. New York: Cambridge University Press, 2007.

Lees, Colin, and Sue Ralph. "Charitable Provision for Blind People and Deaf People in Late Nineteenth-Century London." *Journal of Research in Special Education Needs* 4, 3 (2004): 148–60.

Le Galès, Patrick. *European Cities: Social Conflicts and Governance*. Oxford: Oxford University Press, 2002.

Lehan, Richard D. *The City in Literature: An Intellectual and Cultural History*. Berkeley: University of California Press, 1998.

Letters from Scotland: by an English Commercial Traveller. Written during a Journey to Scotland in the Summer of 1815. London: Longman, Hurst, Rees, Orme, and Brown, 1817.

Lettice, I. [John]. *Letters on a Tour Through Various Parts of Scotland, In the Year 1792*. London: T. Cadell, 1794.

Lewis, Mary S. *Antonio Gardano, Venetian Music Printer, 1538–1569: A Descriptive Bibliography and Historical Study*. 3 vols. New York: Garland, 1988–2005.

Lewis, Michael. *A Social History of the Navy, 1793–1815*. London: George Allen and Unwin, 1960.

Lindberg, Kirsten. *Sirenernes Stad København: By- og bygningshistorie før 1728*. Vol.1. Copenhagen: Skippershoved, 1996.

Linebaugh, Peter. *The London Hanged: Crime and Civil Society in the Eighteenth Century*. Cambridge: Cambridge University Press, 1992.

Loades, David. *The Oxford Martyrs*. London: B.T. Batsford, 1970.

Lockhart, John Gibson. *Peter's Letters to his Kinsfolk*. 1819. Edinburgh: Scottish Academic Press, 1977.

Lossen, Max. *Die Reichsstadt Donauwörth und Herzog Maximilian*. Munich: F. Straub, 1866.

Löwith, Karl. *Meaning in History*. Chicago: University of Chicago Press, 1949.

Macarthur, William F. *History of Port Glasgow*. Glasgow: Jackson, Wylie, 1932.

Macky, J. *A Journey Through Scotland. In Familiar Letters from a Gentleman Here, to his Friend Abroad*. London: J. Pemberton and J. Hooke, 1723.

Mah, Harold. *Enlightenment Phantasies: Cultural Identity in France and Germany, 1750–1914*. Ithaca: Cornell University Press, 2003.

Manley, Lawrence. *Literature and Culture in Early Modern London*. Cambridge: Cambridge University Press, 1995.

Maquet, Jaques. *The Aesthetic Experience: An Anthropologist Looks at the Visual Arts*. New Haven: Yale University Press, 1986.

Marcus, Abraham. *The Middle East on the Eve of Modernity: Aleppo in the Eighteenth Century*. New York: Columbia University Press, 1989.

Marsden, George M. *The Outrageous Idea of Christian Scholarship*. Oxford: Oxford University Press, 1997.

Martin, W.R. "The Eye of Mr. Ruskin: James's Views of Venetian Artists." *Henry James Review* 5 (1984): 107–16.

Martin-Fugier, Anne. *La vie elégante, ou la formation de tout-Paris, 1815–1848*. Paris: Fayard, 1990.

Mathews, Patricia. *Passionate Discontent: Creativity, Gender, and French Symbolist Art*. Chicago: Chicago University Press, 1999.

Mauersberg, Hans. *Wirtschafts - und Sozialgeschichte zentraleuropäischer Städte in neuerer Zeit, dargestellt an den Beispielen von Basel, Frankfurt a.M, Hamburg, Hannover und Munchen*. Gottingen: Vandenhoeck und Ruprecht, 1960.

Maxwell, Richard. "Henry Mayhew and the Life of the Streets." *Journal of British Studies* 17, 2 (1978): 87–105.

Mayhew, Henry. *London Labour and the London Poor*. 4 vols. 1861–62. Reprint. New York: Dover, 1968.

Mayhew, Henry, and John Binny. *The Criminal Prisons of London and Scenes of Prison Life*. 1862. Reprint. London: Frank Cass, 1968.

McClain, James L. *Kanazawa: A Seventeenth-Century Japanese Castle Town*. New Haven: Yale University Press, 1982.

McClain, James L., and Wakita Osamu, eds. *Osaka: The Merchants' Capital of Early Modern Japan*. Ithaca: Cornell University Press, 1999.

McClain, James L., "Space, Power, Wealth and Status in Seventeenth-Century Osaka." In *Osaka: The Merchants' Capital of*

Early Modern Japan, ed. James L. McClain and Wakita Osamu, 44–79. Ithaca: Cornell University Press, 1999.

McClain, James L., John M. Merriman, and Ugawa Kaoru, eds. *Edo and Paris: Urban Life and the State in the Early Modern Era*. Ithaca and London: Cornell University Press, 1994.

McClendon, Muriel. *The Quiet Reformation: Magistrates and the Emergence of Protestantism in Tudor Norwich*. Stanford: Stanford University Press, 1999.

McEwen, John. "A Room of her Own." *Art in America* 74 (June 1986): 111–14.

McLeod, Mona Kedslie. *From Charlotte Square to Fingal's Cave: Reminiscences of Journey through Scotland, 1820–1824, by Krystyn Lach-Szyrma*. Edinburgh: Tuckwell Press, 2004.

McNeill, William H. *A World History*, 4th ed. Oxford: Oxford University Press, 1999.

[McPherson, Charles]. *Life on Board a Man-of-War; Including a Full Account of the Battle of Navarino. By a British Seaman*. Glasgow: Blackie, Fullarton, 1829.

McWhirter, David. *Henry James's New York Edition: The Construction of Authorship*. Stanford: Stanford University Press, 1995.

Melville, Herman. *Moby-Dick, or The Whale*. New York: Modern Library, 2000.

Metzner, Paul. *Crescendo of the Virtuoso: Spectacle, Skill and Self-Promotion in Paris during the Age of Revolution*. Berkeley: University of California Press, 1998.

Meyer-Fong, Tobie. *Building Culture in Early Modern Yangzhou*. Stanford: Stanford University Press, 2003.

Michman, Jozeph, Hartog Beem, and Dan Michman. *Pinkas: Geschiedenis van de Joodse Gemeenschap in Nederland*. Ede: Kluwer Algemene Boeken, 1985.

Miller, Amy. *Dressed to Kill: British Naval Uniform, Masculinity and Contemporary Fashions, 1748–1857*. London: National Maritime Museum, 2007.

Milton, John. *Paradise Lost*. In *John Milton: Complete Poems and Major Prose*. Ed. Merrit Y. Hughes. New York: Macmillan, 1957.

Misra, S.C. "Some Aspects of the Self-Administering Institutions in Medieval Indian Towns." In *Studies in Urban History*, ed. J.S. Grewal and Indu Banga, 80–90. Amritsar: Department of History, Guru Nanak Dev University, 1981.

"Miss Spence and the Bagman." *Blackwood's Magazine* 3 (1818): 428–38.
Misson, Maximilien. *A New Voyage to Italy: With Curious Observations on Several Other Countries, as, Germany, Switzerland, Savoy, Geneva, Flanders, and Holland ... Done out of French*. London, 1699.
Mitterwieser, Alois. *Geschichte der Fronleichnamsprozession in Bayern*. Munich: Knorr and Hirth, 1930.
Moeller, Bernd. *Imperial Cities and the Reformation: Three Essays*. Ed. and trans. H.C. Erik Midelfort and Mark U. Edwards, Jr. Philadelphia: Fortress Press, 1972.
Montorgueil, Georges. *La parisienne peinte par elle-même*. Paris: Librairie L. Conquet, 1897.
Morrison, Arthur. *Tales of Means Streets*. Chicago: Academy Chicago Publications, 1984.
Muir, Edward. *Civic Ritual in Renaissance Venice*. Princeton, NJ: Princeton University Press, 1981.
– "Images of Power: Art and Pageantry in Renaissance Venice." *American Historical Review* 84 (1979): 16–52.
– *Ritual in Early Modern Europe*. Cambridge: Cambridge University Press, 1997.
Mukherjee, S.N. "Bhadralok and Their Dals - Politics of Social Faction in Calcutta, c. 1820–1856." In *The Urban Experience: Calcutta: Essays in Honour of Professor Nisith R. Ray*, ed. Pradip Sinha, 39–58. Calcutta: Riddhi-India, 1987.
– "Class, Caste and Politics in Calcutta, 1815–38." In *Elites in South Asia*, ed. Edmund Leach and S.N. Mukherjee, 33–78. Cambridge: Cambridge University Press, 1970.
Mukund, Kanakalatha. "Caste Conflict in South India in Early Colonial Port Cities, 1650–1800." *Studies in History* n.s., 11 (1995): 1–27.
Mumford, Lewis. *The Culture of Cities*. New York: Harcourt Brace, 1938.
Murdoch, Alexander, and Richard B. Sher. "Literacy and Learned Culture." In *People and Society in Scotland*, ed. T.M. Devine and Rosalind Mitchison, 1:127–42. Edinburgh: John Donald, 1988.
Nagle, Jacob. *The Nagle Journal: A Diary of the Life of Jacob Nagle, Sailor, from the Year 1775 to 1841*. Ed. John C. Dann. New York: Weidenfeld and Nicolson, 1988.
Nakagawa, Hisayasu. "Approaches to the Study of 18th-Century Cities: In Search of New Possibilities for Comparative Research." In *Cities in the 18th Century: Comparison between European and Japanese Cities*. International Symposium in Chiba University, 15–16 December 1998, 7–19. Chiba: Chiba University, 1999.

Naquin, Susan. *Peking: Temples and City Life, 1400–1900*. Berkeley: University of California Press, 2000.

Naujoks, Eberhard. *Kaiser Karl V. und die Zunftverfassung: Ausgewählte Aktenstücke zu den Verfassungsänderungen in den oberdeutschen Reichsstädten, 1547–1556*. Stuttgart: W. Kohlhammer, 1985.

Neddermeyer, Uwe. *Von der Handschrift zum gedruckten Buch: Schriftlichkeit und Leseinteresse im Mittelalter und in der frühen Neuzeit* Wiesbaden: Harrassowitz, 1998.

– "Was hat man von solchen confusionibus ... recht und vollkömmlichen berichten können?' Der Zusammenbruch des einheitlichen europäischen Geschichtsbildes nach der Reformation." *Archiv für Kulturgeschichte* 76 (1994): 77–109.

Nehring, Neil. *Flowers in the Dustbin: Culture, Anarchy, and Postwar England*. Ann Arbor: University of Michigan Press, 1993.

Nenadic, Stana. *Lairds and Luxury: The Highland Gentry in Eighteenth-Century Scotland*. Edinburgh: John Donald, 2007.

The New Picture of Edinburgh for 1818, Being a Correct Guide to the Curiosities, Amusements, Public Establishments, and Remarkable Objects in and Near Edinburgh. Edinburgh: W. Whyte, 1818.

Newte, Thomas. *Prospects and Observations on a Tour in England and Scotland: Natural, Oeconomical, and Literary*. London: G. and J. Robinson, 1791.

Nicol, John. *The Life and Adventures of John Nicol, Mariner*. Edinburgh: William Blackwood, 1822.

Nord, Debra Epstein. *Walking the Victorian Streets: Women, Representation and the City*. Ithaca: Cornell University Press, 1995.

Norling, Lisa. *Captain Ahab Had a Wife: New England Women and the Whalefishery, 1720–1870*. Chapel Hill: University of North Carolina Press, 2000.

Nye, Robert. *Crime, Madness, and Politics in Modern France: The Medical Concept of National Decline*. Princeton, NJ: Princeton University Press, 1984.

Oberman, Heiko. *The Reformation: Roots and Ramifications*. Trans. A. Gow. Grand Rapids: Wm. B. Eerdmans, 1994.

Ogborn, Miles. *Spaces of Modernity: London's Geographies, 1680–1870*. New York: The Guilford Press, 1998.

Ongaro, Guilio Maria. "The Chapel of St Mark's at the Time of Adrian Willaert, 1527–1562: A Documentary Study." PhD diss., University of North Carolina at Chapel Hill, 1986.

Ortiz, Fernando. *Cuban Counterpoint: Tobacco and Sugar*. 1940. Reprint. Durham: Duke University Press, 1995.

Ostrow, Steven F. *Art and Spirituality in Counter-Reformation Rome: The Sistine and Pauline Chapels in S. Maria Maggiore*. Cambridge: Cambridge University Press, 1996.

Owen, David. *English Philanthropy, 1660–1960*. Cambridge, MA: Harvard University Press, 1964.

Paley, Morton. *The Continuing City: William Blake's Jerusalem*. Oxford: Clarendon, 1983.

Parkinson, C. Northcote. *Portsmouth Point: The Navy in Fiction, 1793–1815*. Liverpool: University Press of Liverpool, 1948.

Paster, Gail Kern. *The Idea of the City in the Age of Shakespeare*. Athens, GA: University of Georgia Press, 1985.

Paulson, Ronald. *Rowlandson: A New Interpretation*. New York: Oxford University Press, 1972.

– *Hogarth*. Vol. 1: *The Modern Moral Subject*. New Brunswick: Rutgers University Press, 1991.

Pearl, Valerie. "Change and Stability in Seventeenth-Century London." *London Journal* 5 (1979): 3–34.

Pemberton, Charles Reece. *The Autobiography of Pel. Verjuice*. Ed. Eric Partridge. London: The Scholartis Press, 1929.

Perkins, Leeman L. *Music in the Age of the Renaissance*. New York: W.W. Norton, 1998.

Phalèse, Pierre. *Musica divina*. Antwerp: n.p., 1583.

[Pichot, A.]. *Historical and Literary Tour of a Foreigner in England and Scotland*. London: Saunders and Otley, 1825.

Pinkney, David H. *Decisive Years in France, 1840–1870*. Princeton, NJ: Princeton University Press, 1986.

Pinol, Jean-Luc. *Histoire de l'Europe urbaine*. 2 vols. Paris: Éditions du Seuil, 2003.

Pippin, Robert B. *Henry James and Modern Moral Life*. New York: Cambridge University Press, 2001.

Plessis, Alain. *The Rise and Fall of the Second Empire, 1852–1871*. Trans. Jonathan Mandelbaum. Cambridge: Cambridge University Press, 1985.

Polk, Keith. "Orologio, Alessandro." *The New Grove Dictionary of Music and Musicians*. Ed. Stanley Sadie and John Tyrrell. 18:748. London: Macmillan, 2001.

Pomeranz, Kenneth. *The Great Divergence: China, Europe and the Making of the Modern World Economy*. Princeton, NJ: Princeton University Press, 2000.

Portsmouth Jack's Garland. Newcastle, 1785.

Posnock, Ross. *The Trial of Curiosity: Henry James, William James and the Challenge of Modernity*. New York: Oxford University Press, 1991.

Pound, John. "Government to 1660." In *Norwich since 1550*, ed. Carole Rawcliffe and Richard Wilson, 35–62. London: Hambledon and London, 2004.

Poverty in the Victorian Age: Debates on the issue from 19th century critical journals. Introduction by A.W. Coats. 4 vols. Farnborough: Gregg International Publishers, 1973.

Prasch, Thomas. "Photography and the Image of the Poor." In *Victorian Urban Settings: Essays on the Nineteenth-Century City and Its Contexts*, ed. Debra N. Mancoff and D.J. Trela, 179–94. New York: Garland, 1996.

Pratt, Mary Louise. *Imperial Eyes: Travel Writing and Transculturation*. London: Routledge, 1992.

Prentice, Rina. *A Celebration of the Sea: The Decorative Art Collections of the National Maritime Museum*. Greenwich: National Maritime Museum, 1994.

Proal, Louis. *Le crime et le suicide passionnels*. Paris: Félix Alcan, 1900.

Rabaut, Jean. *Marguerite Durand, 1864–1936: "La Fronde" féministe, ou, "Le Temps" en jupons*. Paris: L'Harmattan, 1996.

Ramaswamy, Vijaya. "Artisans in Vijayanagar Society." *Indian Economic and Social History Review* 22 (1985): 417–45.

Rapoport, Amos. *Human Aspects of Urban Form: Towards a Man-Environment Approach to Urban Form and Design*. Oxford: Pergamon Press, 1977.

Rappaport, Steve. *Worlds within Worlds: Structures of Life in Sixteenth-Century London*. Cambridge: Cambridge University Press, 1989.

Rasch, Rudolf A. "Tollius, Joannes." *The New Grove Dictionary of Music and Musicians*. Ed. Stanley Sadie and John Tyrrell. 25:554–5. London: Macmillan, 2001.

Rawcliffe, Carole, and Richard Wilson, eds. *Medieval Norwich*. London: Hambledon, 2004.

Rearick, Charles. "Introduction: Paris Revisited." *French Historical Studies: Special Issue–New Perspectives on Modern Paris* 27, 1 (2004): 1–8.

– *Pleasures of the Belle Époque: Entertainment and Festivity in Turn-of-the-Century France* New Haven: Yale University Press, 1985.

Rediker, Marcus, and Peter Linebaugh. *The Many-Headed Hydra: Sailors, Slaves, Commoners, and the Hidden History of the Revolutionary Atlantic*. Boston: Beacon Press, 2000.

Reed, Walter. *Meditations on the Hero*. New Haven: Yale University Press, 1974.

Rey, Robert. *Suzanne Valadon: Les peintres français nouveaux, n. 14*. Paris: Éditions de la Nouvelle Revue française, 1922.

Reynolds, Matthew. *Godly Reformers and Their Opponents in Early Modern England: Religion in Norwich, c. 1560–1643*. Woodbridge, Suffolk: Boydell Press, 2005.

Reynolds, Siân. *Paris-Edinburgh: Cultural Connections in the Belle Époque*. Hampshire: Ashgate, 2007.

– "Running Away to Paris: Expatriate Women Artists of the 1900 Generation, from Scotland to Points South." *Women's History Review* 9, 2 (2000): 327–44.

Ridley, Jasper. *Bloody Mary's Martyrs: The Story of England's Terror*. London: Robinson, 2002.

Riot-Sarcey, Michele. *La démocratie à l'épreuve des femmes: Trois figures critiques du pouvoir, 1830–1848*. Paris: A. Michel, 1994.

Rizvi, Sayid Athan Abbas. *Shah Wali-Allah and His Times: A Study of Eighteenth-Century Islam, Politics and Society in India*. Canberra: Ma'rifat Publishing House, 1980.

Roach, Joseph. *Cities of the Dead: Circum-Atlantic Performance*. New York: Columbia University Press, 1996.

Roberts, Mary Louise. *Disruptive Acts: The New Woman in Fin-de-Siècle France*. Chicago: University of Chicago Press, 2002.

Roberts, M.J.D. *Making English Morals: Voluntary Association and Moral Reform in England, 1787–1866*. Cambridge: Cambridge University Press, 2004.

– "Reshaping the Gift Relationship: The London Mendicity Society and the Suppression of Begging in England, 1818–1869." *International Review of Social History* 36 (1991): 201–31.

Robinson, David M. "Banditry and the Subversion of State Authority in China: The Capital Region During the Middle Ming Period (1450–1525)." *Journal of Social History* 33, 3 (2000): 527–63.

Roche, Patrick A. "Caste and the British Merchant Government in Madras, 1639–1749." *Indian Economic and Social History Review* 12 (1975): 381–407.

Rodger, N.A.M. *The Wooden World: An Anatomy of the Georgian Navy*. Annapolis: Naval Institute Press, 1986.

– *The Command of the Ocean: A Naval History of Britain, 1649–1815*. New York: Norton, 2005.

Roe, Sue. *Gwen John: A Life*. London: Chatto and Windus, 2001.

Roeck, Bernd. *Eine Stadt im Krieg und Frieden: Studien zur Geschichte der Reichsstadt Augsburg zwischen Kalenderstreit und Parität*. 2 vols. Göttingen: Vandenhoeck & Ruprecht, 1989.

Rogers, Nicholas. *The Press Gang: Naval Impressment and Its Opponents in Georgian Britain*. London: Continuum, 2007.

Rørdam, Holger. *Danske Kirkelove samt udvalg af andre bestemmelser vedrørende Kirken, Skolen og de fattiges Forsørgelse fra Reformationen indtil Christian V's Danske Lov, 1536–1683*. Vol. 3. Copenhagen: Gad, 1889.

Rosand, David. *Myths of Venice: The Figuration of a State*. Chapel Hill: University of North Carolina University Press, 2001.

Rosand, Ellen. "Music in the Myth of Venice." *Renaissance Quarterly* 30 (1977): 511–37.

Rose, June. *Mistress of Montmartre: A Life of Suzanne Valadon*. London: Richard Cohen Books, 1998.

Rosinsky, Thérèse Diamand. *Suzanne Valadon*. New York: Universe Publishing, 1994.

Rozman, Gilbert. "Edo's Importance in the Changing Tokugawa Society." *Journal of Japanese Studies* 1, 1 (1974): 91–112.

Rudé, George. *Wilkes and Liberty Wilkes and Liberty: A Social Study of 1763 to 1774*. London: Oxford University Press, 1965.

Ruskin, John. *The Stones of Venice*. London: Collins, 1960.

Russell, Gillian. *The Theatres of War: Performance, Politics, and Society, 1793–1815*. Oxford: Clarendon, 1995.

Rye, Walter, ed. *Depositions Taken before the Mayor & Aldermen of Norwich, 1549–1567. Extracts from the Court Books of the City of Norwich, 1666–1688*. Norwich: A.H. Goose, 1905.

Sacks, David Harris, and Michael Lynch. "Ports, 1540–1700." In *The Cambridge Urban History of Britain*. Vol. 2: *1540–1840*, ed. Peter Clark, 377–424. Cambridge: Cambridge University Press, 2000.

Safely, Thomas Max. *Matheus Miller's Memoir: A Merchant's Life in the Seventeenth Century*. Basingstoke: Palgrave Macmillan, 2000.

Saint-Fond, Barthélemy Faujas. *Travels in England, Scotland, and the Hebrides; undertaken for the Purpose of Examining the State of the*

Arts, the Sciences, Natural History and Manners in Great Britain. London: James Ridgway, 1799.

Sartre, Jean Paul. "American Cities." In *The City: American Experience*, ed. Alan Trachtenberg, Peter Neill, and Peter C. Bunnell, 197–205. New York: Oxford, 1971.

Sarty, Léon. *Le suicide*. Nice: Imprimerie Centrale, 1889.

Sauer, Marina. *L'entrée des femmes à l'École des Beaux-Arts*. Trans. Marie-France Thivot. Paris: énsb-a, 1990.

Schafer, R. Murray. *The Tuning of the World*. New York: Knopf, 1977.

Schilcher, Linda Schatkowski. *Families in Politics: Damascene Factions and Estates of the 18th and 19th Centuries*. Berliner Islamstudien 2. Wiesbaden: Franz Steiner Verlag, 1985.

Schilling, Heinz. "Aufstandsbewegungen in der stadtbürgerlichen Gesellschaft des Alten Reiches: Die Vorgeschichte des Münsteraner Täuferreiches, 1525 bis 1534." In *Der Deutsche Bauernkrieg, 1524–1526*, ed. Hans-Ulrich Wehler, 193–238. Göttingen: Vandenhoeck und Ruprecht, 1975.

Schmidt, Heinrich. *Die deutschen Städtechroniken als Spiegel des bürgerlichen Selbstverständnisses im Spätmittelalter*. Göttingen: Vandenhoeck and Ruprecht, 1958.

Schopen, Gregory. "Archaeology and Protestant Presuppositions in the Study of Indian Buddhism." *History of Religions* 31 (1991): 1–23.

Schorske, Carl E. *Fin-de-Siècle Vienna: Politics and Culture*. New York: Vintage Books, 1981.

Schudt, Johann Jacob. *Jüdische Merkwürdigkeiten: Vorstellende Was sich Curieuses und denckwürdiges in den neuern Zeiten bei einigen Jahr-hunderten mit denen in all* IV. *Theileder Welt, sonderlich durch Teutschland zerstreuten Juden zugetragen. Sammt einer vollständigen Franckfurter Juden-Chronik ...* / Frankfurt am. Main: S.T Hocker, 1714.

Schwab, Heinrich W. "*Italianità in Danimarca*: Zur Rezeption des Madrigals am Hofe Christian IV." In *Europa in Scandinavia: Kulturelle und soziale Dialoge in der frühen Neuzeit*, ed. Robert Bohn, 142–5. Frankfurt: Peter Lang, 1995.

Schwerhoff, Gerd. "Das Kölner Supplikenwesen in der Frühen Neuzeit: Annäherungen an ein Kommunikationsmedium zwischen Untertanen und Obrigkeit." In *Köln als Kommunikationszentrum: Studien zur frühneuzeitlichen Stadtgeschichte*, ed. Georg Mölich and Gerd Schwerhoff, 473–96. Das Riss im Himmel: Clemens August und seine Epoche, 4. Cologne: DuMont, 2000.

Scioppius, Kaspar. *Emmanuel Thaumaturgus Augustae Vindel. hoc est relatio de miraculoso corporis Christi sacramento, quod Augustae in S. Crucis ecclesia servatum est*. Augsburg: n.p., 1612.

Seeger, Peggy, and Ewan MacColl, eds. *The Singing Island: A Collection of English and Scots Folksongs*. London: Mills Music, 1960.

Seigel, Jerrold. *Bohemian Paris: Culture, Politics, and the Boundaries of Bourgeois Life, 1830–1930*. New York: Penguin Books, 1986.

Seltzer, Mark. *Henry James and the Art of Power*. Ithaca: Cornell University Press, 1984.

Sennett, Richard. *Classic Essays on the Culture of Cities*. New York: Appleton–Century–Crofts, 1969.

– *Flesh and Stone: The Body and the City in Western Civilization*. New York: W.W. Norton and Company, 1994.

Shapiro, Ann-Louise. *Breaking the Codes: Female Criminality in Fin-de-Siècle Paris*. Stanford: Stanford University Press, 1996.

Sherman, Stuart Pratt. "The Aesthetic Idealism of Henry James." *The Nation* 104 (5 April 1917): 393–9.

Shirley-Fox, John. *An Art Student's Reminiscences of Paris in the Eighties*. London: Mills and Boon, 1909.

Showalter, Elaine. *Sexual Anarchy: Gender and Culture at the Fin de Siècle*. New York: Penguin Books, 1990.

Siena, Kevin P. *Venereal Disease Hospitals and the Urban Poor: London's "Foul Wards," 1600–1800*. Rochester, NY: University of Rochester Press, 2004.

Simkins, M.E. "Ecclesiastical History." In *The Victoria History of the County of Norfolk*. Vol. 2: *The Victoria History of the Counties of England*, ed. William Page, 213–314. Folkestone, Kent: Institute of Historical Research, University of London, 1975.

Simpson, Kenneth. *The Protean Scot: The Crisis of Identity in Eighteenth-Century Scottish Literature*. Aberdeen: Aberdeen University Press, 1988.

Singh, M.P. *Town, Market, Mint and Port in the Mughal Empire, 1556–1707 (an Administrative-cum-Economic Study)*. New Delhi: Adam Publishers, 1985.

Skrine, Henry. *Three Successive Tours in the North of England, and the Great Part of Scotland. Interspersed with Descriptions of the Scenes they Present, and Occasional Observations on the State of Society, and the Manners and Customs of the People*. London: W. Bulmer & Co., 1795.

Smith, Alison. *The Victorian Nude: Sexuality, Morality and Art*. Manchester: Manchester University Press, 1996.

Smith, Bruce R. *The Acoustic World of Early Modern England: Attending to the O-Factor*. Chicago: University of Chicago Press, 1999.

Smith, Jeffrey Chipps. *Sensuous Worship: Jesuits and the Art of the Early Catholic Reformation in Germany*. Princeton, NJ: Princeton University Press, 2002.

Snell, Robert. *Théophile Gautier: A Romantic Critic of the Visual Arts*. Oxford: Clarendon Press, 1982.

Soergel, Philip M. *Wondrous in His Saints: Counter-Reformation Propaganda in Bavaria*. Berkeley: University of California Press, 1993.

Stansell, Christine. *American Moderns: Bohemian New York and the Creation of a New Century*. New York: Henry Holt and Company, 2000.

Starn, Randolph. "Renaissance Redux." *American Historical Review* 103 (1998): 122–4.

Stewart, Mary Lynn. *Women, Work, and the French State: Labour Protection and Social Patriarchy, 1879–1919*. Kingston: McGill-Queen's University Press, 1989.

Stieve, Felix. *Der Kampf um Donauwörth im Zusammenhänge der Reichsgeschichte: Der Ursprung des dreißigjährigen Krieges, 1607–1619*. Munich: M. Rieger, 1875.

Storm, John. *The Valadon Drama: The Life of Suzanne Valadon*. New York: E.P. Dutton, 1958.

Stow, John. *A Survey of London. Reprinted from the Text of 1603*. Ed. Charles Lethbridge Kingsford. 1971. Vol. 1. Reprint. Oxford: Clarendon, 2000.

Strauss, Gerald. "Success and Failure in the German Reformation." *Past and Present* 67 (1975): 30–63.

Stuart, Kathy. *Defiled Trades and Social Outcasts: Honor and Ritual Pollution in Early Modern Germany*. Cambridge: Cambridge University Press, 1999.

Stubbs, Ken, ed. *The Life of a Man: English Folk Songs from the Home Counties*. London: English Folk Dance and Song Society, 1970.

Styles, John. *The Dress of the People: Everyday Fashion in Eighteenth-Century England*. New Haven and London: Yale University Press, 2007.

Sweetman, Will. " 'Hinduism' and the History of 'Religion': Protestant Presuppositions in the Critique of the Concept of Hinduism." *Method and Theory in the Study of Religion* 15 (2003): 329–53.

Swetschinski, Daniel M. *Reluctant Cosmopolitans: The Portuguese Jews of Seventeenth-Century Amsterdam*. London: The Littman Library of Jewish Civilization, 2000.

Swinth, Kirsten. *Painting Professionals: Women Artists and the Development of Modern American Art, 1870–1930*. Chapel Hill, NC: University of North Carolina Press, 2001.

Symons, Arthur. "The Blind Beggar." *Poems by Arthur Symons*. Vol. 1. London: Heinemann, 1927.

Takashi, Kato. "Edo in the Seventeenth Century: Aspects of Urban Development in a Segregated Society." *Urban History* 27 (2000): 189–210.

– "Governing Edo." In *Edo and Paris: Urban Life and the State in the Early Modern Era*, ed. James L. McClain, John M. Merriman, and Ugawa Kaoru, 41–67. Ithaca and London: Cornell University Press, 1994.

Teahan, Sheila. "Engendering Culture in The American Scene." *Henry James Review* 17 (1996): 52–7.

Temple William. *Observations Upon the United Provinces of the Netherlands. By Sir William Temple of Shene, in the County of Surrey, Baronet, Ambassador at the Hague, and at Aix la Chappellè, in the year 1668*. London: Printed by A. Maxwell, 1673.

Thomas, Alison. *Portraits of Women: Gwen John and Her Forgotten Contemporaries*. Cambridge: Polity Press, 1994.

Tittler, Robert. *The Architecture of Power: The Town Hall and the English Urban Community c. 1500–1640*. Oxford: Clarendon Press, 1991.

– "The Incorporation of Boroughs, 1540–1558." *History* 62 (1977): 22–44.

Tobin, Beth Fowkes. *Picturing Imperial Power: Colonial Subjects in Eighteenth-Century British Painting*. Durham: Duke University Press, 1999.

Tobin, William. "Léon Foucault." *Scientific American* 279 (July 1998): 70–8.

– *The Life and Science of Léon Foucault: The Man Who Proved the Earth Rotates*. Cambridge: Cambridge University Press, 2003.

Topham, Edward. *Letters from Edinburgh; written in the years 1774 and 1775*. 1776. Edinburgh: West Port Books, 2003.

Torgovnick, Marianna. "Spirituality: Modernism's Other?" Paper presented at the Modern Language Association Conference, Washington, DC, 29 December 1996.

– *Primitive Passions: Men, Women, and the Quest for Ecstasy*. New York: Knopf, 1997.

Trotter, Thomas. *Medicina Nautica: An Essay on the Diseases of Seamen*. London: T. Cadell, Jr. and W. Davies, 1797.

Tufts, Eleanor. *Our Hidden Heritage: Five Centuries of Women Artists*. New York: Paddington Press, 1974.

Tulard, Jean, ed. *Dictionnaire du second empire*. Paris: Fayard, 1995.

Turner, Victor. *From Ritual to Theatre: The Human Seriousness of Play*. New York: PAJ, 1982.

van der Sprenkel, Sybille. "Urban Social Control." In *The City in Late Imperial China*, ed. G. William Skinner, 609–32. Stanford: Stanford University Press, 1977.

van Eijnatten, Joris. *Liberty and Concord in the United Provinces: Religious Toleration and the Public in the Eighteenth-Century Netherlands*. Leiden: Brill, 2003.

van Leuve, Roeland. *Werelds Koopslot, of de Amsteldamsche Beurs*. Amsterdam: Jacobus Verheyden, 1723.

van Nierop, Henk. "Popular Participation in Politics in the Dutch Republic." In *Resistance, Representation and Community: Origins of the Modern State in Europe*, ed. Peter Blickle, 272–90. Oxford: Oxford University Press, 1997.

van Strien, Kees. *Touring the Low Countries: Accounts of British Travellers, 1660–1720*. Amsterdam: Amsterdam University Press, 1998.

Vecchi, Orazio. *Le veglie di Siena*. Venice, 1604.

Vetter, Conrad [a.k.a. Andreae]. *M. Conradi Andreæ &c. Volcius Flagellifer. Das ist: Beschützung vnd Handhabung fürtreflicher vnd herlicher zweyer Predigten von der vnleydenlichen vnd Abschewlichen Geysel Proceßion, erstlich gehalten, hernach auch in Truck gegeben durch den Kehrwürdigen, vnnd Wolgekerten Herrn M. Melchior Voltz Lutherischen Predicanten zu Augspurg bey Sant Anna*. Ingolstadt: In der Ederischen Truckerey, durch Andream Angermayer, 1608.

Vlessing, Odette. "The Excommunication of Baruch Spinoza: The Birth of a Philosopher." In *Dutch Jewry: Its History and Secular Culture, 1500–2000*, ed. Jonathan Israel and Reinier Salverda, 141–72. Leiden: Brill, 2002.

Volcius, Melchior. *Zwo Christliche Predigten, von der abscheulichen Geisselungsprocession, welche jährlich im Papsthumb am Charfreytag gehalten würdt*. Tübingen: in der Cellischen Truckerey, 1607.

von Bezold, Friedrich. "Zur Entstehungsgeschichte der historischen Methodik." In *Aus Mittelalter und Renaissance: Kulturgeschichtliche Studien*. Munich/Berlin: Oldenbourg, 1918.

von Glahn, Richard. "Municipal Reform and Urban Social Conflict in Late Ming Jiangnan." *Journal of Asian Studies* 50 (1991): 280–307.

von Pöllnitz, Freiherr, Ludwig Karl. *The Memoirs of Baron Charles Lewis von Pöllnitz: Being the Observations He Made in his Late*

Travels from Prussia thro' Germany, Italy, France, Flanders, Holland, England, &c ... In Letters to his Friend ... / Tran. Stephen Whatley, London: Printed for Daniel Brown, 1737.

Wade, Mara R. *Triumphus Nuptialis Danicus: German Court Culture and Denmark - The "Great Wedding" of 1634*. Wiesbaden: Harrassowitz, 1996.

Wahrman, Dror. *The Making of the Modern Self: Identity and Culture in Eighteenth-Century England.* New Haven: Yale University Press, 2004.

Walker, Mack. *German Home Towns: Community, State and General Estate, 1648–1871*. Ithaca: Cornell University Press, 1971.

Walker, Susan S. *The Invention of the Model: Artists and Models in Paris, 1830–1870*. Aldershot: Ashgate, 2006.

Walkowitz, Judith R. *City of Dreadful Delight: Narratives of Sexual Danger in Late-Victorian London*. Chicago: University of Chicago Press, 1992.

– "Going Public: Shopping, Street Harassment, and Streetwalking in Late Victorian London." *Representations* 62 (Spring 1998): 1–30.

Ward, Joseph P. *Metropolitan Communities: Trade Builds, Identity, and Change in Early Modern London*. Stanford: Stanford University Press, 1997.

Watson, Thomas. *Italian Madrigals Englished.* London: n.p., 1590.

Weber, Eugen. *France: Fin de Siècle.* Cambridge, MA: The Belknap Press of Harvard University Press, 1986.

Weber, Max. *The City*. Trans. Don Martindale and Gertrud Neuwirth. New York: The Free Press, 1958.

Weber, Wolfgang. *Priester der Clio: Historisch-sozialwissenschaftliche Studien zur Herkunft und Karriere deutscher Historiker und zur Geschichte der Geschichtswissenschaft 1800–1970*. Frankfurt/Bern/New York: Peter Lang, 1984.

Weinberg, Robert. "The Pogrom of 1905 in Odessa: A Case Study." In *Pogroms: Anti-Jewish Violence in Modern Russian History*, ed. John D. Klier and Shlomo Lambroza, 248–89. Cambridge: Cambridge University Press, 1992.

Weinstein, Arnold. *Soul and the City: Art, Literature, and Urban Living.* Course No. 484. Audio Download. Chantilly, VA: The Teaching Company, 1999.

Weisberg, Gabriel P., and Jane R. Becker, eds. *Overcoming All Obstacles: The Women of the Académie Julian*. New Brunswick, NJ: Rutgers University Press, 1999.

Whaley, Joachim. *Religious Change and Social Toleration in Hamburg, 1529–1819*. Cambridge: Cambridge University Press, 1985.

White, Paul Whitfield. *Theatre and Reformation: Protestantism, Patronage and Playing in Tudor England*. Cambridge: Cambridge University Press, 1993.

Williams, Kate. "Nelson and Women: Marketing, Representations, and the Female Consumer." In *Admiral Lord Nelson: Context and Legacy*, ed. David Cannadine, 67–92. New York: Palgrave Macmillan, 2005.

Williams, R. Vaughn, and A.L. Lloyd, eds. *The Penguin Book of English Folk Songs*. London: Penguin Books, 1957.

Williams, Raymond. *The Country and the City*. New York: Oxford University Press, 1973.

Wilson, Kathleen. *The Island Race: Englishness, Empire and Gender in the Eighteenth Century*. London: Routledge, 2003.

– "Nelson and the People: Manliness, Patriotism, and Body Politics." In *Admiral Lord Nelson: Context and Legacy*, ed. David Cannadine, 49–66. New York: Palgrave Macmillan, 2005.

Winner, Viola Hopkins. *Henry James and the Visual Arts*. Charlottesville: University of Virginia Press, 1970.

Winton, John. *Hurrah for the Life of a Sailor! Life on the Lower Deck of the Victorian Navy*. London: Michael Joseph, 1977.

Withington, Robert. *English Pageantry: An Historical Outline*. 2 vols. Cambridge, MA: Harvard University Press, 1918–20. Reprint, New York: Arno Press, 1980.

Wolfart, Johannes C. *Religion, Government and Political Culture in Early Modern Germany: Lindau, 1520–1628*. Basingstoke: Palgrave, 2002.

– "Sex Lies and Manuscript: On the 'Castration' of the Lindau Archives." In *Shell Games: Studies in Scams, Frauds and Deceits, 1300–1650*, ed. M. Crane, R. Raiswell, and M. Reeves, 271–85. Toronto: Centre for Reformation and Renaissance Studies, 2004.

Wordsworth, William. *The Prelude: A Parallel Text*. Ed. J.C. Maxwell. Harmonsworth: Penguin, 1971.

– *The Prelude or Growth of a Poet's Mind*. Ed. Ernest de Selincourt. 2nd ed. Oxford: Clarendon, 1959.

– "The Recluse, Part First, Book First: Home at Grasmere." *The Complete Poetical Works*. London: Macmillan and Co., 1888; Bartleby.com, 1999. Available at www.bartleby.com/145 (viewed 17 February 2009).

– "Steamboats, Viaducts and Railways." *The Complete Poetical Works of William Wordsworth: Student's Cambridge Edition*. Ed. A.J. George, 721. New York: Houghton Mifflin, 1904.

Wu, Duncan, ed. *Romanticism: An Anthology with* CD-ROM. 2nd ed. Oxford: Blackwell, 1998.

Yeldham, Charlotte. *Women Artists in Nineteenth-Century France and England: Their Art Education, Exhibition Opportunities and Membership of Exhibiting Societies and Academies, with an Assessment of the Subject Matter of their Work and Summary Biographies*. 2 vols. New York: Garland Publishing Inc., 1984.

Yeo, Eileen. "Mayhew as a Social Investigator." In *The Unknown Mayhew*, ed. E.P. Thompson and Eileen Yeo, 51–96. London: Merlin, 1971.

Yonemoto, Marcia. *Mapping Early Modern Japan: Space, Place and Culture in the Tokugawa Period, 1603–1868*. Berkeley: University of California Press, 2003.

Youngson, A.J. *The Making of Classical Edinburgh, 1750–1840*. Edinburgh: Edinburgh University Press, 1993.

Zola, Emile. *The Masterpiece (L'Oeuvre)*. 1886. Translated by Roger Pearson. Oxford: Oxford University Press, 1993.

Zylberberg-Hocquard, M.H., and E. Diebolt, eds. *Femmes et travail au dix-neuvième siècle: Enquêtes de la Bataille syndicaliste, Marcelle Capy–Aline Valette*. Paris: Syros, 1984.

Contributors

MELANIE A. BAILEY is an assistant professor of history at Centenary College of Louisiana.

MARY A. BLACKSTONE is a professor in the Department of Theatre and the director of the Centre for the Study of Script Development at the University of Regina.

GLENN CLARK is an assistant professor in the Department of English, Film and Theatre at the University of Manitoba.

SASKIA COENEN SNYDER is an assistant professor of modern Jewish history at the University of South Carolina.

BERNARD COOPERMAN is the Louis L. Kaplan Chair of the Meyerhoff Centre for Jewish Studies and is an associate professor of Jewish history in the Department of History, University of Maryland.

ALEXANDER J. FISHER is an associate professor of music at the University of British Columbia.

CHRISTOPHER FRIEDRICHS is a professor of history at the University of British Columbia.

SUSAN LEWIS HAMMOND is an associate professor in musicology and music history in the School of Music at the University of Victoria.

ROBIN HOOPLE was a professor of English at the University of Manitoba until his death in 2006. He taught American Literature for over thirty years and became a noted expert on the work of Henry James. He authored and co-edited books on James plus numerous articles on American and Canadian Literature, and was a founding editor of the journal *Mosaic*.

JULIE JOHNSON holds a PhD from the Department of History at Queen's University in Kingston, Ontario.

PETER LAKE is university distinguished professor of history and professor of the history of Christianity, Divinity School, at Vanderbilt University.

ISAAC LAND is an assistant professor of history at Indiana State University.

JUDITH OWENS is an associate professor and the head of the Department of English, Film and Theatre at the University of Manitoba.

PAM PERKINS is a professor in the Department of English, Film and Theatre at the University of Manitoba.

JON SAKLOFSKE is an assistant professor of English at Acadia University, Nova Scotia.

GREG T. SMITH is an associate professor of History at the University of Manitoba.

VANESSA WARNE is an associate professor in the Department of English, Film and Theatre at the University of Manitoba.

JOHANNES C. WOLFART is an associate professor of religion, College of the Humanities, at Carleton University.

ARLENE YOUNG is a professor in the Department of English, Film and Theatre at the University of Manitoba.

Index